KU-272-003

TICKLE THE PUBLIC

SOUTH NOTT' COLLEGE

C70·172

20811·6

LIBRARY

ACC NO : 20811-6
TITLE : TICKLE THE PUBLIC ONE
AUTHOR : ENGEL M

DDC(1) : 070.172

WITHDRAWN

NEW COLLEGE NOTTINGHAM

261211

TICKLE THE PUBLIC

ONE HUNDRED YEARS OF THE POPULAR PRESS

Matthew Engel

Tickle the public, make 'em grin,
The more you tickle, the more you'll win;
Teach the public, you'll never get rich,
You'll live like a beggar and die in a ditch.

VICTOR GOLLANCZ

LONDON

Illustration credits. Page 1: above, *Daily Mirror*/British Library; below, *The Sun*/John Frost. Page 2: above and below left, Hulton Deutsch; below right, *Daily Mail*/ John Frost. Page 3: above, Hulton Deutsch; below, *Observer*. Page 4: above, Hulton Deutsch; below, Popperfoto. Page 5: above, Hulton Deutsch; below, Popperfoto/Reuter. Page 6: above left and below, Hulton Deutsch; above right, Popperfoto. Page 7: above, Mirror Group Newspapers; below, Express Newspapers plc. Page 8: above, *Daily Mirror*/John Frost; below, *News of the World*.

First published in Great Britain 1996
by Victor Gollancz
An imprint of the Cassell Group
Wellington House, 125 Strand, London WC2R 0BB

© Matthew Engel 1996

All rights reserved. No part of this publication may be reproduced or transmitted in any form or by any means, electronic or mechanical including photocopying, recording or any information storage or retrieval system, without prior permission in writing from the publishers.

The right of Matthew Engel to be identified as author of this work has been asserted by him in accordance with the Copyright, Designs and Patents Act, 1988.

A catalogue record for this book is available from the British Library.

ISBN 0 575 06143 X

Typeset by Rowland Phototypesetting Ltd
Bury St Edmunds, Suffolk

Printed and bound in Great Britain by
Butler & Tanner Ltd, Frome and London

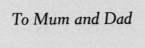

To Mum and Dad

Contents

Preface

Brian Inglis once wrote that a Fleet Street journalist who had not worked for the *Daily Express* was like a soldier who had never marched to the sound of gunfire. He was talking, of course, about the old broadsheet *Daily Express*, now diminished physically, metaphorically and statistically. But it would be equally apposite to make the same remark in the 1990s about a Fleet Street journalist who has never worked for *The Sun*.

Either way, I am that soldier. I have spent almost twenty-five years committing journalism, most of that time on one newspaper: *The Guardian*, generally regarded as the most gentlemanly regiment in the army. For part of that time, I was the cricket correspondent, generally regarded (by non-cricket correspondents) as the cushiest of all Fleet Street billets. So, to stretch Inglis's image, I have spent my journalistic war as the rough equivalent of a skiving Aldershot pay clerk.

As it happens, I have performed more journalistic tasks than most, including marching (or cowering, anyway) to the sound of gunfire. But my direct experience of the papers which are the matter of this book has been confined to freelancing and a few daily reporting and sub-editing shifts. While doing the research, I began to regret this in the way I regret other experiences I would have loathed but would like to have behind me – running away to sea, for instance.

Most histories of newspapers, however, are written by academics, with no direct experience at all of the practice of journalism. So this is not an apology. I believe I learned to read via the *Daily Mirror*, which may explain a lot. I have worked alongside journalists on pop papers for many years. I have enjoyed their company, their help and their friendship. I have admired their tenacity and their professional skill. I have come to realize that it is a great deal easier working for a paper like *The Guardian* where one is, in essence, writing for one's chums, than for a newspaper with whose readers one might not instinctively identify. Journalists working for the popular press generally have to learn to empathize with their readers, which is why they get told to think of 'the people in the back streets of Derby' (the *Daily Express* c.1935); 'the wife of a Sheffield bus conductor' (the *Daily Mirror* c.1960); or 'the bloke you see in the pub – the right old fascist who wants to send the wogs back' (*The Sun*, allegedly, c.1985).

I believe that writing for a mass audience is not an intrinsically debased form of literature but, in theory, the highest and most noble form. But it has become debased. Over a hundred years much of British journalism turned into an institutionalized force for distortion and half-truth. What follows is not a formal history. But I hope it sheds some light on how it happened.

Acknowledgements

My first thanks go to the past and present editors of *The Guardian*, Peter Preston and Alan Rusbridger. I am not sure they agreed happily to my effective disappearance from their pages for a year – I hope not, anyway – but, sensing my need to write this book, they agreed readily, and I am very grateful to them. My thanks, too, to Vivien Green and Sean Magee, for their faith in the project, to Gillian Bromley, for making the text a great deal better than it would have been, to Andy Denwood, producer of the accompanying BBC Radio Four series, for his support and enthusiasm – and, above all others, to my wife Hilary (not least for her own in-house editing service) and my son Laurie, who I hope will realize one day that 'Goawaydaddysworking' is not actually all one word.

The research for this book has been done in a number of different libraries. Geoff Smith and Brian Huff of the Newspaper Library at Colindale went beyond the call of duty in the assistance they gave me, and the book could not possibly have appeared without them. I am grateful also to the staff at St Bride's Library (especially Nigel Roche), Cambridge University Library and the British Museum in Great Russell Street. At Cambridge I had the special delight of reading back numbers of the *Daily Star*, in its quasi-pornographic phase, next to someone trying to research nineteenth-century Russian literature. At the British Museum I was able to fulfil an ambition by working under the great dome of the Reading Room; it is a tragedy that future generations of writers will not have this privilege. My thanks also to Brian Cathcart, for lending me the substantial collection of newspaper books collected by the late Alex Maxey; I am sorry Alex was not here to share his knowledge as well.

I am also grateful for the help, inspiration and information given by a large number of people, including the friends and colleagues whose anecdotes lodged in my brain long before I ever knew I was going to do this, and the people who very kindly agreed to be interviewed for the book and/or the radio series. Some of them wish to remain anonymous; some of them may have to, because I have accidentally forgotten to include their names. Many thanks to them all, including: Cyril Bainbridge, Steve Barnett, Julia Barton, Bill Bateson, Scyld Berry, David Bishop, Richard Bourne, Pat Collins, Lord Cudlipp, Reg Cudlipp, Professor James Curran, Christopher Douglas,

Eamon Dyas, Anne-Marie Ehrlich, Sir David English, Reg Foster, Vic Giles, Geoffrey Goodman, Roy Greenslade, David Hadert, Murray Hedgcock, Nick Hiley, Derek Hodgson, Chris Horrie, Melanie Hudson, Catherine Hurley, John Jackson, Jonathan Keates, Graham King, Shan Lancaster, Jim Lewthwaite, Kelvin MacKenzie, Helen Martin, Henry Maxwell, Professor Anthony Morris, Frank Nicklin, Andrew Nickolds, Sir Edward Pickering, Chapman Pincher, Clive Porter, Marjorie Proops, Claire Rayner, Neil Russell, John Sharpe, Bernard Shrimsley, Norman Smart, Ian Todd, John Turner, Lloyd Turner, Tim Wapshott, Keith Waterhouse, Alan Watkins, Audrey Whiting, Philip Wrack and (as usual in alphabetical lists, last, but not least) Donald Zec. None of these people should be blamed for what follows.

Broadsheets and Tabloids: A Note

In the 1990s it is common to use the terms 'tabloid press' and 'popular press' as synonyms, to be contrasted with the 'broadsheet' or 'quality' press. This is a relatively new distinction: in the late nineteenth century, as this book shows, it was the morning papers that were considered respectable, while evening papers were the disreputable ones. Of the five titles which form the heart of this book, all bar the *Daily Mirror* began as broadsheet-sized papers. *The Sun* became tabloid in 1969, the *Daily Mail* in 1971, the *Daily Express* in 1977 and the *News of the World* in 1984. Hence the word 'tabloid' is used sparingly.

Currency: A Note

Britain switched to decimal currency in 1971. The penny (1d) in use before that is equivalent to five-twelfths of a modern penny (1p), i.e. there were 240 to £1 instead of 100. The *Daily Mail*, which cost ½d when it was launched in 1896, cost 35p at the beginning of 1996; this is 168 times its original price. So it goes.

PART ONE

'Is there much more of this, mate?'
The Popular Press before 1896

Prologue

A journalist traditionally spends vast amounts of time searching for the perfect intro, the opening paragraph that will capture the essence of the story he is writing, hook the readers' attention until he has finished with them, and perhaps miraculously be good enough to win the writer an Award, a pay rise and a literary reputation.

The intro of the millennium was written in 1649:

> Tuesday, January 30. This day the King
> was beheaded, over against the Ban-
> quetting House by Whitehall.

Unfortunately, the crispness of the reporting was not matched by the title of the publication: A *Perfect Diurnall of Some Passages in Parliament and the Daily Proceedings of the Army*. The intro of the previous millennium was the somewhat better-known sentence:

> In the beginning God created the heaven
> and the earth.

This would, however, be rejected by a modern journalist. The Reuters news agency, which will not allow its staff to report unprovable assertions, would amend it to: 'In the beginning God created the heaven and the earth, according to normally reliable sources.' The chief sub-editor of a modern popular newspaper would reject it because the timescale was not immediate enough. It would probably end up in the paper as 'God created the heaven and the earth last night.'

This demonstrates one way newspapers can get things wrong. It also makes the point that news has existed since humans first acquired the ability to communicate, maybe since the first invertebrate discovered dry land and somehow had to convey the information to the rest of the community back in the primeval swamp. And it ties in with the theory put forward by Kennedy Jones, editor of the *Evening News* in the 1890s and for many years right-hand man to Lord Northcliffe, the founder of the *Daily Mail*.

Displaying greater breadth than one finds in most volumes of journalists' memoirs, Jones drew on the scholarly theory that the second and third chapters of Genesis were written long after the first, which, following its

dramatic start, does become rather matter-of-fact. In contrast, the next two –
dealing with the Garden of Eden – are lush with storyteller's detail: 'And the
eyes of them both were opened, and they knew that they were naked; and
they sewed fig leaves together, and made themselves aprons.'

How, asks Jones, would the writer of the opening chapter have dealt with
this?

> Certainly he would not have paused on this supreme instant to describe
> the dress of the sinners, the very material, the cut and style of it, for all
> the world as though he were a modern society reporter at Ascot on Gold
> Cup Day. Yet the story has endured and will endure through the centuries
> by reason of these human touches.
>
> To this hour and to the end of time Adam and Eve live and move in
> man's imagination because their garments were described at a moment
> when most writers would have thought it more seemly and dignified to
> have hung a moral round the necks of our first parents than an apron
> round their waists.

Jones was leading on to some very specific blowing of his own trumpet. It
was the *Daily Mail*, which he helped found in 1896, which broke out of the
conventions of Victorian journalism and brought daily news to the breakfast
tables of the mass of the British public rather than to a tiny elite. The first
edition of the *Mail*, published on 4 May 1896, marks the real beginning of
British popular journalism. The telling of the Adam and Eve story, said Jones,
'illustrates fitly the news instinct, the journalistic touch, which, during the
middle years of the nineteenth century had all but disappeared from the
daily press on account of the obsession with politics, and which made possible
the immediate success of the newspaper with the human note'.[1]

Had Jones been writing at the end of the twentieth century he might have
noticed that these two chapters of Genesis have even more in common with
popular newspapers as they developed later, being full of veiled references
to sexual intercourse ('therefore shall a man leave his father and his mother,
and shall cleave unto his wife: and they shall be one flesh'), insults that stop
just short of libel ('Now the serpent was more subtil than any beast of the
field which the Lord God had made') and bogus quotes ('And the serpent
said unto the woman . . .'). Indeed, he might have added that the whole story
was almost certainly a work of imaginative fiction anyway, and could thus
easily have made the front-page splash in a modern popular paper. Frank
Harris, also a former editor of the *Evening News* but better remembered these
days as a Victorian sexual athlete, once remarked to the politician Arthur
Balfour:

'All the evils of the age come from Christianity and journalism.'

'Christianity, of course,' replied Balfour, 'but why journalism?'
He should be living at this hour.

I

The journey from the *Daily Mail* of Northcliffe and Jones, which became
Britain's best-selling paper as soon as it was founded, to the modern *Sun*, the
best-selling paper a hundred years later, is the main business of this book. It
is necessary also to say something of the history of the newspaper before the
Mail to understand how we got out of the primeval swamp and then, some
might say, climbed back in again.

There were nine national daily newspapers in Britain at the beginning of
1996. (A tenth, *Today*, founded in 1986, closed in November 1995.) Of these
nine, two have been founded in the last twenty years (the *Daily Star* and
The Independent); a third, *The Guardian*, was for most of its 175 years a
provincial paper. Each of the others has spent a sustained period as the
best-selling paper in the country, an era for which its methods were just right,
which it instinctively understood and even embodied. On each occasion this
era ended when the leading paper was undercut, as it were, by a rival that
was able to gather in a new section of society, below the level captured by
the former best-seller – and understood the message of the anonymous verse
that went round Fleet Street in the nineteenth century:

> Tickle the public, make 'em grin,
> The more you tickle, the more you'll win;
> Teach the public, you'll never get rich,
> You'll live like a beggar and die in a ditch.

Thus *The Times* led from the Napoleonic era until 1855, when the *Daily
Telegraph* overtook it by appealing to the middle classes. In 1896 that was in
turn overwhelmed by the *Daily Mail*, which was beaten by the *Daily Express*,
which was beaten by the *Daily Mirror*, which was beaten by *The Sun*. The
process by which this happened is not just the history of a few newspapers;
it is a sort of history of the last hundred years in Britain.

More than two thousand years before *The Sun*, the Romans are alleged to
have had daily reports called *acta diurna*. In England, Henry VII warned
against 'forged tydings and tales' in 1486, ten years after Caxton set up his
printing press, beginning the endless battle between spluttering authority
and unruly media. And from 1542 onwards the Privy Council was taking

action against individuals for 'seditious', 'unfitting' or 'unsemely worddes' and 'evil opinions'.[2]

In Tudor times, people who needed news – merchants, ministers, and the like – would pay newswriters to keep them informed. Information was always especially important in times of conflict, and there were plenty of those. There were strict laws against unlicensed printing, but pamphlets and news ballads strayed into circulation throughout the sixteenth and early seventeenth centuries. In the 1620s what were known as the news-books or *corontos* began to appear more or less regularly, bringing news from Holland and Germany – foreign affairs being safer and less likely to be censored by the representatives of what was then a very touchy British monarchy than comment on home news.

As authority broke down during the Civil War years, the first regular papers began to appear. For instance, *Mercurius Aulicus*, on the King's side, and Parliament's *Mercurius Britannicus* gave competing versions of events. The Roundhead writers particularly enjoyed reporting the death of Sir Ralph Hopton, the most feared of the King's early generals – so much so that they reported it on several different occasions.[3]

Control of the press remained relatively loose under Cromwell, but was fiercely reasserted by Charles II, in his determination that the story of the preceding decades would not be repeated. Most of the old laws restricting newspapers were brought back in 1662, and grew even sterner under his brother James II. But within weeks of James's ejection from the throne and the country in 1688, six newspapers sprang up to challenge the official *London Gazette*.

The Bill of Rights in 1689 guaranteed freedom of speech and freedom of debate in Parliament, but the press was not considered worth a mention, in contrast to the American constitution a century later. The British concept of liberty developed before newspapers were fully formed, which possibly explains why press freedom has always been considered so marginal to it. In 1695, however, the liberal philosopher John Locke successfully argued for the abolition of the Licensing Act that controlled the press, and for the next seventeen years there was a brief but luxuriant flowering that produced Britain's first daily paper, the *Daily Courant*, in 1702, as well as Daniel Defoe's *Review*, *The Tatler* and *The Spectator*.

The urge of the executive to control the press, so central to British history that it might be considered innate, soon resurfaced. In 1712 the first Stamp Act was introduced, taxing the press at a basic rate of a penny a paper. It was apparently a response to one irritating piece in the *Courant*. With the new tax taking a large slice out of newspapers' profits, journalists henceforth eked out their income by taking bribes. Sir Robert Walpole, who in 1715 assumed the position that was to develop into that of Prime Minister, not merely paid journalists to support him, he bribed Defoe to write pieces that ostensibly opposed him.

Though the tax was increased at regular intervals,[4] there were soon newspapers everywhere:

> For, soon as morning dawns with roseate hue,
> The 'Herald' of the morn arises too,
> 'Post' after 'Post' succeeds, and all day long
> 'Gazettes' and 'Ledgers' swarm, a motley throng.
> When evening comes she comes with all her train,
> Of 'Ledgers', 'Chronicles' and 'Posts' again.

When the *Daily Universal Register*, later better known as *The Times*, started in 1785, the year George Crabbe wrote this poem, it brought the total of London morning papers to nine, as in 1996. And it was accepted that they were corrupt:

> Some, champions for the rights that prop the crown;
> Some, sturdy patriots, sworn to pull them down;
> Some, neutral powers, with secret forces fraught.
> Wishing for war, but willing to be bought.[5]

Though it was not high-minded, British journalism at the end of the eighteenth century was at least good fun. The stern Libel Act of 1792 increased the risks of the profession, as it was meant to do, but it took prosecutions out of the hands of ministers and gave writers and printers the right to a jury trial. This lent the whole business of libel a certain whimsicality, which it has never lost; but in those days the perversity of juries tended to be exercised in favour of the press rather than against it.

Newspapers did manage to antagonize His Majesty's enemies as well as his ministers. During the brief intermission in the French Wars in 1803, Napoleon was said to be 'extremely hurt to find that his endeavours to conciliate had hitherto produced no other effect than to increase the abuse with which the papers in England continually loaded him'.[6] Hop Off, You Frog, as *The Sun* would put it several generations later.

The press, said the profession's most high-mindedly Victorian historian, were run in those days by 'besotted geniuses ... the business of their profession keeping them out of their beds half the night, they kept out the remaining half of their own choice; and the little hours were consumed in tavern hilarity ... [but] the reign of the rackety ones was drawing to a close.'[7] More's the pity. Thereafter, for the best part of a century, rackety and besotted genius was smothered under layers of respectability. The process was never as complete as earlier historians like to think, but the effect was to deny information to much of the British public long after it was ready for it, and perhaps to stifle the development of the press enough to ensure that it never did grow up properly.

II

The long war against the French naturally stimulated the demand for news, and before Napoleon was beaten one newspaper had emerged ahead of all the rest. The *Daily Universal Register* had been started by John Walter in 1785 primarily as a means of demonstrating a new printing system called logography. This involved using pieces of metal displaying not single letters or figures, but whole words or groups of numbers; it was designed, in particular, to avoid errors when giving the results of the national lottery.[8]

Logography lasted just seven years: only a paper with a very limited vocabulary could live with such a system. *The Times*, as the *Register* became in 1788, has survived more than two hundred, by heading in the opposite verbal direction. From an early stage it recognized that news was the essential element of a newspaper, which had not been wholly obvious to all the agents and agitators who had previously conducted the business of journalism. And it was rewarded, soon after it acquired its new title, with a dramatic story that was to run and run:

FRANCE.

———

CONFINEMENT
of the
KING, QUEEN,
and
ROYAL FAMILY
and
THE ATTEMPT TO MURDER THE QUEEN.

It took more than a quarter-century for the consequences of that upheaval to unravel on the plains of Waterloo. During those years Walter's son, John Walter II, established *The Times*'s reputation, both by lifting it above the general slime of corruption and by a piece of business innovation that was to prove a great deal more worthwhile than logography: the steam-driven press. The machine was brought in by subterfuge to a private room in Printing

House Square to avoid sabotage by the print workers, who would lose jobs and money through this new technology. On 29 November 1814 Walter, to avoid any Luddism, produced the paper in secret and then informed his workers. One hundred and seventy-four years later history at *The Times* would repeat itself, when Rupert Murdoch destroyed the power of the print unions once and for all by covertly moving his newspapers to Wapping.

The profits generated by this first, forgotten exercise in union-busting enabled Walter to improve *The Times*'s reporting services so that it rapidly acquired a circulation that far outstripped its rivals. It kept that position, without challenge, until 1855. In the early 1850s it was selling up to four times as many as its main rivals – the *Morning Herald*, *Morning Chronicle* and *Morning Post* – added together. Two successive great editors, Thomas Barnes and J. T. Delane, led the paper from 1817 to 1877 and gave it an authority that has never been matched. Until 1887, when it was duped into making unfounded allegations against the Irish leader Charles Parnell, it was regarded as close to infallible.

But it was still read only by a tiny minority of the nation, even allowing for the fact that the copies the news-hawkers delivered to the coffee-houses were each read by several people. The circulation of *The Times* passed 30,000 only in 1848, at a period when the population of the United Kingdom was 27 million. The discrepancy used to be explained away by saying the masses were illiterate, but this is false. *The Times* escaped from the ruck of rackety papers, and became a world-famous institution, not by tickling the taste of the public, but by becoming a paper aimed solely at an elite, who were presumed to be too grown up to be tickled.

In the early days, *The Times*'s instincts were as rackety as anyone else's, and not merely in the matter of taking political bribes. One of the paper's first illustrations, in April 1806, was a diagram, looking rather like a Cluedo board, of the house at Greenland Dock where Isaac Blight had been sensationally murdered. It conducted feuds with its rivals with a robustness that soon disappeared from the press until the Murdoch *Sun* appeared on the scene: 'That squirt of dirty water, the Chronicle,' it fulminated one day, to be described in return as 'the poor old Times, in its imbecile ravings'. The Irish leader Daniel O'Connell referred to *The Times*'s 'venal rascality', and was called back 'an unredeemed and unredeemable scoundrel'.[9] Its coverage of the feud between George IV and Queen Caroline, the Chas and Di of the 1820s, was gloriously disrespectful. 'There never was an individual less regretted by his fellow-creatures than this deceased king,' it eulogized on the day of George's funeral in 1830. 'What eye has wept for him? What heart has heaved one sob of unmercenary sorrow?'

Palmer's *Index to The Times*, the Baedeker's of nineteenth-century history, would start its alphabetical listings, unless there happened to be a reference to Aberdeen or (less often) Abolition of Capital Punishment, with the heading ACCIDENTS, as in 1828:

— at Astley's Theatre, an Actress falling off her Tight Rope on which She was Walking and Seriously Injured.

— at Glocester, to three Workmen being Suffocated by Foul Air in a Vault they were clearing out.

— Mdlle Sontag, by her falling down the Stairs of the Hotel de l'Europe, from Treading on a Peach Stone, and falling down Ten Steps Injuring Herself Severely.

— Mr. Lane, the artist, at the Horse Bazaar, Grays Inn Lane by falling through one of the Skylights and so Dashed to Pieces.

— Singular Circumstance of the Explosion of an Urn at a Tea Table.

— Jack Ketch,[10] from a Piece of Meat at his Dinner, nearly Suffocating him, at Hull.

Page 3 of *The Times* in the 1820s was not unlike page 3 of the modern *Daily Telegraph*. Hidden within its grey columns, all human life lurked. The following court report, from 5 February 1828, by the simple sparseness of the narrative, beats anything in Dickens:

MARYLEBONE

John Bursell, the son of an ornamental painter . . . was charged by William Ridding, the parish beadle, with having behaved disorderly in Marylebone Church on Sunday evening.

The beadle said the conduct of the young people had been complained of, and Dr. Spry, the rector, ordered him to look after them. For that purpose on Sunday night, he disguised himself, by putting aside his laced coat, and went amongst them, and he found the young gentleman at the bar, and a young woman, behaving very improperly.

Mr. Rawlinson [magistrate]—What were they doing?

Beadle—Smiling in each other's faces.

—Was that all?

—No, your worship, they took liberties.

—What liberties?

—Took hold of each other's hands, and talked as if they were courting, like.

Lord Montford [magistrate] asked the beadle what they said. The beadle said he did not hear.

—Were you far from them?

—No, close, my lord, but they did not know me in my plain coat.

—Did any of the congregation complain?

—No, my lord.

Mr. Rawlinson—How long did they talk together?

—Nearly a minute.

—Nearly a minute! Fifty and some odd seconds, barely long enough to say 'How well that gentleman reads.' Well, what did you do?

—I laid hold of him, pulled him out of

church and sent him to the watch-house. —To be locked up for the night? —Yes.

Mr. Rawlinson said to the beadle: 'It is my opinion that you acted very indiscreetly . . . To the defendant: 'You are discharged, sir.'

Beadle—Please, your worship.

Mr. Rawlinson—I will not be answered. The case is decided.

It is all there: the insolence of office and the innocence of youth, even the improbably happy ending, shining through the generations more powerfully than literature.

But *The Times* was changing: it acquired agents in Alexandria, Boulogne, Malta and Marseilles. It was gaining the ear of statesmen, rather than their cash. On this breadth of coverage and political authority it built its power. As it did so it lost interest in Marylebone, or at any rate the rougher end of it. *The Times* might well run a thundering leader on the power of parish beadles and behaviour in church, and if there were a parliamentary debate on the subject it might report the speeches almost verbatim; but it no longer reported much from what you might call ground level. It still did not ignore the more sensational court cases, though it began to underplay them. The paper grew in size, from four to eight or even more pages. Its opinions were more often offered in support of authority than against it ('ever strong upon the stronger side', as the liberal writer William Hazlitt said, a description that has stood the test of the years); but, whichever way it faced, *The Times* was concerned more with political leaders than with the sons of ornamental painters. Whether or not it had the interests of the working man at heart, it had no interest in appealing to him.

In 1839 *Palmer's Index* still had its share of the dramatic and offbeat:

ACCIDENTS —at the Aberdeen Gasworks from the Great Water Tank bursting.

—a child, at Chittlehamholt, from a Pig Eating both its Hands &c.

—at Olveston Church, from the Clock weight falling down and Disturbing the Preacher in his Sermon.

HEREFORD FAIR —an Elephant at, Swallows a Gentleman's Diamond Ring.

PHENOMENON, RARE —a Magnificent Quintuple Rainbow.

PHENOMENON, SINGULAR —a Cow has a Calf with two Heads, four Ears, four Eyes, two Necks, two Spines and two Stomachs.

But such reports tended themselves to be rare phenomena. They were swamped by pages of references to Civil Actions, dutifully reported at enormous length. On 27 August 1855, as William Howard Russell sent his dispatch from the camp before Sebastopol where he was pioneering the craft of war reporting, *The Times* ran an entire column beginning as follows:

BRITISH ARCHAEOLOGICAL ASSOCIATION

The association concluded their proceedings at Newport last night when, Sir Fortunatus Dwarris having taken the chair, Mr Black delivered a lengthened and interesting lecture on the ancient system of keeping exchequer accounts by means of tallies . . .

A column in *The Times* in 1855 contained approximately 2,000 words. So the twenty-five columns of PARLIAMENTARY INTELLIGENCE, plus four columns of comment on the debate, that it carried on 25 January 1855 amounted to more than half the length of this book. It is impossible to believe that even the likes of Sir Fortunatus Dwarris, ensconced in his compartment on the Great Western Railway for the journey back from Newport, could have excavated their way through those twenty-five parliamentary columns – still less the thirty and three-quarter columns (61,500 words) that appeared three days later.

III

And what of the 99.9 per cent of the British population who did not buy *The Times*? We know now that most of them could read, contrary to the old theory that the popular press, exemplified by the *Daily Mail*, emerged only in response to the growth in literacy created by the Education Act of 1870. Even in 1840, 70 per cent of the men and half of the women could sign their names on marriage registers, and this figure was rising rapidly well before 1870.[11] Working people learned to read in all kinds of ways: Sunday Schools, dame schools, charity schools, fireside Bible reading – or through the cheap literature brought by hawkers and pedlars. This included the chapbooks of popular ballads and stories which were sold through the streets by the 'chapmen', and (most popular of all) the Last Dying Speeches of convicted murderers. Public executions were the nearest thing Britain had to a national sport in the first half of the nineteenth century, and the story of the Confession and Execution of Corder, who murdered Maria Marten in the Red Barn, is said to have sold over a million copies in 1828.[12]

Now, this figure is pretty incredible. The circulation figures of legal, stamped newspapers can be fairly accurately gauged up to 1855, when stamp duty was abolished, because the Government kept a record. From then on until after the Second World War, when the Audit Bureau of Circulations took a firm grip, they have to be treated with great scepticism. There is only the patchiest evidence of the true sales figures of illegal and quasi-legal publications in the early nineteenth century. So divide that figure of a million by ten, or even twenty, remembering that each copy would have been passed from hand to hand, and read aloud in pubs and barbers' shops by the literate to the less literate: it still represents a far more potent form of communication than *The Times*.

This huge audience did not buy daily newspapers, in the first place because stamp duty made them prohibitively expensive – *The Times* cost seven old pence in the 1820s when that might be a third of a farm labourer's daily pay – and secondly because they were dull. But in the decades after Waterloo there was enormous interest in the radical papers like the *Political Register*, edited by William Cobbett, *Black Dwarf* and the *Poor Man's Guardian*. They railed against repressive government, and generated huge sales. Because they did not have the Government stamp they were illegal; but they still outsold the legal press.[13]

Cobbett's *Register* is estimated to have sold up to 60,000 in the agitated winter of 1817, ten times *The Times*'s figure. The eruption of journalism from underground was volcanic and the flow of words unstoppable. Again, it is important to note that, for the working class, newspaper reading was even less of a private habit than it was higher up the social scale, so the sales figures, however unreliable, hugely understate the true readership. In Manchester in 1833 John Doherty's Coffee and Newsroom served a choice of ninety-six newspapers, legal and illegal.[14] Elsewhere, groups of workers would club together to buy a paper that would be passed from hand to hand.

As politics became calmer, the underground papers faded away – to the relief of the Government, which encouraged legal journalism with a reduction in stamp duty from 4d to a penny, and a cut in the advertising duty from 3s 6d to 1s 6d. From the rubble, another powerful and ultimately more durable strand of popular journalism emerged, one that has never lost its affinity with the rackety pre-Victorian tradition. This was the Sunday press, which was to point the way more clearly than anything else to the real newspaper revolution – not one for which the radicals might have agitated, but the one the *Daily Mail* initiated.

IV

In 1995 *The Observer* issued a T-shirt – a promotional medium not available in the eighteenth and nineteenth centuries – proclaiming itself Britain's Original Sunday Paper. It is the oldest now in existence, but it was certainly not the original. This was actually the *Sunday Monitor*,[15] founded, rather surprisingly, by one Elizabeth Johnson round about 1779. A whole string of imitators followed quickly, including *The Observer* in 1791. One of those imitators, the *Sunday Morning Herald*, loftily dismissed its rivals as weekly papers rather than dailies and said it would provide the same service as a daily newspaper. It failed. Thus the American tradition, that a Sunday newspaper was a bigger, fatter version of the same paper that came through the door six days a week, never had a chance. In Britain Sundays were to be different.

The poet–vicar George Crabbe nailed that difference for ever in 1785:

> Then lo! the sainted Monitor is born,
> Whose pious face some sacred texts adorn;
> As artful sinners cloak the secret sin,
> To veil with seeming grace the guile within,
> So moral essays on his front appear,
> But all is carnal business in the rear.

And in essence nothing has changed in more than two centuries: carnal business and secret sins remain the business of the popular Sunday press, and though the veil of morality has become almost wholly moth-eaten over the years it has never entirely been tossed away.

But on a British Sunday the hypocrisy has never been all on one side. The papers had to fight constant skirmishes against sabbatarians, or those purporting to be sabbatarians. These battles were sometimes resolved by changing the official time of publication to Saturday, with editions produced on Friday or even Thursday; in any case, before the railways, it would often be close to the middle of the following week before the coaches could get the papers to the more distant parts of Britain.

Distribution was always a problem. In 1820 the London newsboys petitioned the House of Lords to abolish Sunday papers because of their 'tendency to the destruction of public morals' and because they distracted people from attending divine service; they did not actually say they wanted the day off.

Later, Victorian sabbatarianism grew more entrenched, especially out of town; and W. H. Smith, which now began to dominate the sale of newspapers, did not want to operate on Sundays either. So the papers set up their own system, using 'horn-boys', whose noise could drown out church bells.

Some of the papers did not waste time even trying to 'cloak the secret sin'. The *Weekly Dispatch* (founded in 1801 and surviving, as the *Sunday Dispatch*, until 1961) remarked casually that it was no worse to be a clergyman than an infidel, and employed the roisterer Pierce Egan to write descriptively about boxing, racing and wrestling, as well as about murders. In 1825 Egan, or a staunch disciple, reported on a bare-knuckle prize-fight at The Old Barge House opposite Woolwich. It was supposed to be between Lenney and Young Sam, but Lenney was in jail; these fights were on the very fringes of the law, and magistrates could intervene at any moment. Instead £5 was collected from the crowd as prize money and Harry Jones, the sailor boy, came forward to box a '*seedy cove*' called Captain Corderoy. The *Dispatch* printed what was then slang in italics; most of it is now safely entrenched in the language:

Seconds: Barney Aaron and G. Western for Jones; two Piccadilly *cads* for Corderoy.

Round One, The Captain seemed to belong to the half-pay list; for it was evident from an inspection of his frame, that he was on *short-commons*. Jones seemed anxious to give him a *belly-full* and commenced action immediately on coming to the scratch by offering a left-handed facer. Corderoy, however, who possessed a *little bit of science*, turned off the hit, and a few stops occurred on both sides. A close: Jones fibbed, and both went down.

So it went on, in great detail, until the eighth, when 'Jones took innumerable liberties with the Captain's mug, which was now pinked all over.' However, at this point our correspondent seems to have got bored or drunk, and merely reported:

The remainder of the battle afforded no points of detail. Jones had it all his own way; and Corderoy, after *coming on* with considerable game, but no chance, till the twenty-first round, resigned the contest.

Sometimes, Egan's boxers had *gravy* distilling from damaged *squinters* before they were hit again on the *larboard goggle*. The *Weekly Dispatch* also had columns on pigeon-shooting, cocking and bull-baiting.

Not all the Sunday papers were quite so determinedly unrespectable, but they were almost uniformly radical in their politics, and they played their part – like the unstamped papers – in galvanizing opinions on the Reform

Bill of 1832, the first tentative step on the road towards a universal franchise. And they were all read by people who had neither the time nor the money to buy a daily. The tradition grew that Sunday papers took more licence than daily papers, even as Victorian attitudes superseded the old laxity and the official Sunday became stricter. This paradox was usually resolved by the use of the hypocrisy-weapon. Respectable churchgoers would return home for their regular dose of Sabbath salaciousness.

There were a confusing number of people called Bell involved in the Sunday paper business. Robert Bell of *Bell's Life in London* was not related to the Robert Bell who edited the *Weekly Dispatch*, nor to John Bell, of *Bell's Weekly Messenger*. John Bell disinherited his son, John Browne Bell. When his father died, the disinherited Bell started *Bell's New Weekly Messenger*, which included what may have been the first two Sunday supplements, *The Reviewer* and *The Commercialist*. His advertising was shameless: '60,000 persons read it every week – contradict it who can.'[16] Here is a true founding father of modern British journalism. In 1843 John Browne Bell went on to start a new paper: the *News of the World*.

The previous year a young compositor called Edward Lloyd started what became known as *Lloyd's Weekly News*, and in 1850 George Reynolds began *Reynolds's Weekly Newspaper*, 'a Journal of Democratic Progress and Social Intelligence'. Along with the *News of the World*, these became the most widely read papers of Victorian England, superseding *Bell's Life*, the *Weekly Dispatch* and the *Weekly Chronicle*. In effect, they represented a fusion between the traditions of the radical press and those of the original Sundays; and they burst through to the mass circulations made possible by the abolition of stamp duty, the spread of the railways, and the arrival of cheaper paper and the rotary press.

By 1854 the *News of the World* had already established its own traditions:

FRIGHTFUL TRAGEDY IN SOHO.

HORRID MURDER AT BARNSLEY.

MELANCHOLY SUICIDE OF A CITY SOLICITOR.

THE ALLEGED POISONING OF A FAMILY AT BERMONDSEY.

THE HORRIBLE MURDER AT EAST ACTON.

These headlines might have appeared even in *The Times*. It was the relentless procession of them that made the *News of the World* so different, along with the space given to columns of cases from London magistrates' courts, from the horrific to the outwardly routine. The whole gives an extraordinary insight into the innards of Victorian England:

LAMBETH: DISTRESSING CASE OF CHILD MURDER BY ITS MOTHER.

HAMMERSMITH: GROSS OUTRAGE BY A GANG OF GIPSIES UPON TWO LADIES.

WESTMINSTER: MORE FLOWER-PICKING AT CHELSEA.

The last of these was a case of lilac-picking in the grounds of Chelsea College: a crime punished by a fine of £1 or fourteen days' imprisonment. Begging got even shorter shrift:

WORSHIP STREET: FLEECING A TAR.

BOW STREET: DRUNKEN BEGGARS.

William Clare, an ill-looking fellow, with large rough whiskers, and Margaret Clare, his wife, were charged with begging in Chancery Lane and being drunk . . . It was proved that the prisoners had been both committed previously; and, in fact, had never pursued any other avocation than that of mendicants for years. Mr Jardine [the magistrate] said it was a pity the good people who threw away their money in street charity could not be compelled to spend a week or so in the metropolitan police courts to witness the practical results of their benevolence. Here were two of the worst characters, who had thrived on the system, and were drunk every night, and although such cases came to light every day, and the public were warned from all quarters, still indiscriminate relief continued to be given, and the class whom they encouraged – the drunkards, thieves and imposters of London – were triumphant against all public interference, legislative enactments, and every means yet devised to suppress the scandalous nuisance. The male prisoner was committed to hard labour for three months, and the woman for one month.

Occasionally, the cases would take a step outside the routine and into the realms which the *News of the World* would make famous.

LAMBETH: A LADY AND HER SWEETHEART.

James Gray, a young man of respectable appearance, was placed at the bar, on a charge of stealing a pianoforte and other property belonging to Miss Georgina Hastings of Kensington . . . Counsel: 'Have you been on terms of intimacy with the prisoner?' Miss Hastings: 'Yes, sir, but not of improper intimacy.'

SHOCKING CHARGE AGAINST ANOTHER ROMAN CATHOLIC PRIEST.

At Haverfordwest Sessions, the Rev. Patrick Kelly was charged with having committed rape on Mary Sullivan, a girl of about 14 years of age . . . 'Mr Kelly bolted the door . . . He then went into the vestry room and called me in . . . he laid hold of me by the hand. I pulled my hand loose, and I went to run through the passage and he ran after me before I could have time to go down into the passage. The room was up two steps and before I could get down he pulled me back by the frock and I fell down. (The witness here gave evidence which proved the capital offence.)

There was something world-weary about the use of 'another' in that headline.

All these court reports were given at enormous length in the close type of the day; occasionally the penny-a-line correspondents had to draw a veil, as happened again in that case when the surgeon was called as a witness:

Mr Luke C. Hislop (surgeon): 'I examined the person of Mary Sullivan, professionally.' This witness gave evidence which proved that there had been violation of the person. The evidence, however, is unfit for publication.

It is quite surprising, though, to discover what was sometimes considered fit for publication.

INFAMOUS ABDUCTION OF A BELGIAN FEMALE.

Adolphus Harrison, a low-looking fellow of shabby exterior, was accused of conspiring to defile and seduce a woman, Alice Leroy, sixteen and a half years of age. She was brought to London to live with Madame Denis in Vauxhall Bridge Road. 'Madame Denis said to the gentleman "This is my sister," ' Miss Leroy told the court. 'She said to me "You must remain". Madame Denis then took the gentleman's hand and put it down my breast. The gentleman said "Leave me alone with your sister . . ." '

It seems safe to assume that fellows, low-looking and of shabby exterior or otherwise, were placing their hands down sixteen-year-old girls' breasts long before 1854. This may, however, be the first time they did so in the pages of English newspapers: *Lloyd's* and *Reynolds's* had the story as well.

This report does seem rather more explicit than was the *News of the World* norm at the time. A contemporary newspaper historian called it 'the calmest of the cheap weeklies',[17] and was gratified to note that it was outselling the most violent, *Reynolds's* (one assumes he was talking about its politics), by more than two to one. The *News of the World* sold 5,673,525 copies in 1854 – that is, in the whole year: rather fewer than it was later to sell in a week.

But that still meant more than 100,000 copies every Sunday, which was an extraordinary circulation for the time. And it was rising fast, because it was not just hands down breasts that sold papers in 1854. This extract comes from the paper of 19 November, more than three weeks after the event, but is still resonant almost a century and a half afterwards:

THE EARL OF LUCAN'S SPIRITED REPORT OF THE BATTLE.
Balaclava, 27 October 1854

My Lord – I have the honour to report that the cavalry division under my command was seriously engaged with the enemy on the 25th, during the greater part of which day it was under heavy fire; that it made a most triumphant charge against a very superior number of the enemy's cavalry, and an attack upon batteries which, for daring and gallantry, could not be exceeded. The loss, however, in officers, men, and horses, has been most serious.

This was, of course, Lucan's official report on the Charge of the Light Brigade. The *News of the World* did not have its own correspondent in the Crimea – only *The Times* had that – and it had to rely on second-hand sources. But since one of the functions of a Sunday paper was to draw together the news of the week for a readership that did not have access to other media, this was quite normal. On this occasion it took from the *Morning Chronicle* a slightly less biased comment on the triumphant charge than was obtainable from Lord Lucan: 'By an imbecile command, a misconception as to its nature, or by some mysterious circumstance, the flower of the British Army were thus led to certain butchery.'

War news was not just a matter of passing interest to the British working class; it was after all their sons who were being butchered. The Napoleonic Wars had nurtured the early growth of Sunday papers, and the conflict in the Crimea gave it renewed impetus. R. Power Berrey, later the newspaper's assistant editor, recalled how his grandfather would drive his horse into Neath every Saturday morning from the South Wales village where he lived, buy the *News of the World* when it arrived off the train, then sit in his trap and read the news from the Crimea to the assembled crowd.[18] The public appetite for newspapers was turning into hunger.

Elsewhere in the world this hunger was being sated, above all in the United States, where the history of the press may be seen as identical to the history of the press in Britain, but in reverse. American visitors to Britain in the 1990s are shocked by the riot of competing libertine tabloids. Nearly all their own newspapers are now serious, cautious, self-regarding, long-winded and rather pallid. Except for the fact that they are almost always local monopolies as well, that gives them a great deal in common with the newspapers that dominated Victorian middle-class breakfast tables. In contrast, nineteenth-century American newspapers were cheap, ferociously competitive, rude, sensationalist, scurrilous and insulting – much like the British popular press today.

The press played an important role in the American War of Independence and emerged from it protected by the Constitution, and the freest in the world. Penny papers arrived in New York in 1833; they were satirical about goings-on in society, and even a little bit saucy. It was 1855 before the abolition of stamp duty in Britain made penny newspapers even a possibility. Parliament allowed it to happen only after a fierce debate. Nor did the arguments in favour of abolition owe much to American concepts of liberty: a cheap press, it was presumed – by Gladstone, among others – would enable journalists to educate the working man.[19] The object was to teach the public, not tickle it. Alarmed conservatives, perhaps looking across the Atlantic, still claimed the abolition of the tax would let loose atheism, infidelity, sedition and blasphemy, all preached by a cheap and corrupt press. But this was Victorian England. What actually happened was the *Daily Telegraph*.

V

All the histories state that the *Telegraph* was founded by one Colonel Arthur Burroughes Sleigh in pursuit of a vendetta against the Duke of Cambridge. This does, however, have the smack of a later invention by the paper's Peter Simple column. The vendetta did not permeate the *Telegraph*; later newspapers would make their campaigns a great deal more obvious.

Sleigh's paper – the *Daily Telegraph and Courier*, as it was first called – did have two crucial innovations. The existing papers – which meant primarily *The Times*, the *Daily News*, the *Morning Advertiser*, the *Morning Chronicle*, the *Morning Herald*,[20] the *Morning Post* and *The Standard* – had responded to the end of stamp duty merely by dropping their price from 5d to 4d, removing the cost of the penny stamp (except for *The Times*, which still charged an extra ha'penny). Any extra profits accruing from the abolition of advertising duty, which came at the same time, they intended to keep. The *Telegraph* cost only 2d. It promised to rely less on parliamentary reporting, printing only 'the pith and marrow of debates' rather than the 'lengthened reports in the columns of our contemporaries'. In the first issue, Parliament still rated two and a half columns out of four pages. But the headlines had a whiff more of the *News of the World* than of *The Times*:

EXTRAORDINARY AFFAIR AT CROYDON.

THE LATE RIOT AT PENGE.

THE DARLINGTON SLOW-POISONING CASE.

HORRIBLE CASE OF CHILD-STARVING.

The second day's paper carried an approving quote from a rival called *The Leader*: 'Altogether, the humbler classes may congratulate themselves upon being thus enabled, by the removal of the stamp, to have for so small a sum so good a record of contemporary events.' The humility of the classes involved seems to have been decidedly relative. Tuppence was still too expensive for most people, though it was not expensive enough for Sleigh, who soon defaulted and was obliged to sell the paper to his printer, Moses Levy, already the proprietor of the *Sunday Times*.

On 17 September, believed to be the day Levy took over, the price went down to a penny. Three days later the paper was claiming a circulation second only to *The Times*: 'This journal not only circulates with the million, but it is taken in the very highest circles.' The word million should, once again, not be taken literally, but the *Telegraph* was probably selling 50,000. 'We have been enabled, single-handed, and alone in the field,' it claimed, 'to contend against prejudice, and prove the truth of the arguments in the House of Commons . . . that the unfettered press would not, of necessity, become a licentious one.'

Well, not yet, anyway. The *Telegraph* in those early years was rather free-spirited, more advanced in its opinions, some might say, than it would be 140 years later: against capital and corporal punishment, in favour of reforming the House of Lords, decidedly pro-Liberal – it was the *Telegraph* that called Gladstone 'the people's William'. Politically, it only began to move rightwards in the mid-1870s. As an in-house history noted indulgently: 'Young newspapers are not unlike young men.'[21]

It was a young reporter's paper, too, and produced a new generation of journalists known as the 'young lions'. One man emerged as the king of this part of the jungle: the *Telegraph*'s star reporter, George Augustus Sala, an extraordinary, wayward, Bunteresque figure who bestrode British journalism in the second half of the nineteenth century to an extent that is all the more terrifying to a modern journalist when one considers how utterly forgotten he is now. Rightly forgotten, it has to be said, because his chief skill was windbaggery. 'Your smart reporter,' wrote Sala's biographer,

did not speak of coffee, for instance, but of the fragrant berry of Mocha. Blood, of course, was the crimson stream of life, a dog's tail his caudal appendage, and the oyster had been temporarily banished in favour of the succulent bivalve. And for this unfortunate change one member of the *Daily Telegraph*'s staff of 'young lions' was largely if not wholly responsible: Sala himself.[22]

This technique spread throughout the paper. Parliamentary coverage might be slightly curtailed, but nothing else was. As the *Telegraph* grew rich and as fat as *The Times* – eight or twelve pages – an important court case could easily rate eight columns, or 15,000 words. Modern readers, accustomed to skipping the dull bits, may find this next passage difficult but it is necessary to give something of the flavour of the nineteenth-century newspaper. This was part of the *Telegraph* account of the wedding of the future Edward VII at Windsor on 11 March 1863:

It will thus be seen that nothing had been spared to render the interior of the chapel worthy of the brilliant ceremonial which was so soon to grace its precincts. The noble structure, however, is in itself so architecturally beautiful, and its normal decorations are of so stately a character, that when the whole appeared in unison, the *coup d'oeil*, illumined by the chastened radiance penetrating through the stained glass of the memorial window, and of the casements in the adjacent chapel – now flickering on the spiracles of the stalls – now bringing the embossed work on the communion plate into gorgeous, golden light – now bathing with a mild suffusion the pallid alabaster – now casting the recesses of the stalls into nebulous shadow – and now finding the full field of rich colour to disport itself – approached, as we have hinted, if anything of the kind could so approach, to sublimity. It is curious to mark how the accidental disposal of accessories will frequently enhance artistic effect in a far greater degree than will the most careful and premeditated juxtaposition of light and shade; and if for a moment the vast masses of carved woodwork on either side of the chapel gave it, laterally, a somewhat mournful appearance, the mere act of the vergers, as they went round placing the white programmes of the ceremonial on the ledges of the desk were sufficient to give instantaneous relief to the eye, to bring forward objects that had hitherto been lost in shadow, and to produce a most noticeable effect of *chiaro oscuro*.

About 7,000 not dissimilar words precede this passage; another 10,000 were to follow, plus about 3,000 in the leader columns. The reporter (or, one hopes, for the sake of everyone's sanity, reporters; since there were no by-lines, there is no way of knowing) must have returned to the office in London and written his copy in longhand before it was sent to the printer. Those of us who worked in journalism in the days when reports were typically sent over via a copy-typist on the other end of a telephone will be familiar with the weary sigh and the phrase: 'Is there much more of this, mate?' It would be hard to imagine plucking up the courage to say: 'Only another 17,000 words, mate.' Yet someone liked it: this edition allegedly sold 207,000 copies,[23] an unprecedented figure anywhere in the world.

Verbosity was an established Victorian trait. The middle class had servants, and no cinema, radio or television; they had the time to read long novels. But the works of Dickens, Eliot and Trollope still come alive for the modern reader because they speak to us down the years about timeless truths of human nature. Did anyone actually wade through all this *Telegraph* treacle? Did they really want to read it, or did they just put up with it because there was nothing better? We have to wait until 1896 and the *Daily Mail* to get the answer.

But the *Telegraph* did mark another step on the road to a truly popular journalism. It was bought by the very ancestors of the suburban ladies and Lt-Cols (rtd) who still buy it today, the great British complaining classes: when Mr Pooter wanted to moan about the behaviour of a cabbie, it was the *Telegraph* he decided to write to. It was a rather Pooterish paper for rather Pooterish people. And there were moments when it hit the nerve-ends of Victorian society as surely as Trollope ever did, and not just in the classified advertisements for false teeth ('clinically prepared . . . without springs or wires . . . sharp edges avoided'). Perhaps its most direct hit came in 1868, when a case involving Belgian girls in London led to a leader which denounced prostitution without ever mentioning the word:

> The public does not underrate the evils of that ghastly travesty of human passion — that blasphemy of human love — which sets this trade afoot, maintains its consignees and *entrepreneurs*, makes the evening and the night shameful in our street, and poisons the moral blood of society . . . the monster vice which feeds on the manhood and womanhood of our race . . . colossal abomination . . . central curse of our time . . . this sorrow and pest . . . there is a noble army of kind and high hearts waiting to march against the Devil of Lust and his hateful works. What it awaits is a leader . . . and the new powers of the people's House of Commons.

It is hard to imagine anything less likely to be advocated by the modern *Daily Telegraph*, with its post-lapsarian view of human nature, than the idea of the Devil of Lust being overcome by an army of kind and high hearts and the powers of the people's House of Commons. It may have been an aberration even then, because, a week later (26 June 1868), it returned to the topic and began to consider the matter more realistically, noting that 'the customers in this market-place of the Devil' were young men who ought to marry, but were unable to do so because of 'the outrageous expectations of parents on behalf of marriageable daughters, and the inflated sumptuary ideas of the ladies themselves'.

Thus began 'Marriage or Celibacy?', a debate that raged in the *Telegraph* letters column for a full month, getting within a whisker of mentioning subjects that were never mentioned in Victorian society, let alone its newspapers, while maintaining the veneer of discussing only its more overt obsession: money.

Sir— . . . I maintain it is impossible in our station to live in anything but genteel beggary on £100. Why, it is not the wages of a respectable mechanic.

An eldest daughter.

Sir— . . . I would not advise any girl to leave her parents' roof, where she has been tenderly cared for, to marry on less than £200 a year.

One who married on £120 a year.

Sir—The single point in favour of these imprudent marriages is that they save a young man from sin. What necessity obliges him to sin? . . . If he is obliged to restrain his lust for wealth and his lust for drink, can he not equally restrain his lust for sensuality?

A matron.

Towards the end, the correspondence began to focus on emigration as the answer to the younger generation's financial problems, and the paper concluded on 30 July: 'England is no longer big enough for its inhabitants' – a rather downbeat end to the march against the Devil of Lust. As an argument, it was not very good business either: London newspapers could not make money from people who vanished to Canada or New Zealand. But more of England's inhabitants did seem to be buying the *Telegraph*, even going by the rather dubious figures of the late nineteenth century: 140,000 by 1861, past 200,000 in 1876, 300,000 in 1888: close to 1 per cent of the population, rather than *The Times*'s 0.1 per cent.

It was not very rapid progress, and the paper did not appear to be interested in selling to the respectable mechanics or their prospective brides, though a penny newspaper would, allowing for lower taxes, take no more of a £100 annual income than would a 45p newspaper for someone on the national average wage in 1996. But after the 'Marriage or Celibacy?' debate the *Telegraph* retreated rapidly to the routine business of Victorian newspapers. Its news service was improving, thanks to the invention of its namesake the electric telegraph. The *Telegraph* received the news of Lincoln's assassination on 26 April 1865, eleven days after it happened, when the first sketchy telegrams arrived by ship. Six years later, it received the news of the Great Fire of Chicago via Reuters at once. It just refused to get very excited about it. The *Chicago Tribune* screamed:

FIRE!

Destruction of Chicago.

2,600 Acres of Buildings Destroyed.

Eighty Thousand People
Burned Out.

Incendiaries and Ruffians
Shot and Hanged
By Citizens.

and so on, for another ten decks – the best it could do at a time when it was still technically impossible to run a headline across more than one column. In London, the *Telegraph* contented itself with a simple GREAT FIRE IN CHICAGO, along the lines of THE LATE RIOT AT PENGE. Now, of course, the fire was a better story in Chicago than it was anywhere the *Telegraph* circulated. But American papers had been running multi-deck headlines since the Mexican War of 1846, and not even the beheading of the monarch in Penge would have induced the *Telegraph* to produce a fifteen-deck headline.

Nevertheless, it was still considered by some way the most adventurous of the London newspapers. In 1873 it sponsored archaeological research in Nineveh to find the missing fragments of the cuneiform account of the Flood. Then, after the editor, John Le Sage, had met Stanley in Marseilles on his way back from finding Livingstone (and incidentally – to prove that British journalists were not entirely stupid – extracting some rather good quotes that were supposed to be exclusive to the *New York Herald*), it co-sponsored, with the *Herald*, Stanley's next expedition. It also backed the exploration of Kilimanjaro and Lionel Decle's march from the Cape to Cairo. And it regularly touched the hearts of its readers in a thoroughly modern fashion, raising funds for the starving in Lancashire (1862–3) and Paris (1871).

But every time the *Telegraph* dared to depart from the norm of English journalism, it would quickly scurry back to routine and stay there. In the words of one historian: 'One may perhaps infer that the desire to emulate marked both the readers and the proprietors.'[24]

VI

In 1882, however, the *Daily Telegraph* stumbled across a journalistic crock of gold. It was grey and enormous, and, when first sighted by a reporter, all six tons of it was in the road outside Regent's Park refusing to budge.

This was Jumbo, already the best-known animal in London Zoo. London children of the 1870s had ridden on his back as surely as their modern equivalents go to McDonalds. He was known as a character, with a weakness for buns, and the occasional beer and whisky besides. The Zoo had sold him for £2,000 to the American circus owner, P. T. Barnum, and he was being led away from his 'wife' Alice to Millwall Docks when the *Telegraph* reporter caught the moment:

> ... one of the most pathetic scenes in
> which a 'dumb animal' was ever the
> chief actor. The poor brute moaned
> sadly, and appealed in all but human
> words to his keeper, embracing the man
> with his trunk, and actually kneeling
> before him. Jumbo's cries were soon
> heard in the elephant house, where poor
> Alice was again seized with alarm and
> grief ...

Eventually, the elephant's tormentors had to give up and he was led back home, where

> ... the joy of Alice knew no bounds,
> her delight being expressed with clumsy
> gambols round her compartment.

This was real journalism! The outcry, naturally, was immediate. 'A national disgrace', wrote E.S. of Shepherd's Bush. A clergyman wanted the people of London to rise as one man to stop 'this cruel, inhuman bargain'. They might have been talking about prostitutes again. But a child of eight joined in: 'I have had many beautiful rides on him. I'm sure there are many mammas and papas who would subscribe and pay the £2,000 to keep dear Jumbo here.' And not only mammas and papas: 'six little friends' offered a shilling each. Even some Fellows of the Royal Zoological Society were baffled by the sale of their chief attraction. If the *Telegraph* could raise £6,000 for the starving in Lancashire, there would have been no problem at all raising £2,000 for a cause far dearer to its readers' hearts.

But there was a problem: the deal had been done. Le Sage, the editor, sent a telegram to Barnum: EDITOR'S COMPLIMENTS. ALL BRITISH CHILDREN DISTRESSED AT ELEPHANT'S DEPARTURE. HUNDREDS OF CORRESPONDENTS BEG US TO ENQUIRE ON WHAT TERMS YOU WILL KINDLY RETURN JUMBO. ANSWER PREPAID UNLIMITED — LE SAGE. As the *Telegraph*'s leader column put it: 'Will he not listen to the cry of the children? We all expect a gentle answer.'

The actual reply was perhaps a clue to the fact that Jumbo would not be the only national treasure heading for America over the next century or so: MY COMPLIMENTS TO EDITOR DAILY TELEGRAPH AND BRITISH NATION. FIFTY MILLIONS OF AMERICAN CITIZENS ANXIOUSLY AWAITING JUMBO'S ARRIVAL. MY FORTY YEARS' INVARIABLE PRACTICE OF EXHIBITING BEST THAT MONEY CAN PROCURE MAKES JUMBO'S PRESENCE HERE IMPERATIVE. HUNDRED THOUSAND POUNDS WOULD BE NO INDUCEMENT TO CANCEL

PURCHASE — BARNUM. Gentle answer? It would have saved the *Telegraph* money had he simply cabled GET LOST.

There was a frenzy of a sort certainly seen since, but never before. There were questions in Parliament. There were Jumbo hats, Jumbo ties, Jumbo cigars and Jumbo songs:

> Jumbo said to Alice: 'I love you';
> Alice said to Jumbo: 'I don't believe you do,
> For if you really loved me, as you say you do,
> You wouldn't be going to Yankeeland and leave me in the Zoo.'

Everyone was convinced that the rough types of Yankeeland would treat Jumbo badly. Some of the Fellows of the Society took the committee to court on the grounds that they had not been consulted, and Jumbo briefly became that most forlorn of Victorian creatures: a ward in Chancery. That was a temporary hitch. The only real problem for the Zoo was finding a way of securing Jumbo's consent, or at least a method of tricking him into a movable cage. As preparations towards that end continued, both parties to the bargain were doing splendidly. Attendances at the Zoo rocketed – 24,000 on 24 March, compared to 1,700 on the corresponding Monday the previous year: at sixpence a head, the Zoo made more money in a couple of days than Barnum was paying; meanwhile, the American papers, then so much livelier than the British in pouncing on this kind of story, were giving Jumbo enormous publicity.

Barnum's final ploy was to sign up Jumbo's keeper, Matthew Scott, who did seem to have a special rapport with the elephant. Finally, Jumbo was led away in a special cage. The *Telegraph* reported his portage to the docks as if it were a royal funeral: 'Everywhere, everybody hears today the tidings "Jumbo's gone."' It quoted a dockside tough: 'I feel as if I could sit down and cry.' Jumbo sailed aboard the *Assyrian Monarch*, accompanied by Scott – and a representative of the *Telegraph*, who filed reports obsessively: 'Off Dover, Sunday: Jumbo has proved himself a very good sailor.' 'Off Scilly, Monday night: Wind North-West with a fresh breeze. All well on board.'

The Zoo's defence of its actions through all this had been very limp indeed. The secretary, P. L. Sclater, wrote a pretty feeble letter to the paper about Jumbo becoming a source of anxiety. But the Jumbo story was a precursor of twentieth-century journalism not only because it was a rattling good yarn, milked for all it was worth, and nothing to do with Parliament or the law courts; the *Telegraph* was also, at the very least, highly selective with the facts. The Jumbo–Alice love affair was imaginative nonsense: the two elephants had never even shared a cage. The other side of the story was that around the age of 20, male elephants begin to suffer great pain from the sexual condition called 'must'; Jumbo was potentially dangerous. In 1871 another African elephant had crushed its keeper,[25] and the Zoo was very anxious to avoid a repetition – partly to avoid criticism from the *Telegraph*, which had been very stern over a nasty incident involving a rhino.

On the other hand, the British animal-lovers were quite right: the Americans were beastly. To make sure Jumbo got into his specially built railway car when he arrived, Barnum positioned two other elephants behind to shove him and a man on top to bash him on the head with a crowbar and force him to duck inside. For three years Jumbo was billed across North America as 'the largest elephant that ever lived' (which was rubbish) until he was being led across a railway line in Ontario one day in 1885 and the unstoppable force, a freight train, finally met the immovable object. Both train and Jumbo were wrecked.[26]

The Jumbo story was not an attempt to fill the paper during a thin patch. It ran all through winter and early spring, and meanwhile the world was not standing still:

POLITICAL CRISIS.

EXPECTED RESIGNATION
OF MR GLADSTONE.

ATTEMPT TO SHOOT THE QUEEN.

BRADLAUGH EXPELLED FROM
PARLIAMENT.

EARTHQUAKE IN COSTA RICA.

GREAT LOSS OF LIFE.

The author of the Jumbo pieces got no by-line, no Journalist of the Year award. But, according to J. Hall Richardson, who joined the paper as a junior reporter that year, he was Godfrey Turner. On another occasion Turner was sent, along with Richardson, to cover a big colliery explosion at Barnsley. The press were writing in one big room.

'Listen to this, boys,' Turner shouted, and he read out some passages he had just written.
'But there is not one word of truth in that,' the others protested.
'Well, what does it matter?' replied Turner. 'It is jolly good copy.'[27]

It is instructive that Richardson, writing half a century later, when such methods were becoming the norm, felt the story worth telling. Turner seems, like the Jumbo story, anachronistic – a throw-forward: cheerfully amoral, casually mendacious, he may be regarded as a true father of modern British journalism.

VII

Richardson's memoirs, like those of other Victorian journalists, suggest that with no big headlines, no pressure to write a cracking opening paragraph, plenty of room to report the intricacies of stories and late-night deadlines leaving plenty of time to write, there seems to have been minimal pressure to report anything other than the truth as the reporter perceived it. The result of this comfortable method of working was a generation of journalists unable to communicate clearly, let alone succinctly, and often incapable, as we shall see, of even gathering the facts properly.

However, newspapers preferred to tell deliberate lies only about their political opponents or their circulation figures. By the late 1880s the *Telegraph* was claiming above its leader column:

LARGEST CIRCULATION IN THE WORLD.

THE SALE OF
THE DAILY TELEGRAPH
AMOUNTS TO AN AVERAGE WHICH,
IF TESTED,
WILL SHOW AN
EXCESS OF HALF A MILLION
COPIES WEEKLY
OVER ANY OTHER MORNING PAPER.

The modern scholar Lucy M. Brown, who did test those figures, suggests that the *Telegraph* was probably only about 50,000 a day, i.e. 300,000 a week, ahead of its nearest rival, *The Standard*. But the *Telegraph* was to tell much bigger lies in this respect in the future. It claimed the largest circulation until 1903, seven years after everyone knew the *Daily Mail* had overtaken it.

By prevailing standards, the *Telegraph* did seem innovative. It was actually a thinner paper in the 1880s than it had sometimes been, usually just eight pages. But it could pull out all the stops when necessary. For the divorce case of the century, in 1886, involving Lady Colin Campbell and five co-respondents – two dukes, a general, a leading physician and the head of the London Fire Service – there were sixty-two columns over seventeen days. And the paper left out all the salacious bits.

Around this time the *Telegraph* acquired its own private wire from Paris to London and began a daily feature entitled PARIS DAY BY DAY, which it ran in the most prominent position, next to the leader page. Here it stayed every day for years, since the news came more or less free. The lead story of the moment might be from New York, Berlin or Whitechapel, but still PARIS DAY BY DAY occupied the plum position in the newspaper. Before the decade was out, it acquired a twin called LONDON DAY BY DAY, but somehow this was altogether drearier: 'Julia, Countess of Jersey, has sent out cards for a small party this evening.'

In 1887 the *Telegraph* organized a party in Hyde Park for 30,000 children to coincide with the Queen's Golden Jubilee:

... surprise, delight, unmistakeable happiness were stamped on every young face ... They clustered like swarming bees round the Punch and Judy shows ... they raced and romped ... there was kiss-in-the-ring – the boys too shy to kiss just at first, but were soon put up to that daring duty by the demure little damsels ... 'oh, dear, oh, dear,' a small thing in a white mob-cap and yellow gloves from Archbishop Tenison's School was heard to sigh, 'I wish it would never be night. I shan't be able to play with half the things here ...'

And it seemed as though night never would fall on the Queen – or the *Daily Telegraph*.

Every summer now the paper would lighten its pages, as it had twenty years before, with a lengthy correspondence. In 1889 there was 'An Angelic Quire' – i.e. should women be choristers? – and 'The Battle of Life', an argument between optimism and pessimism; in 1890 the question of capital punishment was superseded by a rather racier argument about matrimonial agencies.[28] None of these, however, matched 'Is Marriage a Failure?', to some extent a re-run of the earlier 'Marriage or Celibacy?' debate but one that attracted, so the paper claimed, 27,000 letters in the summer of 1888. This was picked by the paper, very self-consciously, from an article in the *Westminster Review* by Mrs Mona Caird, an early feminist who said marriage was a vexatious failure: 'unjust to the woman, dehumanising to the man'. She wanted to move on to a higher and less tyrannical relationship between the sexes. Many *Telegraph* readers did not:

Sir—I advocate marriage because I have
long experience of its blessings.
British matron, Maida Vale.

Some of the letter-writers daringly touched on the possibility of free love, though if any of them advocated it, theirs must have been among the 26,000 plus that never got printed:

> *Sir*—'Free marriage' would, I am satis-
> fied, cause the wildest vice. Crime, mur-
> der and degeneracy of the human race
> would be the result.
> > *Patriot, Aldridge Road Villas,*
> > *Bayswater.*

The correspondence ran from 9 August to 29 September, when the paper summed up: 'It goes without saying that the burden of this stupendous correspondence has proved to be overwhelmingly in favour of marriage.' Even so, there was, in this as in all the *Telegraph*'s nineteenth-century diversions from the straitened path of Victorian journalism, just a hint of the impishness that characterized its early years and was to become the defining quality of successful popular journalism.

But only a hint. The *Telegraph*'s correspondences were conducted during what was then a very silly season indeed, because the papers were so dependent on Parliament and the law courts, which were on vacation. It was as though the bonds that constrained British journalism were relaxed, very temporarily, in the way a strict schoolmaster might allow the boys to lark about at the end of term. Elsewhere, braver journalists were beginning to break free of the bonds for ever. So preoccupied was the *Telegraph* with the marriage question in 1888 that it was slow to pick up the fact that the real news was coming out of Whitechapel, and it was very big news indeed. Other papers were becoming quicker on the uptake.

VIII

The *Daily Telegraph* began penny journalism in Britain and was thus able to dominate the newspaper industry from 1855 to 1895, as *The Times* had dominated it for the previous forty years. Ha'penny journalism is supposed to have begun in Britain with *The Echo*, a London evening paper owned by J. Passmore Edwards, a businessman, temperance campaigner and philanthropist. *The Echo* had cottoned on to the significance of events in the East End in 1888 five weeks before the *Telegraph*, on 7 August.

MYSTERIOUS TRAGEDY IN
WHITECHAPEL.

A WOMAN BRUTALLY
MURDERED.

The body lying in a pool of blood on the
first-floor landing . . . up to one o'clock
no clue of any kind had come to the
knowledge of the Commercial Street
police authorities . . .

Nor has any clue come since: not a definitive one, anyway. But throughout
the autumn of 1888 the police and the evening papers clutched excitedly at
straws as the series of murders attributed to Jack the Ripper went on. *The
Echo's* headlines gave the flavour. On 11 September:

THIS DAY'S NEWS.

THE EAST END TRAGEDY.

LATEST DETAILS.

PISER IN CUSTODY TODAY.

PIGGOTT CLOSELY WATCHED.

IS HE A LUNATIC?

The American-style decks, and the frank sensationalism, were classic
examples of what had been defined and denounced in May of the previous
year in the magazine *Nineteenth Century* by the poet and critic Matthew
Arnold as 'New Journalism'. This is a phrase that recurs from time to time:
in the 1960s it became identified with the counter-culture and with journalists
who were breaking the profession's then traditions – particularly in their use
of words previously considered, in different ways, taboo, most notably 'fuck'
and 'I'.

There is still some debate about who first brought the 1880s version of
New Journalism to Britain, though it is clear that the infection spread from
America and the carriers were the London evening papers. One school of
thought favours W. T. Stead, the Puritan showman who became editor of
the *Pall Mall Gazette* in 1883, and two years later began his series entitled
'The Maiden Tribute of Modern Babylon' which set out to expose child
prostitution. While the *Telegraph* might have invited its readers to have a
jolly old chinwag on the subject, Stead went out and got the facts for himself,
in the process making himself technically guilty of abduction, for which he
served three months in jail. He also introduced American methods of display

into his paper: larger headlines, line illustrations – photographs were still impossible to reproduce at speed – and crossheads to break up long reports. (Stead went down with the *Titanic* in 1912, thus missing, as has been pointed out, his best ever story.)

Another theory lays greater stress on the role of *The Star*, the evening paper founded by the Radical, T. P. O'Connor, in January 1888, just after he had come back from America. His Confession of Faith, which appeared in the first issue of *The Star*, is the frankest of all manifestos for the journalism that was to come:

We believe that the reader of the daily journal longs for other than mere politics; and we shall present him with plenty of entirely unpolitical literature – sometimes humorous, sometimes pathetic; anecdotal, statistical, the craze for fashions and the arts of housekeeping and now and then, a short, dramatic and picturesque tale. In our reporting columns we shall do away with the hackneyed style of obsolete journalism; and the men and women that figure in the forum or the pulpit or the law court shall be presented as they are – living, breathing, in blushes or in tears – and not merely by the dead words that they utter. Our ideal is to leave no event unrecorded; to be earliest in the field with every item of news; to be thorough and unmistakeable in our meaning; to be animated, readable and stirring.

What was still very nineteenth-century was the earnestness with which *The Star* stated its aims, and the frankness of its partisanship:

> *The Star* will be a Radical journal. It
> will judge all policy – domestic, foreign,
> social – from the Radical standpoint.

And indeed, its by-election coverage, for instance, left no doubt that the paper meant what it said:

VICTORY!

WE WALK IN AT SOUTHAMPTON.

But *The Star* was animated all right, both in its politics – 'The few dozen lines of drivel known as the Queen's Speech' (9 February 1888); 'The organised hypocrisy that at present styles itself the Government' (9 June 1888) – and in other matters: 'If Marion Terry has shown that good acting can cause to be forgiven a large nose, Lady Monckton has demonstrated the same fact concerning a large mouth .' It had headlines like:

SKIMPY SKIRTS AND SHORT WAISTS.

and

IS OUR MARY ILL?[29]

By 25 May, issue no. 110, it was claiming the 'Largest circulation Of Any Evening paper in the Kingdom' under the title-piece. It printed its news on page 1 and it printed it as boldly and brassily as the typefaces of the time allowed.

Morning newspapers did not conduct themselves in this fashion, and a distinction began to be discerned between morning newspapers, which were respectable, and evening newspapers, which were not, rather like the difference between broadsheets and tabloids that exists today. This perception lasted at least until 1936, when George V's physician manipulated the King's death to ensure that it caught the morning papers' deadlines and was handled more sedately. He was, by then, rather behind the times in his knowledge of journalism.

In 1888 the distinction was very real. But Sunday newspapers had been going their own way for a hundred years. The New Journalism, in a sense, had always been here; it was now merely breaking out of its bounds. And the evening papers did have fun with the great story of 1888. Poor old Piser and Piggott, the alleged lunatic, were merely among the first of a myriad of suspects, and *The Echo*'s headlines tell the tale of blighted hopes:

13 September	POLICE SAID TO BE ON TRACK.
27 September	A MAN GIVES HIMSELF UP.
1 October	IMPORTANT DISCOVERY.
2 October	ARREST AT CHINGFORD.
4 October	PURSUING AN AMERICAN.
6 October	SUPPOSED MURDERER'S PORTRAIT RECOGNISED: THE POLICE ON HIS TRACK.
7 October	DOZEN MEN ARRESTED – AND DISCHARGED.
10 October	ANOTHER IMPORTANT CLUE.
17 October	SUSPECTED MURDERER TRACKED: EXPECTED CONFESSION.

and then, sadly:

17 November	POLICE VIGOUR UNREWARDED.

Through the yellowing pages, down the generations, accompanied by the swirling of London fogs and the clip-clop of the hansoms, one can hear the voice of Inspector Lestrade of the Yard, confidently briefing the press, having grasped hold of the wrong end of the stick every time. Alas, the real-life Lestrades had no Holmes to help them out. But they were confident, the late Victorians. And this included the old-fashioned daily journalists, who were so slow on to the Ripper story, as they were with so many others. Within a few years, however, they were going to get a very nasty jolt indeed.

PART TWO

Ta-ra-ra-boom-de-ay!

The *Daily Mail* Era

Prologue

Geoffrey Tempest is a struggling writer, who suddenly inherits £5 million from an uncle who says he has sold his soul to the Devil, and the money was his reward. Tempest meets a mysterious foreign prince, buys a horse that wins the Derby, marries an earl's beautiful daughter and – thanks to his wealth – gets his book published.

His bride, Lady Sibyl, tells Tempest she is evil: 'I am passionate, resentful, impetuous – frequently unsympathetic, inclined to morbidness and melancholy . . . I am a contaminated creature, trained to perfection in the lax morals and prurient literature of the day.' He finds she is right. She is false to him ('O infamous woman! Have you no shame?') with the prince, who, naturally, turns out to be the Devil. Tempest leaves his wife ('Further intercourse between us is impossible'). She takes poison. He is swindled out of all his money.

This is the gist of a novel called *The Sorrows of Satan* by Marie Corelli. It was published in November 1895, and went through ten editions before the end of the year and a further twenty-two in 1896. In 1909 it was in its fifty-fifth edition. These days it is probably not read by fifty-five people a year.

There is nothing erotic about *The Sorrows of Satan*. But Corelli had an instinct for the popular fancy. The book, said Corelli's biographer, Brian Masters, was 'read avidly in the servants' hall and surreptitiously by middle-class ladies'.[1] Perhaps the modern analogy would be with Jeffrey Archer, a man with even less literary ability but precisely the same instinct for public taste and self-publicity.

Corelli was a genius at that. *The Sorrows of Satan* would have been routinely savaged by the critics in all the smart magazines and the newspapers, but for the fact that Corelli had been caught that way before. She insisted that a special notice went out with the book: 'NO COPIES OF THIS BOOK ARE SENT OUT FOR REVIEW. Members of the press will therefore obtain it (should they wish to do so) in the usual way with the rest of the public.' It *was* savaged, but amid a great deal of publicity.

Corelli's revenge on the critics is one of the sub-plots of the novel. Once Tempest has money he is told that, for £40, an agency will 'boom' his book by inserting paragraphs in up to 400 newspapers. This is accompanied by an asterisked footnote which says simply 'A fact'. There is a minor villain, a corrupt critic called McWhing. And the heroine ('feminine . . . graceful . . . dainty . . .

unaffected . . . vivacious . . . happy . . . studious . . . perfect taste') is a best-selling lady novelist who is called Mavis Clare, thus, by an astonishing coincidence, sharing the author's initials. Tempest, out of jealousy, gives her book a nasty review, but she is entirely serene. At the end all he has left is a kindly letter from Mavis: ('It pressed against my heart, a shield against all vileness.')

Corelli was shameless, but she knew all about 'booming'. The book was brilliantly marketed, in a single volume instead of the three that had previously been commonplace. The fuss even eclipsed the trial of Oscar Wilde, which was taking place at the same time. An obsequious warder at Reading Gaol is supposed to have asked Wilde:

'Excuse me, sir, would Marie Corelli be considered a great writer?'

'From the way she writes,' Wilde replied, 'she ought to be here.' In 1956 Cyril Connolly in the *Sunday Times* called *The Sorrows of Satan* 'unbearable and unreadable'.

Yet probably hundreds of thousands of people bought this book. They could all read. But in 1895 there was not a single morning newspaper published in England that catered for readers who might like Marie Corelli. The *Daily Telegraph*, with its occasional bouts of correspondence on marriage, was the only paper that even remotely considered the interests of people who might not be men, and men of affairs at that, and might not be obsessed with reading verbatim reports of parliamentary debates, foreign and financial reports, criticism of the higher forms of artistic endeavour and – now and again, if it did not miss the story – details of the more sensational sort of crimes. Each report was typically presented to them at enormous length in grey, pictureless columns. The population of the United Kingdom was now almost 40 million. The morning newspapers sold little more than a million copies between them.

Marie Corelli may be almost forgotten now. But the man who realized that there was a market in selling newspapers to the Corelli-reading classes created a revolution that transformed the nation. Perhaps he did more than anyone to create the modern British democracy of the next hundred years – for better and worse.

I

Alfred Harmsworth was born in Dublin in 1865, the son of an indigent, boozy barrister of the same name and a fearsomely determined woman from a Protestant business family, born Geraldine Maffett. He was the eldest of fourteen children. Three died in infancy; two of the others became viscounts, one a baron and two more baronets. The family moved to London and lived mostly in St John's Wood. The children grew up rumbustiously while the father's career faded, and their circumstances drifted into shabby gentility.

When Alfred was eight, their next-door neighbour, George Jealous, who was editor of the *Hampstead and Highgate Express*, gave him a printing set. At fifteen, he founded the *Henley House School Magazine* ('Edited by Alfred C. Harmsworth'), professionally printed, priced 3d. In the first issue he wrote: 'I have it on the best authority that the HHS Magazine is to be a marked success.' In the second he commented: 'I am glad to say that my prediction as to the success of this magazine proved correct.'[2] Corelli and, presumably, Harmsworth would have called it booming; these days we would call it hype. Whatever the word, this was someone who instinctively understood its importance.

At sixteen, Harmsworth left school and impregnated his mother's house-maid. He was sent to Europe for a while, as travelling companion to a clergyman, to convalesce after pneumonia, so it was said. When he came back, his mother would not have him in the house; this was only a brief interruption in the most intense relationship of his life. He roomed with an old schoolfriend, Max Pemberton, and wrote for magazines. He became editor of a publication called *Youth* and then, aged twenty, of *Bicycling News*, which was covering the craze of the time and involved in a circulation battle akin to those fought by computer magazines in the 1990s. He also wrote for *Tit-Bits*, the snippets magazine which was one of the harbingers of the popular press revolution, started in Manchester in 1881 by George Newnes, the former owner of a vegetarian restaurant. In 1888 Harmsworth married Mary Milner, from another family with pretensions but no money. The following year his father was to die, aged fifty-two, from cirrhosis. At the wedding, his mother said through her tears: 'They will have so many children and no money.'[3] She could not have been more wrong. Though the couple remained married, all four of Harmsworth's children were illegitimate. And money very soon ceased to be a problem.

Shortly after the wedding, Alfred Harmsworth achieved his first ambition and found someone willing to back his plans to start a rival to *Tit-Bits*. Originally called *Answers to Correspondents*, later *Answers*, it began with issue no. 3, making it look as though the snappy paragraphs really were responses to genuine enquiries from previous issues. These magazines flourished on facts, or something very close to them, preferably but not necessarily odd ones.[4] Successful popular journalism in the late twentieth century has been based on the contraction of readers' interests to not much more than sex and television. In the late nineteenth century the horizons of ordinary British people were constantly being expanded: their country was completing the construction of the largest empire the world had ever seen; the railways were opening up possibilities of travel; the telegraph and telephone meant information could be transmitted instantly. Harmsworth himself was insatiably curious about what was around him. He was not alone.

Answers was not an immediate triumph. It bumbled along with a circulation around 30,000. Harold Harmsworth gave up his steady clerk's job to play Sancho Panza to his brother Alfred's Quixote and kept expenses under control, as he was to do all his life. The story, often told whether true or not, goes that the two of them were walking along the Embankment and met a tramp who told them that happiness was £1 a week for life. So, in 1889, *Answers* ran a competition offering precisely that as a prize. Competitors had to guess how much gold and silver would be in the Bank of England on a given day. They also had to have their entries countersigned by five witnesses. All figures involving Alfred Harmsworth should be treated with caution. But it was said that 700,000 people entered, which meant that more than three million may have been involved in the countersignatures, and would therefore have heard about *Answers*. Two hundred and five thousand bought the issue which published the result. The winner was Sapper Austin of Southampton. He married his sweetheart on the proceeds and died of tuberculosis eight years and four hundred Harmsworth pounds later.[5]

From here, the two Harmsworths built their empire. They were an extraordinary pair: Alfred, quixotic, quick-witted, a heaven-sent journalist; Harold, cautious, pessimistic, calculating. Alfred's instinct was always to spend money – indeed, the whole mentality of Fleet Street may be traced back to this impulse – Harold's to try to save, cut back, buy cheap paper, save pennies. This is a shorthand encapsulation of the two men's characters. Harold's is in many ways the more enigmatic and intriguing and, after Alfred's death in 1922, it becomes crucial to this history. But as a partnership they were devastating.

Over the next six years they began magazines at a rate of about two a year, starting with *Comic Cuts* (a name which passed into the language, and remained there long after the magazine had passed out of existence) and continuing with *Chips, Forget-Me-Not, Home Sweet Home, Union Jack* and *Pluck Library*, whose very names breathe their niche in the market. Neither of the Harmsworths was yet thirty and it was said they already had the biggest publishing company in the world. In August 1894 they bought a failing London newspaper, the *Evening News*, and rapidly made it as successful as everything else they owned.

There was no question that Alfred Harmsworth was ambitious. But the direction of his ambition remained uncertain. In March 1895 he stood as Conservative candidate for Portsmouth, buying one of the local newspapers to help him on his way, as casually as a lesser man might have bought a copy of it. He lost, and never again attempted the chancy method of seeking power

through election. Early the following year the Harmsworths began producing
dummy issues of a new national newspaper, which they eventually decided
to call the *Daily Mail*. On 4 May 1896 it burst into life.

II

Looking back from the 1990s it is impossible not to get a little misty-eyed
over life in London in the 1890s:

> The newsvendors shouted of the latest cricket scores or of ''Orrible Mur-
> ders' and called you 'Captain', the piano-organs played, the hansoms
> trotted by, their lights a golden glow like fireflies along Piccadilly, and the
> gas-lamps flickered or the new-fangled electric globes shone bluey-grey
> over the pleasure-seekers of London ... a gay, care-free, light-hearted
> throng, whose tomorrow would be as today, as yesterday.[6]

That, of course, assumes they did not become the victims of the 'orrible
murders. But for the middle classes there were all sorts of possibilities. The
rail system was virtually complete; it was possible to stay in a first-class hotel
for half a crown at night; eating out was becoming popular. It was a brief,
glorious interlude when swift, safe and reasonably comfortable travel was
possible, but the air was not yet filled with exhaust fumes. Cycling was all
the rage for men and women (Daisy, Daisy, give me your answer, do),
and people were healthier as a result. The favourite song of the day was
Ta-ra-ra-boom-de-ay and the catchphrase Hi-tiddly-hi-ti-ti-ti-ti!

Conditions were improving even for those who were not part of the gay,
carefree throng. According to the historian of feminism Pat Thane, women
could feel 'a potential for control over their lives that was historically unprecedented'.[7] They were starting to work in shops and post offices and elementary
schools; middle-class women were playing an increasing role in public life,
on bodies like the Poor Law Boards, instead of sitting at home in their lace
dresses and corsets, sewing decorously and reading Marie Corelli. Working
people were enjoying a better life: the eight-hour day was starting to come
in; agricultural wages were rising; food prices had been falling for twenty
years. Meat, sugar, tea, jam and bananas were becoming staples; fish and
chip shops were spreading across the country. And though Charles Booth's
Life and Labour of the People in London tells blood-curdling stories of life
among the underclass, conditions were improving even in the slums. This
was no longer the London of Dickens, nor even of Booth's predecessor in

these investigations, Henry Mayhew, thirty years earlier. There were sewers and there was drinking water. It was after the drains but before the trenches; in some ways, there may never have been a happier time to be alive.

And there was a choice, before the *Daily Mail*, of eleven different morning newspapers. There were also competing papers in the major provincial centres, two business papers (the *Financial Times* and the *Financial News*), various sporting dailies and nine London evenings. It was a magnificent selection. Unfortunately, all the morning papers had one thing in common: they were useless.

For a start, they were incompetent at the basic task of newsgathering. Nearly a century later Lucy M. Brown researched the gales that blasted Europe around the New Year of 1895. When the wind eventually dropped, reports of the ships that had failed to arrive began to accumulate in papers like the *Telegraph*. In total, more than 400 people must have died. But not a single national paper bothered to collate the individual reports, let alone get any eye-witness accounts or demand to know whether such a toll could have been avoided. 'This suggests,' Brown wrote, 'as well as an indifference to human loss of life, the haphazard and casual way in which news, outside certain standard topics, tended to be put together.'[8] Even contemporary critics had noticed the papers' failings: 'It is only a few months ago that a Jewish theatre in London was the scene of a dreadful loss of life at quite an early hour of the night, and next day not a solitary line about it appeared in any London morning newspaper. The manager of the theatre had omitted to send notice to the reporters that the catastrophe was to happen.'[9]

The dailies were also incapable of relating to their potential readers. Seven of them were very well established. *The Times*, still charging 3d and somewhat in eclipse, had retained some of its reputation but not its readership. Then, at a penny, there was the *Morning Post*, the High Tory upstairs–downstairs paper;[10] the *Daily Telegraph*, which by now claimed THE LARGEST CIRCULATION IN THE WORLD, perhaps the only pithy phrase in the entire paper; the Liberal supporters, the *Daily News* and *Daily Chronicle*; the business-oriented *Standard*; and the *Morning Advertiser*, owned by the licensed victuallers and retreating from being a general paper into becoming a news-sheet for pubs.[11]

The industry had changed remarkably little since the abolition of stamp duty, yet the conditions in which it operated had been revolutionized. Paper, which once had to be processed from old rags – German peasants' cast-offs, it was said – could now be produced from wood-pulp at a fraction of the cost. (The difference can be seen in the files of old newspapers: those from the earlier part of the nineteenth century are still in beautiful condition, while papers of a hundred years later are yellowing and flaking away.) The mechanical Linotype composing machines transformed the process of putting the words on to the paper. The steam presses, as surreptitiously installed by *The Times* in 1814, were gradually replaced by rotary presses capable of mass production; these transformed the process of getting the paper on to the streets. The railways transformed the process of getting the paper to readers anywhere in the country, and made truly national newspapers possible.

The four newcomers had seen something of the gap in the market that Harmsworth saw, but had failed to grasp the formula. The *Daily Graphic*, started in 1890, was the first to use a significant number of illustrations – still line drawings rather than photographs – but a penny was too expensive for its potential public. *The Morning* and the *Morning Leader* had both started in 1892 at a ha' penny, but neither had got the balance right. Harmsworth's partner Kennedy Jones spotted what was wrong with *The Morning* straight away. He noted that, in the eighteenth century, *The Times* had succeeded while a rival called *All Alive and Merry* had not. *The Morning* 'had a cheap look as well as a cheap price . . . there must be an indefinable dignity which at the glance stamps a paper as a responsible organ . . . though the British public worships cheapness it abhors the appearance of cheapness.'[12]

Finally, there was the *Daily Courier*, which Newnes of *Tit-Bits* launched eleven days ahead of the *Daily Mail* as a spoiler. It was even smaller than a modern tabloid: magazine-sized. Like the *Mail*, it specialized in running one-paragraph reports and indeed began calling itself A Paragraph Newspaper. But it cost a penny and its paragraphs were boring. The day the *Mail* started, the *Courier* led its Summary with the news that the Prince of Wales had visited the Royal Academy on Saturday. When the *Courier* reached issue 98, on 15 August, it ran the following paragraph:

> The Season being over with the Proro-
> gation of Parliament, publication of the
> Daily Courier, which is mainly a social
> journal, will be suspended for the
> present.

And suspended it has remained.

They were hopeless, all of them, old and new. On the day the *Daily Mail* started, the *Daily News* – 'The Largest Circulation of any Liberal Paper in the World' – carried lengthy accounts of both the Booksellers' Dinner and the Camera Club Dinner. Hamilton Fyfe, later editor of the *Daily Mirror*, wrote that the newspapers of the time sent reporters to these events not because anyone was much interested but because 'we always send to that'.[13] Two days later, the *News* had a 15,000-word account of a routine day's proceedings in Parliament. The *Standard* gave 2,000 words to a leader article about Persia and Russia, exactly 100 of them in one sentence. Then there was the *Daily Chronicle*, which claimed the largest circulation of any daily paper in London.[14] A year earlier, on the day W. G. Grace became the first cricketer ever to score a hundred first-class hundreds, the *Chronicle* had begun the first of its dozen leader articles: 'Is it not time that there should be a distinct process of what the Germans call *Aufklärung* within the Liberal Party?'

One of the articles did deal with Grace, but it was well behind the one considering M. Edmond de Goncourt's Diary (Volume Eight). On 4 May 1896 the *Chronicle* began its cycling column:

> The Wheel Club held its reception at its headquarters, Hertford House, Bolton Gardens, South Kensington on Saturday afternoon. The house itself is a very commodious and old-fashioned one, and the grounds are large, including rows of deserted greenhouses and stables.

Who on earth was interested in the greenhouses? This was not the property column. There were twenty-two leading articles – twenty-two! – the shortest of them a hundred words on the weather ('The wheat crop on well-favoured and well-drained soils is looking very well'), the longest about 1,500 words on a magazine article by Professor Brander Matthews, 'On Pleasing the Taste of the Public'. The leader-writer explained, or attempted to explain, that Professor Matthews was wondering 'whether Gresham's Law might be as potent in art as it is in finance, the inferior product driving out the superior, as the bloody shows of the arena in Rome finally extinguished the Latin literary drama'. Then he lashed out with the dripping scorn that must have won awfully golden opinions back in the Junior Common Room: 'Several queries of this sort might be dropped, each fully as helpful as the Professor's. As whether the continued depreciation of the rupee accounts for the fact that Charley's Aunt is still running.'

Well, by exquisite irony, it happened that as that leader was being written the bloody shows were indeed preparing to enter the Fleet Street arena and drive into the darkest corners not only the Latin literary drama but de Goncourt's Diary (Volume Eight), Camera Club dinners, cycling reports that began with a description of the commodious headquarters and the kind of undergraduate clever-dickery that had hitherto passed muster as leader-writing. At last, someone did intend to tickle the public.

III

The jackdaw mind that produced *Answers* produced a jackdaw newspaper. Almost nothing in the *Daily Mail* was original. What Alfred Harmsworth did was to get all the elements right. He lined up the three bells on the fruit machine, where the proprietors of *The Morning* and the *Courier* etc. had got only one or two. The content was right; the price was right; the technique was right.

The most unexpected thing about the *Daily Mail* was not what it was, but what it was not. Through the late winter and early spring of 1896 the *Mail* produced dummy editions that looked very much like the kind of paper a modern designer, given the technological constraints of the time, might have produced: the words DAILY MAIL across the top in rather flashy bold capitals; a headline across the page in the largest typeface available; and a cartoon dominating the front page in the position where even the staidest modern broadsheet would have the day's main photograph. It must have looked fairly advanced stuff.

Yet when the paper was actually published, none of this happened: the newspaper that was to set the tone for the next hundred years looked exactly like the newspapers of the previous hundred years. It was a broadsheet, of course;[15] the words *Daily Mail* were in steady, reliable Old English typeface; the front page was covered with advertisements – it might have been *The Times* or the *Telegraph*. This was precisely the idea. One of Northcliffe's many dicta on journalism was that the man in the street (earning maybe £100 a year) was 'tomorrow's £1,000 man – so he hopes and thinks'.

'For months before 4 May, we produced a great many private copies of the paper,' Harmsworth recalled later. 'In some of these were inserted all sorts of grotesque features with which to delude any of the enemy who might be awake. We saw to it that he got these copies.'[16] The modern design must have been the grotesque features. The *Mail*'s conservatism in these matters was not a passing aberration. It was not until the First World War was under way that the *Mail* began to include cartoons with any regularity; it was not until the outbreak of the Second World War, after even the *Telegraph* had succumbed, that the *Mail* put news instead of adverts on the front page; and the title-piece of 1896 has survived more or less unchanged until 1996. In the conformist society of the 1890s people on the horse omnibuses and the smoky trains wanted to be seen reading a paper that did them credit. On either side of the words *Daily Mail* were boxes saying 'A Penny Newspaper for One Halfpenny' and 'The Busy Man's Daily Journal'. Cheap without the appearance of cheapness.

The months of preparation had not been wasted. The paper looked as though it knew what it was doing, in a manner that was matched ninety years later when *The Independent* also produced dozens of dummy issues before presenting itself to the public. The *Mail* also had some cracking news stories on its very first day: one might argue that they constituted an early warning of the kind of stories the popular press would make its own, combining triumphalism,

SOUDAN.
BRILLIANT BRITISH VICTORY.

xenophobia,

PRETORIA PRISONERS.
SEARCHED BY THE BOERS.
PUBLIC SYMPATHY.

and, of course, crime,

READING MURDERS.
SENSATIONAL LETTERS OF CONFESSION.

in about equal proportions. But it was the skill behind what modern newspaper executives are inclined to call 'the package' which was so compelling. The little one-paragraph items that had dominated *Tit-Bits* and *Answers* were now adapted to the business of news. There were columns of political gossip,

> The precincts of the House of late have been brightened by an unusual number of pretty women . . . possibly the attraction may be the large percentage of well-groomed and well turned-out 'young bloods' that the last General Election brought in.

society gossip,

> The pretty Lady Downshire has not given up horse riding for cycling.

cricket gossip, racing gossip (by Robin Goodfellow, a name still used in the paper) and cycling gossip,

TODAY'S WHEEL
CAUSERIE.

The number of actors and actresses who
cycle nowadays is astounding.... It is
a matter of common knowledge that
Seymour Hicks and George Edwardes
worked out most of the plot of 'One of
the Best' while riding tandem in beaut-
eous Berkshire.

A good deal of the paper's inspiration came from setting out to appeal to
100 per cent of the adult population instead of the usual 50 per cent. On
page 7 there was 'The Daily Magazine' including 'Woman's Realm': 'Today's
Dinner' ('White Soup, Cold Lamb, Mint Sauce, Mashed Potatoes, Marmalade Pudding, Sweet Sauce'), 'Hints for Housewives' ('Instead of trying to
revive a dead fire with paraffin, try a teaspoonful of sugar'), 'Toilet Hints'
('Anxious or angry thoughts at bedtime are ruinous to good looks, for the
scowl they produce has eight hours to engrave itself on the face') and a
column called 'Strange Doubles' ('Queen Nathalie of Servia has a double
in the keeper of a small grocery shop').

There was also a serial, or a feuilleton, as it was rather preciously known,
'Beauregard's Shadow'. Other newspapers had tried serials before, often with
big-name writers; they never got them right. This was anonymous, but it was
organized like a modern soap opera:

> ... 'Why, yes Morgan,' she said. 'But
> why do you call me a young lady of
> importance?'
> 'Because, my dear, you have just
> inherited half a million of money.'
> (To be continued in tomorrow's *Daily
> Mail.*)

And tomorrow, and tomorrow, and tomorrow. Until 30 May, when the *Mail*,
with the instinctive cunning that its rivals lacked, not only ended 'Beauregard's Shadow' but, in the same issue, started its successor, 'Married in June'.

Now, this was clearly not a paper aimed at the lumpenproletariat. The
writer of the recipe wrote: 'I am presuming that your Sunday joint was a roast
shoulder of lamb', which would still have been a fairly bold presumption for
much of the British population. But nor was it aimed only at the handful of
people interested in politics. The *Mail* did not have twenty-two leading
articles. There was apparently some discussion about whether it should have
any at all. It settled for three, one of them on the law forcing motor cars to
be preceded by a man carrying a red flag. 'Exquisite nonsense,' said the *Mail*.

The law was repealed before the year was out, which still seems rather a pity. Most of the papers of the time were overtly partisan organs, committed to the stereotyped battle between Conservatives and Liberals, ins and outs, which meant a great deal to Trollope's less engaging characters and very little to real people. The new paper was, on the face of it, almost apolitical. And it appeared not to take its own opinions all that seriously. This did not last.

There was one further element in the *Mail*'s success, which was at least as important as the editorial content. While the dummy issues were being prepared, the *Mail* was advertising heavily elsewhere. In issues two and three, it reprinted a stack of complimentary comments: from other newspapers, from Mr Gladstone, from Mr Beerbohm Tree and from Albert Trott, captain of the touring Australian cricket team. The second issue also contained an announcement signed by E. Layton Bennett, Fellow of the Institute of Chartered Accountants, to the effect that the circulation of the *Mail*'s first paper was 397,215, 'a world's record for a first number'. This figure has subsequently been quoted in at least two dozen books on journalism, usually along with the information that Alfred Harmsworth, after seeing through the first two days' issues, went home and slept for twenty-two hours, and that the paper was so popular crowds besieged the office in Carmelite Street throughout the first day.

Let us tread carefully here. Perhaps E. Layton Bennett is still alive somewhere at the age of 140 and not beyond suing for his professional reputation. But in 1914 Harmsworth himself – Lord Northcliffe as he had by then become – began a campaign to force his rivals to produce honest circulation figures, pointing out that sixty days were needed for the newsagents to get their returns back to the paper for the auditors to come up with accurate figures. Even today, with computerization, it takes several days for papers to come up with exact numbers, because they depend on the efficiency of the wholesalers and newsagents in processing their unsold copies; and the monthly audited figures take a fortnight to come through. The idea that every street vendor, railway station bookstall and corner newsagent, especially in all those regions beyond the Home Counties where sales of London papers remained haphazard, could have fed their sales figures back to E. Layton Bennett within the first twenty-four hours is absurd.

It is possible that 397,215 papers did indeed circulate, in the sense that they were printed, and that many ended up, unsold, where they started, in the *Mail* office. It is not possible that Bennett could have known that 397,215 – and not 397,214 or 397,216 – had been sold to the public. It is also possible that people really did besiege the offices and were not hired from the 1890s equivalent of Mobs-R-Us. Doubtless E. Layton Bennett was an honourable man. But Alfred Harmsworth knew, as Marie Corelli knew, the importance of 'booming'. He had known it since he edited the *Henley House School Magazine*: 'the *Daily Mail* is to be a marked success . . . my prediction has been proved correct.' Ta-ra-ra-boom-de-ay! The *Mail*'s first circulation figures have to go down as the first whopping lie of the popular press's century; the first, it has to be said, of many.

IV

But there can be no dispute about the *Mail*'s journalism in its early days. As he did with *Answers*, Harmsworth expanded his readers' horizons.

A critic of newspapers, writing in 1895, had noted how news from the United States had actually diminished since the invention of the Atlantic telegraph.[17] In the old days, papers were content to wait for the mails and would then print lengthy letters of American doings. The papers of the 1890s might print all kinds of guff but they did not want to print ancient guff, so American news was usually confined to brief cables. The *Daily Telegraph*, happy to print two columns of Paris news because it came on its private wire, would not go to the expense of doing the same from America. Alfred Harmsworth, when his brother Harold did not actually restrain him, was eager to invest in news whatever the cost. And he did so.

A year later, on the *Mail*'s first anniversary ('Today's dinner: Cabbage Soup, Lamb Chops'), Northcliffe wrote a signed message in the self-congratulatory style that was to become familiar:

The warmth of the reception of the new methods of the Daily Mail brought about a number of much-needed changes in the working arrangements of other journals. American news had hitherto been almost entirely neglected . . . India rarely mentioned . . . And apart from the local nature of the unimproved London daily, there was the drawback of its verbosity. The Press had not kept pace with the people in quickness and movement, in the desire to obtain the largest result with the smallest loss of time . . . the Master, has in fact, learned a good deal from the Pupil.

This was perfectly fair comment. Within three weeks of the *Mail*'s launch, the *Daily Chronicle*, for instance, had introduced a twelve-page paper on Saturday with illustrations and its own rather long-winded women's columns. The change was not universal – that same day *The Standard* still managed to devote 6,000 words to a report of the coronation of Czar Nicholas II, most of which comprised a list of Russian officialdom and the order in which it processed. And this was nothing compared to its equally turgid 80,000 words on the Queen's Diamond Jubilee a year later. *The Standard* was to die even more quickly and more bloodily than the Czar,[18] and just as deservedly.

One has to presume that E. Layton Bennett's monthly figures over the next few years were something like accurate, because of the degree to which the *Mail* slipped into popular culture and song, in a way perhaps not matched until Page Three of *The Sun* moved into national consciousness in the 1970s:

> I'm a lady, don't forget,
> All I say
> Is in the Daily Mail next day.
> Dances, music halls and plays,
> Drawing rooms and smart soirées.
> Henley, Goodwood and Paree
> Owe their great success to me.[19]

and

> While we have Joseph,[20]
> The corn in Egypt will never fail
> He's a statesman and a brick too
> And what he says, he'll stick to
> By kind permission of the Daily Mail.[21]

Bennett audited the *Mail*'s circulation as settling down to 170,000 in its first month, then rising again very steadily: 300,000 by 1897; above 400,000 by 1898, enough to claim 'The Largest Circulation in the World'; 600,000 by 1899; over a million at the more dramatic moments of the Boer War – indeed, almost a million and a half on 23 January 1901 when Queen Victoria died – before settling back around 700,000 for most of the years before the First World War.

It seems to have been either an exhilarating or a terrifying place for a journalist to work, depending on one's temperament and Northcliffe's mood. The *Telegraph* had a rule that 'the editor cannot be seen by anyone'.[22] One imagines him flitting among the shadows like the Ripper. The young lions were now all very ancient, and unenthusiastic about encouraging any cubs. The *Mail* had a policy that any likely young reporter was given a trial 'on space' by Kennedy Jones, i.e. he was paid for what got into the paper. According to Hamilton Fyfe, this made Jones the most hated man Fleet Street has ever known: people said that the *Mail* sucked young men's brains, then threw them away.

But these brains did produce some great journalism. The *Mail* had the good fortune that its first month saw two of the decade's most resonant murder trials. The Reading murders that produced the SENSATIONAL LETTERS

OF CONFESSION on the new paper's first day were particularly dreadful, and resulted in the conviction of Amelia Dyer for the murder of three infants she was supposed to be minding. On 23 May, after she was sentenced to death, the leader-writer was able to list some of the great villains of the century and add:

> Nothing in the ghastly record of these monsters of crime touches our heart with quite the same thrill[23] of wrathful sorrow as the story of the Reading murderess, for her victims were the most helpless of God's children — little children newly born.

One day earlier, the Muswell Hill murderers had also been sentenced to death. This case involved the murder for money of Henry Smith of Muswell Lodge; it was a grubby little affair, though it is said locally that the publicity was partly responsible for Muswell Hill's popularity as a suburb.[24] While waiting for the verdict, one of the murderers, Fowler, leapt on his accomplice Milsom and tried to kill him. Now this was a good story for all the newspapers, and made for them too, since the reporters were also waiting in court. But *The Times*, which had lost its early taste for a good murder, tucked the account away at the back of its broad acres of parliamentary reporting, and the *Morning Post*'s account was so perfunctory one must assume the reporter had nipped out for a pint and been too idle to try to catch up. No one reported it with the *Mail*'s magnificent relish:

> With a terrific blow of the left hand he knocked Milsom against the side of the dock, and struggled violently to clutch him by the throat. He had succeeded in plucking him by the hair, when Milsom, crouching and trembling, and looking round with terrified eyes, partly slipped and partly dodged out of his grasp.
>
> In an instant, the half-dozen constables appointed to guard the men in the dock were on their feet. Quickly they grappled with the infuriated prisoner. Hither and thither in the roomy dock they swayed, and again and again the herculean ruffian broke from their grasp. No word did he utter, his teeth set hard, his eyes flashing like a wild beast's, his hair dishevelled, his clothes torn, his brawny throat exposed.

It is necessary to pause here, first to take a breather, and then to consider journalistic technique. For even the *Mail* retained the custom of the time by reporting this incident halfway down the long (even in the *Mail*) chronological account of the proceedings. This practice had already vanished in the United States, where reporters were expected to get the news into the first paragraph. As late as 1913 one press critic attacked the American system. R. A. Scott-James contrasted a first paragraph from the *Daily Chronicle*:

> An extraordinary story of the mysterious
> disappearance of a trade union leader
> was told yesterday by Mr Percy Young,
> general secretary of the Amalgamated
> Union of Hotel, Club and Restaurant
> Workers.

with one from an unnamed American paper:

> Mrs Milton Siegfried of West Front
> Street had one ear partly blown off and
> suffered serious cuts and bruises about
> the head, face and hands today in an
> explosion which wrecked the kitchen.

It is the most fixed rule of modern journalism that the second example is good, if not for Mrs Siegfried, and the first one terrible: since at least the 1930s trainee reporters have been instructed to get the news in the first paragraph even before being told how to make the office tea. Scott-James argued this was all wrong:

> The only interest in this story [Mrs Siegfried's] lies in its horror. But the horror is entirely exhausted before the story is half told. After this first sentence it is impossible to add a word which can increase or maintain the sensational interest. From the point of view of the most popular and sensational journalism such a method of narration – a deliberate method – is artless, and defeats its own ends.[25]

This assumes that people read newspapers as they would a detective novel, which is nonsense. Anyway, headline writers had been giving the game away since journalism began. People were not expected to read through several columns to see if anything unusual happened to Mr Lincoln the night he visited the theatre.

In this respect, as with its staid design, the *Mail* was stuck in the nineteenth century. It was also scrupulously non-salacious. And one senses that it set out to report the news scrupulously too. For years, critics would not allow it to forget a false report of a massacre of British subjects in China during the Boxer Rebellion in 1900, and it was rechristened the Daily Liar. But all the evidence is that this was an honest, if very bad, mistake. Northcliffe was mortified. However, the *Mail* was the first tough school of news reporting, and in these circumstances reporters do start to cut corners on the road to the truth. But it undoubtedly produced great journalism, great writing even. The Harmsworths were young and fresh: 'Why, they're only boys,' cried a shareholder when they climbed the podium for the company's annual meeting. The staff were young, too. The *Mail*'s first great reporting star was G. W. Steevens, who made his name as a descriptive writer in the big foreign stories of the *Mail*'s first four years. He died of fever at the siege of Ladysmith, aged twenty-nine. Alfred Harmsworth is said to have sobbed uncontrollably when he heard the news, raced down to Steevens's widow and refused to forgive himself for sending her husband to his death. 'The Chief' must have been an astonishing man. And the journalists who came through this process of having their brains sucked seem to have done so by leaving their cynicism with the hall porter. In the early years, before his attention came to be diverted, Northcliffe's personality suffused the paper. And the memoirs of him by his former employees which came out regularly in the years between his death in 1922 and the Second World War are extraordinary for their starry-eyed hero-worship. The very mention of his name turned hard-bitten hacks into simpering sycophants.

'The Chief was certainly "a hero" to us smaller fry on the Daily Mail.'[26]

'I believe he recognised goodness as not merely a beautiful but as *the* beautiful thing.'[27]

'He cared nothing for his own life except in so far as his life might be of use to his country.'[28]

'He smiled that kindly, boyish smile that made us all love him.'[29]

'Why, in his . . . office he keeps a cupboard full of toys for the kiddies who happen to be brought there.'[30]

It seems improbable that these sorts of remarks will characterize the reminiscences, when they appear, of the employees of, say, Rupert Murdoch.

Perhaps they all believed, as did the spiritualists like Louise Owen, Northcliffe's secretary, and the journalist Hannen Swaffer, that the Chief was up there watching, and taking notes. But perhaps he truly was as charismatic as they make him sound. Even the one self-consciously debunking biography – *Northcliffe, Napoleon of Fleet Street* by Harry J. Greenwall – has to go in for a lot of grudging admissions. The description that rings truest is F. W. Wile's: 'The Dr Jekyll in him always outweighed the Mr Hyde. But . . . the Chief, in his Hyde moments, could be . . . as tyrannical as Nero.'[31]

The most extraordinary manifestation of the Hyde side of his character is the story of the race for the editor's chair. For the *Mail*'s first three years, Northcliffe himself edited the paper, helped by S. J. Pryor. When the Boer War broke out in 1899 Pryor was sent to South Africa to organize the war coverage; when he came back he found that Thomas Marlowe had been recruited from *The Star* as managing editor. It was now unclear which of them was in charge, so they would race each other every morning to get to the editor's chair first and stay there, with Northcliffe looking on and enjoying the joke. Marlowe emerged victorious: it is said he got up earlier and had the foresight to bring sandwiches for his lunch; maybe he also had the stronger bladder. He remained editor until 1925, with increasing authority, as Northcliffe became distracted, first by other newspapers, then by his quest for political power, then by madness, then by death.

V

On 9 June 1902 ten teenagers, nine girls and a boy, died in a fire in the City of London. They were employed in a workshop owned by the General Electric Company on the fifth floor of a building in Queen Victoria Street. The *Daily Mail* reported as follows:

> The most shocking feature is perhaps the fact that while the victims were yet shrieking at a fifth-floor window, while they were waving to the crowd in their agony, while thousands of persons stood appalled at the spectacle, a hand fire-escape, six or ten feet too short, was reared hopelessly against the building, and the firemen had to look on – impotent – as people were sacrificed.

The early phase when the *Mail* was not sure whether or not it had opinions of its own was well and truly over. Within days it had begun a campaign against the man it held responsible – Commander Wells, chief of the London Fire Brigade: 'The experiment of choosing a naval officer to manage the fire brigade had been a hopeless and costly failure.' The battle was fought quite civilly, but relentlessly, spilling over casually into the headlines of the news columns:

THE HEADLESS BRIGADE.

THE CASE AGAINST COMMANDER WELLS.

THE FIRE SCANDAL.

FIXING THE BLAME.

FIRE BRIGADE NEGLECT.

and so on. Less than two months later, an inquest jury did fix the blame. But it fixed it squarely on the 'gross legal negligence of the General Electric Company', which had stored a large amount of inflammable material on an upper floor with no fire escape. But this was not the angle the *Mail* wished to emphasize, and it was forced to trumpet, clearly contorting itself in the process, the jury's lesser criticisms against Wells's Brigade.

In one sense this was incipient popular journalism at its very best, capturing the human element of a tragedy, and crusading to ensure it is never repeated. Modern Western society does regard life as something infinitely more precious than the Victorians did; never again could hundreds of people die at sea or in a Jewish theatre and not be noticed. It is impossible to ignore the role the popular press has played in enhancing public safety by reporting dramas like this in a way that transforms them from bare statistics into human tragedies. Any *Mail* reader would have sensed that ten families had been unnecessarily bereaved and that Something Ought To Be Done.

On the other hand, here in the ashes of the Queen Victoria Street fire was the direction in which the popular press would take its concern: find an angle quickly, regardless whether it was justified by the full facts or not. The *Mail*'s reporting was boxed in by the line it had chosen. However scrupulous Northcliffe's intentions, this way facts get twisted. It was a sign of things to come.

The attack on Commander Wells was not the *Mail*'s first campaign. Very early on, it decided that the London tram system was wastefully run; and it was keen, reasonably enough, for the Metropolitan Police to put telephones in its police stations. Sometimes there would be jolly little money-raising exercises. Some of the campaigns, like the air races, the sweet-pea contest, Standard Bread and the *Daily Mail* hat, of all of which more anon, would pass into national folklore. One led the paper not merely into error but into disaster.

In the autumn of 1906 Northcliffe began his campaign against the soap magnate, Lord Lever, who had formed a Soap Trust to raise prices. For weeks the paper ran heartrending stories about the consequences of such a move. One was by Edgar Wallace, who found a poor washerwoman who was losing 1s 6d a week because of the Trust: 'The rise in the price of soap means all the difference between bread and butter for my children and dry bread.' The *Mail* also listed the soaps which were outside the Trust and encouraged the public to buy them – Royal Primrose, John Knight's Washing Soap, Fels Naphtha, Margerison's Carbolic, Albion Milk and Sulphur, Hedley's Hyssop and Bulrush.

The campaign worked in that Lever abandoned the Trust and began an advertising campaign to try to win back lost ground. However, he did not put any adverts in the *Mail*, which then returned to the attack and repeatedly accused Lever of selling short-weight. At this point Lever got fed up, briefed two of the best barristers in the land, Sir Edward Carson and F. E. Smith, and sued. The washerwoman could not be produced; Carson said this was not surprising, because to lose 1s 6d she would have to be using ninety-six bars of soap a week. The libel damages alone came to £50,000, then a record, and equivalent to about £1 million in 1996; the costs and loss of advertising doubled that.[32]

The *Mail* was not much deterred. Its campaigns came thicker and faster; they also became more overtly political. The innocent even-handedness of the *Mail*'s early editions soon vanished as its proprietor realized the extent of his power. The Government paid him the traditional compliments: he became Sir Alfred Harmsworth, Bt, in 1904, Lord Northcliffe in 1905 and Viscount Northcliffe in 1917. It might be argued that the ownership of a great popular newspaper leads inevitably to megalomania:[33] and Northcliffe owned more than one. Before the First World War he had the two biggest-selling newspapers, the *Daily Mail* and the *Daily Mirror*,[34] the oldest surviving Sunday paper, *The Observer*, which he sold, and the most influential of the elite papers, *The Times*, which he acquired secretly in 1908. He certainly became a megalomaniac. He was also too volatile, too journalistically quick-witted, to tie the paper specifically to a political party or cause. Indeed, he missed the first great political battle of the century by wavering on tariff reform; the *Daily Express*, which started in 1900, picked up that banner.[35]

But the right-wing partisanship that became the paper's hallmark was taking shape. To some extent, it went against some of Northcliffe's own radical reflexes. But after the Liberal election victory of 1906 the paper soon began to slide into hatred of the Government. From an early stage particular venom was reserved for the 'wastrels' in local government. The *Mail*'s modern readers would feel very comfortable with the attacks on waste, which were to become far more extreme when Northcliffe died and his brother Harold (who became Lord Rothermere) took complete control. The campaigns on this subject might reflect Rothermere's influence even in the early days. But there was something classically *Daily Mail* about the Fat Boy of Peckham, John Trundley. He was too unfit to walk to school, so in 1906 the 'wastrels' built him 200 yards of special tramway – the sort of decision that might be rejected by a sensible modern council precisely because of the withering scorn it would attract from the *Daily Mail*.

Perhaps the most obsessive *Mail* campaign began very discreetly on 9 January 1911, with a brief report – below a shipwreck with no fatalities off the Scillies and a small earthquake in Central Asia – about the squire of Rolleston-on-Dove, Staffordshire, who had introduced his villagers to the then almost forgotten delights of wholemeal bread. The squire's name was Sir Oswald Mosley. His grandson, also Sir Oswald, was to become rather more famous as the leader of Britain's Fascists, and was also to become a *Mail* hero. This Sir Oswald, however, was a jolly, ruddy-faced old soul who still dressed like a squire of the 1840s, and used to keep twenty-four greys to pull his own coach. This emerged when the *Mail* despatched one of its best descriptive writers, Percy Izzard, to see him. Mosley was old-fashioned, reported Izzard, yet progressive: 'He believes that the fashion for eating white bread is causing the physical degeneracy of the nation.'

Any mention of physical degeneracy was a cue for Northcliffe. It was one of his pet subjects. According to Hamilton Fyfe, he instructed Marlowe, as editor, to print an article on what became known as Standard Bread every day for a year. Marlowe came close to carrying out the instruction. Day after day someone new would support the campaign. On 27 January the splendidly named nutritionist Dr J. C. Thresh gave his backing. Two days later J. Lyons & Co. agreed to manufacture Standard Bread. Soon there were lists of bakers in every town who would supply loaves to the standard demanded by Dr Thresh and his colleagues. On 10 February three whole pages were given over to adverts, puffs, lists of aristocratic wholemeal-bread-eaters (the Countess of Arran, the Countess of Cottenham, the Countess of Dunmore, the Countess of Selkirk, the Countess of Ranfurly . . .) and a lot of self-congratulation. The headmaster of the King's School, Ely, reported that his boys 'had escaped from the bondage of white bread' while, as the story droned on into April, the boys of Beccles College were reported to have grown at a rate of three and a half inches a year the previous term instead of the usual two inches due 'to the nutritious effects of Standard Bread'. By now there can have been very few people in England who had not been asked for their opinion, although dear old Sir Oswald was quite forgotten. But someone was worse off: 'The man in charge of the stunt narrowly escaped death in two forms – from exhaustion and at the hands of his exasperated colleagues.'[36] The campaign failed in the end, anyway: according to Hannen Swaffer, bakers seized the opportunity to flog off their sweepings and call them brown bread.[37]

The paper was now generally up to sixteen broadsheet pages per day. Even so, it is a wonder there was any room for other news because, at the same time, the *Mail* was in its sweet-pea period. On 7 February it compared the craze in sweet-peas to the old tulip-mania in Holland. To what extent this was an existing phenomenon that was reflected and harnessed by the newspaper, and to what extent it was actually invented, is hard to judge from this distance. But the *Mail* claimed 38,000 entries for its £1,000 prize for the best blooms. This went to Mrs Fraser from the Manse at Sprouston in the Scottish Borders; her husband came third. They spent the money on a new chancel for their kirk.[38]

By now, the *Mail* could hardly report anything without getting in on the action. Just relaying the news was not enough; it had to be at the centre of it, flexing its muscles, proving its potency. In the first few months of 1912 alone it was raising money for a new YMCA building in London, trying to drum up crowds to watch Humperdinck's 'The Miracle' at Olympia, fighting the inadequacies of the telephone system – not surprisingly, since Northcliffe was constantly on the phone cajoling his staff – trying to find poultry that laid more eggs, and giving a Gold Cup for roses at the Chelsea Flower Show. In April 1912 came the most dramatic peacetime story of the era:

TITANIC SUNK.

FEARED LOSS
OF
1,500 LIVES.

But within two days the *Mail* was steaming away from the straight facts and into its own appeal to raise money for children left fatherless by the disaster. It raised £57,000 in five weeks, but was so busy publicizing its fundraising that it gave short shrift to the stories that were starting to emerge about the *Titanic*'s inadequate lifeboats. At other times it collected money to entertain overseas athletes coming to London for the 1908 Olympics, or to send Barry the sculler to the world championships in Australia, or (in 1909) to alleviate distress among the old horse-cabmen, who had been ruined by motors.

The concern for the horse-cabmen was a bit of an aberration, for what fascinated Northcliffe most was anything new. In that brief, happy period before war obliterated everything, progress may have seemed wholly beneficial. Even something as dreary as the motor omnibus (Northcliffe, in one of his sweet old-fashioned touches, would never permit the abbreviation 'bus') seemed to offer a freedom that was impossible in a tram. But Northcliffe was Toad-like in his enthusiasms. In 1901 the Gordon Bennett Cup for automobiles racing between Paris and Bordeaux engendered great enthusiasm in the *Mail*, even though all the competitors were French, and the local peasantry was described as very apathetic. In 1903, the *Mail* gave the Wright brothers' first flight only a couple of paragraphs under the heading BALLOONLESS AIRSHIP. But in 1906, when a Brazilian aviator called Santos-Dumont persuaded another plane to leave the ground for a few moments and the *Mail* gave it another two paragraphs, Northcliffe thundered down the inadequate telephone system that the paper was to take notice. 'Don't you realize what this means? Britain is no longer an island.'

On 17 November 1906 the *Mail* offered £10,000 to the first person to fly from London to Manchester. It was to be three and a half years before the prize was won. By that time Northcliffe's point had been proved by the memorable headline and byline:

MY FLIGHT.

By Louis Blériot, Dover, Sunday.

Blériot won £1,000 from the *Mail*. The £10,000 went to another Frenchman, Louis Paulhan, who flew from Hampstead to Manchester in twelve hours. The *Mail*'s second £10,000, for flying 1,000 miles round Britain in 1911, went to another Frenchman, André Beaumont. His only serious rival was yet another Frenchman, Jules Vedrines. There were three Britons in the competition; they were 'plucky and sportsmanlike', said the *Mail*, i.e. they got licked.

By now there were prizes for everything to do with planes, and the *Mail*'s rivals were joining in. Almost every week there were aviation meetings, which attracted crowds of enthusiasts and huge publicity. The *Mail*'s 'Aviation Notes' said the sport was 'degenerating into a vulgar and degrading scramble after money'. This was either a very brave coded dig at the *Mail* proprietor or, if it represented the paper's official line, a spectacular loop-the-loop. But the *Mail*'s obsession with aviation was not just a circulation ploy. There was a greater game afoot. 'Man, the all-conquering, who shall overcome all things, save only death, has achieved his greatest triumph' said the paper in an editorial after Blériot's flight. 'He has conquered the air ... We trust our countrymen will recognise the lesson of this portent.'

Not exactly. The chief British contender for the London–Manchester prize, Claude Grahame-White, was actually asleep when Paulhan started his plane. There was a certain obvious symbolism in this. Since its inception the *Mail* had been saying that the British were plucky and sportsmanlike, but dozing in a world that was full of danger. It was a theme sustained with outstanding consistency, as the *Mail* was very quick to point out in August 1914, when, on the face of it, it was proved stunningly right.

VI

**GREAT BRITAIN
DECLARES WAR
ON GERMANY.**

SUMMARY REJECTION OF
BRITISH ULTIMATUM.

ALL EYES ON NORTH SEA.

INVASION OF BELGIUM.

The day war broke out in 1914, there were scenes of great enthusiasm in London.

... 10,000 people in front of Buckingham Palace when the King and Queen, the Prince of Wales and Princess Mary came out on the centre balcony. After frantic cheers of loyalty, the crowd sang with great fervour the National Anthem ... a white-haired lady riding in a motor-car and waving the Union Jack was surrounded by enthusiastic clubmen in Pall Mall ... when the ultimatum was read at a matinée at the London Hippodrome the audience rose and sang the National Anthem for twenty minutes.

Had they but known what was to follow, the scenes might have been very different. No one on the streets of London had any conception of what a war might be like. Britain itself had not been threatened since 1815, and the difference between Waterloo and the Somme represented the passage of far more than one ordinary century. The war was to destroy so much, including, arguably, the *Daily Mail*'s journalistic dominance. Yet it also marked the peak of Northcliffe's power.

From its earliest days there had been a strand of the *Mail*'s reporting which suggested that war was the only game worth bothering about. Here was the boy-wonder reporter G. W. Steevens in the war between Greece and Turkey in 1897:

Domokos, May 19

A band! I had an idea that bands never went into action nowadays, but this was unquestionably a band ... a real complete military band. And behind it, striding out, erect, elastic, almost supernaturally un-Turk, came the brigade from Adrianople ... attacking the last Greek stronghold this side of the old frontier ...

There was half a column of this jolly stuff, with a lot of emphasis on their Mauser rifles, before Steevens came to the nub, reporting that out of about 4,000 in this brigade, more than 1,000 ended the day dead or wounded.

... They came limping and groaning past my fire all night. In the morning the cornfield was sown anew before it was reaped, with dead young men in new uniforms, and beside them, just out of reach of clutching waxen fingers, Mauser rifles.

Dead Turks have never been of enormous concern to the average British newspaper reader. But 1897 was the apogee of British imperialism. The Empire which Britain had famously acquired in a fit of absence of mind became a more central concern than it had ever been before. The *Mail* played a part in both reflecting and cementing that process, by investing money in reporting, as Northcliffe said in his first anniversary message, 'Empire rather than Parish'.

On 23 June 1897, the Queen's Diamond Jubilee, the symbolic celebration of it all, the *Mail* proclaimed:

> We ought to be a proud nation today, proud of our fathers who founded this empire, proud of ourselves who have kept and increased it, proud of our sons, whom we can trust to keep what we hand down and increase it for their sons and in turn for their sons' sons . . . How many millions of years has the sun stood in heaven? But the sun never looked down on the embodiment of so much energy and power.

No one seemed to enquire much what all this energy and power might be for. When Steevens reported on Kitchener's capture of Omdurman in 1898, he did so with undaunted freshness, vigour and, above all, enthusiasm.

> 'When Allah made the Sudan,' say the Arabs, 'he laughed.' You can almost hear the fiendish echo of it crackling over the grilling sand. And yet – and yet – there never was an Englishman who had been there, but was ready and eager to go again.

Steevens's report of the actual victory was written after he had spent fourteen hours on horseback, by the light of Vestas successively lit for him by friends. And the leader-writer was just as mustard-keen:

> Kitchener has done it. That masterful master of military tactics has achieved his purpose . . . And he has done it brilliantly.

It is a little hard for us now to remember why it was we wanted Omdurman in the first place. The *Mail* explained:

> We have lifted from the Sudan the curse
> of savagery which for years has
> oppressed it . . . But does it all end here?
> Assuredly not . . . The Equatorial Prov-
> inces southward — even to Uganda —
> need the wholesome breath of this pion-
> eering force of civilisation. The country
> needs to be opened up to the commerce
> of the world. And the path from Cape to
> Cairo must be made straight.

Straightening that path began a long way from Omdurman. That same month, September 1898, there was an exchange of letters in the paper about corporal punishment.

Sir—Thrashing by schoolmasters without the parents' permission should be put down with a heavy hand, and woe betide any individual daring to thrash a boy of mine . . . The 'old school' was in many ways a brutal institution.

Justice

Sir—I hope, nay, I feel sure that people like 'Justice' are rare. Their system is one calculated to make a boy into that delightful being known as a 'prig' whose chief feature is respect for nothing but his own skin. May the day be far distant when the hearty, fearless, merry British boy of today is replaced by a whining, insubordinate young prig, always on the look-out for injustice and grievances.

A Teacher

There was never any doubt where the *Mail* stood on this matter, four-square for heartiness and fearlessness. But all that energy and power of the Jubilee was about to receive a very severe jolt. The Boers refused to lie down as readily as tribes on the edges of the British Empire were expected to do. For most people, there was not much triumphalism about this war. There was for the *Daily Mail*, though.

Many of the Liberal papers were sympathetic to the Boers. J. A. Spender of the *Westminster Gazette* was remonstrating with Northcliffe in his office one day about his policies. Northcliffe pointed to the *Mail*'s circulation graph: 'No, Spender, you are wrong. See here, up, up, up.' Though the war caused immense damage to the British Empire's self-esteem, it left the *Mail* more puffed up with pride than ever. Eight days after war was declared, the *Daily Mail* War Express was started, getting the papers to the Midlands and the North by breakfast-time. Shortly afterwards the paper began printing an edition in Manchester.

The *Mail*'s combination of money and ingenuity made it a formidable operator in the business of war reporting. After Steevens died it discovered a new star reporter, the ex-soldier Edgar Wallace, who, long before he disgraced himself over soap, not only wrote with unusual sympathy of the lot of the ordinary Tommy suffering on the Veld but exercised a great deal of journalistic skill: hence the *Mail* scoop on the peace talks at Vereeniging, when Wallace suborned one of his old soldier pals who was guarding the encampment to send him coded messages by waving different-coloured handkerchiefs.

And its imperialist editorial line chimed with the mood of the time. The *Mail* commissioned Kipling to write a war poem. When he came up with 'The Absent-Minded Beggar', which was not quite what they had in mind, the paper made a virtue of it, and opened the Absent-Minded Beggar Fund for soldiers; Kipling kicked it off by donating his £250 fee, and it raised £100,000. The *Mail* was able to attack with impunity both the pro-Boer elements in the Liberal Party on the one side and the fuddy-duddy War Office on the other, sometimes simultaneously. In the 1900 general election the 'Little Englanders' who opposed the war were crushed, and the *Mail* danced on their graves:

> They are as obsolete as the muzzle-
> loading artillery which cumbers so many
> of our ships and fortresses . . . Imperial-
> ism is the true and living force of our
> political life of today.

When the Secretary of State for War, St John Brodrick, tried to punish the paper for publishing unauthorized information by banning it from running official casualty lists, it simply ignored him.

As London went berserk on the night the world's news organizations had announced that Mafeking was relieved, the War Office was refusing to say anything.

> The whole town cheered and shouted
> and whistled and roared until you forgot
> it ever had a beginning, and lost all
> thought of any end. The clubs were blaz-
> ing with cressets and spangles. Pall Mall,
> from the bottom of St. James's Street,
> looked like a pit of white-hot gold. And
> the War Office – yes, it still had 'no
> news'. Dear old War Office!

Next morning the *Mail* ran a leader that summed up a great deal more than just the feelings of that moment. It has the smack of Northcliffe himself:

WHY THE FOREIGNER DOES NOT REJOICE WITH US.

The rejoicings will not be without practical effect. Just as the South African war swept out of literature the unhealthy, introspective novel, just as it destroyed the trade of baleful writers and thinkers, so it brought about a recrudescence of the national spirit which, when kept within due and proper bounds, tends to national order and national greatness. The effect . . . on the young is incalculable . . . It is a fact, and a suggestive one to the foreigner, that though we may be a nation of shopkeepers – and very good ones, too, though a little old-fashioned – and though we do not brag or bluster about military ardour, the feet of our Colossus are not made of clay.

This was strong stuff from a nation that was struggling to subdue a handful of Afrikaners. But the *Mail*'s Britain was coming into clear focus: a gentle, peace-loving nation (quite how it had conquered a quarter of the globe remained mysterious), slow to anger and hampered by incompetent bureaucrats, but one that would always prevail if riled. And once the Boers had been dealt with, there was never any doubt which foreigner the *Mail* expected to do the riling.

VII

The Oval Test between England and Australia in August 1902 is still recognized as one of the greatest cricket matches of the century. England won by one wicket, Gilbert Jessop scored a hundred and, with the last pair at the wicket and fifteen runs still wanted, George Hirst supposedly said to his partner Wilfred Rhodes: 'We'll get them in singles, Wilf.'[39]

'Feverish with excitement,' the *Mail* reported, 'twenty thousand people watched the great and triumphant struggle' as 'the indomitable pluck of Englishmen' turned almost certain defeat into victory. Well, maybe 19,999 people were excited. In addition to the anonymous cricket reporter, the *Mail* claimed to have sent along a visiting Frenchman, one Henri de Nousanne. M. de Nousanne was not feverish, merely liverish.

Tiresome and ugly! That is to but feebly express what cricket is. It is absolutely idiotic . . . your 'national sport' – and you may thank heaven for it – is not cricket at all, it is the sea, the finest of all. As for cricket, its vogue can only be a simple question of enthusiasm, fashion or autosuggestion . . . You are willing to remain, motionless, silent, gloomy, hardly paying attention . . . and this monotony, this silence, this weariness of the whole business does not drive you away! . . . In sober truth, you are there solely because you have never troubled to reflect on what you are doing and because you do not know how to employ your time to better advantage. Take stock of yourselves a moment! You are literally hypnotised by that green lawn and the dozen men on it throwing about a ball. It is as if you had been eating haschisch . . . Aberration of intellect! Amusing simplicity! Long since, we in France renounced these infantile sports once and for all.

It was perhaps unfortunate for the *Mail* that they should have chosen to run this rant the day after a finish that ranks with the Leeds Test of 1981 in the game's annals. There have been enough boring days' cricket when it might have been more convincing. But only a little more convincing. One does not have to be unduly cynical to start thinking that 'Henri de Nousanne' might not be exactly a hundred centimes to the franc. He comes over as just the sort of pastiche Frenchman one might expect a *Daily Mail* hack to imitate if instructed to do so.

This was not the first exercise of its kind. A year earlier, in July and August 1901, the *Mail* had run a series of pieces entitled 'England Through German Eyes' under the thoroughly unimaginative name of Max Schmidt. The *Mail* published a disclaimer to the effect that Schmidt's views were nothing to do with the paper. But, on the contrary, they had everything to do with the paper: 'Schmidt', as he was doubtless intended to do, drew attention to the contrast between easy-going England, where the pro-Boers could argue their case unhindered, and the autocracy and growing militarism of Germany:

> You protect those who comfort your King's enemies, you treat with civility those who most foully traduce his officers and men, you smile at treason, you have pleasant words for traitors! Are you growing deaf, blind and toothless? Upon my word, one hardly knows what to think.

The German army, Schmidt pointed out, existed to defend the fatherland. It was not, like the British army, 'a comfortable loafing-place for young gentlemen with more money than intellect'.

Sometimes an American dimension would creep into the *Mail*'s nationalism. After an athletics contest between Britain and the United States a few weeks later, it pointed out that the Americans did take the whole thing more seriously than we did, the British being more interested in a good game than in victory. But there was only one real enemy: Germany. This had been Northcliffe's pet theme even before the paper was founded. In 1893 he ran a series in *Answers* by William Le Queux called 'The Great War in England in 1897'. A *Mail* writer was talking about the Germans' 'inherent brutality' in August 1896, when the paper was only three months old. In 1897, after Le Queux's Great War had failed to materialize on time, G. W. Steevens had been sent to Germany and wrote a sixteen-part series entitled 'Under The Iron Heel'. The Kaiser, he said, had 'a face at once repulsive and pathetic, so harsh and stony was it, so grimly solemn . . . He looked like the man who had Never Laughed.'

When the Boers finally surrendered, Northcliffe's anti-German preoccupation became the *Mail*'s theme song. There were many variations but the basic melody remained the same: Germany was arming with a view to destroying the British Empire; the Kaiser was an aggressive dictator; the Prussian generals wanted to invade England; the Government (especially after 1906, when the Liberals were in power) was culpably, bordering on treasonably, complacent; the British army and navy were hopelessly inadequate, and unaware of the significance of developments in the air; the British people were asleep, hypnotized by the green lawn, preferring a good game to victory, comforting the King's enemies. Deaf, blind and toothless!

The *Mail* was attacked, above all, for scaremongering. After war was declared in 1914, there was a brief pamphlet skirmish between one of Northcliffe's bright young men, Twells Brex, and the Liberal journalist A. G. Gardiner, editor of the *Daily News*. Brex listed the *Mail*'s 'scaremongerings' to emphasize how right the paper had been about the Germans, in contrast to papers like the *Daily News* which had consistently denied any possibility of war with Germany. There were two prongs to Gardiner's riposte. One was that the *Mail* had itself been inconsistent, which was entirely unconvincing; he had to mine very deeply indeed in eighteen years' worth of newspapers to come up with the very occasional nugget that might be construed as pro-German. The other was the more serious: that the *Mail* had been not just scaremongering, but warmongering. 'It has been the policy of the Daily Mail on this side of the North Sea, and of certain German jingo organs on the other side, to inflame public opinion in each country by stories of the hostile designs harboured by the other nation. Next to the Kaiser, Lord Northcliffe has done more than any other man to bring about the war.' Addressing Northcliffe, he went on: 'Your claim to be the true prophet of war does not call for dispute. It has always been your part to prophesy war and cultivate hate. There is nothing more tempting to a journalist than to be an incendiary. It is the short cut to success, for it is always easier to appeal to the lower passions of men than to their better instincts.'

In 1914 Northcliffe still owned the two largest-selling newspapers, the *Mail* and the *Daily Mirror*; for six years he had also owned *The Times*, with its hold on the elite, and had increasingly been taking command of its editorial direction. About half the national daily papers bought in Britain were his papers, a proportion never subsequently matched: Beaverbrook controlled only a fifth at most; the International Publishing Corporation reached its peak in the early 1960s under Cecil King (Northcliffe's nephew), at around 40 per cent; Rupert Murdoch, in the mid-1990s, has around a third. No one has ever exercised such a hold on the nation's newspaper readership as Northcliffe did.

Those crowds that sang the National Anthem so fervently outside Buckingham Palace and inside the Hippodrome, the clubmen who were so enthusiastic in Pall Mall . . . would they have been so keen had more of them been reading Gardiner's pessimistic broodings in the *Daily News*? Was all the scaremongering, in effect, a self-fulfilling prophecy?

VIII

For the *Daily Mail*, the First World War was actually long overdue. In the spring of 1906 it had begun publishing what it called 'The Invasion of 1910' by Le Queux, prophet, as *Answers* readers would remember, of the non-existent war of 1897. This time he was assisted by the *Mail's* naval correspondent, H. W. Wilson, and supported by the military hero Lord Roberts. What the *Mail* called in advance 'this intensely interesting narrative' described how the Germans landed on the east coast and issued one of those proclamations beloved of Germans in both fact and fiction, warning that spies and saboteurs would be shot. It was signed:

> The General Commanding The North
> German Army Corps
> *von Kronhelm*
> *Beccles, 2 September 1910*

Obviously, von Kronhelm was not aware that the boys of Beccles were extra strong because they had been eating Northcliffe's wholemeal bread. The fiction was thickly spread with propaganda, and the odd pay-off for Le Queux's chums:

As every despatch was read, sighs, groans and curses were heard . . . The Government were responsible for it all, was declared on every hand. They should have placed the Army upon a firm and proper footing. They should have encouraged the establishment of rifle clubs to teach the young man how to defend his home . . . they should have listened to those forcible and eloquent appeals of Lord Roberts, England's military hero, who, having left the service, had no axe to grind. He spoke the truth from patriotic motives because he loved his country and foresaw its doom. And yet the Government and the public had disregarded his ominous words.

The story goes that Le Queux, Wilson and Roberts came up with a militarily sensible line of invasion through the countryside to the capital. But this was no use to the *Mail*, which, while it did wish to alert the population to the nature of the danger, also wished to sell more papers and therefore wanted as many place-names as possible to add local interest. So Le Queux's Germans kindly obliged, amending their invasion route to suit the *Mail*'s circulation department.

SCENES IN SHEFFIELD.

LANDING OF THE GUARD AT KING'S LYNN.

BATTLE OF PURLEIGH.

INVADERS CHEERED AT CHARNWOOD FOREST.

On and on went the Germans, and Le Queux, relentlessly, through the English springtime, amid the grave and gay doings of the real world, as recorded elsewhere in the *Daily Mail*: San Francisco was devastated by an earthquake; Vesuvius erupted; Asquith, the Chancellor, took a penny off tea; a magistrate in Halifax noted that there were never any bald criminals; Paderewski stopped a performance of the Moonlight Sonata to tell two ladies to shut up; there was sunshine; there was snow.

All through April the Germans advanced:

BATTLE OF HARLOW.

GERMAN ATTACK AT EPPING.

And then, at last:

THE SIEGE OF LONDON.

On 8 May Le Queux excelled himself by getting fourteen London place-names into his first twelve lines. But he droned on, through the best part of a million words, six days a week, until 4 July, when the Germans were at last repulsed with a peroration about the criminal weakness of the Army Council and the Admiralty and the moral tone of the nation.

Le Queux's epic coincided with – and helped to fuel – perhaps the greatest of all the scares of a German invasion, a periodic feature of British life that dated back at least to 'The Battle of Dorking', published in *Blackwood's Magazine* in 1871. Erskine Childers's *Riddle of the Sands*, published in 1903, had been one literary outcrop. Feelings would surface again when *An Englishman's Home* by Guy du Maurier was a big West End success early in 1909. It was then all satirized by P. G. Wodehouse in *The Swoop!*, in which only Clarence MacAndrew Chugwater, Boy Scout, realizes the nation's danger, which is announced in the stop press columns thus:

FRY NOT OUT 104, SURREY 147 FOR 8.

A GERMAN ARMY LANDED IN ESSEX THIS AFTERNOON.

LOAMSHIRE HANDICAP: SPRING CHICKEN 1; SALOME 2; YIP-I-ADDY 3. SEVEN RAN.[40]

Even the *Mail* seemed to grow weary of Le Queux, but it was by no means tired of the iniquity of the Germans. In June, while the fictional forces were besieging London, the paper sent the writer Bart Kennedy to Germany to produce a series called 'In The Fatherland', which went on almost as long as Le Queux's war, though its conclusions were obvious right from the start. It was not the sort of piece journalists write for the benefit of a tourist board which has allowed them a free trip:

> Golden bells ringing out over the calm-flowing Rhine. Out over the beautiful town and the beautiful waters. Out over grim forts of destruction. They ring out over glinting murder-steel, over great, dark engines of death. These glorious cathedral bells were carrying a message to a people armed to the teeth. For this strangely beautiful land of the Rhine was a land ripe with the powers of death and evil.

This went on for fifteen days. In Goslar, in the Harz Mountains, Kennedy sat and watched the German officers as they

> swanked and swaggered about along the quiet streets . . . I used to sit and watch the officers reverentially by the hour. It was after all a privilege to be living in the Middle Ages. Let it not be thought for a moment that I have the least intention of being rude to the delightful German people. They must like their swanking, clanking officers or they would not have them.

While both Le Queux and Kennedy were in full cry, a group of forty-eight German newspaper editors came to London, invited by the journalist W. T. Stead. Many of these editors' papers, the *Mail* remarked, were 'sadly anti-

English in tone', but it insisted: 'We have no desire to treasure up a sense of injury.' Indeed not. Any of the visitors who opened the *Mail* might, however, have noticed that during their visit von Kronhelm was arresting much of the population of Islington and the British cavalry was defending Sydenham Hill. This was Part Three of Le Queux's work: 'The Revenge'.

Anti-German feeling flared periodically in the *Mail* over the next eight years. In October 1908 the Kaiser agreed to an interview in a British paper. This, not surprisingly, was a scoop the *Mail* missed; he talked to the *Daily Telegraph*:

You English are mad – mad as March hares. What has come over you that you are so completely given over to suspicions quite unworthy of your great nation? What more can I do than I have done? . . . My heart is set on peace . . . Have I ever been false to my word? . . . My actions ought to speak for themselves but you listen, not to them, but to those who insinuate and distort them. It is a personal insult which I feel and resent. To be forever misjudged, to have my repeated offers of friendship weighed and scrutinised with jealous, mistrustful eyes, taxes my patience severely. I have said time after time that I am a friend of England. Your press – or at least a considerable section of it – bids the people of England to refuse my proffered hand and insinuates that the other holds the dagger. I repeat that I am a friend of England, but you make things difficult for me.

And the press lord with the mistrustful eyes went on making things difficult for the Kaiser.

Much of the political debate of these years centred on the pace of rearmament. It is a curious quirk of history that the period which was freest of it was probably the summer of 1914. All the newspapers, including the *Mail*, were convinced there was going to be a war:

10 July	DECISIVE MOMENTS.
11 July	READY FOR ACTION.
13 July	THE CLIMAX AT HAND.
16 July	THE SUPREME MOMENT.
18 July	THE KING AND THE CRISIS.

But this was nothing at all to do with the Germans: the Ulster Protestants were arming to resist Home Rule violently. The assassination of the Archduke Franz Ferdinand in Sarajevo, the spark that ignited the First World War, was reported in the *Mail* purely as a foreign story, and there was no suggestion anywhere that it might somehow imperil the peace of Europe. On 22 July, with war a fortnight away, the paper carried a vague foreign report about strained relations between Austria and Serbia, followed by the languid footnote:

> It may be pointed out that undue impor-
> tance should not be attached to the series
> of panics on the Vienna Bourse as a
> symptom of the situation. The experi-
> ence of the first Balkan War taught that
> a certain class of financiers abroad is
> always ready to take advantage of a state
> of political tension to bring about an arti-
> ficial drop in prices.

The weather forecast was warm and sunny, with just a hint of thunder later.

It was on 25 July, ten days before war was declared, that Germany began to knock Ulster out of the headlines and, as Winston Churchill memorably put it: 'The parishes of Fermanagh and Tyrone faded back into the mists and squalls of Ireland.' When war started, the paper quickly collected itself, though the proprietor did not.

IX

The *Daily Mail* read the war right – right, that is, in the newspaperman's sense of not being caught out by any ascertainable facts and being in tune with the way the public wanted to interpret those facts. But on the day war was declared, there was a bizarre deviation. Blinded by his own propaganda about a German invasion of Britain, Northcliffe wrote a leading article opposing the British Expeditionary Force, headed NOT ONE BRITISH SOLDIER TO LEAVE BRITAIN'S SHORES. Marlowe, the editor, wrote another, supporting the BEF, and stood his ground. There was an impasse and the paper was forty-five minutes late when Northcliffe accepted the patriotic line of the day and gave in.

From that moment the *Mail*'s resolve did not waver. Its war map was on sale within days (price 6d); within a fortnight its staff photographer, Herbert A. Maunder, had sent back the first pictures from the front. But it was a strange time. On 25 August the following headlines appeared on the *Mail*'s main news page, page 5:

FIERCE FIGHT IN CHARLEROI.

IT IS ANNOUNCED THAT NAMUR HAS FALLEN.

SHELLING OF A BRITISH DESTROYER.

BRITISH CASUALTIES.

The headlines on page 7 included:

LEVEL GAME AT GRAVESEND.

ONLY 12 RUNS BETWEEN WARWICK AND KENT.

County cricket was continuing as though nothing was happening, certainly nothing that would not be over by Christmas. But the real level game was to go on for more than four years, and the graves would never end. The leader that day said:

> Since 1896 the Daily Mail has perpetually warned the people of this country that Germany meant to make this war. Do the British people even now understand what is upon them? . . . Abroad, wherever we turn our eyes, the young men without exception are in the fighting line. With us, too many of them are looking on at cricket matches or lolling at seaside resorts with the women and children.

Three days later the *Mail* published a picture of the crowd at Lord's: 'People are anxious to see the type of men who look on in the cricket field while the manhood of Europe is in the battle field,' said the caption. 'Further selections', it added menacingly, 'will be published.'

On 12 September it tried a different method:

YOUR KING AND COUNTRY WANT YOU
Words and Music by Paul A. Rubens

Oh we don't want to lose you
But we think you ought to go
For your king and your country
Both need you so.

We shall want you and miss you,
But with all our might and main
We will thank you, cheer you, kiss you
When you come back again!

The fact that it was a question of if, rather than when, anyone might come back was not much discussed at this stage. But to rally the fainthearts the main headline that day was

NEWS OF VICTORY ALL ALONG THE LINE.

along with the encouraging information, repeated for some weeks to come, that the King and Country song could be heard that night sung by, for instance, Miss Jessie Broughton at the South Shields Empire, Miss Blodwen Butcher at the Kursaal, Harrogate, and Miss Edith Beverley at the Bijou Theatre, Hythe.

For the most part the paper's tone was sombre and sober, in keeping with its status, which was soon emblazoned above the leader column:

THE PAPER THAT PERSISTENTLY
FOREWARNED THE PUBLIC ABOUT
THE WAR.

And Northcliffe never pretended it was going to be over quickly. The *Mail* continued to do its journalistic as well as its patriotic duty. It did not slavishly follow authority. Northcliffe railed against censorship, and on 21 May 1915 personally turned on Kitchener in the most important and influential leader article of the war.

Lord Kitchener has starved the army in France of high-explosive shells ... The admitted fact is that Lord Kitchener *ordered the wrong kind of shell* – the same kind of shell he used largely against the Boers in 1900. He persisted in sending shrapnel – a useless weapon in trench warfare. He was warned repeatedly that the kind of shell required was a violently explosive bomb which would dynamite its way through the German trenches and entanglements and enable our brave men to advance in safety. The kind of shell our poor soldiers have had has caused the death of thousands of them.

That day the *Mail* was burned on the Stock Exchange. Businessmen met and solemnly promised never to read the paper again, and someone pinned a notice on the paper's City office proclaiming: 'The Allies of the Huns'. But Northcliffe was right: and five days later the Ministry of Munitions was created, with Lloyd George moving from the Exchequer to sort out the crisis. The Hun insult was absurd; indeed, the *Mail* probably did more than anyone to popularize the word Hun, which was not a term much used in the trenches.

Long after the last spectator had left Lord's in 1914, the *Mail* harried anyone who had still not caught on that they jolly well ought to go, and demanded the introduction of conscription. The burning on the Stock

Exchange gained a nice symmetry when the *Mail* gleefully claimed, in June 1916, that it was being regularly burned by extreme socialists:

The incendiary process appears to be a simple one. It consists in the gathering together, on some street corner or other coign of vantage, of members of that curious tribe of loafers who always emerge from mysterious nowheres on the occasion of such happening as a runaway horse or the hoisting of a safe. The wild-eyed orator brandishes our unfortunate journal, passes the Resolution (which is always carried unanimously by the Slackers) to the effect that the German system of compulsion is inimical to the liberty of the subject and then proceeds to his task of destruction. The very fact that these little mobs can be formed so readily shows that there are still many people in this country doing very little work, and is in itself an additional argument for taking the shirker by the neck and making him do something.

For the first two years of the war, moreover, the *Mail* went on making it clear that the slackers and loafers were not only on street corners, they were running the country.

Northcliffe himself was everywhere, intriguing in Whitehall, inspecting the Western Front, supporting the generals against the politicians. At some point between 1915 and 1922 he descended from self-obsession into clinical insanity. When and how this happened is a matter of dispute, as is his precise role in the machinations that ousted Asquith from Downing Street and put Lloyd George there instead. Northcliffe, however, believed he had effected the change of leadership. In May 1917 Lloyd George asked him to head a permanent British War Mission in the United States; this appointment was widely attacked, but had the inestimable advantage for Lloyd George of getting Northcliffe out of his way. He returned and appears to have been offered the Air Ministry, which went to Rothermere instead; he then became Director of Propaganda in Enemy Countries.

When the Armistice came, Northcliffe demanded a place at the peace conference. Lloyd George refused to give him one. Instead, in April 1919 he attacked Northcliffe in Parliament. Without mentioning his name, he spoke of 'diseased vanity' and touched his forehead with his hand in a gesture that everyone understood at once. That one jerk of the Prime Minister's hand did more damage to Northcliffe's pretensions to political power than a thousand fulminating articles. Three years later the greatest, most dominating, journalist Britain has ever known was dead.

Alfred Harmsworth, Viscount Northcliffe, had changed the business of newspapers beyond recognition. Now the war had changed the world; and people began to want a different kind of newspaper. The British public emerged from the most serious trauma in the nation's history in a very unserious mood. And the man who took over Northcliffe's mantle was the man who grasped that.

PART THREE

On the Sunny Side of the Street

The *Daily Express* Era

Prologue

Ralph D. Blumenfeld – known throughout Fleet Street as R.D.B. – was an American-born journalist. He first came to Britain in 1887 to cover Queen Victoria's Golden Jubilee for the United Press; but he hung around and gradually, like Henry James, became more English than the English.

From the start he was a well-known man about town, met everyone in London worth knowing, and recorded his thoughts in a diary. In 1887 he reported on the new invention produced by Frederick Wicks of *The Times*, which cast and set type mechanically. Blumenfeld was unimpressed. 'I doubt if type-setting by machinery will ever be as efficient or indispensable as hand-setting.' In 1900 he met Charles Yerkes, the underground railway entrepreneur. 'He predicted to me that a generation hence London will be completely transformed; that people will think nothing of living twenty or more miles from town, owing to the electrified trains. He also thinks that horse omnibuses are doomed. Twenty years hence, he says, there will be no horse omnibuses in London.' Blumenfeld considered all these propositions and concluded: 'Although he is a very shrewd man, I think he is a good deal of a dreamer.' The following year there was an idea that firemen might abandon the wild cries they traditionally made on the way to fires. He rejected it. 'They have always yelled Hi! Yi! and they always will.' By 1909 most people were excited by Blériot's flight across the Channel and the possibilities aeroplanes created. Blumenfeld was not. 'These things represent a foolish waste of money. Besides, flying the Channel means nothing after you have done it. You can't carry goods or passengers.' Up to a point, Mr Blumenfeld.

The new century was to bring with it a new newspaper, one that was to acquire a reputation for being regularly and sometimes spectacularly wrong about what was going to happen next, and indeed what was already happening, a newspaper that eventually was to provide such headlines as:

MARTIN BORMANN IS ALIVE

HAILSHAM PREMIER

and

CHARLES TO MARRY ASTRID – OFFICIAL

This was the *Daily Express*. R. D. Blumenfeld, who had been news editor of the *Daily Mail*, became foreign editor of its new rival in 1902 and editor in 1904. He was to be a crucial figure through the first three decades of the *Express*'s existence and the early stages of its phenomenal success.

The *Daily Express* was the first, though not the last, paper to triumph by proving it did not actually matter whether what you said was right or wrong, as long as you said it with conviction and *élan*. In the inter-war years this simple discovery was to transform journalism, from a craft adhering to the principles established by Lord Northcliffe into something closer to a business where principles hardly mattered at all. But newspapers were, in the process, about to become a lot more fun. Hi! Yi![1]

I

The *Daily Express* was not founded by Ralph Blumenfeld, nor by Lord Beaverbrook, who owned the paper throughout the years of its ascendancy. It was started by C. Arthur Pearson, the least-known of the late nineteenth-century popular press tycoons, perhaps the least gifted, but by common consent quite the nicest.

Pearson was only thirty-four in 1900 but already well known as publisher of such magazines as *Pearson's Weekly* and *Home Notes*. He moved into newspapers four years after the Harmsworths, who had also started by making their money in magazines and had then made such a success of the *Daily Mail*. The existing newspapers, which had been so staid and boring in 1896, had been terrified and confused by the *Mail*, but none of them had had the wit to challenge it properly. Pearson saw, quite correctly, that there was a living to be made operating in the *Mail*'s shadow – just as, many years later, the *Daily Sketch* would get by for decades as a pale imitation of the *Daily Mirror*, and, still later, the *Daily Star* would make a living as tepid competition for *The Sun*.

But no popular newspaper can ever have started with quite such polite and modest charm. In February 1900 Pearson wrote to the trade paper *The Newspaper Owner and Modern Printer*: 'If you think the matter of sufficient general interest, will you be so good as to announce that I am going to produce a London morning newspaper in a few weeks' time. It will be called the *Daily Express*. Its price will be a halfpenny.'

Even the name was not exactly original, the word 'express' having been made topical in newspaper terms by the trains in which Northcliffe was sending the *Mail* all round the country. There had been a *Daily Express* before: in 1877 one had been founded to see 'whether there was a demand for a church paper, conducted on church principles and designed for the perusal of churchmen'. The answer was No – the first *Daily Express* lasted four months – but it is fair to assume Pearson was not thinking of that.

On 7 March 1900, a month after his diffident letter to the magazine, the *Newspaper Owner* interviewed Pearson: 'I think I have hit upon some good ideas but the great difficulty in connection with a new paper is to think of something worth doing that has not been done before.' Indeed, he was still asking for ideas after the paper started, but was obliged to report sadly that, while he had been flooded with letters offering suggestions, not one had been usable.

The paper started on 24 April. Its adverts announced: 'The *Daily Express* will not pander to any Political Party. It will aim to PLEASE, AMUSE and INTEREST, by gathering News and Witticisms all the Wide World Over.' It began with a simpering report on a visit to Ireland by the ageing Queen Victoria and an equally abject, though far more pointed, dispatch from Berlin: a message of goodwill to the new paper from the Kaiser. 'Tell the British people that my one hope now and always is the promotion of international peace.' One of the Kaiser's ministers interpreted this a little more forcefully for the *Express*'s Berlin correspondent: 'It is in the pin-pricks from the Press of our own and your country that the great difficulty of diplomatists will be found.' The sub-text appeared to be that if the *Express* was less beastly to the Germans than that horrid *Daily Mail*, it might receive the odd favour in return.

There was the customary high-minded letter from the Proprietor: Pearson promised that the paper 'will not provide a parade-ground for marshalling the feuds of any individual . . . We have no axes to grind, no personal ends to serve.' This did not prove binding on the paper's most famous proprietor, who could have renamed it the *Daily Axe-Grinder*. But the main thrust of Pearson's message, by pure fluke, did prove a reliable guide to the future philosophy of the *Express*. He promised news, and whenever possible it would be good news.

For choice, we will tell you of the comedy of life, putting the minor tragedies in the background . . . Somehow, it is a newspaper tradition to love the darkness more than the light, to put the bad news in bigger letters than good news, make capital out of the sudden ending of life, the catastrophe of the household, all the bitterness and sorrow that make life look black. In our young, fresh, candid way we will try and do better than that and to pick out the one ray of sunshine peeping through the clouds, the one flower blooming away among the weeds of life . . .

The *Express* kept its promise. Long after Pearson had gone, it would regularly insist there were flowers growing through concrete and sunshine at midnight.

In the meantime, Pearson had one more tangible idea. The *Express* was the first national daily in Britain to last any length of time putting news on the front page, the policy which Northcliffe had so deliberately eschewed, although it was commonplace in America, and in the London evening papers. This did not immediately thrill the British public and it cost Pearson dearly: the *Mail*'s page 1 adverts brought in massive revenue. Typographically, the *Express* was infinitely more daring than the *Mail*; within a year it was regularly running double-column headlines. Northcliffe was convinced such tricks made a paper look cheap. The *Newspaper Owner* disagreed. The *Express*, it said, was best summed-up in the word 'respectable . . . no one who reads it, even in a first-class railway carriage, need feel ashamed of being seen in possession of a halfpenny newspaper.' It even considered that Pearson had even kept his promises about sunshine: 'Readers of the *Daily Express* have had to go a whole week without contact with police-court or other squalor, and are, we imagine, no worse for the deprivation.'

Pearson never had Northcliffe's flair, and some say he was an incompetent manager. He rushed around the building doing everything, even carrying bundles of paper to help out, instead of ensuring the proper running of each department. Supposedly, Northcliffe was the man with the Napoleon complex. However, according to one theory, it was Pearson who, in one crucial respect, was Napoleonic: 'He never consolidated his victories, making each enterprise pay the cost of its successor, but passed from one incomplete achievement to another, ever putting more and more to the hazard . . . the strength of the Harmsworth press was all in the foundations; Pearson reared a showy superstructure on an inadequate and shifting bottom.'[2]

There was something of the Robert Maxwell about Pearson solely in the sense that if it printed, he wanted it. In 1904 he bought *The Standard*, the dreary old businessman's paper, and its companion, the *Evening Standard*. The evening paper would eventually fall to Beaverbrook, and survive and flourish. Pearson did nothing to find the morning title a new and younger audience. 'Damn this East wind,' he remarked, walking down Shoe Lane one bitter morning, 'that means at least six more readers gone.' He was convinced that he had won *The Times* in 1908; Northcliffe congratulated him publicly, but kept negotiating privately, and won the day. Most journalists who had worked for both, and there were a good many, seemed to regard this as a good thing. In any case, Pearson was now starting to lose his eyesight. He sold his papers and began to devote himself to good works. He established the St Dunstan's home for blind ex-servicemen and raised huge amounts for charities. This earned him a baronetcy rather than the peerage traditionally given to newspaper proprietors who do really great work, like supporting the Government. He died dreadfully, in 1921. Taking a bath, he slipped, knocked himself out on the tap, and drowned. He was only fifty-five.

Pearson was ruled by his heart even as a newspaper owner: he would reinstate sacked drunks if they had a sob story about their children. He was, said his biographer, kind, simple and obvious.[3] In those early days the *Express* was never edited with the ruthlessness that characterized the *Mail*, where words and men were equally expendable; if a story, or a reporter, failed to make it on the *Mail*, it or he would quickly cross the road to the *Express*.

The formula in both papers was very much the same, and, like the *Mail*, the *Express* did tend to bang on rather. The first issue contained a 2,000-word report from Hesketh Prichard: WHERE BLACK RULES WHITE – A Visit to the Almost Unknown Republic of Hayti. Each one of the next forty-eight issues also had 2,000 words from Hesketh Prichard on the Almost Unknown Republic of Hayti. The following year Prichard was despatched to find the Giant Sloth of Patagonia, which one likes to think could have been a ruse to get rid of a tedious correspondent. He came back, having merely discovered a new sort of puma.

But the paper soon had a campaign to call its own: Pearson became the chief press ally of Joseph Chamberlain in his battle for tariff reform, an issue that was to play a huge role in the *Express*'s later history. It was running page 1 slogans like TARIFF REFORM MEANS THE ANTIDOTE TO SOCIALIST POISON or TARIFF REFORM GIVES THE FOREIGNER THE CHANCE TO PAY SOME OF OUR TAXES. Lord Beaverbrook would have been proud, except that at this stage he was still in Canada, making his fortune, and had possibly never heard of the *Daily Express*.

The paper also quickly developed a respectable news service of its own: when the Russo-Japanese War broke out in 1904 it had correspondents in nineteen Far Eastern cities. And it did tell its stories with a lighter touch; as one observer put it, whereas the *Mail* would run a headline saying SATIS-FACTION IN CONSTANTINOPLE, the *Express* would have TURKISH DELIGHT. A story about drapers protesting to the Prime Minister about his wife wearing French dresses was headed 10, GOWNING STREET, which the *Mail* would never have allowed. And one gets an inkling that its standards of accuracy were a great deal laxer.

On 23 August 1902 the *Express* reported, in graphic detail, a summer holiday tragedy in Filey Bay, Yorkshire, where five children – three sisters and their two cousins – were drowned by the incoming tide.

Through the shallows the five children had paddled to the tallest mound they could find. They were digging away busily at this, and all the time the water rose stealthily and unobserved round them. Their hillock was a castle with a moat round it. It became an island in the midst of a little sea. Suddenly one of the women looked over and saw what was happening. At the same moment the children saw the surging waters and began to call out piteously . . .

The mothers' efforts to save them failed, said the *Express*.

> ... The last that was seen of the drowned
> children was the two elder holding up
> the two little ones in a brave effort of
> love. Then came a great wave, the cries
> ceased suddenly and, save for a fleeting
> glimpse of white in the frothing water,
> the children were seen no more.

A harrowing story and, in newspaper terms, dramatic stuff. But how did the *Express* know all this? The police were doubtless obliging. But an accurate description could only have come from the two grief-stricken mothers – yet if a reporter had spoken to either, he would surely have quoted them; and it seems improbable they would have been in any state to give picturesque descriptions. The *Mail* reported the same case factually, with the added but authentic-sounding detail that a man had drowned close by earlier that same morning, which the *Express* carelessly missed. One is forced to conclude that the *Express* was not unhappy about helping along the infant Fleet Street tradition of imaginative fiction.

II

In September 1910 Ralph Blumenfeld, by then editor of the *Daily Express*, met Max Aitken at a lunch in London. Aitken asked him incessant questions and, according to Blumenfeld, the two transplanted North Americans rapidly became close friends. Aitken had only just arrived in London, and was cutting a dash in a way that was possible only for someone who came from outside the class system and could not be pigeonholed, particularly someone who had the most astonishing quantities of money, energy, native wit, curiosity, ambition and, above all else, *chutzpah*.

William Maxwell Aitken, first Baron Beaverbrook, was born in 1879 in Maple, Ontario, the fifth of ten children of a Scots Presbyterian minister who had emigrated to Canada, and an Irish-Canadian mother. He grew up in Newcastle, New Brunswick, in conditions of some harshness and hardship, but not as much as he would later maintain. He became the local correspondent of a Newfoundland paper and, like Northcliffe before him, started his own school newspaper – though this one was shut down when the Revd. Aitken discovered him desecrating the Sabbath by working on it at 2 a.m. on a Sunday.

At sixteen Max Aitken became articled to a lawyer in nearby Chatham. Then he became a businessman, making money quickly and moving even faster. In 1905 he cancelled his subscription to the *Presbyterian Witness*. He married, moved to Montreal, bought companies and sold them, becoming involved in a particularly murky set of deals concerning the Canada Cement Company. Aitken decamped to London, arriving in late July, when everyone who was anyone had gone away. He acquired not a Rolls-Royce but the Rolls-Royce company, 'to keep boredom and uncertainty at bay',[4] though he soon sold out. There were even more interesting things afoot.

Aitken rapidly formed a friendship with Andrew Bonar Law, another son of a New Brunswick Presbyterian manse, a leading tariff reformer and the man who the following year would become leader of the Conservative Party. The new arrival was precisely the sort of fellow Bonar Law wanted to attract into the party. He was dynamic; he was keen on tariff reform as a means of strengthening the bonds of Empire; and he was very, very rich. Even allowing for this, it still seems barely credible that Bonar Law should have found him a winnable constituency in time for this outsider to stand in the election that December. But he did, and Aitken became MP for Ashton-under-Lyne less than six months after coming to England. By the following summer he had a knighthood.

In contrast to all this, Aitken's entry into journalism was uncharacteristically stealthy, even cautious, though one version is that at that first lunch meeting Aitken's opening gambit was: 'You're Blumenfeld, aren't you? How much do you want for your paper?' 'Not so fast,' said Blumenfeld.[5] It was not done so fast. As he went blind, Pearson turned the *Express* into a public company, with Blumenfeld as general manager as well as editor. The paper was said to be selling 400,000 copies a day. But this was less than half the figure of either the *Mail* or Northcliffe's newest success story, the *Daily Mirror*, and the paper was desperately short of capital. George Johnston, the proprietor of Bovril, put in some money, which may have helped him save on his huge advertising bill, and Bonar Law offered Conservative Party funds to help. Blumenfeld righteously turned this idea down, though later he had to be less scrupulous. Then he approached Aitken, with a supporting letter from Bonar Law, on the steps of the casino at Monte Carlo. Aitken wrote him a cheque for £25,000. One of the great adventures in journalism was under way.

For a long time little happened. In 1911 Aitken did take control of *The Globe*, one of London's half-dozen evening papers,[6] an old-fashioned political sheet which aimed at exercising discreet influence on the ruling class through its leader columns rather than through mass circulation. Blumenfeld helped him try to make it more popular; they almost doubled its circulation, but 37,000 was still less than a tenth of the number sold by either *The Star* or the *Evening News*.

The *Express* soon got into more crises, and Aitken put in more money. In November 1916 he bought out Johnston and took control, though it was kept quiet because, like Lord Northcliffe, he was deeply embroiled in the wartime plot to overthrow Asquith as Prime Minister. In the midst of all this, Aitken told Northcliffe of his ambitions. 'How much are you worth?' the great man is supposed to have asked. Aitken gave him a figure. 'Well, you will lose it all in Fleet Street.'

III

Northcliffe did not lose his money, merely his sanity. In 1921 he appointed the *Mail*'s head porter, Bob Glover, as advertisement director. The Chief thought the adverts, with their garish illustrations, often of ladies' underwear, made his paper look cheap, and he wanted an ordinary man's opinions on the subject.[7] By 1922 he was sick and raving. He spent the year travelling, and became convinced he had been poisoned by a Belgian ice cream. (The *Mail*, according to folklore, bore a grudge against Belgium for decades.) His cables to the *Mail* and *Times* offices became increasingly crazed and were intercepted and ignored. The managers and editor of the *Daily Mail* did their best in difficult circumstances. At one point two of the *Mail*'s most senior employees, Sir Andrew Caird, who controlled the finances, and the journalist W. G. Fish, were suing him for libel. Northcliffe's last call to the *Mail* was an instruction to the night editor to rescue him from his sick room, where he was locked in. On 14 August 1922 he died. His funeral was in Westminster Abbey. Crowds lined the street all the way from the abbey to the burial ground, St Marylebone Cemetery.

One of his last messages was telephoned to the manager of *The Times*: 'Have you seen Gordon Robbins in Fleet Street wearing a tall hat, strutting up and down? He is trying to become editor of the *Daily Mail* at a salary of £5,000 a year. But he won't. He has been rude – that young man has – to my relatives. Find out why he wears a tall hat. Tall hats are only to be worn on special occasions. I know more than you think. My men tell me.'[8]

Northcliffe had become obsessed with hats. Two years earlier he had obliged the *Mail* to conduct perhaps its most famous and most fatuous stunt. On 31 August 1920 the paper announced: 'There is a great monotony about the hats of modern man. Hardly a man in England is satisfied with his hat. The Daily Mail will give £100 for the best design for an all-the-year-round hat . . . hats must be practical and wearable.' On 12 October there was a further announcement that 40,000 entries had been received. But this was not said or displayed with the old pre-war conviction that bludgeoned the nation into buying brown bread or the right brand of soap. It had the look of a mumbled fib. Eight days later there was a winner, Mr A. O. Hopkins of New Cross, who designed an improved version of the bowler that could be copied in silk, plush, felt, straw or even ('for the cheaper trade') wool.

Quite possibly, in normal circumstances, Mr A. O. Hopkins's improved bowler might have swept the country. But it was now The *Daily Mail* Sandringham Hat. Orders were said to be 'colossal'. That was definitely a fib. 'The thing was going badly,' wrote Tom Clarke, the *Mail* news editor, in his diary for 1 November 1920. 'The public refused to be ordered about on the matter of hats. Were it the best hat in the world, given away free, people would not risk ridicule by wearing it.' A furious Northcliffe abused Clarke for his coverage of the stunt, partly because a reporter, in desperation, had said the hats had been seen at Mile End. Northcliffe said this was 'bad taste' – he wanted it in the *West* End. Winston Churchill had agreed to pose in a free one, and so had ex-King Manoel of Portugal, who was well known in Fleet Street for being game to do anything for publicity.

'Some of the fellows in the office,' wrote Clarke, 'especially ambitious youths looking for promotion, who have heard the Chief's jesting threat to have a Carmelite House hat inspection, wear a Daily Mail hat on duty, but keep a less conspicuous article in which to travel home to their distant suburb. I hope the Chief doesn't ask me if I'm wearing one. I simply haven't the courage.'[9] The Hon. Mrs Charles Craven was persuaded to say 'Charming, perfectly charming!' when she saw a *Daily Mail* hat. But the hat stories were rapidly tucked away among the Latest Wills, a report that badgers were flourishing in Berkshire and the doings of Mr Asquith, gone from power four years earlier and now very old news indeed.

The hat fiasco was symbolic. The *Daily Mail* was still the paper to read to see what novelty and nonsense it would come up with. A new hat! Whatever next? Its news service was supreme. Its circulation was still rising; indeed, it took its biggest leap ever in the year Northcliffe died, passing one and three-quarter million. The *Mirror* had fallen away, and the *Mail* was again unchallenged as Britain's (or perhaps, as it regularly claimed, the world's) biggest-selling daily paper. But newspaper sales generally were rising fast and the *Mail* now held the number one position by default, until it could be overhauled by a paper as well in tune with the new era of jazz and wireless and flappers as the *Mail* had been with the age of Ta-ra-ra-boom-de-ay.

Britain, and its young men in particular, had had more than four years of being horrified, terrified, bored and bossed about. Three-quarters of a million men had not come home from the war. Two hundred thousand more, soldiers and civilians, were to die in the winter of 1918–19 from influenza. Those who did come through wanted some fun.

When the Armistice had come, at the eleventh hour of the eleventh day of the eleventh month, it was not wholly certain that it was the end of the war; and the world was still full of other dangers that offered a far more plausible source of conflagration than the events of 1914. The Bolsheviks now in control of Russia were talking of world revolution and the West was intervening, if half-heartedly, to overthrow them. It was not impossible that there would be a revolution in Britain: the labour unrest that was to culminate in the General Strike of 1926 began soon after the fighting stopped. The old order of masters and men was just one of the certainties that died in the war. Churchgoing began to decline dramatically, partly perhaps because material comforts were growing, partly no doubt because faith was not a flower that flourished among the Flanders poppies. 'God as an all-wise Providence was dead; blind Chance succeeded to the Throne.'[10]

But faith had not been shaken in the offices of the *Daily Mail*. It had had a triumphant war. For the first eighteen years of its existence the paper had warned its readers against Germany while the liberal press pouted and prevaricated. And if anyone had any different version of events, they were now keeping very quiet. 'It is to the everlasting honour of our country that in the hour of decision she turned against the voices which bade her purchase ease with shame,' the paper trumpeted the day after the Armistice. There was also the latest Roll of Honour of Officers Killed: Barclay, Capt. G. R.; Boyce, 2nd Lt C. W.; Broad, Capt. F. B. . . . The newspapers were reduced to six pages by rationing; there was no room to list the non-commissioned dead.

Northcliffe's grip on reality and his own newspaper may have been diminishing, but the paper retained his authentic touch. Throughout the summer months of 1919 it published in a box above its leader columns the following quotation, attributed to a Swiss-German, Carl Rosemeier.

THE WARNING.
THEY WILL CHEAT YOU YET,
THOSE JUNKERS! HAVING WON
HALF THE WORLD BY BLOODY
MURDER, THEY ARE GOING TO
WIN THE OTHER HALF WITH
TEARS IN THEIR EYES, CRYING
FOR MERCY.

The *Mail* headlines still regularly referred to Huns, and its pages were certainly not demobilized. On 23 June 1919, after the Germans had scuttled their fleet in Scapa Flow, there were six Huns in various headlines and one in a caption. The action was 'an act of war, automatically annulling the Armistice'. A week later the Treaty of Versailles was signed, and the *Mail* issued a Golden Peace special issue. But it still printed the warning about the Junkers. (The only British paper to suggest that the principles enacted at Versailles were fundamentally wrong, and that the vengeful nature of the victors' demands, not the Germans' inherent duplicity, would bring about disaster, was said to be the socialist *Daily Herald*, which at that stage nobody read.)

The *Mail* was carrying on where it had left off, but its feel for history was no longer so assured. In April 1919 it gave massive coverage to Hawker and Mackenzie-Grieve, a pair of aviators who were attempting to fly the Atlantic and win the £10,000 prize the *Mail* had promised before the war. They failed to arrive in Ireland, and for days were feared lost. In fact, they had been picked up in the Atlantic by a Danish boat that had no wireless. The news that they were safe was greeted with national *Mail*-orchestrated rejoicing. They travelled by train from Thurso to King's Cross and were met by huge crowds at every station. Two months later a pair of RAF men, Captain Alcock and Lieutenant Brown, did fly the Atlantic. But their plane had no wireless, and the *Mail* had not followed their flight. They won the prize, knighthoods and a place in history. However, they had failed to provide a running story, and the publicity was rather flimsy and grudging. When Charles Lindbergh made the first *solo* Atlantic flight in 1927 it was widely assumed he was making more of a breakthrough than he actually was.

The paper still retained something of its light touch and skill at self-advertisement, though its vaingloriousness was becoming absurd. There is a piece of paper preserved from just after the war on which Northcliffe had scribbled down various slogans: Daily Mail, Never Stale; Hail, Hail, the Daily Mail; and, best of all, Daily Mail, Million Sale. In August 1920 the paper invited the children of Britain to spend their summer holidays arranging the following words and figures, 'DAILY MAIL WORLD RECORD NET SALE 1,121,790', into a design in a place visible to the public. 'You may use sand or stones or, if in the country, moss, flowers or any rustic medium,' said the *Mail*, helpfully, and added various suggestions: 'How would you like to try an aeroplane, going up, up, up, like the Daily Mail record net sale?'

That same month it put on another stunt, this time not for the kiddies, and one which Northcliffe would surely never have allowed had he retained his former grip. The central figure was Councillor Donald Clark of Tonbridge, an arch-prude and opponent of mixed bathing, who hit the papers by suggesting that in the interests of decency men and women should swim in skirted costumes. SKIRTS FOR MEN! shouted the *Mail* headline. The fun was just beginning. The *Mail* sent Councillor Clark on a tour of seaside resorts. He was so shocked by what he saw, he kept on looking. There was Bournemouth:

> In some cases I saw what was, to my
> mind, most repulsive – namely men
> holding their partners for the ostensible
> purpose of teaching them to swim, but
> in reality doing nothing of the sort . . .

And naturally he was 'horrified' by Brighton:

> . . . They undress promiscuously in the
> open, and apparently it is permissible for
> any Peeping Toms to assemble on the
> parade east of the pier to watch the
> performance . . .

By now the *Mail* had made him a star. In Southsea (where it was 'as if they
had never heard of the word "modesty"') he was compelled to resort to
'various small disguises' to stop people coming up and discussing the subject
with him. In Shoreham a party of young girls did discuss it:

> But their criticisms lacked logic. They
> made the statement that the modern girl
> has so poor a chance of marriage, owing
> to the scarcity of men, that it does not
> matter what she looks like when bathing,
> and they informed me that my ideas on
> the subject are all 'tommy-rot'.

In Blackpool – 'flimsily-clad men and women disporting themselves' – someone stuck him on the back of a donkey.

On 19 August the *Mail* ran the startling headline

ALL YOUNG ENGLAND AT IT.

But this was a reference to the kiddies' Net Sale competition. A party of Boy
Scouts had managed to get the figure 1,121,790 on the summit of Snowdon.
By now, the *Mail* may well have left the figure behind. For the first time
since Northcliffe deliberately barred the idea after the dummy issues in 1896,
the *Mail* began to run regular cartoons. In the war there were drawings billed
as cartoons, but these were very earnest, very continental, drawings by Louis
Raemakers, which were accompanied by laborious explanations, rather than
jokes: 'This fine drawing recalls the victory of Hercules.' Now Tom Webster
emerged, primarily on the sports pages, where he invented the very British
figure of the Horizontal Heavyweight and rapidly became one of the highest-
paid men in Fleet Street. There were even occasional touches of fairness in
the political coverage. In the 1918 election, one of the most hysterical of the

century, Northcliffe donated a column to the Labour Party to say whatever it wanted, because it did not have its own newspaper.

But this was not a precedent. The *Mail* was to turn savagely against this new force in British politics. While Northcliffe was alive, there was always a hint of the unexpected in the *Mail*'s responses, first because he was a brilliant journalist, later, maybe, because he had gone crazy. When he was succeeded by his brother Rothermere the paper's election coverage set into a mould from which it has never emerged. 'The British Labour Party, as it impudently calls itself, is not British at all,' scowled a leading article on 30 November 1923, just before the election that led to the first Labour Government. 'It has no right whatever to its name. By its humble acceptance of the domination of the Sozialistische Arbeiter Internationale's authority at Hamburg in May it has become a mere wing of the Bolshevist and Communist organisation on the Continent. It cannot act or think for itself.' Labour's respectable leaders were merely a front for a load of 'notoriety-hunters, bookworms, "high-brows", discredited professors and dons, professional Atheists . . . and haters of their fellow men'.

The *Mail*'s campaign was to reach its peak, or its nadir, at the following year's election when it published the famous purported letter from Grigori Zinoviev of the Communist International saying: 'It is indispensable to stir up the masses of the British proletariat.' This was sent to the Communist Party, not the Labour Party, and is now generally, though not unanimously, regarded as a forgery, concocted by White Russian émigrés, with the help of the Foreign Office, Conservative Central Office, and the *Mail*:

CIVIL WAR PLOT BY SOCIALISTS' MASTERS.

MOSCOW ORDER TO OUR REDS.

GREAT PLOT DISCLOSED YESTERDAY.

The paper explained: 'Moscow issues orders to the British Communists . . . the British Communists in turn give orders to the Socialist Government, which it tamely and humbly obeys.'[11] The story was given to other papers as well, presumably because scooping the opposition was not the object of the exercise; there was a bigger game afoot.

Labour lost power in the election, but its vote actually rose by a million; the Conservatives got a majority because the Liberal poll collapsed, thus suggesting that the Red Scare had rather less effect than is generally assumed. Voting figures, like circulation figures, are sometimes unhelpful to the perpetuation of historical myths. One does sense, however, that it was the men who had actually served in the trenches and been ordered around for four years who wearied most quickly of being hectored at their peacetime breakfast tables.

IV

While all this was going on, the *Daily Express* was not yet even yapping at the *Mail*'s heels. In 1920, wrote the future editor Beverley Baxter, the *Mail* staff still looked down contemptuously on the *Express* like the Spaniards on a galleon sneering at the *Revenge*. The paper operated from poky offices in Shoe Lane. The site of the great black-glass building that was to become the *Express*'s home and Fleet Street's most conspicuous landmark was occupied by an older institution: the sausage shop, or to be precise the SPO shop, which sold sausages, potatoes and onions from great steaming trays in the window. (It had no telephone, which made it an especially attractive retreat for reporters trying to stay out of range of their news editors.)

But by now the former Max Aitken was slowly turning himself into a full-blown press lord. He acquired the barony and the name Beaverbrook in 1916; he discussed his coat of arms with Rudyard Kipling, who said he should make the beavers *regardant* more ferocious.

The beavers stirred, however, very slowly. By 1917 there is written evidence that Beaverbrook was starting to give Blumenfeld orders. In 1918 he started the *Sunday Express*. There was none of the sabbatarian outcry that thwarted Northcliffe's plans two decades earlier, but Blumenfeld thought the project absurd, and even Beaverbrook could not have been that wholehearted: he only gave the new paper a staff of six. Nevertheless, between 1919 and 1922 he invested £200,000 in the *Express* organization. One of Beaverbrook's early triumphs was persuading Gordon Selfridge, the department-store tycoon, to advertise in the paper. By September 1919 Selfridge's was pushing its Raincoat Week and advising that anyone who could not get to town only had to phone Gerrard 1. Beaverbrook did not have Northcliffe's Victorian inhibitions about advertising.

The *Express* became fractionally more bold in its presentation and definitely more forthright in its tone. On 20 March 1919 Beaverbrook wrote the first of his many unsigned manifestos. He began with the traditional guff about independence and freedom and equality. Then he became more specific: the *Daily Express*, Beaverbrook declared, 'believes in the abolition in peacetime of the Government's controls brought in by the war. It will uphold the right of people to advance their own interests and shape their own lives, and will oppose all attempts to interfere with the simple and healthy pleasures of the nation.' If it is possible to find a link between the newspaper Beaverbrook turned into the greatest in the world and the dull, subservient rag that it later became, it is in that simple piece of philosophy. Northcliffe's *Mail* would demand that the slackers and loafers get into line but would perhaps, on a good day, shed a tear for their human failings; Beaverbrook's *Express* would never be that bothered one way or the other. The North American influence was very strong: it was a paper of rugged individualism. Increasingly the British were moving out of the cities, climbing on the trains and the tubes provided by the dreamer Yerkes, and going home to Tudorbethan semis in the suburbs where once there were green fields. The great landowners who owned the fields were selling up; their new liquidity did not carry with it the old feudal rights and responsibilities.

Meanwhile, the country was becoming increasingly dominated by the south-east. The population of Lancashire, for instance, was virtually static between 1921 and 1937; that of London and the Home Counties rose by 18 per cent. There was a new class, often far removed from their roots and their families, from both the certainties of the countryside and the jolly squalor of the Victorian city. By an instinct as sure as Northcliffe's, Beaverbrook developed a paper that appealed to them, and to a far wider public as well. 'Beaverbrook never had a conscious marketing strategy, and never needed one,' said his most recent biographers; 'he produced a newspaper that would interest *him*.'[12] It was not an instant triumph, as the *Mail* had been, but its rise was inexorable.

Around 1922 the *Express*'s circulation overtook that of the *Daily News*, which was stuck with the collapsing Liberal Party; that year it started to make a profit. About five years later it climbed ahead of the *Daily Mirror* to become the *Mail*'s obvious rival. The *Express*'s readership became to a remarkable extent a cross-section of the country as well. It was still considered respectable enough to read in first-class railway compartments, partly because people were becoming rather less fussy about what strangers on trains thought of them.

It also built a strong following among the working class. Perhaps the paper's most enduring constituency was to be the working-class Conservative voter, either deferential by nature or maybe a bit cussed: in the *Express* the large minority who disliked trade unions before it became fashionable to do so could find solace and soul-mates. But a great many Labour voters read it too; some of them never seemed to notice its politics, no matter how stridently Beaverbrook was blaring. The six-page papers of the end of the First World War had quadrupled in size by the start of the next one, so the politics was a great deal less noticeable than it used to be; there was so much else to read. A parliamentary reporter called Philpott once resigned because of Beaverbrook's obsession with the Empire. Blumenfeld was shocked: 'I'm surprised you take your politics so seriously.'[13]

Many of Beaverbrook's tricks were straight lifts from Northcliffe. In 1922 he ran a £1,000 competition asking people to guess when the *Express* circulation would pass a million; each entry had to have four countersignatures. Two hundred thousand people were said to have entered, so a million people may have heard of the *Express*, though it would be 1926 before a million of them bought it. But in many respects he went beyond Northcliffe, who wanted his papers to be bright, truthful whenever possible and, above all, dignified. With Beaverbrook the brightness was all-important. On 28 May 1920 the *Express* ran a leader whose opening paragraph ran:

The world is becoming better.

It went on: 'In spite of Bolshevism, in spite of our gloomy prophets, in spite of personal and national greed, humanity at large is steadily gaining the heights of progress. The universal mind is abroad with its hatred of injustice and tyranny and with its love of fairness and good will to men . . . Humanity moves on.' Indeed it does. Next day, the *Express* obtained what was said to be the first wireless communication ever received and printed in a newspaper office:

Redcar 1.30 – Foolery 100 to 8, Carlean 4 to 1, Bucksphere 100 to 8. Twelve ran.

Actually, this was not even news, as the meeting happened several days earlier. But it was appropriate. People wanted to believe that the world was becoming better and they wanted to enjoy themselves. As a prediction for the next two decades optimism was as wrong as Blumenfeld's views on underground railways, but it was a perfect recipe for selling newspapers to people content to imagine that Beaverbrook was right.

In 1922 he had given a speech in Sheffield on 'The Sensational Press'. He did not shrink from the title.

It is the duty of newspapers to advocate a policy of optimism in the broadest sense and to declare almost daily their belief in the future of England. Optimism is a frail and tender flower springing from some crevice in the barren rock of depression. Expose it to the east wind of analysis, or the cold sleet of criticism, and it will surely die. Sustain it with the hot breath of confidence and the glowing warmth of courage and it will flourish.[14]

'A newspaper is like a young and beautiful girl,' he said, opening a Women's Exhibition in 1922. 'The *Daily Express* is only twenty-one years of age . . . but this beautiful girl is dancing her way through life.' It was actually twenty-two, but women and newspapers are entitled to little fibs on such subjects without being exposed to the east wind of analysis.

Oh, how we danced! A cast of characters began to emerge as the dramas of the 1920s were played out in the *Express*'s pages. There was Christabel Russell, who bore a son even though her husband, the Hon. John Hugo Russell, had failed to consummate the marriage. It was not clear who the father was because her admirers included 'Greeks, slim silky Argentines, four young men in the Oxford and Bucks Light Infantry and a Dago young man with a Marcel wave'. There was Mrs Smith-Wilkinson, who died in 1924, having spent £30,000 a year on clothes while giving her third husband eight shillings a week to live on bread and dripping. There was Zaghlul Pasha, the Stormy Petrel of Egypt. There was Lady Dorothy Mills, who lived for a month among the Human Leopards, the cannibals of Northern Liberia. 'I found the cannibals very cheery,' she said, 'and they made no attempt to molest me . . . They do not usually like eating a woman, as they find her flesh very bitter; a male thigh aged about 14 or 15 is the best food.' There was Dare-devil Davo, who dangled 200 feet in mid-air above Oxford Street. And there were Jack Hobbs, Coco Chanel, Malcolm Campbell, Tutankhamun, Louis Armstrong, Dixie Dean, Horatio Bottomley, Stanley Baldwin and his pipe, the infant Princess Elizabeth and, now and again, a funny little German with a moustache.

There was George Carpentier, the French heavyweight, who was sensationally beaten in 1922 by Battling Siki of Senegal. 'Carpentier is broken-hearted,' reported Victor Breyer (Special to the *Daily Express*), 'and on calling at his home after the fight I found him crying like a child. "These coloured men are not made like us. They are abnormal."' That was the way the French were expected to take defeat. There were characters who were starting to appear on the infant wireless: in April 1926 Nora Bradbury could be heard playing the pianoforte on 6BM from Bournemouth. And there were the inanimate characters from the Saturday small ads: the 'Boilabath' immersion bath heater for £3 12s 6d and lucky elephant hair rings for 3s 6d.

There was a second cast of characters whose names did not appear in the *Daily Express*, sometimes because they were friends of the proprietor and he was doing them a favour by suppressing their troubles or, more often, because they were his enemies and he was suppressing their successes. It was not all that easy to tell the characters who were mentioned in the news columns from those who were starting to appear in the 'By The Way' column by Beachcomber, which began as a light comment on current events and turned into a private farce that went on for fifty-one years in the hands of J. B. Morton, inventor of Dr Strabismus (Whom God Preserve) of Utrecht, Mr Justice Cocklecarrot, Captain Foulenough, Dr Smart-Alick of Narkover and the Filthistan Trio from Thurralibad.

Possibly he invented Zaghlul Pasha, Mrs Smith-Wilkinson, Dare-devil Davo and the funny little German as well. You could never quite be sure in the *Express*. 'Sixty Horses Wedged In Chimney', as Beachcomber once wrote; 'The story to fit this sensational headline has not turned up yet.' But it might easily have done.

The General Strike came and went: 'The crisis will pass – and will pass quickly. The Government are completely competent to meet the situation. Keep calm and support the Government.' The crisis did pass, to be succeeded by scores of others in that twenty-one-year hiatus between cataclysm and cataclysm. But in the *Express* the band played as allegro and fortissimo as it could to drown out the cries of a tormented world. One month after the Strike the main headline, streaming across page 1 in what was now accepted *Express* style, read:

RAIN FORECAST FOR THE TEST MATCH.

That was about as gloomy as the *Express* wished to get.

V

Blumenfeld was said to be the only man in the history of the *Daily Express* who could deal with Beaverbrook on something like equal terms. Naturally, Beaverbrook eventually pushed him aside, though he was careful to shove him upstairs with various titles like editor-in-chief and chairman. R.D.B's improbable replacement was Beverley Baxter, who formerly sold pianos in the Canadian north. In London he met Beaverbrook, who was a fine judge of Canadian chancers and, on the slenderest evidence, offered him a job as a leader-writer. Baxter was not interested. The story goes that, by coincidence, they travelled back across the Atlantic on the same liner. After the ship's concert, Beaverbrook sent him a message: 'My Dear Baxter: I have heard you sing. More than ever I advise you to take up journalism.'

So Baxter came back. He showed some facility at writing the uplifting little leaderette that was a staple of the *Express*'s opinion column and was sent to the *Sunday Express*, where he made his reputation by buying up the memoirs of the jockey Steve Donoghue and the letters of Mrs Edith Thompson to her murderous lover. Circulation went up. Baxter was promoted to managing editor of the daily. He said later that Beaverbrook was fed up with people who knew more about journalism than he did and wanted someone who knew less.[15]

Baxter was famously calm. He was usually seen in the office in his dinner jacket, on his way to somewhere far more glamorous. One morning in 1931 he got his customary wake-up call from Beaverbrook.

'Well, it has come.'

'What's come?'

'The crisis. It is here.'

Britain, Baxter eventually gathered, had gone off the Gold Standard.

'Where will you be this morning, Baxter?'

'I think I'll go to Ranelagh and knock a golf ball about for an hour.' He had received four further messages in four holes before he gave up and went to the office.

Until 1927 Beaverbrook ran the paper from the *Express* building. Thereafter he relied on the telephone and E. J. Robertson, yet another Canadian, who occupied a role in the Beaverbrook organization similar to that which the Scotsman Sir Andrew Caird had played for Northcliffe. Robertson first came to Beaverbrook's notice when he carried his bags in a Toronto hotel; he was known in the office as 'the bell-hop' (Baxter was 'the piano-tuner'). He interpreted Beaverbrook's instructions by saving pennies wherever possible – he banned commas from cabled news copy after working out that 200 commas cost £3 – thus enabling Beaverbrook to tell employees whenever it suited him that he was a man of boundless generosity, forever being thwarted by the skinflint Robertson.

VI

The *Mail*, meanwhile, was proceeding in all kinds of unorthodox directions. The following invitation went out for The Memorial Hall, Farringdon Street on Saturday 16 May 1925: 'Northcliffe invites his old colleagues particularly of the mechanical, printing and publishing staffs To Hear His Message of Hope to the World. Admission Free. All are Welcome.' At the time Northcliffe had been dead for almost three years.

The invitation was contained in a penny pamphlet published by the Chief's private secretary Louise Owen, who had already established herself as the high priestess of the Northcliffean cult both by publishing a booklet just after his death – 'Those little souls who carped at him? What have they done for humanity? Will their names echo round the world, live in history?'[16] – and by contesting his will on the grounds that Rothermere had been allowed to buy his brother's shares too cheaply. She lost and was described by the judge as 'an extremely dangerous woman', which is the sort of thing judges are prone to say about the slightly batty and litigious.

The 1925 pamphlet, *Northcliffe's Views Upon The Christ*, was 'Given to Louise Owen, through Automatic Writing, and the Trance Mediumship of Mrs Osborne Leonard, on 22 March 1925'. Mrs Leonard, who operated from a cottage in East Barnet, was in touch with a decidedly mellowed Chief. 'Mere worldly success, mere material gain, is nothing if one loses one's soul in the getting . . . service, mutual *service* and co-operation can cleanse the world of all its ugliness.' Whether Mrs Leonard was genuinely in touch with Northcliffe's spirit or not, it has to be said that this is a line of thinking that had never appeared in the leader columns of the *Daily Mail*. One might also note that the least authentic touch was at the end of the invitation to Farringdon Street: 'Admission Free. All are Welcome.' Northcliffe would surely have charged a ha'penny and offered a prize for something or other.

But spiritualism was a major preoccupation in the 1920s, and understandably: so many wives, so many mothers, had been bereaved in the war which Northcliffe himself had so relished. And Louise Owen was not even the most famous person in communication with the Chief. It is a curiosity that Fleet Street journalists – sceptical by professional necessity, cynical by inclination – should have produced a long line of spiritualists, beginning with W. T. Stead and going on via the socialist journalist Robert Blatchford to Pat Duncan, chairman of Odhams, publishers of *The People*, who received instructions from his proprietor Lord Southwood both before and after Southwood's death. (Other enthusiasts included Conan Doyle and Sir Edward Marshall Hall KC, whose name had years earlier been regularly reduced to M. Hall in the *Mail* while Northcliffe was feuding with him.)

The most prominent journalistic believer was Hannen Swaffer, who was briefly editor of *The People*, but more famous as a columnist, dramatic critic and all-round Fleet Street character, a role he played to the full, cultivating a wide-brimmed hat, black stock and long hair. Frank Owen, the editor of the *Evening Standard*, called him the Pope of Fleet Street: Northcliffe, who employed him in a variety of roles, called him Poet. In 1922 Swaffer gave up drinking and began to dicker with spiritualism. Two years later he was convinced, and he was among those who received various improbable Northcliffean messages on the horrors of war and the need to nationalize the press. Members of the interlocking spiritualist circles which Louise Owen and Swaffer frequented also claimed that Northcliffe was present at *Mail* editorial meetings and undergoing his own purgatorial suffering in being unable to intervene. Rothermere, he is supposed to have said at one seance, was 'following public opinion instead of leading it . . . he has no vision of the future, as to how things are going'.

Another time the message came through this way: 'The *other paper*, Swaffer.' There was no question which other paper he meant; the *Express* was the *Mail*'s obvious rival even before Northcliffe died. 'Did you see the changes in the *other paper* on Monday?' asked Swaffer. 'Yes,' said the voice. 'It's going to be very good.' Another time he complained about the *Mail*. 'Too many advertisements . . . Interest your public first.'[17] Rothermere, however, was not listening to his dead brother; or to anyone else, much. And he had no idea how to interest the public.

VII

On the face of it, the *Daily Express* and the *Daily Mail* were engaged in furious no-holds-barred combat throughout the 1920s. In 1928 Beaverbrook called it 'a life and death struggle' – a struggle beyond death if you believed the spiritualists. The earthly reality was a little more subtle. Rothermere had encouraged Beaverbrook to buy the *Express* in the first place, presumably not imagining it would ever become a threat. After Northcliffe's death, Rothermere set up the Daily Mail Trust as a public company. Beaverbrook took a large stake in the Trust, becoming the second largest shareholder, and the Trust took a large stake in the *Express*. 'Since the Trust, which greatly prospered, paid substantial dividends, whereas the *Express* did not, the effect of the arrangement was that the Trust helped to finance the expansion of the *Express*.'[18]

The *Mail* was now run by Panza without Quixote. Its decline was by no means obvious. When, in the autumn of 1924, a twenty-one-year-old journalist from South London, Reg Foster, joined the paper 'on space', the *Mail* was still the giant of Fleet Street. And the office still had the authentic Edwardian flavour. 'There was this wonderful reporters' room – a large panelled room, well away from the news room – with a phone with a handle on the wall and a big roaring fire and a bell you could ring for boys, who'd bring beans on toast and marmalade on toast. If the news editor wanted you he'd either ring the phone or he'd panic down the corridor with his coat tails flying.'[19]

But Rothermere, whose favourite denunciatory word was 'Squandermania', was squandering the inheritance. He rarely visited Carmelite House, the *Mail*'s headquarters; James Dunn, one of the paper's star reporters, said he only met him once.[20] And, unlike Beaverbrook, he made no attempt to influence the news or features. He did, however, direct the paper's political preoccupations into all kinds of sluggish and murky channels. From the start, the *Mail* was very taken with Mussolini. Sir Percival Phillips, the paper's special correspondent, was writing glowingly of the Fascists' triumph within weeks of Northcliffe's death in 1922.

It is a wonderful epic, this story of a
long, weary struggle against heavy odds
... Patriotism has become a sacred
thing, and self-sacrifice the noblest of
virtues. Party creeds have been put aside.
The doctrine of the Fascisti, 'Our
country and not ourselves' is being practised as well as preached in a way that
the people of other countries may well
contemplate and profit by.

The paper's tame naval expert, H. W. Wilson, wrote an equally glowing
introduction to a collection of Phillips's articles: 'Fascism must win if only
because it is founded on love, while Communism is founded on hatred, and
good is always ultimately stronger than evil. Indeed, so high are the ideals of
Fascism that it will be difficult for mere men to live up to it.' But Mussolini
had more than a theoretical appeal for the *Mail*. 'He is rationing departments
in money and officials, and doing precisely what the *Daily Mail* has suggested
a hundred times should be done by Government departments here.'[21]

It is too easy with hindsight to mock people who flirted in the 1920s and
1930s with either of the century's two great ideological cul-de-sacs. Many
people were distracted by the enticing possibilities offered along the paths
that led to fascism or communism. But Rothermere kept on the same road
long after the scenery had become hideous; and, as far as the *Mail* was
concerned, his greatest flaw was his insistence on leading the paper down
other dead-ends that could not possibly be of interest to anyone apart from
himself.

In 1927 he took up the cause of Hungary, which had supported Germany
in the First World War and was duly punished in the Treaty of Trianon.
Rothermere became a hero in Budapest, which fed his vanity and harmed
no one, and in the *Daily Mail* the Hungarians were hailed as heroes, regularly
and at length, which must have wholly baffled the readers. Nor was it just
the 1924 election campaign that the *Mail* spent in a screaming hysteria about
Red Plots; they provided a constant and recurring theme that filled its pages
while the *Express* was having fun. In December 1924 the paper succumbed
to that new-fangled American innovation (first brought to Britain a few weeks
earlier in the *Sunday Express*), the crossword. Even here, there was a certain
sternness of tone. 'The puzzles are not only a game,' the *Mail* insisted, 'they
have considerable educational value.'

Of all the press lords, Rothermere is the most enigmatic. He stares out at
us from the pages of history, looking a bit like Dr Watson, played as a
complete ass by Nigel Bruce in the old Basil Rathbone versions, a bit like
The Very Fat Man Who Waters The Workers' Beer and, frankly, a bit like

Lord Emsworth's pig. Most written portraits of him are equally unflattering because journalists generally regarded him with contempt. Even the lick-spittles who produced books idolizing the very ground whereon Northcliffe walked usually got off the floor in time to aim a few blows at his curmudgeonly brother.

Yet he may have been a more sympathetic figure than he looked. He had three sons, two of them killed in the war; during his miserable stint as Air Minister in 1917–18, his eldest son Vyvyan was dying of wounds sustained at Cambrai. His wife had been carrying on with his younger brother St John, who was paralysed in a car crash on his way back from a tryst with her. She then left to live in France. If Rothermere was a professional pessimist, perhaps he had good cause.

An unusually – perhaps uniquely – kind picture appeared just after the Second World War from the pen of Collin Brooks. 'Ah,' Rothermere had said to Brooks at an early meeting, 'you thought I was a brazen-faced old man sitting in a corner counting his gold.' In fact, according to Brooks, he was an omnivorous reader who loved cathedrals, gardens, Italian art and the Brontës; a man of simple tastes whose favourite food was beef sandwiches, tinned fruit and seed-cake. 'His prevailing mood was politically one of the deepest pessimism, and personally one of almost uproarious satirical mirth.'[22] This rings true – partly because Brooks goes on to make some devastating criticism of Rothermere's journalism. His priorities were indeed wildly cock-eyed. In 1928 the chairman of the Conservative Party had to report to the Prime Minister that the *Daily Mail* would support Labour at the next election unless Baldwin slipped a sentence of support for Hungary into his next speech.[23]

Rothermere seems to have become obsessed with the suggestion that the Berry brothers, Lords Camrose and Kemsley,[24] had the largest press empire in Britain. So he started his own chain of provincial evening papers to fight them, bloodily, city by city. It must have been the last time in history when local newspapers had any glamour about them. At any rate, on 31 July 1929 the *Mail* plugged a forthcoming article with the drum-roll of a title: THE GLORIOUS HUNDRED DAYS by Viscount Rothermere. The story of Napoleon, perhaps? Not quite. 'It is the stirring epic of the *Evening World*, Newcastle.'

The conventional wisdom was that this was complete folly. Similar stirring epics up and down the kingdom inevitably ended in a compromise, with a lot of closures portending agreed local monopolies. Thirty years later all competition among English provincial evening newspapers effectively ceased and each town and city had one monopoly paper, invariably run on the more normal Rothermerean principle of minimum costs. Thanks partly to his battle in the late twenties, a good many, in decent-sized cities like Hull,

Plymouth, Derby and Leicester, were in the hands of Rothermere's descendants. These were all highly profitable right through the 1970s, precisely the time when Fleet Street was becoming a vast sink of lunatic labour practices sucking money down the plughole. Rothermere's son was able to survive in the business; Beaverbrook's son, his interests concentrated in Fleet Street, was not. In the long term, Rothermere's activities saved the dynasty; in the short term, the *Mail* went to pot.

At the time of the Hundred Days nonsense, the *Mail* had sent the snob Beverley Nichols to the races at Goodwood. 'Naming no names,' he reported, 'I observed in the paddock suits which looked as though their owners had been feeding hens in the rain, overcoats which had seen better days . . . and a quite horrifying selection of jumpers. One had a momentary impression that the rag, tag and bobtail had, after all, rebelled and swarmed over the barriers.' Someone had to write for the rag, tag and bobtail. The *Mail* was effectively quitting the contest.

VIII

Beaverbrook's character continues to exercise an extraordinary fascination. Cecil King, later head of the *Daily Mirror*, thought that 'he was the first evil man to figure in British public life for a very long time.' Malcolm Muggeridge also used the word 'evil' – in the specific context of Beaverbrook's habit of developing and encouraging people's weaknesses, usually sexual or alcoholic. Chesterton called him Caliban. Hugh Kingsmill, deliciously, christened him Robin Badfellow. Alan Wood thought he was 'in essentials a Marxist'. While running often phenomenally vindictive anti-Labour newspapers he acted as a patron to the far left: to both Aneurin Bevan and Michael Foot, and their newspaper *Tribune*. Scores of people relied on his generosity; yet he was remembered at the Lord Beaverbrook Hotel in New Brunswick because he never left a tip. William Davis learned that he was a man who could never be bluffed. Tom Hutchinson said he should always be bluffed: a local reporter was once asked by Beaverbrook how many laying hens were in his neighbourhood, spluttered out a figure at random and was immediately appointed agricultural correspondent of the *Daily Express*. Michael Foot's wife Jill Craigie said Beaverbrook's nature was 'infinitely complex, contradictory, whimsical, a nature on which the last word can never be said'.[25]

On that point at least everyone can agree. Likewise, no one denies his brilliance as a journalist, or as a manipulator of journalists. Northcliffe was a journalistic visionary; it is not clear that Beaverbrook had any vision at all.

Yet though he had no profound knowledge of how newspapers were produced either, he had an instinct for the public taste that never faltered. A great deal of his style was borrowed from the previous champion: the clipped, telephonic commands; the ever-flowing stream of memos; the obsessiveness. But, crucially, he was unencumbered by the constant concern for accuracy and ethical conduct that was the rock of all the Northcliffe papers.

He was also the hardest-working journalist in history, in the sense that he never stopped. Malcolm Muggeridge says that you always knew which society lady he was trying to entice into bed because there would be an instruction to write a flattering paragraph or two about her; if his efforts failed, a different account would be sent. Rothermere's extra-marital life also seems to have been rather lively, involving a great many showgirls and large quantities of champagne, which the girls probably needed to make the experience bearable. It was, however, conducted with great discretion and provided no copy whatever for the *Daily Mail*.

The Beaverbrook set was just an extension of the newspaper. Journalists would be wined, dined and flattered until such point as his love was withdrawn. He saw himself as the spider at the centre of a web of power and intrigue, and he loved being there. He told the 1949 Royal Commission on the Press that he ran his papers for propaganda, and this line has regularly been quoted ever since. But that in itself was of course propaganda. He ran his papers, above all, for the sheer joy of it. The *Daily Express* was fun because he was having fun. He once rang his gossip columnist: 'Driberg? . . . Lord Lloyd is very angry with you. He did not like what you wrote about him this morning. He is very angry with me also. I can bear Lord Lloyd's anger. I *rejoice* in Lord Lloyd's anger. It does not distress me at all. At all. Goodbye to you.'

IX

Megalomania is the occupational disease of newspaper proprietors; the coal dust of their idiosyncratic form of power enters their lungs with an insidious inevitability. The manifestations of the sickness vary. Sometimes they come to believe, like William Randolph Hearst – and, in his early Portsmouth adventure, Northcliffe – that people who buy a newspaper will wish to elect the paper's owner to office. Sometimes, like Northcliffe in the First World War, they believe that politicians listen to them not because they are influential but because they are wise. Sometimes – often – they over-estimate not only their wisdom but also their influence, as Cecil King did in 1968 when he had lost faith in Harold Wilson and assumed that a few harsh words from him on the front page would immediately cause millions of *Mirror* readers to do the same.

In 1929 the owners of the *Daily Express* and the *Daily Mail* launched a campaign that combined elements of all three delusions. After close to a full five-year term, Baldwin's Conservative Government lost the 1929 general election, and the second minority Labour Government took power. Beaverbrook and Rothermere now began to manoeuvre feverishly against Baldwin, using the argument that had dogged the Tories for almost a century: free trade vs. protection. Beaverbrook beat the drum that Pearson had first tapped in the early days of the *Express*, but now he thumped it with the sound of thunder. He demanded Empire Free Trade – it took a mind like Beaverbrook's to begin a campaign for protection and call it free trade. This was the Empire Crusade. The history of the next few months is convoluted and barely credible. Beaverbrook recruited Rothermere as an ally and the two press lords really did seem to think they could take over the country. Their aims were not even identical: Rothermere was far more interested in countering 'Squandermania' and the Bolshevik threat than he was in the Empire.

Baldwin placated Beaverbrook by offering to hold a referendum on the subject when he returned to power. 'March the Fourth, 1930', began the next day's leader in a prediction spectacularly wrong even by *Express* standards, 'will be remembered in the political history of the country for generations to come.' When Beaverbrook realized Baldwin had not the slightest intention of holding a referendum, he turned on him with redoubled fury. On 29 March 1930 the Red Crusader, the enduring symbol of the *Daily Express*, appeared at the top of page 1.

By all objective accounts, Beaverbrook became increasingly erratic and power-crazed. Certainly his daily newspaper did. On 31 January 1931 the *Express* reported on the inaugural Empire Crusade meeting in the East Islington by-election campaign.

One question stood out long after the turbulence of the first by-election meeting had gone. 'Does this mean . . . a war in the Conservative Party?' a man asked Lord Beaverbrook from the gallery.

Lord Beaverbrook's eyes flashed. He took a quick step forward to the front of the platform.

'If,' he began, and his voice rang in the back of the hall. 'If the Conservative Party does not accept the policy of Empire Free Trade . . .'

There was a pause.

'Yes!' he thundered.

The hall rocked with cheers.

And Lord Beaverbrook's candidate, Brigadier-General Critchley, came second to Labour, beating the official Conservative. There had been other triumphs, like South Paddington, when the Beaverbrook candidate won:

THE EMPIRE WINS SOUTH PADDINGTON.

Less convenient results, such as East Renfrewshire, were buried in dark corners of the *Express* by dutiful sub-editors.

But the Crusade did not strike a chord only with Beaverbrook's hired hacks. Capitalism was obviously in crisis. Far more outlandish cures were also in fashion, and were regularly spouted in the pages of the *Daily Mail*. It was a moment in history when a well-organized and well-funded by-election campaign might have persuaded people to vote for *anything*. And protection was a cause that had long attracted the Conservative rank and file. Beaverbrook spoke tirelessly, up and down the country. Howard Spring observed him at a meeting in Darwen, Lancashire, and described him in the *Manchester Guardian* as 'a pedlar of dreams'. Beaverbrook liked that.

Meanwhile, the *Express*'s circulation kept going up. One is forced to conclude that this had little or nothing to do with its political beliefs. The *Mail* was so bamboozled that it called for Beaverbrook to become Prime Minister and made the Crusade its main news story twelve days running. But amid the quarter-truths of the *Express*'s coverage of the Empire Crusade, Beaverbrook was also putting out the most appealing popular newspaper Britain had ever seen. The morning after he flashed his eyes and thundered on the platform at East Islington, *Express* readers also learned that the King of Sweden had refused to let his son marry his teenage lover; a Swindon railway foreman who dabbled in the stock market had left £44,000 (equal to a modern million); a woman in Harlesden had been practising her dance steps by the canal and fallen in; the Duchess of Sutherland had apologized to a pilot whom she had blamed for the death of her daughter in a crash; there was a gun battle following the arrest of Al Capone in Argentina; and there was copious coverage of the Schneider Trophy air race and the North-amptonshire blazing car murder. It was all good stuff. Even Northcliffe's unquiet spirit seemed finally silent: Dean Inge of St Paul's denounced spiritualism as belonging 'to the barbarous childhood of the human race'. No one needed to ask Northcliffe how it should be done any more. There was a new master of journalism, alive, and kicking at everything in sight.

The Crusade passed away in the spring of 1931, at the by-election of St George's, Westminster. Baldwin thought of quitting the leadership; then he thought of resigning and contesting the leadership himself; instead he boxed Beaverbrook and Rothermere into a corner. He made the power of the press lords the issue of the election. Even if he lost, the Conservative Party could not get rid of him without being seen to truckle to Beaverbrook and Rothermere.

Their papers, he said,

are not newspapers in the ordinary acceptance of the term. They are engines of the propaganda for the constantly changing policies, desires, personal wishes, personal likes and dislikes of two men. What are their methods? Their methods are direct falsehood, misrepresentation, half-truths, the alteration of the speaker's meaning by putting sentences apart from the context, suppression, and editorial criticism of speeches which are not reported in the paper . . . What the proprietorship of these papers is aiming at is power, but power without responsibility – the prerogative of the harlot throughout the ages.

These words, the most famous Baldwin ever spoke, were never reported in the *Express*, though Baxter, the editor, covered the meeting himself. Thus the paper proved Baldwin's point for him. The Conservative candidate, Duff Cooper, beat Beaverbrook's candidate, Sir Ernest Petter, by 17,242 votes to 11,532. (Cooper's wife, Lady Diana, was one of Beaverbrook's favourites, which made him rather ambivalent about this by-election.) Baldwin made a few piffling concessions towards imperial preference in his programme for the next election, and the *Express* claimed triumph. But this war was over, and Beaverbrook had been routed. Its most enduring legacy was probably the figure of the Crusader.

The editor of the *New Statesman*, Kingsley Martin, had seen it all coming. The average newspaper reader, he said, was either tired or busy: 'he looks at the headlines and reads the snappy paragraphs just as willingly as he stands for a few minutes on a corner to watch a street acrobat . . . But the spectators are not impelled to put either the physical or the verbal exhibitionist into ministerial office.'[26] Beaverbrook was now able to devote his attention to the real press war. And headlines and snappy paragraphs were only part of the weaponry.

X

The first great circulation gimmick offered by newspapers was free insurance. Sir George Newnes's *Tit-Bits* led the way, insuring against railway accidents in the 1880s. The *Daily Chronicle* is said to have been the first daily to take up the challenge, and the *Daily Mail* leaped in at the beginning of 1914, offering to protect 'regular readers' (defined as those who had an order at a newsagent's) against mishaps not just on a train but also on a 'public omnibus (horse or motor driven), tramway car, cab or passenger steamer'. There was no mention of the kind of threat that, in 1914, was soon to prove infinitely more dangerous than any public omnibus or tramway car. But the *Mail's* scheme was an advance on anything earlier, because it did not apply only on the days when the paper was published. Previously, it was not advisable to get injured on a Sunday.

Through the 1920s, popular papers had to offer free insurance to be competitive. Circulation managers liked insurance; advertising managers did not, because there was a fair bit of anecdotal evidence that people were ordering papers and never reading them, or sometimes not even collecting them from the shop.

The space devoted to plugging insurance gave the papers a curiously gloomy quality. This applied even to the normally relentlessly upbeat *Express*, whose morale-boosting message to its readers one summer's morning in 1922 was that it was the only paper which would insure them against appendicitis. There followed a list of twenty-one names who had each received a tenner for their troubles: 'Mr Kingsbury of 77, Brook Street, Kennington; Mrs Buckle of 27, Bristowe Road, Hounslow; Major Palmer of 25, Richmond Park Crescent, Bournemouth; Mr Small of 499, Barking Road, Plaistow . . .' Already the *Express* could appeal to majors in Bournemouth as well as to the Mr Smalls of Plaistow. There were four columns of £4 a week payments for total temporary disablements, and £2 a week for a further list of sufferers from shingles, chicken-pox, sunstroke (in places like Biggleswade, if you please), mumps, scarlet fever, diphtheria, whooping cough, measles and scurvy (well done, Mr H. Roach of Rhymney!). It was a sort of sickness bingo. There was a macabre fascination in these announcements and people may well have read them like lists of magistrates' court defendants in local papers, just to see if anyone they knew had got scurvy. And the newspapers were filling a gap: in 1922 there was no all-embracing welfare state to help sick people through bad times.

If necessary the message would be hammered home in a more personal way. Involvement in the insurance business meant the papers employed large staffs of canvassers, out there trudging from door to door on a smile and a shoeshine; many of them were ex-naval officers, axed in defence cutbacks and glad even of this demeaning work. If there was a large pay-out, then canvassers would descend on the lucky/unlucky reader's neighbourhood, pressing home the advantage. Naturally, they would be followed by rival canvassers. In 1928 *The Economist* reported cases of streets being bothered by representatives of a dozen different papers in the same week. Reporters knocking on doors in search of a story might well have the door slammed in their face as soon as they mentioned their paper, because people assumed it was yet another canvasser.

At that stage both the *Express* and the *Mail* were offering £25,000 if a registered reader and his wife were killed in a railway accident. One wonders if unscrupulous children began to encourage their parents to take unnecessary journeys on rickety branch lines. The offer was soon reduced, and for two years this jackpot was limited to £10,000. But every now and again there would be further announcements about new categories of disaster the schemes would cover. By 1930 the *Express* was offering £50 for death at work and gun fatalities, £100 for dead pedestrians and cyclists and £250 – say £10,000 today – for drowning on holiday; and Mr T. Anslow of Limerick did precisely that. Lucky Mrs Anslow! The *Express* refrained from phrasing it quite that way, but it would not have been out of keeping with the general tone.

Even in the late 1920s the papers' insurance work was extended by a number of free gift schemes. They also began to offer four-figure cash prizes for competitions, especially for the new craze of crosswords. Often there was a cash stake, and in 1931 the *Herald, Mail* and *Mirror* pushed their luck over a Derby competition, in which the *Mail* offered a £7,500 first prize. They fell foul of a legal technicality and were each fined a piffling £30 by magistrates – enabling the *Express*, which was not involved, to run a magnificently high-horse leader: 'The legal aspect of the case is of small importance compared to the journalistic ethics involved. The spectacle of newspapers actually making heavy profits out of money hazarded by the public in a preposterous gamble . . . is one that can only lower newspapers generally in the estimation of the public.'

But by then the stakes had already been raised in a gamble of impudence and desperation unrivalled even in the Fleet Street casino. The *Daily Herald* had started in 1911 as a strike sheet produced by the London print workers and was turned into a daily paper in 1912 by George Lansbury and Ben Tillett. It went weekly during the war and was relaunched as a daily shortly afterwards, when it became something of a *succès d'estime*, highly regarded for the quality of its writing. But it had no money and had to be bailed out by the Labour Party and the TUC.

As the newspaper combines grew stronger through the 1920s, the *Herald* still could not compete, certainly not in the matters of insurance and gifts. The working class were happy enough to vote Labour, but the party was not yet in a position to match the capitalist press in the matter of providing £10 a week for appendicitis sufferers. And many large firms simply refused to advertise in the *Herald*. Ernest Bevin was instructed to solve the paper's problems, which brought him into contact with the press lord who later took the title Viscount Southwood.

Behind this bland and rather *goyish* title lurked J. S. Elias, a polite Jewish businessman of homespun tastes. He started as a jeweller's errand boy and became successful in publishing, so it was said, by producing magazines that Mrs Elias liked to read by the fireside. While Beaverbrook and Rothermere stalked the fleshpots of the world, Elias spent his holidays with his wife in the Grand Hotel, Eastbourne, listening to the Palm Court orchestra.[27] Elias was no socialist; but, as the owner of Odhams Press, he was in the print business. And business was business. He had formerly printed the scandalous magazine *John Bull*, owned by the scoundrel Horatio Bottomley. He also printed *The People*, which meant he had presses that were under-used during the week. The Labour Party's money was as good as anyone else's, indeed rather better than Bottomley's. A deal was done. Odhams took 51 per cent of the capital, but allowed the TUC to fill the paper with whatever propaganda it wanted provided the commercial side was left to Elias.

The *Herald* was relaunched yet again on 17 March 1930 and at once went out to play with the big boys. It began its own insurance scheme, hired good writers at substantial salaries and tasted blood within weeks: the two great Liberal papers, the *Daily News* and the *Daily Chronicle*, were forced to merge as the *News Chronicle*. Almost instantly the *Herald*'s circulation leaped from barely 250,000 to above a million. The paradox was that this was not enough. The *Express*, on the way up, was just passing the *Mail*, on the way down, but both were selling around one and three-quarter million, while the combined *News Chronicle* started at around one and a half million. And the *Herald* found it harder than any of these to get advertising, partly because of political prejudice, partly because of the cold calculation by the advertising agencies – and they were getting more scientific – that *Herald* readers had less money to spend. Elias reasoned that the paper had to sell two million copies a day to succeed, and he set out to do just that.

Part of the effort was conducted by traditional horny-handed Labour Party methods. Bevin made five speeches on behalf of the party and the paper every weekend. Part of it involved a recognition that even the most devoted member of the Labour Party might be a little more of a capitalist than he liked to pretend: any party member who signed a hundred readers for ten weeks received £3 15s for himself and £2 10s for the local party. But above all there were the inducements for the readers themselves. They were given gifts, or at any rate bribes. This was a development the other newspapers could not afford to ignore, and thus began the most intense circulation war in British newspaper history.

This war was not fought primarily in the pages of the papers; it was fought on the well-scrubbed doorsteps of industrial Britain. Since the gifts were available only to newly registered readers, the last thing the papers wanted to do was alert the poor saps who were paying over their penny to be entertained or told what to think by Beaverbrook, Rothermere or even Ernest Bevin. Canvassers were instructed never to approach anyone registered as a reader of their own paper. But in fact many of the saps were a great deal smarter than the would-be manipulators. The papers were not buying the readers' loyalty; they only had to sign up for a few weeks. Then they could switch, and get another gift from someone else.

It was a war – at least, that was the word used the whole time in the trade paper, *World's Press News*, along with other relevant terms like 'ammunition', 'ceasefire' and 'armistice'. But it was more like a war of the 1980s or 1990s, Lebanon or Bosnia, perhaps: there were incessant 'peace talks'; truces would be arranged, then break down, and the fighting would resume more bloodily than ever while onlookers wrung their hands and muttered about the madness of it all.

The first time the proprietors agreed to stop offering further gifts, Elias got round the agreement by offering large reference books like dictionaries, *The Home Doctor* and *The Handyman*, printed in vast quantities at a low unit cost on Oldhams' own presses. Then he offered a complete collection of the works of Dickens, sixteen volumes in cloth or imitation leather. The *Herald* started to creep closer to Elias's target of a two million sale. At this point the other proprietors cried Foul! and, on 7 March 1933, called a famous meeting at the Savoy Hotel, attended by the heads of the *Express*, *Mail*, *Herald* and *News Chronicle*. Beaverbrook demanded that Elias withdraw the Dickens offer. Elias refused, and was about to leave. Beaverbrook confronted him. 'Elias,' he said. 'This is war – war to the death.' And he drew an imaginary Crusader's sword and made the gesture of running it through Elias, who smiled and departed.

And so *Express*, *Mail* and *News Chronicle* readers also got offered the works of Dickens. That is why – to this day – it is very easy to pick up cheap Dickens collections second-hand, usually in close to mint condition because even in the 1930s the attention span of the British public was no longer up to *Bleak House* or *Martin Chuzzlewit*. From that point the papers ran riot. The canvassers offered boots, tea sets, cigarette cases, cutlery, toy trains, dolls, mackintoshes, mangles and mincing machines. The *Herald* dished out ladies' underwear; the *Express* gave away 10,000 pairs of silk stockings. It was said that an entire family could be clothed from head to foot if they could only bear to spend a penny a day on the *Daily Express* for eight weeks.[28]

The *Daily Mail* warned its shareholders about 'unavoidable sacrifices' but in this war, as in any other, the poor bloody infantry suffered most. One canvasser replied to an advert for people 'of exceptional selling ability' and turned up to find forty other men, all of whom were engaged without any questions being asked on a wage of £3 a week plus bonuses. 'After knocking at a few dozen doors we discovered that the general public was heartily fed up with newspaper canvassers, and any orders granted were given out of sympathy ... in other words the job became one of not salesmanship but purely and simply glorified begging.' The company showed no sympathy whatever and regularly sacked people after three days' work.[29]

The *Herald* got to two million first, but only just ahead of the *Express*. And when the debris of durables and scanties was finally cleared, as it was, slowly, from 1934 onwards, it was the *Express* that forged ahead, for the simple reason that it was actually a better and more interesting newspaper, which in the end is rather cheering. The free gift and insurance schemes continued until the real war; and after that the state took on more responsibility for people who were sick or distressed. The press lords had failed when they tried to usurp the business of government but, in providing basic insurance, they had been fulfilling one of the functions later recognized as a responsibility of government. It is rather a neat irony.

XI

On 2 April 1930, while Lord Beaverbrook was busy trying to bring down the leader of the Conservative Party, the following story appeared on the front page of the *Daily Express*:

DANCING GIRL BURNED TO DEATH IN FILM STUDIO.
FATAL LAST LOOK IN HER MIRROR.

Tragedy came into the make-believe world of talking pictures at the Twickenham Film Studios yesterday.

Pretty golden-haired Anita Fay Tippett, a 20-year-old chorus girl in 'Here Comes The Bride' at the Piccadilly Theatre, and dancer in the new film 'Spanish Eyes', was so severely burned when her flimsy gown caught fire against an electric radiator in a dressing-room at the studios, that she died in the Royal Hospital, Richmond . . .

It has to be said that within a very few years no one on the *Express* would get away with a second paragraph as wordy as that one. But here was the perfect Fleet Street story of the inter-war years, when glamour and tragedy so often went together. That very day the *Express* also reported the death of the Duchess of Leinster, former Gaiety Girl Mary Etheridge, found gassed in a London flat. This sort of thing happened all the time: Isadora Duncan was garrotted when her long scarf was trapped by the wheels of a car; airships and aeroplanes fell regularly and spectacularly out of the sky; gallant aviatrices vanished without trace. Chorus girls in flimsy gowns were good news for the papers, however gruesome the circumstances. Miss Tippett, *Express* readers learned, had only just heard the call 'Set-up. Dancers please.'

> ... The girl turned to the mirror when
> she heard the call and glanced to see that
> her make-up and her hair were as they
> should be. As she bent down to look into
> the glass her skirt came into contact with
> the glowing wires of the radiator. She
> was ablaze in a moment . . .

This is fascinating detail. However, there had been only one other person in the room at the time, one Donald Calthrop, and he was, as the *Express* faithfully reported, too ill to talk. So this plausible account of Miss Tippett's last moments presumably came from that most inexhaustible of all journalistic sources, the reporter's imagination – the same database that had provided such a vivid account of the Filey Bay tragedy in the *Express* twenty-eight years before.

At that time, it was a bit of a rarity. But now there was no Northcliffe to hammer home to his reporters the importance of accuracy and integrity; and these high ideals were never close to Beaverbrook's heart. Newspapers were under unprecedented commercial pressures. Journalists were well paid but with minimal job security. It was inevitable that corners were cut. Although there was an element of hocus-pocus about the circulation war of the 1930s, many of the readers sucked in were genuinely new ones. The overall number of buyers rose, and never fell back. Thus the process that had been going on for more than a century continued towards the point when daily newspapers saturated the market, and all Britain read a paper. The papers had to retain the attention of these new readers as they ate their breakfast with the utensils so thoughtfully provided by the gift schemes.

Critics of the ha'penny papers before the First World War carped about their triviality. Now they cost a penny, and triviality was wearily accepted. Complaints focused instead on their inaccuracies and their shoddy reporting methods. Hamilton Fyfe, the former editor of the *Daily Mirror* and *Daily Herald*, wrote in 1936 that the habit of pestering people related to the victims of tragedies began on one national paper (he does not say which, but circumstantial evidence points to the *Express*) and was taken up by the others out of fear. He goes on to tell the story of a group of bereaved women pursued by reporters across the country and into a hotel where they were pestered at regular intervals with demands for information. They were advised to stay in their rooms, where theoretically they should have been safe.

But not a bit of it. The bedside telephone soon started to ring. 'This is the —— wishing to speak to Mrs ——.' The photograph of the dead woman was pushed under the bedroom door with a paper requesting to know if it were a correct likeness. One of the reporters actually applied for a bedroom close by for himself so as to be able to pounce upon the ladies the moment they appeared in the morning.[30]

Fyfe also noted the *Express*'s particular cavalier way with facts. On 30 October 1931 a photograph appeared of a crane unloading cases of gold sent from the United States to France; on 24 November the same picture appeared, only this time it purported to show Soviet butter being sent to Britain. He went on to cite the splendid case of the Empire Day pageant of 1932. The early editions of the paper on 25 May had the classic *Express* headlines

THRILLING CLIMAX TO EMPIRE DAY.

THOUSANDS CHEER HISTORIC SCENES.

above a detailed account of the day: '. . . the slender figure of a girl robed in white, representing Peace, stood enthroned before us in a single beam of white light . . . We sang as darkness fell.' Later editions, alas, had to reveal the truth:

HYDE PARK PAGEANT CALLED OFF.

But all the papers were cutting corners, such as when a prominent surgeon died while preparing to go to a private house to perform an operation (*News Chronicle*); while visiting a friend (*Daily Herald*); in an operating theatre awaiting a patient (*Express*); and in the middle of an operation (*Mail*). On that occasion, the *Express* was the one that got it right. At other times – and this was not such a new development – the facts were conditioned by the paper's political outlook, such as the figure for the 1933 budget deficit: £3 million in the more-or-less pro-Government *Express*, £32 million in the definitely anti-Government *Herald*; or the Danzig elections, which were both a TRIUMPH FOR NAZIS (*Daily Mail*) and SHOCK FOR NAZIS (*News Chronicle*). And there was a caption for a picture taken at a march of the unemployed, which showed 'A casualty during a disturbance between hecklers and socialist supporters' (*Express*) or 'Ambulance men attending a fainting case' (*News Chronicle*).

Even the supposedly respectable newspapers were not above a little spin of their own. When a group of Russians visited London they 'all had a drawn and hungry look which follows privations and obvious suffering' in the vigorously right-wing *Morning Post*, but looked 'very much like well-to-do Lancashire artisans, sturdy and obviously healthy' in the more sympathetic *Manchester Guardian*.[31]

Reporters acquired a reputation as fairly hard-bitten brutes, and their attitudes radiated outwards. The following dialogue from the reporters' room of a big London daily in 1928, between a small newsboy who rushed in and the reporter he accosted, is said to be true and probably is:

> 'Case of suicide. Worth half a crown, Guv'nor.'
> 'Police told yet?'
> 'No, 'course not.'
> 'Woman?'
> 'Yep.'
> 'Young?'
> 'Mother of five.'
> 'Oh . . . Why did she do it?'
> 'Booze.'
> 'Where?'
> 'Down in Stepney. I came running right here.'
> 'Stepney – that's no good. Any last letter?'
> 'No, she forgot.'
> 'For God's sake, don't tell me she just put her blooming head in a gas oven?'
> 'Sorry, Guv'nor, that's what she did. But it's worth half a dollar, honest, Guv'nor. And I brought it here straight away, same as they told us. It's my mother, Guv'nor.'[32]

It was the age of classic crime stories and murder cases: the Brighton trunk murders (numbers one and two), the Cheltenham torso, the body on the Crumbles . . . The big names from Scotland Yard's Murder Squad and the big-name reporters could be on a case for weeks, and the reporters had to keep coming up with fresh angles. There was a certain amount of scope for what Reg Foster, reasonably enough, called 'harmless fun'. 'I mean, somebody might find a blood-stained garter in a ditch,' he said, 'and take it to the police. Marvellous story but no relevance at all to the investigation.'

But round these cases would also lurk some of Fleet Street's least fine: the picture-snatchers, whose sole job was to get pictures of people involved in big cases, by whatever means. 'The *Daily Mail* had one of the best picture-snatchers of his time,' Reg Foster recalled, 'a very urbane gentleman with a silver-top walking stick. He would talk his way into a house and used the line that is true really, that the publication of this picture might help the police, and that I'll send it back. Sometimes they did and sometimes they didn't.'[33] Other picture-snatchers used more direct methods: they just stole them.

Press intrusion was a constant source of complaint in the 1930s. St John Ervine wrote to *The Times* in 1933 after he had been woken by a journalist at 2 a.m. to be asked where Bernard Shaw was at that moment. He had a list of other, more serious, grievances including several instances of the bereaved being harassed 'in the nauseous pretence of offering sympathy'. In 1936 Charles Lindbergh and his wife came to England to seek privacy after the trial of their baby's supposed kidnapper. They were met at the quayside by hundreds of journalists and were forced to hole up at the Adelphi Hotel.

By 1932 the Church was starting to get very agitated about the excesses. 'The cheap press,' said the Archbishop of Canterbury, Dr Lang, 'is one of the invasions into home life which are presenting to growing boys and girls conceptions of life far different from those their mothers would wish them to hold.'[34] The Bishop of Salisbury, as lesser figures are inclined to do, put it more strongly: 'What does the cheap press talk about? Absolutely nothing except dirty sex affairs, murders and accidents, and all that goes for an unclean and unhealthy life. The cheap press is a menace to the nation.'[35] Had they but known what the rest of the century was to bring, they might have been less censorious.

But criticism was coming from all quarters. More telling, perhaps, was a piece by the American journalist Westbrook Pegler, who said the worst of the British press had now sunk beneath American levels. This was some achievement, given the American press's reputation in the 1920s. Pegler was not concerned about the immorality of British papers, or even their intrusiveness; he thought they were just careless, incompetently written and naïve, regularly falling for the oldest tricks: 'Miss Merle Oberon, a moving picture actress, broke into print with the news that her lips had been insured for $100,000, a gag which no self-respecting Press agent would have the effrontery to offer the most gullible American news desks at this late date.' It got printed in London.[36]

The intelligentsia as a whole was starting to regard popular newspapers with the mixture of horror, contempt, secret fascination and wry detachment that would redouble in force during later periods of press excesses. The following verse by Douglas Cole, published in the *New Clarion* in July 1932, seems to me as fresh and relevant now as it was then. It should be sung to the tune of 'What Shall We Do With The Drunken Sailor?'

> *The Song of the Press*
> What shall we put in the daily paper?
> What shall we put in the daily paper?
> What shall we put in the daily paper?
>   Early in the morning?
> Workers on the dole who guzzle
> Communists who need a muzzle,
> All the winners and a crossword puzzle,
>   Early in the morning.

What shall we put in the daily paper?
Suicide of a linen draper,
Duchess poisoned by noxious vapour,
    Early in the morning.
Awful international crisis;
Idiot reader wins three prizes.
See how the British public rises
    Early in the morning.

Shove 'em all down in the daily paper,
Cabinet Minister cuts a caper.
Architect felled by his own sky-scraper,
    Early in the morning.
Some of it's truth and some is lying
What's the odds if the public's buying?
Journalists never leave off trying,
    Early in the morning.

XII

On the same day as it carried its report on the death of the chorus girl Anita Tippett, the *Express* also ran a story about a master mariner in Whitstable who left all his money to German disabled soldiers because 'England was going to the dogs'.

Indeed it was. The popular papers now devoted considerable space on the sports pages to the new craze of greyhound racing, then familiar enough to be known sometimes as 'greycing'. People were equally taken by the Irish Hospitals' Sweepstake, which had displaced the old Calcutta Sweep, and papers would devote whole pages to lists of winners. England was also going roller-skating, a uniquely cyclical craze, and, from 1929, ice-skating. Its children were playing with yo-yos. England was going to the talkies; Beverley Baxter claimed that the *Sunday Express* was the first London paper to realize that film news was of more general interest than theatre news, and its daily sister cottoned on fast. England was going to Lyons Corner Houses (a good source of advertising).

England was also going hiking, a word that came into vogue around 1927. The *Express* fed this interest by publishing pictures of Colourful England. Unfortunately, the technique was too primitive to allow more than one colour at a time, and when Grove Mill, near Watford, was portrayed in its verdant glory, everything had to be in different shades of green, including the sky. It would take more than half a century to develop the techniques of getting full colour on to large quantities of newsprint produced at speed.

England was listening to the wireless, too, and on 2 November 1936 the *Express* critic Jonah Barrington reported on the BBC's new television service, which opened at 3 p.m. the previous day without a hitch: 'I have watched it with interest for two hours, I have a bad headache, and I am looking forward to returning to my radio.' Underneath was an advert for Elliman's Embrocation, showing an elderly couple with the slogan: 'After all, old friends are best.' (There is a story that around 1926 John Logie Baird went into the *Express* office anxious to show his new invention to the editor. Baxter, in keeping with the paper's reputation for percipience, sent down a message: 'Get rid of that lunatic. He may have a knife.')

The nation smoked. Round Wimbledon time in 1933 the *Express* had an advert depicting two tennis players. 'My wife and I smoke roughly 450 between us weekly. They do not affect our breathing and we come off the courts comparatively fresh . . . Athletes favour CRAVEN "A" Cigarettes because Craven "A" do not "cut" the wind nor do they affect the throat or breathing.'

And England was beginning to splinter. J. B. Priestley, in his *English Journey*, published in 1934, identified four nations. There was the old England, with the parson and squire, which could still just about be found; nineteenth-century industrial England; and the new England of the arterial roads and the bungalows. 'In this England, for the first time in history, Jack and Jill are nearly as good as their master and mistress.'[37] The fourth England was that of the unemployed, but there was very little sign of them among the bungalows, or in the pages of the *Daily Express*. For those in work, and that was always the overwhelming majority, the 1930s were, like the 1980s, a time of unprecedented prosperity and opportunity. It was the era of Amy Johnson, and of Madame Lupescu (the paramour of King Carol of Romania); of Gandhi, Bradman, Belisha Beacons, the St Neots Quads and a now slightly less funny German with a moustache.

The *Express* did write about people who led lives remote from most of their readers, but if these were unemployed it was only because they were the idle rich. At regular intervals newspapers would claim that they were reinventing the idea of gossip columns, but the more they changed, the more they seemed to stay the same. After the First World War the *Express* had 'Table Talk' by Patricia, full of stories about London emptying and filling up again, according to the season, or rather The Season, in keeping with the illusion, which *Express* readers seemed happy to share, that most of them lived their own lives by the social calendar.

This was followed by 'The Dragoman', who was sometimes slightly more non-U. When the editor of that retired, Beaverbrook instructed his deputy to change the emphasis. Thus on 12 May 1933 the following appeared under the heading THESE NAMES MAKE NEWS:

> Social chatter about the eccentricities of gilded half-wits is dead. Occasionally I may ornament my page with the photograph of some lovely but idle debutante. This will be for decorative purposes only. In general, any woman who is 'in Society' and has no other justification for her existence, will be out of this column. I believe this experiment is on the right lines.

The new columnist was Tom Driberg, who a few weeks later took the *nom de plume* William Hickey. Driberg's subsequent reputation, as a biographer of Beaverbrook, a left-wing Labour MP, an alleged Russian spy, and, above all, as a promiscuous homosexual with a particular taste for sucking working-class penises in gentlemen's lavatories, has given his column a lasting place in newspaper history. Undoubtedly it took on a more subversive edge, which appealed to both the proprietor and the public. But it had to be filled every day, and much of the content was not all that different from everything that had gone before.

Although there was a wider range of material in the newspapers of the early 1930s, they retained something of the Victorian mystique. The *Express*, wrote Hugh Cudlipp, was respectability itself. 'People were divorced in their columns in the same droves as in other newspapers, but it was hard to discern just why they had parted. For the darker offences the sentences were duly recorded, but no evidence was published which might embarrass or intrigue the most innocent member of the family.'[38]

The philosophy behind this was contained in the *Express* style book, which was issued to the public under the title *Do's and Don't's for Reporters and Sub-Editors* in 1930 by Blumenfeld, who by then was chairman of the *Express* and presumably had little else to do. Blumenfeld said they were as he had produced them a generation earlier, and had stood the test of time. Indeed, much of the advice would be recognized as standard practice in 1996 (though a modern sub-editor would hardly put two apostrophes in *Don't's*): 'Put the *essential point* of the "story" in the headline (avoiding abstractions) but remember that the *ideal headline* while "telling the story", should leave the reader with the desire to read the story itself. With this object use freely words like *mystery, secret, tragedy, drama, comedy, scandal* and *human*.'

Then came the words and phrases the *Express* was not allowed to use. These included:

Don't Use	Alternative
Abortion	Illegal operation
Adultery	— was cited as co-respondent
Amazing	
'Bus	Omnibus
Disgusting	
Gashed his throat	
Gentleman	Man
Grim tragedy	
Gruesome	
Lady	Woman
Nasty gash	
Seduced	Betrayed or deceived
Shocking	
Society ladies	
Tram	Tramcar

Driberg and, indeed, Beaverbrook, in their very different ways, were leading extremely unrespectable lives, and the readers in the bungalows might have thought the details amazing, shocking and, in Driberg's case, rather disgusting. They were not ready to hear about any such matters. Or at least, they were *thought* not to be ready to hear about such matters, which is what counted.

Above all, discretion still prevailed in the case of the Royal Family, because it suited the proprietors to keep it that way. All through the summer of 1936 a sizeable minority of the population knew that Edward VIII was cruising on a yacht with Mrs Simpson. Anyone who had access to overseas newspapers, which were analysing the subject in enormous detail, would have known. Anyone who received *Time* magazine would have wondered why his copies had bits scissored out by the distributors, who claimed that the libel laws were involved. It was 3 December before the saucepan boiled over and the story finally got into print.

There was an eight-day crisis, and even in that short time the *Express* managed to misread developments badly more than once. On 8 December it ran the headline END OF THE CRISIS, on the grounds that Mrs Simpson was ready to withdraw. Beaverbrook was heavily involved with the King's cause, and when the crisis did end, with what soon came to seem like historic inevitability, the *Express* 'deeply deplored' the abdication.

XIII

It was not much of a welcome for the new monarch, George VI, from the paper read by more of his subjects than any other. That was now beyond dispute. On 1 July 1933 the *Express* had passed the two million mark. For a time after that, it did fall back again. But by 1937 it was racing away from the opposition. A few weeks after the two-million triumph, the laid-back Baxter resigned as editor. He was already feeling office-political pressure from a very different kind of journalist, who had recently been appointed as assistant editor before his thirtieth birthday: Arthur Christiansen.

According to Cecil King, Beaverbrook privately gave Baxter the credit for the *Express*'s success: 'The *Express* was a hard paper, like the *Daily Mail*. And then along came Baxter with all his hypocrisy (chuckle) and it was just what the paper needed.'[39] Christiansen had never tuned pianos in the Canadian Arctic. He had started on the *Wallasey and Wirral Chronicle* as an inky-fingered sixteen-year-old, came to London and eventually got Saturday sub-editing shifts – to this day, one of the best routes towards a staff job in Fleet Street – on the *Sunday Express*. He made his name in 1931, when the R101 airship crashed near Paris just as the final editions of the Sunday papers, and the journalists who produced them, were going to bed. Christiansen's flair and industry gave the *Express* four special editions and something very close to a scoop. From then on, Beaverbrook had him marked for stardom and quickly sent him to Manchester to run the *Daily Express*'s northern edition. He remains perhaps the most famous of all twentieth-century British newspaper editors.[40]

The 1930s was an era of very self-conscious modernization, of clean lines, from streamlined trains and mechanized cafeterias to Art Deco. In America, typographers were somewhere close to the cutting edge of this trend, and in 1929 John E. Allen began campaigning in the print trade paper *Linotype News* for a new approach to headlines, based on the principle that the newspaper reader 'doesn't read, he glimpses'. This was perhaps the crucial (if depressing) realization on the road from the popular newspapers of the nineteenth century to those on the brink of the twenty-first. But Fleet Street was slow to cotton on. The papers, after all, were giving away the works of Dickens, which were not designed for glimpsers. The look of newspapers changed slowly in Britain largely because Northcliffe, who revolutionized everything else, was so attached to columns of grey type.

The papers of 1930 did look different. They were much brighter – more modern, if you like – than those of 1900, partly because the First World War had produced news far too grave to be contained in single-column headlines; partly because of the effect of picture papers like the *Daily Mirror* and the *Daily Sketch*; partly because of American influences; partly because of the general lessening of inhibitions throughout society. But it all happened in a very haphazard way. British newspapers *circa* 1930 looked a mess.

Christiansen was passionately interested in typography in a way that would have bewildered editors of an earlier age, who considered such matters the preserve of the printers. He was editor of the *Daily Express* for almost a quarter of a century, from 1933 to 1957, perhaps the most momentous quarter-century the world has ever known. In his autobiography, he confesses that looking back to major events of the 1930s 'my memory stirs little'. Then he picks up on one headline:

TODAY'S DAILY EXPRESS IS DIFFERENT

The clue is that the headline did not say

TODAY'S DAILY EXPRESS IS DIFFERENT.

'I remember that all right. It was the day that the *Express* reshaped its style *and omitted full stops* from its headlines . . . the Head Printer thought the whole idea outrageous.'[41]

Christiansen changed the *Express* in far less subtle ways, and quickly. To a newspaper design historian, he transformed the paper's use of the Ludlow Century range by using the Century Bold and Bold Extended up to 72 point, insisted on horizontal stress, strength below the fold, headlines in upper and lower case and the use of a 'kicker' story with a four-line ulc sans heading in the middle of the page.[42] These sort of phrases can now be parroted by anyone who has ever attended a journalism training course or bluffed their way through a sub-editing shift. To the reader, they meant bigger headlines and a livelier-looking newspaper. Christiansen bulldozed many of the changes through in August 1933, while Baxter was still nominally in power; within three years he had transformed the whole look of the paper. And no one has ever made a popular broadsheet look better.

But it is unfair to think of Christiansen as just some sort of typographical trainspotter. He confessed to having been an 'indifferent, frightened' reporter but he was a fearsomely hard and hard-nosed editor, who knew what he wanted and exactly how he wanted it, and usually had it rewritten by members of what became an army of sub-editors.

According to critics: 'Information and opinion were served piping hot and pre-digested . . . which might not stimulate the brain but was pleasing to the palate.'[43] 'A slick synthetic product . . . that adjusted the facts to Christiansen's dictum "Make the news exciting, even when it was dull." '[44] Christiansen himself did not really disagree: 'That was the technique . . . Make the unreadable readable, find the news behind the news. Find the news even before it happened . . . Be first, be there!'[45]

And he had a great many other dicta. His 'bulletins' appeared almost daily, a continuing tutorial in modern popular journalism, an art form that Christiansen was himself inventing as he went along. To help the process, he devised two characters: The Man on the Rhyl Promenade and The People in the Back Streets of Derby. Read en masse these bulletins are wearisome, hectoring and often contradictory:

> The Man on the Rhyl Promenade Says: What's this Chateau Yquem and garlic stuff in the *Express* today? My champagne touch is a bottle of Guinness and a plate of winkles.

and

> I wonder what luxury vegetable Fortnums are selling today and what price they are? There is often a lot of news to be got out of shop windows.

and again:

> Are we not in danger of becoming a nagging paper?

His staff may have thought so. But, as A. J. P. Taylor later put it in a different context: 'No one was consistent in the 1930s,'[46] least of all in the *Daily Express*. It was part of its roguish charm.

Express reporters found themselves transformed into big names, given substantial expense accounts (though not necessarily high wages) and massive projection in the paper in return for providing raw material for the great news sausage-machine in the great black building that replaced the old Fleet Street sausage shop. Indeed, they usually had bigger names than when they started, because Beaverbrook did not like any Tom, Jack or Harry writing for his newspaper. Thus Tom Delmer became Sefton Delmer, Jack Gourlay became Logan Gourlay and Harry Pincher became Chapman Pincher. The words that appeared under these by-lines may well have been cobbled together in the office, the style of writing adjusted to please Christiansen, the opinion to please Beaverbrook. For the reporters, it was a Faustian deal. If they failed, they were fired. No one believed in Christiansen's journalistic prowess more than he did himself: 'The staff seemed incapable, whether by accident or design, of producing a good newspaper when I was not there.'[47]

But the biggest Faustian deal was the one which enabled Christiansen to continue this process for so long. If he harried his staff, that was nothing to the process of telephonic torture he had to accept from Beaverbrook: 'No week, no day, no hour conformed to any pattern, except that the telephone constantly rang.'[48] And there was never any doubt who was calling. It might be praise; it might be blame; it might be a leading article; it might be a gossip paragraph; it might be a blatantly nonsensical piece of political judgement. Whatever shape it took, Christiansen had to use his staff and his skill to purvey it to readers of the *Daily Express,* and he did so.

Nineteenth-century editors had fabled power, but still, usually, had to edit with the grain of the paper's declared political allegiance. Modern editors all express their views within constraints imposed by their proprietors' prejudices. Christiansen accepted being politically spayed because the romance of having his own opinions on subjects beyond the presentation of news did not interest him. He said he only quarrelled with Beaverbrook once: in 1944 over the question of whether Sir Oswald Mosley (the Fascist, not the bread campaigner) should be released from detention. Christiansen's objection was solely on the grounds that the *Mail* had lost readers before the war by supporting Mosley.[49] Years later he explained on television: 'The policy was laid down by the proprietor, Lord Beaverbrook, and I was the man who made the policy attractive to the people by presentation.'[50]

But what about when that policy was nuts?

XIV

In the summer of 1939 the following headlines appeared in the *Daily Express*:

1   FINANCIER'S HORSE DRINKS LIQUID SUET
2   SLIMMING MADE GIRL STEAL
3   DRAMA OF HUGE SEAGULL FOUND IN EGG-CUP
4   I'LL BE MAYOR AND STILL SELL FISH AND CHIPS
5   RACE FOR THE SHORE, CRIES BEWILDERED
     BILLIARD-MARKER AS COW BURSTS
6   THEY USED GLAND TONIC 3,000 YEARS AGO
7   ACTRESS SWALLOWS TOWN HALL
8   NO WAR THIS YEAR

The odd-numbered headlines were spoofs, from a Beachcomber column on 1 July; the even-numbered ones are all real. Numbers two, four and six appeared over various news items in early July. Number eight appeared on 7 August, above a canvass of *Daily Express* reporters round Europe on their views of the prospects for the months ahead. Only two departed from the general line; the correspondent in Warsaw said the Poles were so confident of peace that business was picking up.

This was just about the last throw of the dice in a game the *Express* had been playing for more than three years. As Taylor said, no one was consistent in the 1930s. What was consistent was the way in which the paper read by more Britons than any other was prepared to emphasize what it wished to be the truth rather than what it feared. Scholars, generally literal-minded Americans, have pored through the Fleet Street papers of the era with the harsh light of hindsight looking for trends of thought that did not really exist. The newspapers floundered, as did democratic politicians and the people they represented. People who had lived through the most ghastly war in history to so little purpose were understandably reluctant to rush towards another. Was that so shocking?

Rothermere, an instinctive authoritarian, was attracted by Fascism from the start and that conditioned the *Daily Mail*'s responses. For six months in early 1934 the paper formally supported the Blackshirts, and there were many favourable mentions of Hitler. But the *Mail* was run too incompetently to be anyone's reliable ally, under either Rothermere or his son Esmond, who officially took control in 1932. The paper edited by one man, Tom Marlowe, from 1899 to 1926 had fourteen editors in the next forty-five years, and five in the 1930s alone. One incumbent was said to have got the job because he was so good at finding Parisian girls for old Rothermere's delectation. But the *Mail* did not suppress the news of Germany's excesses and it strongly advocated rearmament – indeed, this may have been more damaging in the pacific atmosphere of the mid-1930s than anything else: Rothermere had to deny he was making money from air and armament shares.[51]

The *Express*'s problems were different. As early as 4 May 1931 it had carried an interview with Hitler, and Sefton Delmer claimed to be the first foreign journalist ever to enter the Nazi HQ in Munich. He was shown around by Count du Moulin, Major Roehm's 'charming' young aide-de-camp:

> We peeped into a room where four officers were bent in consultation over a set of maps. 'They are discussing the war,' said Count du Moulin. 'Which war?' I asked. 'The next war,' he grinned! . . .

Delmer was received by Hitler, wearing a blue serge suit, in his large cream and red private office, where he insisted that he did not want a return to

1914 frontiers or Germany's lost colonies, but wanted Germany to be treated as an equal, with a right to expand into the 'empty spaces' on her eastern frontiers. The *Express* did not even carry a leader column commenting on the interview, although eleven days later it did launch an attack on France for its rearmament and chauvinism.

Thus, from this early stage, the *Express* was reading the situation wrongly. Beaverbrook was never attracted by Nazism; the only -ism he wanted to believe in was optimism. The flaw in the *Express*'s coverage of Europe was indifference, shading into self-deception and then, perhaps, to more wilful deception. The black glass offices looking south from 121 Fleet Street stood metaphorically as well as literally on The Sunny Side of the Street.

Leader, 9 March 1936

LET US GET DOWN TO BRASS TACKS

... The Germans have reoccupied the Rhineland ... The question is: Will Britain be involved in war? The answer is NO! There will be no war. And if there were, we should not be involved ...

Leader, 18 March 1936

GO AHEAD!

Get on with your building if you planned it. Extend your activities. Enlarge your commitments. Take on more hands. Why? Because peace will prevail ... Make no mistake about it, the skies are clearing.

By the summer of 1938 the *Daily Express* had acquired a format for broadsheet journalism that has never been surpassed in its technical mastery. Under the words WORLD'S LARGEST DAILY SALE the paper looked fantastic: the headlines demanded attention without screaming; bold type, white space and pictures were all used with total assurance. The material was equally strong, mixing the serious and trivial in an almost perfect blend. On 13 May photographer Stanley Sherman had an exclusive picture of a suspect being manacled having just been captured by police in a haystack. 'Whistle While You Work' was reported to be no. 5 in the radio charts, though nothing like as popular as 'The Lambeth Walk': 'This consists of an exaggerated swagger: tongues may protrude slightly if desired. Peak of the rhythm sends couples three paces back from each other, makes them knock their knees and shout "Oi!"' The *Daily Express* correspondent in Rangoon reported on the birth of quintuplets under the headline:

NEW QUINS' FATHER SAID "AH ME LAY"
(which means 'Hell's Bells')

This was gloriously inventive journalism, even if it was indeed invented.

Unfortunately, the *Express*'s coverage of the only story that mattered was conditioned by an editorial view that was not merely wrong but absurdly so.

23 May 1938
GO ABOUT YOUR BUSINESS
By Lord Beaverbrook
Britain will not be involved with war.
There will be no major war in Europe
this year or next year. The Germans will
not seize Czecho-Slovakia.

That day Tom Driberg picked up on a suggestion in the leader column for a grand show in Hyde Park, using the asterisked points that Christiansen so favoured:

* Water taxis speeding on the Serpentine
* A new Crystal Palace of steel and glass
* Spectacular coloured-fountain dis-
  plays.

'I should like to book a room high up in Park Lane for the summer of 1940,' he added. 'There should be a grand view.' That bit at least the *Express* got right.

On 1 June 1938 Lord Forbes wrote an article assuring readers that the Germans could not afford to try to bomb civilians, because the costs would be out of all proportion to the military results. Only one character in the paper seemed to be reading the situation with an appropriate degree of seriousness: Rupert Bear. When he saw a suspicious plane in his daily cartoon, he reported it at once to Constable Growler.

In September Neville Chamberlain flew to Germany three times to see Hitler. On 17 September an enthusiastic report about the German desire for peace appeared under yet another of those *Express* by-lines that sounded more like addresses than names, this time Selkirk Panton, and the leader column said it again, this time in block capitals:

> For the purpose of reiterating the as-
> surance that is sometimes forgotten
> the *Daily Express* says once more,
> BRITAIN WILL NOT BE INVOLVED
> IN A EUROPEAN WAR THIS YEAR
> OR NEXT YEAR EITHER.

The *Express* was not the only one handing out worthless assurances in September 1938, but it was doing so with an air close to self-parody. The leader
went on:

> We have listened so much to tales of
> strife and confusion in distant lands in
> Central Europe ... We do not wish to
> be disturbed with the threat of it at break-
> fast in the morning. We want to sit down
> to our midday meal in contemplation of
> plenty. And when night comes we desire
> to sleep well and soundly with an
> untroubled heart and without the dream
> of evil.

Those last three sentences, infantile in their petulance and frivolity, contain
the kernel of *Express* thinking, if you can call it that, in the years before
the war. We don't want to be bothered with war, therefore we will not
have it.

Thirteen days later Chamberlain returned from Munich to national rejoicing and a *Daily Express* headline, in the largest type-size ever used in a British
newspaper, saying simply

PEACE!

The American Yellow Press had used its largest type-sizes for war; it was an
advance of a sort.

> *Leader, 30 September 1938*
> Be glad in your hearts, give thanks to
> your God ... People of Britain, your
> children are safe. Your sons will not
> march to battle. A war ... would have
> been the most criminal, most futile, the
> most destructive that ever insulted the
> purposes of the Almighty and the intelli-
> gence of men ...

The next day the headline was:

'YOU MAY SLEEP QUIETLY – IT IS PEACE FOR OUR TIME'

After the weekend, on 3 October, the *Express* reported the takeover of Czecho-slovakia under the headline:

HITLER WILL LEAD MARCH IN TODAY

Next to that was a column headed:

MAKE THIS 'CHEERFUL MONDAY'

It is, however, misleading to say that the *Express* was pro-Nazi, however craven its behaviour. Sometimes Beaverbrook tried to restrain his editors from printing attacks on Ribbentrop, the German ambassador, especially in the *Evening Standard*, always a much more heterodox paper than the *Express*. But when Lloyd George visited Germany in September 1936, and was taken in by Hitler ('a single-minded personality, a resolute will and a dauntless heart'), the *Express* printed his report and gently chided him: 'What a pity that when our distinguished travellers are abroad so many of them see nothing of the suppression that goes on.' The *Express* thought anti-Semitism was wretched and disgraceful; on the other hand, it opposed Britain taking in refugees.

It certainly had the customary Anglo-Saxon prejudices of the time. The reporter Solomon Charing had his name changed to Stephen Charing, against his strenuous objections that he was proud of being Jewish. In private, Beaverbrook would complain that the rest of the press was dominated by Jews who were pushing Britain and Germany into an unnecessary war. 'I estimate that one third of the circulation of the Daily Telegraph is Jewish. The Daily Mirror may be owned by Jews. The Daily Herald is owned by Jews. And the News Chronicle should be the Jews Chronicle.'[52] But this was, I think, the small change of the time, shocking though it sounds now; words like abortion and adultery might be taboo in Blumenfeld's style book, but people had not yet been horrified out of racial insults.

There will be no war this year, the *Express* declared again on 18 July 1939; and on 22 July it said it yet again: 'Experience shows that a battle which is postponed never takes place.' If Beaverbrook was deluding his readers, he certainly deluded himself. On 5 August he sailed for Canada. On 22 August the Nazi–Soviet pact was signed and, on the insistence of his manager, Robertson, he returned to England, grumbling. The next day's *Express* described the situation as 'serious'. Hitler said his patience was almost exhausted, and the *Express* said the same: 'We are sick of these crises. We have had enough. We are not prepared to buy another short respite at the price of surrender.'

And so the war came, as the Abdication had come, and television, and flight, and electrified trains, and everything else the *Express* and Expressmen had said would never happen. Christiansen had evolved the most brilliant technique for telling ordinary people about complex matters in simple terms. But the *Express* had fed them nonsense.

It was a defining moment for British journalism. No paper has ever reached out across the class divide of Britain more than the *Daily Express*; but it could not be trusted. When war was declared, people switched on their radios and got quicker and more accurate information. And another, more potent, form of newspaper was emerging.

PART FOUR

'We're all in the Establishment now'
The *Daily Mirror* Era

Prologue

On a Monday lunchtime in March 1995 about 150 people gathered in the mock-Gothic Lloyd George Room at the National Liberal Club in London. It was not an especially appropriate venue, architecturally or symbolically, but it was a pleasant enough place for a party.

The average age of those present must have been at least sixty-five, probably seventy. If you were looking for someone, people would say: 'He's over there, the grey-haired man.' But they were nearly all grey-haired men. They were, however, uniformly dapper and surprisingly healthy-looking, even though the vast majority supped pints rather than Perrier or even white wine. This was an unexpected tribute both to the life they had led, which Sir Philip Gibbs insisted in *The Street of Adventure* would leave them broken in wind and limb, and to the recovery of the *Daily Mirror* pension scheme, which had been robbed blind when the paper temporarily fell into the hands of a lunatic, Robert Maxwell.

The occasion was a reunion of the people who had been working on the editorial side of the *Daily Mirror* on 9 June 1964. It was not an anniversary or anything, but a couple of the lads, in a very *Mirror*-ish way, thought it would be a good idea to have a celebration. And people were tickled enough by the idea to come along specially, from France, the United States, Spain and, in several cases, Ilford. The significance of 9 June 1964 became clear when facsimiles of the front page were handed out at the door. Stories that might have led the paper on a normal day – FONTEYN'S HUSBAND SHOT IN STREET and SIAMESE TWINS OPERATION DRAMA – were drowned out by the headline

THE MIRROR TOPS 5,000,000

No daily newspaper in Britain had regularly sold that many before; since 1969, when the *Mirror*'s circulation began dropping in the face of competition from Rupert Murdoch's *Sun*, no paper has done it again; it is exceedingly improbable that any paper will ever do it in the future. When the grey-haired men talked about the *Mirror* of the 1950s and 1960s they kept using the same words: 'pride', 'affection', 'enthusiasm', 'the paper had heart'; a librarian said how he used to love coming into work in the morning. Everyone also said the same sort of things about the *Daily Mirror* of 1995 – 'Bloody awful paper now' – though the handful of those present still employed in the organization tended to speak in whispers.

And then everyone quietened, because there was to be one speech. It was made by their undisputed leader, Lord – formerly Hugh – Cudlipp, who had left school in Cardiff at fourteen and risen to be editor of the *Sunday Pictorial* (three times), editorial director of the Daily Mirror Group and chairman of the International Publishing Corporation. Curiously, he had never actually edited the *Daily Mirror*, but he was acknowledged as its presiding genius. At eighty-one, his flair for finding the right words had not left him. The speech was brief, vivid, alternately nostalgic and scathing, a tad indiscreet and perfectly judged.

He said how much fun it had all been. 'Dammit, we had the best writers and cartoonists, all at the top of their form . . . Gathered in this room are the real basic Fleet Street whizz-kids.' He told them how he changed the line on the front page from Biggest Daily Sale to Biggest Daily Sale in the Universe, and Cecil King, then the group chairman, had said: 'How do you know?'

Then he mentioned the people who had run the *Mirror* after he had retired: Clive Thornton, the former building society executive who took over briefly, and went round switching off the lights; Robert Maxwell, at which point he simply crossed himself; and David Montgomery, the current incumbent, responsible for a front page which Cudlipp called 'a multi-coloured kaleidoscopic upchuck'. 'It looks', said Cudlipp, 'as though three passers-by have been eating beetroot and been sick over the front page.' He ended by looking back. 'We were really trying to do *something*.' Then he paused. 'I've forgotten what the bloody hell it was but nobody's trying to do it now.'

The room erupted. Everyone present, possibly even the barmen and waitresses, believed the same: that the *Mirror* of 1964 had been a fantastically successful tabloid newspaper that communicated brilliantly with its readers without being vindictive, intrusive or essentially untruthful, a form of journalism that was destroyed when Rupert Murdoch bought *The Sun* and destabilized the *Mirror*. Is this true? Or is the reality distorted through the haze of nostalgia, like so many of the other images evoked by the *Mirror*'s heyday – cheery Cockneys smiling through the blitz; six penn'orth of chips and you still had change from a tanner; we-wuz-poor-but-we-wuz-happy?

The following day's *Daily Mirror* led with a story about a pop star being found in a 'secret lovenest' and lashing out at the journalists who found them there. The grey-haired men never did spend much time hunting for pop stars' secret lovenests – which is why their paper is remembered with such affection, and why it had to change.

I

All newspaper offices, day to day, are manic places, but the history of the paper is usually a matter of gentle undulations. Papers rise, they fall, they change character, they change direction. But their turns are usually great sweeps, normally discernible only over a period of years. Even the alterations caused when a paper finds a new owner are often invisible to the ordinary reader. The ninety-two-year history of the *Daily Mirror* divides into at least nine separate phases, each of them very different from the others, and usually started not with a gentle shift, but with a sudden lurch.

The *Daily Mirror* was founded on 2 November 1903 by Alfred Harmsworth, shortly to be made Lord Northcliffe, who seven years earlier had made a massive success of the *Daily Mail*, partly because he had designed it with female readers at least partly in mind. The *Mirror* was designed to appeal specifically to women or, at any rate, gentlewomen. The idea of a women's newspaper was not totally novel. In France there had already been a paper aimed at liberated women. And in 1901 an American called Frank J. Warde had told the *Daily Express* that he was thinking of starting a women's paper: the only male connection was to be in the financing because, Warde remarked laughingly, 'though lovely woman is up to running a newspaper she cannot yet keep a secret.' One trusts that, even in 1901, he got his face slapped. Both these projects failed.

The *Mirror*, it was assumed, could not fail; no Harmsworth project had ever failed. Before the launch, the trade paper, *Master Printer and Newspaper Owner*, had questioned whether ladies needed a daily paper and appeared to be about to suggest they did not. Then it reared away from its own logic. 'If the *Daily Mirror* be done well – as it is certain to be – ladies throughout the country will soon think that they need it, whether they do or not, and thinking this, they will want it, and wanting it, they will have it.' The *Mirror*, it said, would be an immediate success.

The new paper provided twenty tabloid-sized pages at a cost of a penny, twice the price of the *Mail*. Harmsworth's inaugural message, a variation on the traditional form, hoped – rather half-heartedly – that the paper would appeal to men as well as women. The *Mirror*, he said, would arrange its material so that 'the transition from the shaping of a flounce to the forthcoming changes in Imperial defence, from the arrangement of flowers on the dinner-table to the disposition of forces in the Far East, shall be made without mental paroxysm or dislocation of interest.'

This rather assumed there was any interest to be dislocated. The *Mirror's* first front page consisted of picture-less adverts for various dressmakers, milliners and furriers. Inside it had lists of DISTINGUISHED INVALIDS (Sir J. Blundell Maple: Improvement maintained. Mrs Cyril Maude: Progressing favourably. Mrs Harry McCalmont: Rather better, but not yet out of danger), FASHIONABLE ANNOUNCEMENTS (Lord and Lady Lucan have returned to Laleham House, Staines), OUR BIRTHDAY LIST (Many happy returns to Lord Cloncurry, Lord Alastair Innes-Ker, Lord William Cecil . . .), WHERE NOTABLE PEOPLE SPENT THE WEEKEND (Princess Louise of Schleswig-Holstein, at Boxmore) and YESTERDAY IN TOWN (Claridge's was exceptionally full).

There were weather reports from Bath, Bournemouth, Harrogate, Biarritz and Cairo, but not Birmingham or Manchester. The crinoline was discussed on page 13. Dishes of the Day were sole à la Savoy, oysters au gratin, rougets à la bordelaise, salade à l'américaine and filets de perdreaux. And there was an extraordinary article entitled OTHER PEOPLE'S UNCOMFORTABLE HOUSES by A Veteran Visitor. This was a prolonged whine by a shameless freeloader which, if intended as parody, was far too subtle. He, or maybe she, complained about forced tipping, barking dogs, and barrack-like bedrooms with no food in them. The author then sweetly added: 'I have taken the opportunity of venting these grumbles in the hope that they will reach the eyes of some of the charming people with whom I shall stay within the next few months.'

The second issue contained the usual Northcliffean apology about overwhelming demand for the paper's first number causing problems with supply. The biggest news was a law report concerning a dispute among corset manufacturers. There had been incessant rain in Bath and Mrs McCalmont was much stronger. But it was perhaps already apparent to Northcliffe that the *Mirror* was very sickly indeed.

Later *Mirror* folklore had it that it was the fault of the stupid women hired to write for the paper, who bickered constantly, needed the three or four men advising them, headed by Kennedy Jones, to keep order, and were too naïve to have acquired the most elementary journalistic defences. Thus the best bits of the early *Daily Mirror* were the ones the men miraculously stopped from getting into the newspaper, like the story about the Drury Lane actor and actress who got married in the afternoon, before 'the usual performance took place in the evening'.[1]

Northcliffe was determined not to appeal to the so-called New Woman, the sort who was anxious to work and vote. Instead he ended up appealing to no women at all. The high-priced women's magazines like *Queen* and *The Lady* had been successful for years. But they had a certain social cachet; no one was going to leave a Harmsworth paper in the drawing room, certainly not where anyone might see A Veteran Visitor's piece. On the other hand, the *Mirror* did not have the same only-just-out-of-reach aspirational appeal that made the *Mail* such a success in the suburbs: lower-middle-class house-wives in 1903 really were not going to cook rougets à la bordelaise.

One historian of the *Mirror* was convinced the disaster was not so much a miscalculation of the market as a result of Northcliffe's well-documented Oedipal obsession: subconsciously, he was starting a paper that would please his mother.[2] What is more palpable is that the *Mirror* was started in an atmosphere of hubris and condescension. SEE THAT YOU SECURE A COPY FOR MADAME, said the advert in the *Mirror*'s brother-paper, the *Mail*, on launch-day, implying that potential readers were incapable of getting their own copies. The nominal editor, Mary Howarth, formerly on the *Mail* staff, was paid just £50 a month, the tiniest fraction of what the senior riders on the *Mail* gravy train were then getting.

II

In January 1904, as the infant *Daily Mirror* gasped for breath, W. T. Stead, one of the great journalistic names of the day, launched the *Daily Paper*, 'for the abnormally scrupulous'. It closed after thirty-two issues.[3] The *Mirror* avoided the same fate, because Northcliffe was not abnormally scrupulous but very fast on his feet. He had made a mistake. He saw the writing on the wall, read it and acted.

Northcliffe had one phenomenal stroke of the luck that attends great generals. Up to now it had proved impossible to get news photographs into daily papers, except by printing at speeds far too slow for the mass market. The *Daily Graphic*, the first picture paper, mostly relied on woodcuts. A Hungarian called Arkas Sapt, formerly editor of Harmsworth's magazine *Home Sweet Home*, came up with the technical solution, making it possible for the *Mirror* to use pictures on one four-page spread.

On 7 January the first, experimental, pictures appeared: of Japanese sailors sighting a gun on a man o' war (this was not, the ladies may have gathered, anything to do with the dispute among corset manufacturers). The Japanese were pointing their guns at the Russians in the Far East; Northcliffe was pointing his at Mary Howarth and her staff. By 21 January the admitted circulation was down to 25,563, and that was copies 'supplied', not necessarily bought. On that day the leader column of the paper that was to become the thunderous voice of working-class radicalism praised the Governor of Mississippi for saying that it was not merely futile to educate the negro, but evil. 'The more "civilised" he becomes, the more rein does he give to his criminal propensities.'

On 26 January the paper was renamed the *Daily Illustrated Mirror*, aimed at both men and women, the price was dropped to the level of the *Mail* and *Express*, a ha' penny, and, in Jones's words, 'Fleet Street's most wonderful changeling uttered its first cry.' Hamilton Fyfe, the former editor of the *Morning Advertiser*, was brought over to sack the staff: 'They begged to be allowed to stay. They left little presents on my desk. They waylaid me tearfully in corridors. It was a horrid experience – like drowning kittens.'[4] The next day the paper was dominated by a fierce full-page picture of the financier Dr Warwick Wright, who had collapsed and died immediately after being convicted of fraud, with the caption *de mortuis nil nisi bonum*, which might have been intended as a wry in-joke about the original *Daily Mirror*. The *Mirror* said Wright had killed himself by smoking a poisoned cigar. Actually, he had done no such thing. But what the heck? This, at last, was real journalism.

There was no further word as to the health of Mrs Harry McCalmont. There was, however, still some unfinished business. The following day the *Mirror* had to announce that its £1,000 prize for suggestions to improve the paper was to be split 200 ways. There was no word of any workable suggestions; the *Mirror* regretted it was not possible to perforate the various features so they could easily be torn out, nor to attach a gummed wrapper so readers could send it to a friend, nor to scent it with a different perfume each day. The real winner should have been Arkas Sapt. Unfortunately, he was notoriously hopeless with money, and he had to sell his invention to the Harmsworths for a few hundred pounds to get out of a jam.

A month later Northcliffe wrote one of the most splendid *mea culpas* in the history of journalism, under the heading

HOW I DROPPED £100,000 ON THE 'MIRROR'.

in which he described the original *Daily Mirror* as 'a flat, rank, and unmitigated failure'. He could afford to be honest; the paper's circulation was now said to be up to 143,000 and rising fast. The word *Illustrated* lasted in the title for only three months, but the paper's new character was to see it successfully through the next two decades. Every day *Mirror* readers would have some new pictorial delight thrust at them. One day it might be the 3rd Company Bengal Sappers and Miners slogging through the Tibetan passes; the next, Tyldesley, having just scored a double century; the next, The Royal Quadrille at the State Ball.

This was very different from the strait-laced presentational approach upon which Harmsworth insisted at the *Mail*. But the *Mirror* quickly turned into a thundering success, first under Fyfe and then under an ex-*Express* and *New York Herald* man called Alexander Kenealy, whose unpretentious flair was exactly right for it. When he died, in 1915, he was described in the paper as The Man Who Saved The Mirror (a phrase unfortunately devalued by being used again in 1991, on the death of Robert Maxwell, who tried to strangle it).

The revamped *Mirror* had the same tireless inventiveness that characterized the *Daily Mail*. A *Mirror* correspondent travelled steerage to America, sharing experiences with the £2 emigrants – perhaps the last time, until Maxwell began cost-cutting, that a *Mirror* correspondent travelled steerage anywhere. Readers were invited to spot the *Daily Mirror* bicycle on the streets of London, with the winner being allowed to claim it; crowds were reported to be so great that the authorities asked the paper to desist. There was a Tram and Omnibus Ticket Competition, with £3,000 in prizes for certain numbers; this was designed to keep the streets clear of litter. In 1906 the *Mirror* put forward the idea of the Boy Army, a militaristic precursor of the Boy Scouts, sending ten teenagers on a training course. This was presumably a response to the invasion scare, which the *Mail* was so enthusiastically promoting that year.

There were the *Daily Mirror* Bees, who lived on the office roof and proved it was possible to get honey even in central London. There was the Performers' Matinee, when the *Mirror* invited buskers to appear in a competition at the Apollo Theatre; the winner, a boy violinist, got a contract on one of the music-hall circuits. There was always something for the kids – buried treasure hunts, sandcastle competitions, poster-colouring competitions (a £10 prize and 1,000 consolation packets of Home and Colonial jelly) – and even something for the unemployed, who were invited to sweep the streets for 3s 6d.

But most of the *Mirror*'s enterprise went into its photography, where it had little competition. This came under what was called the art department, run by Hannen Swaffer with the assistance of a young man called Harry Guy Bartholomew. While the *Mail* still concentrated on words, the cartoons of W. K. Haselden gradually evolved into witty strips in something approaching the modern style. The *Mirror*'s men took enormous risks, as young photographers still do, for the thrill of it all and, in their case, £3 10s a week. They photographed the interior of Vesuvius, climbed Mont Blanc and crossed the Alps in a balloon. It was all fresh, new and different.

One of the *Mirror* staples was the beauty contest. In 1908 the Royal Academy exhibited a painting by Mr Arthur Hacker of that year's winner, Miss Ivy Lilian Close. She was clutching an apple. 'Who is she? What is she? What a lovely creature! Charming! Irresistible, by jove!' These were some of the comments at the Academy, according to the *Mirror*. Modern readers might think her nose was a bit big. Miss Close recommended walking as a beauty aid – rather than the more fashionable cycling – and washing in rainwater. Readers who wished to know more about 'some very interesting incidents in the life of Miss Close' were invited to buy the *Mirror*'s Special Beauty Number, price one penny. I think we can assume that the incidents were not as interesting as all that. Nonetheless, from these modest and well-clothed beginnings, British newspapers began their love affair with the female body. By jove, they did.

The formula gave the *Mirror* the kind of reader Northcliffe was desperately seeking in the first place, and in 1908 Edward Hulton founded the *Daily Sketch* to try to muscle in on the market. The *Mirror* was perfectly respectable. On 16 May 1910 the front page was given over to an exclusive picture of Edward VII's dead body. From this distance, it looks like a pioneering example of the intrusive sneak-photography of the Royals which the paper would adopt so enthusiastically several reigns later. This impression is backed up by the slushy text:

> This last aspect of the earthly tabernacle and soul of the great King, bound to all British hearts by so many ties of duty and affection, will be cherished as a sacred relic in many British homes . . . There is no line in that regal face which has not been made or deepened by care for the destinies of his great people . . .

But cynicism seems to be misplaced. The picture was taken by the court photographer and, apparently, the widowed Queen Alexandra wanted it to be printed only in the *Mirror* 'because', she said, 'that's my favourite.'

It was a lot of other people's favourite too. In 1908 it was claiming a sale close to half a million; in less than six years that was doubled. The philosophy was to show action pictures wherever possible – the horses flashing past the post rather than the winner in repose afterwards. On 21 May 1913 it published what is justly remembered as one of its most famous editions, a special memorial number for Captain Scott, whose body had recently been discovered in the Antarctic. The main shot showed the cairn covering the bodies of Scott and his companions, with Scott's skis planted upright in a pile of frozen snow. Above was a strangely English mackerel sky. There is no action, but it is heartbreakingly moving. Then the *Mirror* skipped lightly back to its normal concerns. The next month, for its 3,001st edition, the paper had seven page 1 pictures of the death of Emily Davison, killed by the King's horse at Epsom. The *Mirror* headline read:

HOW A SUFFRAGETTE TRIED TO SPOIL THE DERBY.

In complete contrast to the angst-ridden *Mail*, the *Mirror* really did seem to believe that life was one long Edwardian summer. On 28 July 1914 it promised its readers a MONSTER BANK HOLIDAY NUMBER ON MONDAY. It was the following day before it gave them even the smallest inkling of what kind of monster might really be confronting everyone after the Bank Holiday.

Three weeks earlier it had run the headline

'DAILY MIRROR' HAS WORLD'S LARGEST CIRCULATION.

though it watered that down in the text to the claim that it was the largest in the English language. It was certainly the largest in Britain: the *Mirror* had probably overtaken the *Mail* in the summer of 1913 somewhere in the 800,000s.

But this is a curious business, for three reasons. The illustrated *Mirror* was racing at full speed down what turned out to be a dead end in the history of British newspapers and its reign as no. 1 seller, at this stage, turned out to be very short-lived. Secondly, its emphasis on pictures also meant that it exercised very much less influence on the political process than any other best-selling paper in the past two centuries. Historians are fond of claiming that popular newspapers are not influential, because members of the elite might not take their views as seriously as they would some thunderous leader in *The Times*; this entirely ignores the much more complex influence they exercise on mass opinion. Readers might discount the battering-ram opinions thrust at them by Northcliffe's *Mail*, Beaverbrook's *Express*, the *Mirror* of the 1950s and 1960s, or Murdoch's *Sun*, but over a period of time they could not avoid being affected by them, or by the drip-drip-drip of biased news selection. The *Mirror* had a minimum of news; and its opinions were played in such a low key that the readers could happily skip past them, and probably did.

The final curiosity is that this is a peculiar case of a proprietor being infuriated by the success of his own newspaper. Northcliffe's official biographers said 'he looked on the Mirror as the bastard of his journalistic family.'[5] Which is splendidly ironic since they suppressed the fact that, as a man with four illegitimate children, he was something of an expert on this subject.

By now, Northcliffe was heavily engaged with *The Times* as well as the *Mail*, and he was taking life more seriously than the *Daily Mirror* was. In early 1914 he had sold his *Mirror* shares to his brother Rothermere for precisely the £100,000 he had lost on the paper in its first few months, and had nothing more to do with it. This, as Northcliffe well knew, was precisely the right way to get rid of a troublesome brat, since Rothermere was bound to ruin it. It took a little while, since the war created a huge demand for pictures, and the jolly *Mirror* was bound to be more popular in the trenches than the sergeant-majorish *Daily Mail*. Indeed, in 1915, when Rothermere heard that Hulton was planning a Sunday picture paper, he brought out the *Sunday Pictorial* in eight days: it became an instant success and lives on, as the *Sunday Mirror*.

III

It is not absolutely clear when the *Mirror's* decline set in, but by 1920 its claims were rather more modest:

CERTIFIED CIRCULATION LARGER THAN THAT OF ANY
OTHER DAILY PICTURE PAPER.

This was, as Hugh Cudlipp later put it, 'a toot on a tin whistle'. It meant it was selling more than the *Daily Sketch* and the *Daily Graphic*. By now, Rothermere's obsession with the need to save money had gone beyond a tyrannical oversight of the office expenses: it dominated the headlines of the *Daily Mirror*. This was not entirely against the national grain: the Anti-Waste League, backed by Rothermere, scored some short-term success at by-elections as a vehicle for protest against Lloyd George's coalition; but Rothermere hammered the message home 'with the same unctuousness and lack of verve as characterise a Sunday evening sermon on the virtues of thrift'.[6]

WASTE SPELLS MISERY.

SAVE OR FACE BANKRUPTCY – OFFICIAL WARNING.

SQUANDERMANIA GIVEN NOTICE TO STOP BY DOVER.

CALL FOR CABINET TO STOP THE SPENDING!

The men who had happily read the *Mirror* when they faced the perils of shot and shell may have had rather different views of what the real waste had been.

The *Mirror* of the 1920s was not without its saving graces. There were Pip, Squeak and Wilfred, 'A Happy Family of Pets Whose Comic Adventures Are Famous Throughout The World'. This was a cartoon which had started with Pip the dog and Squeak the penguin just after the war, and leapt to enormous heights of popularity when they were joined by Wilfred, an inarticulate rabbit whose vocabulary mainly consisted of the phrases 'Gug, gug' and 'Nunc,

nunc'. The Wilfredian League of Gugnuncs had meetings at the Albert Hall
and chanted the Gugnuncs' own Chortle:

> Gug, gug! Nunc, nunc!
> To friends of all degree.
> Give gugly hugs to nuncly gugs
> Of the W.L.O.G.

Even in the emergency sheets produced during the General Strike
(STAND FAST! NO SURRENDER! Rothermere told the Government) the
Mirror's Uncle Dick had to promise the children that Wilfred would soon
be himself again. He is still remembered affectionately, and Wilfred's impact
on some readers seems to have lasted into adult life. In 1928 A. J. P. Taylor
wrote to a friend after an early romantic adventure: 'The Sussex expedition
was attended with all success . . . We both went gug-gug and I dare say
that if she hadn't been feeling a little unwell we should both have gone
nunc-nunc.'[7]

In the 1920s Rothermere, like Wilfred, at least maintained a certain consistency of tone, but in the early 1930s the proprietor found causes that went
beyond Squandermania. On 30 June 1930 he advised readers: 'The need is
for leadership. Lord Beaverbrook has shown the way' which might have
begged the question why on earth they should not switch to Beaverbrook's
own newspaper. Rothermere's reluctance to spend money meant that the
Mirror, like the *Mail*, was slow to keep up with the *Daily Express* and *Daily
Herald* in the free-gift circulation war. And, quite simply, the novelty of a
picture paper had worn off. By now the cinema newsreels could bring people
moving pictures of news events; and the broadsheet papers could get photographs into print every bit as well, and indeed better, since their pages gave
more scope for display.

In many homes it had become the custom to take a picture paper and
another one; but when times were hard the picture paper was the obvious
candidate to go, to save sixpence a week. In any case, the pictures were now
twee rather than dramatic. The *Mirror's* editor from 1931 to 1934 was a
gentle ex-Gloucestershire cricketer called Leigh Brownlee, who was alleged
to be quite useful for getting cricket exclusives but not for much else. There
was speculation that the *Mirror* might close. On 30 June 1932 *World's Press
News* advised all the picture papers to abandon their 'tabloid' (the word was
used, but in quote marks) format and turn themselves into full-size picture
papers. In September 1932 the *Mirror* began experimenting in some provincial editions by going in a different direction – keeping the size but putting
news on the front page.

The good news was that in 1931 Rothermere formally ceased to have control. This could have been the prelude to closure. Indeed, since he was stealthily selling off his shareholding, suspicious minds might have assumed this was about to happen. But he still had sufficient influence in 1934 to get the following reprinted from the *Sunday Pictorial* in the *Mirror*:

GIVE THE BLACKSHIRTS A HELPING HAND
by Lord Rothermere

The British Blackshirt Movement, he said, was suffering 'hysterical abuse and misrepresentation' from 'timid alarmists' and 'panic-mongers':

> ... Very few of these panic-mongers have any personal knowledge of the countries which are already under Blackshirt government ... If they had visited Italy and Germany, as I have done, travelling around and observing the national life in all its aspects, they would find that the mood of the vast majority of the inhabitants was not cowed submission, but confident enthusiasm.

The Blackshirts, said Rothermere, used violence only in self-defence and were not anti-Semites – the Jews did not dominate certain professions in Britain the way they did in Germany.

> ... The British Blackshirts call upon British youth to work for national reconstruction like that which has transformed and revitalised Italy and Germany ...

This was not typical. The *Mirror* actually reported events in Germany with an appalled Believe It or Not tone:

> The queerest General election in history ... To make certain that all Reichstag seats were held by the Nazis, they were the only candidates on the paper! And all votes not wholeheartedly in Nazi favour were declared in advance 'invalid'!

But it was an excellent example of the clash of journalistic ideologies that was about to transform the *Mirror*. By 1934 Harry Guy Bartholomew, last heard of as the assistant art editor in the early days of the paper, had worked his way through the ranks to be appointed editorial director. While John

Cowley, Rothermere's hand-picked chairman, looked on in something close to stupefaction, Bartholomew led the *Daily Mirror* on one of the greatest of all British journalistic adventures.

IV

In the days of the great transatlantic liners, hordes of reporters in fedora hats would rush on board as soon as the ships docked in New York to fire questions at well-known people who were about to hit town. Once, on what might have been a thin day, they discovered a benign old bishop. 'Will you be visiting any night clubs when you are in New York?' The bishop was a little bemused. '*Are* there any night clubs in New York?' Hence the headline: BISHOP WANTS TO KNOW ABOUT NIGHT CLUBS.

So the story goes; and in the New York of the late 1920s anything was possible. From 1925 to 1929 there took place a confrontation not listed in many history books, though it was as bloodcurdling as any of them: 'the war of the tabs' in which three New York tabloid newspapers, the *Daily News*, the *Daily Mirror*, the *Daily Graphic* (otherwise known as the *Daily Pornographic*) fought each other murder for murder, sensation for sensation and, very often, lie for lie. The *Daily Graphic* even had a machine called the composograph, which was a primitive device for faking pictures.

This represents an interesting example of what might be called double cross-fertilization. The New York *Daily News* began, in 1919, as a copy of the *Daily Mirror*; Joseph Patterson, one of its founders, had met Northcliffe when they were both touring the trenches. Within five years it had the biggest circulation in America. Hearst, whose Yellow Press had mellowed with the years, was obliged to start his own *Daily Mirror* to compete, and the *Pornographic* joined in. Amid a million flashes of magnesium sulphate and shouts of hold-the-front-page by green-eyeshaded editors, New York journalism ran amok.

In 1935 the young Hugh Cudlipp, then working on the *Sunday Chronicle*, went for a job interview with the London *Mirror*'s features editor Basil Nicholson. The conversation edged round to the point that the *Mirror* was not the most – how could a young supplicant put it? – well, *exciting* paper in the business. At this point, Nicholson picked up a copy of the New York *Daily News* from his desk and showed it to Cudlipp. There were, he said, going to be some changes at the *Mirror*.

Thus the *Mirror*, having inspired the *News* in the first place, was now in turn reinspired. The *Mirror* sent emissaries to the *News* (a little calmer at this stage than it was in the twenties) to see what could be learned. At the same time they brought in the giant J. Walter Thompson advertising agency, which talked them out of any thought of going broadsheet, arguing that tabloid papers were perfectly designed for the longer commuting distances that were becoming increasingly common: by accident, the *Mirror* was the right paper at the right time. Thompson's support was as important as their guidance, because it meant that the *Mirror* could depend on the backing of advertisers as it took what might otherwise have been a very risky plunge. And so the *Mirror* turned itself into the nearest thing Britain had yet seen to an American-style tabloid. In Britain there was no tabloid war, because no one else was daring enough to do the same.

The ad agency also provided two of the half-dozen people who were to be crucial in the changeover. One was Nicholson, a brilliant but erratic man who moved over to become the *Mirror*'s features editor before the errors outweighed the brilliance and he was displaced by Cudlipp, the young man he hired. The other was Bill Connor, who had previously been expending his talents as the copywriter on the Harpic account. He became the most famous columnist in British journalism, under the name Cassandra.

This, then, was the starting point for Bartholomew's revolution. He was not a man with what you might call a sophisticated world view. His successor, Cecil King, said he was illiterate and drunk – an inaccurate description, Cudlipp now insists: 'he was semi-literate and half-pissed.'[8] He also had a sort of genius – he invented his own system for transmitting pictures – and, in the words of Sir Edward Pickering, a *Mirror* sub-editor at the time, 'an extraordinary flair for conveying his enthusiasm.'[9]

The change took several years. Bartholomew officially took over on 29 November 1933 and immediately stuck on page 1 a picture of a man being lynched in California. But there was still a column from *The Rambler* about Norma Johnston, the famous bell-ringer, 'who delighted her audience with her 49 silver-toned bells'. The British equivalents of the men in green eye-shades could not immediately cast Norma and her ilk into the dustbin of history. Indeed, for a time there were two *Mirrors*: the old team would produce the early editions, then a group of younger sub-editors, under the command of R. W. Suffern, would move in and turn the paper upside down. By November 1934 the news appeared under thick black sans-serif headlines and some of the stories were made to match. When George V died early in 1936 a big, bold headline

DEATH OF THE KING

took up half the front page. It might have been the modern *Mirror* announcing the latest sexual exploit of the star of a television soap opera. But it was perhaps not until the Abdication crisis later that year that the *Mirror* consistently began to give stories full-blast tabloid treatment.

The paper was clearly entering a new era. Dorothy Dix's advice column was syndicated from America and cast aside Victorian morality by giving readers robust daily common sense:

Dear Dorothy Dix,
   I have been married a little more than four years to a woman I love better than anyone else in the world ... But a few days ago she told me that there had been another man in her life before we were married. The other man had fooled her under promise of marriage. She has offered me my freedom if I want it. I feel like taking revenge on the man who wronged her. What shall I do?

Answer: Forget it. Her mistake has been in telling you.[10]

To the American formula, the *Mirror* added a dose of British sentimental-ism. Cudlipp hired as his star feature writer Godfrey Winn, who wrote a column called My Personality Parade in saccharine, even nancy-ish prose. Winn, like James Douglas of the *Daily Express* and Beverley Nichols, was a 'sob-brother'. They had to have dogs or cats, these writers. When Douglas's dog Bunch died, he wrote that he wished he were a child or woman, so he could howl. Winn had no such inhibitions. The major personality in his column, if it was not Winn himself, was often his dog Mr Sponge:

Winn's Day: 4.15 p.m. Tea with Mr. Sponge: It is his lucky day. His master at home, and now he gets a whole plate of bread and butter. For some reason he will not touch white bread, but a piece of brown, butter or no butter, melts in his mouth. Has your dog any funny food tricks too?

'Bunch did well to die,' snarled Malcolm Muggeridge. 'His day was done.'[11] Hundreds of readers wrote in every week in response to Winn's columns. It is not always possible to explain everything in a history of this kind; some things are incomprehensible.[12]

But, slowly, the *Mirror* was pushing the frontiers of British journalism outwards. There was no single proprietor any more to approve or disapprove; and it was being done in the hope that the chairman John Cowley would not really notice. 'It was a gamble, a glorious gamble,' wrote Cudlipp, 'con-ducted in the edgy atmosphere of an unlicensed gaming club expecting a police raid.'[13] All the papers that rose to dominance had a period when they were prepared to rattle the bars of convention; the *Mirror* shook them with tremendous vigour in the late thirties.

Cudlipp himself started the 'Live Letter Box' column, which as 'Live Letters' was to last into the 1990s. The Old Codgers, and their equally fictional staff, George and Lottie, acquired an existence of their own, as real as characters in a radio soap. It was an Answers to Correspondents column – Why are prison vans called Black Marias? How many people does the Royal Albert Hall hold? – with a little extra something. The tone was helpful and warm, but just occasionally, amid the staccato paragraphs that were becoming the *Mirror*'s norm, there might be a cuff round the ear:

> Lonely, of March, Cambs, writes:
>   I'm 23; I save £3 a week, don't smoke or drink.
>   Yet I can't get a girl for love nor money.
>   If I'm not a fairy prince, what am I?
>
> *Answer*: Pretty thundering dull, we should think.

Mirror readers were beginning to see more of women's bodies than they were used to, at least over breakfast. Once Cudlipp put a flash of breast in a springtime picture in the *Sunday Pictorial*. But for young men in the 1930s women's nipples remained largely a rumour. The paper did, however, reveal that women had legs and at least some kind of flesh under their brassieres. More and more often, young women were pictured in flimsy clothes on flimsy pretexts: actress Ann Leslie, flashing her legs up to a foot above the knee, at the Imperial Fruit Exhibition; dainty Tamara Desni, who was about to marry someone called Bruce Seton, which did not wholly explain why her back should be bare on the front page of a newspaper; Miss Irene Burden, London dancer, who displayed her legs and a substantial proportion of her right bosom on page 5, having been awarded £40 damages for injuries received in a taxi-cab accident.

In that case the judge said: 'I am thirsting for more information about cabaret artists. Do they come out after the performance and dance with the customers?' The willingness of judges to say daft things for the benefit of newspaper reporters remains one of the constants of journalism.

V

But still the paper had no certainty of touch. On 29 February 1936 it obtained an interview with the man of the moment. Unfortunately, it believed what he said:

HITLER'S 'LET'S BE FRIENDS' PLEA TO THE WORLD

He denied that violence had taken him to power and said that 90 per cent of the German nation would follow him implicitly, which gave him confidence to ask for peace. 'It is very strange to see in England and in France, people who still think German aggression possible,' said this unfortunately misunderstood figure. The *Mirror*, basking in its scoop, seemed to forget how he had obtained the support of 90 per cent of the country, and its leader column gushed about 'a glow of spring sunshine upon the wintry scene of European confusion'. A week later Hitler marched into the Rhineland. The *Mirror* did not make that particular mistake again; one layer of its ambivalence had been shaken off for ever.

Boldness of display was one side of the equation. But the words acquired a growing confidence in the years before the war. In the conventional sense, the *Mirror* was aiming down-market of the *Express*; but it was, in many respects, a more serious paper. In the fuggy atmosphere of a bare-floored pre-war pub, the *Mirror* was the intelligent chap leaning on the corner of the bar: not lah-di-dah or anything – he liked a laugh, and he definitely had an eye for the girls – but talking a lot of common sense. (In time, he would develop into a real old bore, but that was a long way off.) This was certainly the way the *Mirror* saw itself.

The role was played primarily by the ex-Harpic man Bill Connor, whose Cassandra column developed into the virtuoso solo of the *Mirror*'s great years. For a short while, he toyed with the archness and surrealism of the *Express*'s Beachcomber ('A HEALTH HINT: When soaked to the skin best to change your clothes') before slowly acquiring the tone of indignant crispness that was to last him through three decades. He died in 1967, aged only fifty-seven.

On 30 September 1938, when the war scare faded away, Chamberlain came back from Munich and the *Mirror* ran the headline IT IS PEACE, Cassandra wrote the following:

> Some arrant ass has written to us com-
> plaining that our placard FLEET
> MOBILISES is one that will induce a
> state of panic in the minds of the popu-
> lation.
>
> The time has come for a little straight
> talking.
>
> What else can you say when the
> British fleet mobilises?
> JOLLY JACK TARS GO A-SAILING?

The chap in the pub was a sort of double act, because alongside Cassandra there was the leader column, signed obscurely W.M. and really written by Richard Jennings, who shuffled round the *Mirror* offices in carpet slippers and wrote blisteringly. The leader column he wrote in that same September day's paper remains a masterpiece of the hardest trick in popular journalism: telling the readers an unpalatable truth – unpopular at the time though wholly justified by events – in palatable form, i.e. without veering too far from tickling towards teaching. It was infinitely harder to sell the idea of war to the British public in 1938, with the horrors of the trenches barely a generation behind them, than it had been for Northcliffe to push the same thought to a readership that could still imagine it might be a bit of an adventure. It required a sort of genius. In W.M. it found one.

> Today we do not ask you to plunge back into gloom, but we ask you to agree that the mood ought to be one of confidence with caution. Therefore (again) the mood of resolute preparedness.
>
> Do not relax your defence efforts. Redouble them. Go on hard. It must still be full steam ahead. Bear in mind that we have gained this respite, not because we plaintively argued, reasoned, and explained how right we are, or even how we long for peace. We gained this reprieve because we stood firm.
>
> A great pity that it had to be sought that way – this peace which is our passionate desire and our real aim. But the world isn't a nice place; ruled by kind men and old ladies who wouldn't hurt a fly.
>
> Large parts of it are ruled by men who have proved that they stop at nothing to gain their ends. At nothing but the certainty that if they strike, they will be struck.

It is impossible not to admire a newspaper that could print an editorial like that, when the *Express* was engaged in kidding itself and its readers that Chamberlain really had brought them peace.

The following day the *Mirror* printed the full terms of the Munich settlement with the following taster:

> All who May Enjoy THIS PEACE,
> Must, in Honour Bound, Read and
> UNDERSTAND THE TERMS. They
> are set out in full on page 13.

It is hard to know what effect this had on circulation. But newspapers thrive on self-belief. W.M. began to be billed as The Man Who Made All England SIT UP. The robustness of the *Mirror*'s politics gave credibility to the rest of the paper, in the eyes of the *Mirror*'s own journalists and the rest of the profession, and, ultimately – we have to assume – among the readership as well.

The *Mirror* was not wholly consistent. In September 1938 one columnist, David Walker, was still telling readers that Hitler had worked miracles by dragging the Fatherland back to its feet. But this sort of stuff was becoming rare. By 16 March 1939, when Hitler marched into Prague, the *Mirror* knew precisely what it wished to say. W.M. hit back at the 'Hail-Hitlerite press', who had accused the *Mirror* of pessimism after Munich, and at the Prime Minister, who had talked about not being deflected from his course.

> To millions of humble folk, not in this
> country only, but in America and wher-
> ever the semblance of freedom still
> exists, it will seem that it is Hitler's
> course that has to be deflected.

Just consider that phrase: 'millions of humble folk'. The *Mirror* was beginning to believe it was not only addressing millions of humble folk but even, in a roundabout way, representing them.

Cassandra put it another way under the headline

SOME DAY SOMEONE WILL HAVE TO STOP HITLER: IT MAY BE US

Next month, when Hitler made a radio speech to the Germans, the *Mirror* did not have a corps of correspondents round Europe the way the *Express* did. But it published a picture of a deserted Berlin street, making the point that everyone had been forced to listen. Another day, the paper neatly doubled up its two favourite themes by running a picture of young German girls: 'Healthy young bodies – BUT DISEASED MINDS.'

When the war started, the *Mirror* did not have to do any unpleasant contortions. It had given its readers fair warning. Three days after Chamberlain's famous broadcast, 'Ordinary Bloke' of Ramsgate had a letter published in 'Live Letter Box':

This time it's an ordinary bloke's war . . . And the ordinary bloke's feeling like a man who wants to swat a buzzing blowfly.

There's a pub I know in the country where you can draw your own beer from the cask – grand beer it is, too.

I don't want any Nazi jackboots clumping about its flagged floors.

There's a chop-house in London with high-backed seats and a mouth-watering smell, where the sound of sizzling steaks is music. I don't want that sizzling drowned by blaring bands and the yells of nose-led thugs.

There's a moor in Yorkshire where the cloud shadows dapple the hillside, and the wind is the only sound.

I don't want it defiled by the whip-cracks and screams of the concentration camps.

There's a football team which was going to do great things in the Second League this season.

I don't want to see that football ground strutted over by the parading hordes of oppression.

I didn't really appreciate these things till the past week but I'll soon be off to deal with that blowfly now, and when I've helped to stop his buzzing, I, and a million other ordinary blokes, are going to take care we aren't interrupted again.

It is a pretty safe bet that if 'Ordinary Bloke' did come from Ramsgate, he commuted in to the *Daily Mirror* office every day. Buzzing blowflies and dappled hillsides indeed! But that's what journalists are for, to sum up ordinary blokes' feelings in a way they cannot quite articulate themselves. And that must have done the job pretty well. A few days later the *Mirror* ran a picture of a pair of legs with a hint of bosom attached up a ship's rigging. There was no name, or even a feeble excuse.

A NICE MATE, SAILORS!
We're giving this picture for the sailors
of the Navy. A trim craft, eh? And tell
us, does she know the ropes?

And so the *Mirror* went to war.

VI

But Hitler was just one story. The *Mirror* was full of stories:

HAD £1 A WEEK, RAISED A FAMILY

DANCE GIRL TALKED OF BLACKMAIL – GASSED

ONE-EYED CRIPPLE DUPED WOMEN WITH
THE SAME £2 RING

WHISKY CLOUDY SAYS DEATH FLAT GUEST

WROTE DIARY OF 'A WASTER'; DIED WITH SECRET

The headlines were all genuine. The *Mirror* had no Beachcomber to go in for self-parody. Cudlipp claimed to have written this one:

REVELLER VANISHES FOR DAYS –
COMES BACK AS POP-EYED DRAGON
SHOUTING 'WHOOPEE'! WHAT A NIGHT![14]

You couldn't really parody a headline like that. More often the style was obtuse, in the American manner. The simple, demotic, English tabloid headline was developing only slowly. But tabloid reporting was evolving its style and conventions, which would eventually settle into laws so ironclad that they would supersede all sense and decency. At that stage the *Mirror*'s expectations could come as a shock to youngsters reared on local newspapers, which were still printing columns of facts and listing the mourners at funerals. Donald Zec, who joined the paper in 1938, was immediately sent out to cover a fire in Soho:

That's precisely what I did. I came back and said there was a fire in Soho. I remember the look of utter contempt, and then pity, on the face of the news editor. And he said 'That's not the way we do this.' So another reporter took over the story, and I remember it almost verbatim:

Clad only in her scanties, blonde 17-year-old Sandy something or other climbed along a thirty-foot parapet to rescue her pet cat Timothy, in a fire in Soho last night . . .

And in that brief moment I understood what tabloid journalism was all about. And in particular what the *Daily Mirror* was all about, which was sex, sensation, pets, heroism.[15]

Harry Procter, a more jaundiced observer, put it another way: 'The *Mirror* wanted sex,' he wrote. 'It was not hypocritical about its needs – it was perfectly honest to its employees, its readers and its advertisers.' Procter, as a young reporter, was sent to do a story about a woman who had written to the *Mirror* saying that when she got married, she and a boy born at the same time had accidentally been put in the Forthcoming Marriages rather than the Births column. Procter claims he wrote 'a good, bright story, giving the facts, blowing on them a little perhaps – as one does with cinders to make them glow'.

'What the hell is this?' the night news editor bellowed in to the telephone. He expected to be told the couple now really were going to be married. 'But they're not getting married, sir. They barely know each other and they've got a boy and girlfriend of their own.'
'What the hell do you think I sent YOU down for? You bloody well talk them in to it. Give them a fiver apiece if you like, but they damn well'll have to get married. And for Gawd's sake, hurry, you've already missed the first edition.'[16]

The *Mirror*'s approach completely startled its rivals. Lord Hartwell, working as a gossip writer on the *Daily Sketch*, recalled being shocked when the *Mirror* came out with a story – perfectly true – that Queen Mary had been wearing peep-toe shoes. But the *Sketch* was ever a shockable paper. One of Hugh Cudlipp's favourite stories concerns the prize bull that had what, in his case, were his very public parts airbrushed out of a picture at the insistence of Lady Kemsley, the proprietor's wife. The farmer, furious at this unauthorized castration, sued for damages to the bull's stud potential.

VII

The *Daily Mirror*'s war is largely remembered for one cartoon: Philip Zec's drawing in March 1942 of a man on a raft with the caption THE PRICE OF PETROL HAS BEEN INCREASED BY ONE PENNY – OFFICIAL. The words of the caption were said to be Bill Connor's.

Churchill and his Labour Home Secretary Herbert Morrison were convinced the *Mirror* was saying that profiteers were making money at the expense of the lives of British seamen. The *Mirror* maintained – and Philip Zec's brother Donald maintains to this day – that Zec was merely trying to drive home to the public the vital need to save fuel because importing it cost lives.

It might have been accepted as a legitimate difference of opinion, except that the *Mirror* had been getting under the Government's skin for a long time. Churchill suggested to Morrison that he should close the newspaper, as he was entitled to do under wartime regulations; Morrison, supported by Beaverbrook, argued that the *Mirror* should be given a final warning. Morrison gave the warning to Bartholomew and the editor, Cecil Thomas, in his office. He then gave the *Mirror* full blast in the House of Commons.

> The cartoon in question is only one example, but a particularly evil example, of the policy and methods of a newspaper which, intent on exploiting an appetite for sensation and with a reckless indifference to the national interest and to the prejudicial effect on the war effort, has repeatedly published scurrilous misrepresentations, distorted and exaggerated statements, and irresponsible generalisations. In the same issue the leading article stated: 'All who aspire to mislead others in war should be brass-buttoned boneheads, socially prejudiced, arrogant and fussy.' . . . Reasonable criticism on specific points and persons is one thing; general, violent denunciation, manifestly tending to undermine the Army and depress the whole population, is quite another. Such insidious attacks are not to be excused by calls in other parts of the paper for more vigorous action.

There were all kinds of ironies here: Churchill and Morrison were both old allies of the *Mirror*, and Morrison had been a pacifist in the previous war. The affair was generally held to be a draw: the Government backed away from closure and the *Mirror* eased up on its criticisms, a process helped by Bill Connor's departure to the army. But the wounds stayed raw for a long time, and Churchill hated the paper ever after. From the *Mirror*'s point of view, it was one thing to be called scurrilous, distorted, exaggerated and irresponsible; the paper invited, expected and even welcomed that sort of attack. It was altogether harder when Morrison said the paper was depressing people;[17] for the paper's system of self-belief depended on the fact that it was doing the exact reverse. Here was a nation of Ordinary Blokes battling through against a buzzing blowfly for the sake of dappled hillsides and sizzling steaks, and the brass-buttoned boneheads did get in the way. The *Mirror* fundamentally believed that it was vital to British morale.

The *Mirror*'s war was a specialized version that turned into Britain's guiding folk myth: that of the brave, good-humoured people buckling down to fight Hitler. The *Mirror* was not yet the biggest-selling paper in the country. Paper rationing meant that circulation was pegged to pre-war levels; anyway, there was such hunger for news that all the papers sold out rapidly. But it was becoming enormously popular. Its pagination was cut, as rationing bit, first to twelve pages and then to eight. The infant art of tabloid display was altered to cram everything in. No more would reporters be forced to bribe near-strangers to marry each other to get an inside-page lead. The truth was dramatic enough.

And the *Mirror* had to leave enough room for the cartoon strips: the rabbit Wilfred was still gurgling. And there was Jane, the character who added a new literal meaning to the phrase cartoon strip. Jane dated back to the

Mirror's more genteel days, when she had originally been a busy but discreet girl about town, who would worry, as at Christmas 1934, that her maid was away and there was a pile of washing-up to do. Before the war had started, Jane had become as uninhibited as the paper. Then she went into uniform; or, more regularly, out of it. Now she would be worried that her clothes had unaccountably disappeared while she was taking a cooling dip, and a busload of officers had suddenly turned up. Only in wartime, perhaps, could the millimetre of pen-and-ink nipple or slightly larger frilly knicker that Jane displayed have been regarded as erotic. But it became a cult of extraordinary power, with her picture being emblazoned on tanks and aircraft. 'Worth two armoured divisions to us,' it was said; 'three if she lost her bra and pants.' Jane was part of the nation's belief in itself; she was one of the things that distinguished us from the humourless enemy.[18]

VIII

On 7 June 1944 Jane sat on her bath, naked except for a towel, with her faithful hound Fritz; elsewhere a Zec cartoon showed an Allied soldier kicking down the Nazi door carrying a piece of paper marked:

BILL

FOR THE LONG YEARS OF MURDER, RAPE, ARSON, LOOTING AND ALL THE OTHER FILTHY CRIMES FOR WHICH FASCISM HAS BEEN RESPONSIBLE.

The page 1 headline, in letters which, even for D-Day, were only an inch high, read:

INVADERS THRUSTING INLAND

As the end came nearer, the *Mirror* took on a new tone, captured later that month in 'Question Time in the Mess' by Garry Allighan. This feature, more than anything, summed up the end-of-war mood which the *Mirror* – partly through luck, partly through skill – caught in a manner never equalled in the history of journalism.

Allighan's columns were often very specific, explaining the complexities of Army Form O.1727B or ACI 574/40; at other times he would tell a private to stop whingeing or, alternatively, agree that a sergeant was a bullying brute and, if necessary, the *Mirror* would have a word in high places to do something. On 22 June, however, Allighan announced that he was going to discuss 'the most important question of all – Are servicemen and women being kidded along, or will they get the "better world" for which they have been persuaded by the politicians to fight?' He had a letter from a Corporal Jas. McK, writing from 'somewhere near Caen', which he said was typical of many. 'We don't begrudge one inch of the long, long trail that we're fighting over,' wrote the corporal, probably with a lot of help from Allighan's sub-editing skills, 'nor the dirt and the danger, nor the risks of wounds or worse – so long as we feel certain that, when we've won through, we're going to get what we're fighting for . . . Can we be sure that the politicians – who kidded our fathers with promises in the last war – won't double-cross us after this one's over?'

'Of course you can be sure,' came the reassuring reply. 'Don't let the politicians get away with it this time. You fellows have the power. You have the power to fight – you also have the power to vote.'[19] Allighan did not actually say who they were meant to vote for. Indeed, even when the war ended and the general election was called, the *Mirror* fought its corner with a subtlety that would have been unthinkable in a modern newspaper. It did not actually say Vote Labour. It said Vote for Them, i.e. for the servicemen who were still away and in 40 per cent of cases never had the chance to vote at all. It might have been a slightly ambiguous slogan; after all, Them could also mean all the brass-buttoned boneheads who did not count as Us. But on this occasion everyone was able to crack the code.

The fact that the population in general, and the forces in particular, were going to vote Labour en masse in July 1945 was a better-kept secret than almost any of the wartime stratagems. Certainly neither Churchill nor Attlee had an inkling. The great warrior toured the country, cheered by crowds who idolized him and then calmly went into the ballot box and voted against him. Twelve million people voted Labour, half as many again as at any previous election; and they spattered clues all over the pages of the *Daily Mirror* in the weeks before the election.

Hundreds of letters were printed, almost all of them from people who intended to vote Labour, or at the very least Liberal. There was Colonel Cloutman VC, who wrote to say that, at the RE desert training depot which he had commanded, all the boys had said the issue was the same: Labour stood for the government of the people, for the people, by the people; Conservatism for money interest, sheltering under Churchill's popularity. A woman in Wembley wrote to say her nineteen-year-old son had written to her from Burma: 'I am far too young to vote, but not too young to fight the Japs, and I am entitled to have an opinion. I hope Labour make the grade. Almost every man out here says the same. So vote Labour, mum.' The atmosphere is best re-created by playing the Hovis-commercial section of Dvorak's New World Symphony.

On the eve of poll, the *Mirror's* message to the voters ended simply:

> For five long years the lusty youth of
> this great land has bled and died. From
> Berlin to Burma, through desert and
> jungle, on the seas and in the air, they
> have fought and are fighting still for *you*.
> Vote for Them.

And they did.

IX

On 13 June Harold Nicolson, then National Liberal MP for Leicester West, wrote in his diary:

> The Tories feel that the Forces will all vote for Labour, and that there might be a landslide towards the left. They say the Daily Mirror is responsible for this, having pandered to the men in the ranks and given them a general distrust of authority. The Jewish capacity for destruction is really illimitable. Although I loathe anti-Semitism, I do dislike Jews.[20]

Nicolson deserves a share of the credit – together with the improbable trinity of the Duke of Devonshire, Aneurin Bevan and Emmanuel Shinwell – for spotting what was going to happen. His anti-Semitism smelt no different by whatever name he wanted to call it. It was also inappropriate; Philip Zec was certainly Jewish, but the belief that the *Mirror* was run by Jews apparently derived from a trawl by Morrison through the list of stockholders during the row over the cartoon. This unearthed the fact that the shipowner Sir John Ellerman had a large holding, though he had never exercised any power.[21]

Nicolson's understanding of newspapers was also shaky. Everything in this history points to the fact that newspapers can only influence public opinion if they are working with the grain of it. The *Daily Express* still sold more copies than the *Mirror*. How come no one took any notice of what it said?

Before the war was over, the *Mirror* had extended this very self-conscious sense of solidarity with the population even to its by-lines: It no longer billed Our Political Correspondent, for instance, but Your Political Correspondent – Your Play Critic, Your Own Special Correspondent, On The Allotment with Your Gardening Committee. The *Express* could never have done this, since it was palpably obvious that everyone it employed was Lord Beaverbrook's Own Correspondent, and nobody else's.

Even after war was declared, Beaverbrook was slow to fall into line. He dickered with the idea of a negotiated peace until April 1940. On 6 May that year he at last urged the vigorous prosecution of the war in the *Express*, predicting with the paper's customary flair for getting it wrong that the Germans would not get past the Maginot Line, and British cities would not be bombed. But for once, Beaverbrook was about to back a winner. Four days later he lunched with Churchill, who that night became Prime Minister, and – over the King's protests – made Beaverbrook Minister of Aircraft Production.

Once Beaverbrook had taken to the war, he of course had to take as much of it over as Churchill would allow – as Cabinet minister, as negotiator with Stalin and then as Russia's champion in the West. He joined with the left in demanding a second front in 1942, a view backed by a rosy view of Russia that fits not with any kind of right–left view of the world, but only with the *Express*'s eternal lack of perceptiveness: 'Communism under Stalin has won the applause and admiration of all the western nations ... Persecution of Christianity? Not so ... Racial persecution? Not at all ... Political purges? Of course. But it is now clear that the men who were shot down would have betrayed Russia to her German enemy.'[22]

His newspapers, as ever, reflected Beaverbrook's virtues and flaws. During the war Christiansen's papers were as masterful in the art of compression as they had been in the piping days of peace. On 1 December 1942 there were thirty-four stories on page 1 of the four-page *Daily Express*, as well as one picture, one cartoon, two maps and a Guinness advert. And then there was the copy itself. This was part of Alan Moorehead's report on 15 June 1944, the week after D-Day:

HIDE AND SEEK IN COUNTRY LANES

With the Allied Armies, Wednesday

... In all the villages to the east the Germans are fighting much harder than they have fought before. They are hiding in the old, slate-coloured Normandy houses ... they dig their anti-tank guns into the ditches under the hedges with broken branches to dress over them, and they lie in wait.

Often they have a mortar lodged behind the stout stone walls that surround the kitchen gardens of the farmhouses.

It is largely a game of hide-and-seek. At times the Germans will let a couple of scout cars go by so they can bag someone bigger coming on behind. They will even let a squadron leader bring his tank into the village, and then when he turns in the open turret to beckon on the other tanks, they shoot him dead.

On VE Day the *Express* front page displayed a picture of Churchill among the crowd under the headline THIS WAS THEIR FINEST DAY. Sometimes it is easy to forget just how good popular journalism at its absolute best can be. The *Express*'s most ignominious hour was, however, approaching.

Beaverbrook was Lord Privy Seal in the caretaker administration that held office after the wartime Government broke up. When Churchill accused Labour of planning to set up a Gestapo, Attlee replied that while the voice was that of Churchill, the mind was that of Beaverbrook. In fact, Beaverbrook was not involved in the speech, but it was a fair guess. Churchill's election strategy was bizarre: the Labour leaders – Attlee, Bevin, Morrison – were not unknown quantities; they had been pillars of the wartime coalition for the past five years. This had given them the status that government conveys, but they did not have to shoulder the blame for the direction of policy.

Nothing Churchill did, however, was anything like as bizarre as the *Express*'s attempt to fight his corner. Day after day, in that summer of 1945, the headlines of the *Daily Express* were written in a sort of surreal dream. They focused on the role, not of the party leaders, but of Harold Laski, chairman of the National Executive of the Labour Party which, according to the *Express*, would run the country if Labour were elected. Laski was a plausible villain, being professorial, left-wing, even less photogenic than Attlee and, furthermore, Jewish. On one occasion, they managed to picture Beaverbrook speaking, looking forceful and dynamic, alongside a shot of Laski looking rather like Himmler except for his Hitler moustache. The headlines included:

GAULEITER LASKI

OBSCURE LASKI CAUCUS WILL GIVE ORDERS

CHURCHILL FORCES LASKI SHOWDOWN

SHALL THE LASKI '25' RULE BRITAIN?

Who are they? asked the *Express*. Then it reeled off the names of Labour's Executive: Binks, Burke, Clay, Dobbs, Earnshaw, Heady, Knight, Moody, Openshaw . . . The list might have been more menacing had it included more names like Laski instead of sounding like the Yorkshire batting order. J. E. Binks, an obscure official, was elevated by the *Express* into DICTATOR BINKS.

On other days the *Express* veered between routine adulation of Churchill:

VE DAY ALL OVER AGAIN FOR MR. CHURCHILL

WAR WORKERS HAIL THE WAR WINNER

THE NORTH GIVES HIM HIS GREATEST DAY

and routine Labour-bashing:

SOCIALISM 'EVEN IF IT MEANS VIOLENCE'

SOCIALISTS DECIDE THEY HAVE LOST

The *Express*'s capacity for self-delusion that summer was limitless. Scientific opinion polls did exist but no one took any notice of them. Instead, on election morning, the *Express* ran a headline

LATE SWING TO TORIES

based on a poll asking people who they *thought* would win: 54 per cent Tories; 38 per cent Labour. Given the near-unanimity of supposedly informed opinion that Labour had no chance, the fact that nearly two-fifths of the population thought otherwise ought to have told someone something.

The votes were not counted until three weeks after the election because of the time needed to get the service vote in. This led to a strange hiatus, and allowed the *Express* to keep getting it wrong even after polling. On the morning after the vote, it predicted a three-figure Conservative majority; the following day the figure was said to be seventy, based on 'from-the-spot' forecasting – which failed to take account of the forces' votes. Even when the results were in, and Labour had won by a majority of 157, the *Express* churlishly and bizarrely ran as its main headline

BEVIN FOR POTSDAM

Attlee taking him: Churchill stays here

in a shocked tone, as though the election had been a silly joke which the Labour Party were taking with unreasonable seriousness. As the woman in the Savoy Hotel is supposed to have said: 'This is terrible – *they've* elected a Labour Government and *the country* will never stand for that.'[23] 'How inscrutable are the thoughts of the people . . . The Daily Express does not conceal its disappointment at the result,' wailed that day's leader. The slogan of the moment above the leader column was: 'In Great Britain, nearly everybody reads the *Daily Express*.' And then ignores it.

The accepted explanation of the 1945 result is that people separated Churchill the war hero, as Colonel Cloutman VC had said, from the party he led – and with which, after all, he had a fairly tangential relationship. People remembered not the war but the miseries and blunders that had preceded it. The *Express* was let down by its patent lack of sincerity. Christiansen, the political eunuch, was fulfilling the role Lenin assigned to Stalin in Robert Bolt's play *State of Revolution*: 'He does what has to be done, and doesn't worry about his immortal soul.' Many of the staff were Labour voters but they carried out their briefs, as Christiansen said, 'with professional gusto'. Brian Chapman, the assistant managing editor and a Labour man who later spent many years on the *Mirror*, actually wrote the headline

THE NATIONAL SOCIALISTS

which was gleefully printed. 'I confess,' wrote Christiansen later, 'that at the *Express* office we were carried away with the excitement of the story.' Charged by Hugh Cudlipp with having no political convictions, he pointed out that Cudlipp worked briefly for the *Express* when he quarrelled with Bartholomew: 'A political conviction has to be very deep before a newspaperman is prepared to sacrifice his bread and butter for it.'[24]

None of this seems to have done the *Express* any harm. The circulations of both the *Express* and the *Mirror* rose sharply over the next few years. The *Express* achieved a six-monthly figure above 3,500,000 in the second half of 1946 and passed four million early in 1949. Its main broadsheet rival, the *Daily Mail*, was also climbing, but from a much lower base. It then stuck at around 2.2 million. The *Daily Herald* was a fraction above or below the *Mail* for most of the late 1940s; the *News Chronicle* was already lagging, and failed even to hit 1.7 million.

A duopoly was developing, in which the *Mirror* and the *Express* would dominate the market; this pattern lasted until the end of the 1960s. Journalistically, perhaps, the *Express* was to get better. But in the spring of 1949 the *Mirror* began to sell more copies than its rival. At times in the 1950s its lead would be slender, but never again would the *Mirror* fall behind.

Both papers were so profitable and successful that who held the top-selling spot mattered little except as a point of honour. The newspapers were still the major commercial mass medium and, with newsprint heavily rationed, the demand for advertising space far outstripped supply. This meant that, journalistically, times were still tough and the news had to be crammed in under small headlines and into pages designed out of necessity rather than invention. But Britain was at peace, even if it was of a fearful, uncomfortable kind, and people wanted to have fun again.

X

The fun came in diverse forms. The divorce rate, which had doubled after the First World War, quadrupled after the Second. When the *Report on Sexual Behavior of the Human Male* – the Kinsey Report – was published in 1948, it became an instant best-seller, with its revelatory statistics that 90 per cent of American men masturbated, 56 per cent had been unfaithful to their wives and 37 per cent had achieved orgasm with another man.

Attendance at sporting fixtures reached peaks never approached before or since. Huge numbers of people crammed in to watch Denis Compton, Stanley Matthews and Freddie Mills. In 1947 women enthusiastically adopted the New Look, introduced by Dior in Paris, though it meant longer skirts and the use of far more scarce material. The Government disapproved. Indeed, the sense of official disapproval was everywhere. In 1949 the *Mirror* reported that Colne Council in Lancashire refused to allow a fish and chip shop to open seven doors away from the Town Hall. Alderman Herbert Snell, 75, chairman of Building and Planning, said: 'It wouldn't be right to encourage people to eat chips near the Town Hall. Not dignified, you know.' The previous year the *Mirror* had carried a story about a woman who had tried to knife her husband in the street in Harrogate, but had been stopped by a passer-by with the immortal catchphrase 'You can't do that there 'ere.' It was not necessary to knife your husband to draw that kind of response from officialdom.

Perhaps the ultimate *Mirror* story of the late forties came in the summer of 1949 when the American tennis player Gussie Moran – Gorgeous Gussie – turned up at Wimbledon wearing lace-trimmed panties. The *Mirror* saw it all coming.

GAME, SET AND UNDIES!

by Joanna Davey

To the solid twang of racquet and ball
will be added a new sound . . . the rustle
of ruffles and the frou frou of frills.
Oomph is coming to the Centre Court –
in satin-trimmed frocks and lacy undies
– undies you are meant to see too.

Wholly frivolous, a little bit naughty, but charmingly innocent – it was what people wanted. It was not often what they got outside the pages of the *Mirror*.

In many ways, life was tougher after the war than it had been during: the duration had been extended indefinitely. Bread was rationed for the first time between 1946 and 1948; the winter of 1947, when bitter cold and deep snow combined with a fuel crisis, was the toughest anyone could remember. But the all-in-this-together spirit was wearing decidedly thin.

There was heaps of news: Eastern Europe and China were going uniformly communist; India and Israel were marching bloodily to independence. At home there was a succession of particularly horrific murders, given added piquancy by the drabness of the prevailing background and the starkness of the consequences: murderers still ended on the gallows.

On 4 March 1949, under its largest available headline

THE VAMPIRE CONFESSES

the *Mirror* reported the arrest of one of these murderers, John George Haigh – 'the monster . . . the maniac . . . he cut the throats of the people he had killed and sucked their blood through a lemonade straw.' There was a problem with this report: Haigh had only been charged with one murder and had not actually been convicted of anything; and the *Mirror* had not even bothered to call him an *alleged* monster, maniac and vampire. The lawyers were in clover. 'It is difficult to think of a matter more calculated to prejudice a fair trial,' said Haigh's counsel, Sir Walter Monckton KC. Lord Goddard, the Lord Chief Justice, said that in the long history of this sort of case there had never been one 'of such a scandalous and wicked character'. He was referring to the *Mirror*, not to Haigh, who was indeed a monster and a maniac. The editor, Silvester Bolam, was jailed for three months, though he was quite chipper about it all and – notionally, anyway – continued to edit the paper from Brixton. The *Mirror* modestly reported the sentencing in a single column underneath

BIG BANDS KICK AT
'TOO MANY U.S.
TUNES' ON BBC

The *Mirror* was kicking, but most of the time only gently. When Konni Zilliacus, the left-wing Labour MP, was left off the list of approved party candidates, he said it was 'bloody funny' and the *Mirror* quoted him. On the same front page, 24 February 1949, President Truman used the initials S.O.B. The readership, who appear to have cared nothing about the fairness or otherwise of Haigh's trial, wrote in furiously, under the heading

THOSE WORDS

Assume on arrival home, one is greeted by one's small daughter, aged seven, with the words: 'Hello, you son of a bitch! You forgot my bloody pocket money this morning!' This is not a fantastic supposition. It might easily happen if the Daily Mirror continues to publish such words. – *W. G. E. Rump, Ruislip*.

I am a schoolboy, 11 years old, and a regular reader of your paper. When I pick up the paper I see words I am forbidden to use. Couldn't you put a dash and leave it to the reader to imagine? Because so many children read your paper. – *John Farmer, Hailsham, Sussex*.

The *Mirror* seemed caught between two moods. Sometimes it could still resort to almost Northcliffean pomposity.

Should we allow THESE to open HERE?
From John Godley, Dublin, Wednesday

Whenever there's racing the dregs of Dublin gather at the betting shops. All the boyoes are there – the artful dodgers, the mug punters, the bone idle and the plain crooked ... If cash betting is allowed, the same thing will happen in England ... all the loafers hanging around all day. A new breeding place for petty crime.

The *Mirror* was in some ways suffering the torments of those who achieve their heart's desire. Labour had won the election. 'We are the masters now,' as Sir Hartley Shawcross did not quite say. The *Mirror* was the paper that supported collectivism, the fairness of rationing. It had caught the mood of 1945, and possibly fanned it. As the next election approached, opinion was heading the other way.

Peter Hennessy, looking back from the 1990s, picks out the 1949 Ealing film *Passport to Pimlico*, in which a London suburb declares its independence under Stanley Holloway's leadership and sticks two fingers up at all the people saying 'You can't do that there 'ere'; he felt the film may have been as much a factor in the 1950 election, in which Attlee's majority was cut to single figures, as anything in the papers.[25] The *Express*'s mischievous sympathies would be entirely with the Pimlico rebels; the *Mirror* would, deep down, be on the side of good order.

Occasionally the *Mirror* would break out. In March 1950 it unearthed two spectacular examples of petty bullying from officialdom: Sedgley Urban District Council in Staffordshire threatened to evict tenants who kept pigeons unless they joined the National Homing Union; meanwhile, the education authority at Warrington agreed to limit instruction at the evening class in decorating because the local tradesmen thought amateurs were being taught too much. 'Blithering nonsense and unjustified interference,' thundered the *Mirror*:

> There is too much petty dictatorship by obscure people in this country. It is nothing to do with the Government, whose spokesmen are continually opposed to regimentation in living. But in the nooks and crannies of minor officialdom, people who cannot order their own thoughts seek unreasonably to order the lives of others.

But it was something to do with the Government, and everyone knew it. And this was the sort of story which right-wing newspapers did (and still do) far more often and far better.

Very occasionally, but only occasionally, as the 1940s came to an end, it was possible in the *Mirror's* twelve tabloid pages for there to be a little uninhibited fun involving politicians. On 24 June 1949 it quoted an American entertainer, Howard Sullivan, 21, who was dressed as a girl in a blonde wig and lipstick for a performance of *Ice Cycles of 1949*:

> Over the barrier I went. There in the front was a guy with a lovely bald head. So I gave him a kiss. Then one of the guys says to me 'Do you know who you kissed?' It was Clem Attlee. I said 'What gives? Who's he?' Then he told me he was the Prime Minister.

Nearly half a century on, the incongruity of that incident still makes the mind boggle.

XI

In 1949, 87 per cent of the adult population of Britain read a daily paper; both the *Mirror* and *Express* were read by one adult in four. Mass-Observation reported that half the *Mirror's* readers voted Labour and one-seventh Conservative. As many as a third of its readers, a higher proportion than for any other paper, did not even know which party it supported.[26]

Did politics make any difference at all? There was a swing against Labour in four successive elections in the 1950s, and the *Mirror* trumpet often gave off a very uncertain sound indeed. Yet the *Mirror* of the 1950s represents the apogee of British popular journalism. Reading the files backs up more or less everything the journalists who worked there like to remember. This was a newspaper that, for the most part, told its readers what it believed at the time to be the honest truth. It would explain that truth in simple terms; indeed, its reports were often masterpieces of exposition, and magnificently displayed. At the same time it had a lot of fun, and it was nearly always good clean fun. The *Express* of the 1930s was not honest even to itself; Northcliffe's *Mail* had not quite perfected the art of explaining things simply, and certainly did not display them; the fun in Murdoch's *Sun* is not clean.

But the *Mirror* was a sensationalist newspaper. Silvester Bolam, the editor from 1948 to 1953 who went to jail over Haigh, and so had time to think about such matters, embraced the term with relish, as Beaverbrook had done. When he took over as editor he announced on the front page:

> The *Mirror* is a sensational newspaper. We make no apology for that. We believe in the sensational presentation of news and views, especially important news and views, as a necessary and valuable service in these days of mass readership and democratic responsibility.

On another occasion he put it this way:

> We shall go on being sensational to the best of our ability. Sensationalism does not mean distorting the truth. It means the vivid and dramatic presentation of events so as to give them a forceful impact on the mind of the reader. It means big headlines, vigorous writing, simplification into familiar everyday language, and the wide use of illustration by cartoons and photographs. Every great problem facing us – the world economic crisis, diminishing food supplies, the population puzzle, the Iron Curtain and a host of others – will only be understood by the ordinary man busy with his daily tasks if he is hit hard and hit often with the facts. Sensational treatment is the answer, whatever the sober and 'superior' readers of some other journals may prefer. No doubt we shall make mistakes, but we are at least alive.

It has probably never been put better. Bolam was right to see sensationalism as an ideal, rather than a term of abuse. And the *Mirror was* alive, at a time when several of its rivals were dying (the *Mail* recovered; the *Daily Sketch*, *Daily Herald* and *News Chronicle* did not) and the sober newspapers –

effectively *The Times* and the *Daily Telegraph*, since *The Guardian* was still based in Manchester, and only slowly acquiring a national circulation – believed they had to take superiority to the point of inaccessibility.

But he was also wrong. Sensationalism did mean distorting the truth, because journalists under pressure to get stories into the newspaper and make a living have always distorted the truth, as we have seen: sometimes knowingly, sometimes wilfully, sometimes through incompetence – sometimes just through the editorial process by which a complex and maybe contradictory sequence of events has to be transformed at high speed into a simple, readable, enticing headline. Freelance journalists want to get paid; staff journalists want to stay paid. It is so today; and it was no different in the 1950s.

However, when there were complaints about inaccuracies in the press in the 1950s, it was rarely suggested that the *Mirror*, even though it was clearly the dominant popular newspaper, was the worst offender. In 1955, when two pairs of Siamese twins were born, *The Spectator* reported that in one case the press got into the hospital ward and conducted an auction for the exclusive rights to the mother's story even though she had specifically said she did not wish to see them; in the other the reporters' siege was so pressing that the mother had to move hospitals and an urgent operation was delayed for two days. But these stories smack of Sunday papers; no one implicated the *Mirror*.

When the political journalist Henry Fairlie wrote a critique of the *Mirror* in 1957, he entitled it 'Brilliance, Skin Deep'.[27] He was in no doubt about the brilliance. He said the *Mirror*'s success derived from its journalism, rather than from stunts; it was the only London newspaper that was truly national rather than primarily metropolitan; its personality was 'full of flavour and brilliantly projected'; furthermore, he went on,

> no one, unless he is a perverted prude or does not read the *Daily Mirror* at all, would ever accuse the *Daily Mirror* of being a sexy newspaper. Yet sex is a matter of perfectly normal interest, and the readers of the *Daily Mirror* will find their perfectly normal interest in it satisfied unobtrusively. Sex, in fact, fits into the whole pattern of the *Daily Mirror*'s personality as it fits into the whole pattern of most of its readers' personalities. This is very different from the way in which several Sunday newspapers handle sex.

Fairlie went on to be critical, because that was his job, but the second half of a fairly lengthy piece is infinitely less convincing. He was not greatly enamoured of Cassandra's column – 'he does not have a mind so much as a thesaurus, he does not have feelings so much as reflexes' – and he upbraids the paper, and Cudlipp in particular, for refusing to do much more than reflect readers' prejudices, for failing to advocate policies that its readers might find unpopular. Then he slipped back to a reprise of its virtues:

> It is clean and healthily extrovert; it understands the qualities which make the British working-class decent and civilised. It does the job of catering for its class of readers far better than any other British newspaper has ever done. But if it reflects the good features of the proletarian personality, it reflects the bad ones as well. It is mentally lazy, emotionally sloppy, and incurably insular . . . It gets under the skin of its readers and stays there. But why be satisfied with being skin-deep?

In the mid-1950s people seem to have had high standards and expectations of popular newspapers. In 1955, in the midst of the crisis over whether Princess Margaret should marry Group Captain Peter Townsend, who was divorced, the *Mirror* ran the headline

COME ON, MARGARET

urging her to make up her mind. Sir Linton Andrews, chairman of the Press Council, called it impertinent. 'Surely a member of the royal family has a private life which all decent people should respect? It is purely a matter of human decency.'[28] In short, the *bien-pensant* thinkers had a hard time complaining about the popular daily press in the 1950s. The worst thing people said about the *Mirror* was that it was common. Bolam's successor as editor was Jack Nener (pronounced Neena). He might, as one of his successors, Tony Miles, put it, have been sent from Central Casting to play a tabloid editor: 'crinkly silver hair, dapper bow tie, gravelly voice, gruff warmth, volcanic temperament'.

He was also famously foul-mouthed. 'He was an absolutely awful man to work for,' recalled Audrey Whiting, 'dreadful beyond belief. He swore like a trooper. The language was awful, but it was deliberate. It wasn't until I actually married him and got to know him terribly well that he would laugh.'[29] One story goes that he was having lunch in a restaurant, loudly effing and blinding, when a nearby diner asked him to moderate his language.

'Don't you know who I am?' rasped Nener. 'I'm the effing editor of the effing *Daily Mirror*.'

'I rather thought you might be,' said the other man.[30]

Nener's reign, from 1953 to 1961, must be seen as the high point of the *Daily Mirror* and of British popular journalism. Yet his name is little known except among journalists of that generation. And it remains unclear whether it made that much difference who edited the *Daily Mirror*. The editor took routine decisions and, if necessary, the rap, as Bolam found out. But the policy of the paper came from higher up. Bartholomew, increasingly drunk and irascible, was forced out in a boardroom putsch in 1951. The ringleader, Cecil Harmsworth King, became the new chairman of the *Mirror* group. And thus the son of Northcliffe's sister, Geraldine, took charge of the family's old paper.

King had joined the *Mirror* when it was still one of the family businesses, and his support as a director was crucial when Bartholomew transformed the paper in the 1930s. The family were horrified, and even after the war King's uncle Cecil refused to propose him for the Reform Club.[31] One of King's first acts as chairman was to bring back Cudlipp, who had been forced out by Bartholomew, had sought refuge with Beaverbrook and was on the brink of becoming editor of the *Sunday Express*. King made Cudlipp editor of the *Sunday Pictorial* for the third time, but a year later appointed him editorial director and editor-in-chief of both the *Pictorial* and the *Daily Mirror*.

These job titles can mean almost anything and to this day are sometimes used as a sinecure for ex-editors to avoid public unpleasantness. Cudlipp was clearly in charge. On the days of really big stories he would go into the editor's office, order pork and crackling for lunch, and set to work on some crackling make-ups for the main news pages that night. Thus the great *Mirror* front pages were prepared. Even the bad days were good. It is the *Express* headline for Coronation morning, weaving in the news that Hunt and Hillary had reached the top of the world, that has gone down in journalistic folklore:[32]

ALL THIS – AND EVEREST TOO!

The *Mirror* went for

THE QUEEN'S SURPRISE!

which was followed by news of the 'daring' gown she was going to wear that day. No one remembers it, but that day the *Mirror* sold 7,161,704 copies, every one that it put on sale: more than any British daily newspaper has sold before or since.

XII

In 1951 Churchill had returned to power through a quirk of the electoral system, despite the fact that the Conservatives achieved fewer votes than Labour and despite a *Mirror* campaign of a virulence certainly never matched on that side of the political argument. The slogan was 'Whose Finger on the Trigger?'; the allegation, that Churchill was an irresponsible warmonger. Churchill sued.

This was very different from the *Mirror*'s approach at the 1950 election, which Labour had won with a barely workable majority. Then the *Mirror* had maintained the subtlety of its 1945 campaign but adopted a tone that was paternalistic going on patronizing, with features along these lines: 'We want to talk to the family about polling day – which is tomorrow. Let's take you first, Dad. There is no need to tell you the job isn't finished yet . . .'

There was an assumption in 1950 that Labour would win comfortably enough, as arrogant in its way as the Conservative certainty before 1945. The swing against Labour was strongest in those areas of the south that voted so unexpectedly for them in 1945: *Daily Express*-land, if you like, where people were starting to acquire, or at least crave, the material possessions of the second half of the century – a car, a washing machine and, most significantly, a television. Labour's core support remained solid at the first two elections of the decade; later, as prosperity spread, so the Conservative vote spread with it.

But the *Mirror* circulation, which in 1949 alone had leapt almost a million, from just under 3.7 million in late 1948 to more than 4.5 million, remained very steady throughout the 1950s. The *Mirror*'s six-monthly figures from the Audit Bureau of Circulations, which gave a new reliability to this much-abused branch of statistics, fluctuated throughout the decade only in a very narrow band between 4.4 million and 4.8 million. The *Express* figures were even less variable, never falling below four million but never approaching four and a quarter million.

For the *Mirror*, life went on whoever was in power. Four days after the 1950 election it assured its women readers that there was nothing a good girdle wouldn't put right. This cannot have been absolutely true. On 30 June the paper had to report one of those ghastly sporting days that were to become so familiar in the second half of the century: on the same day, the England cricket team lost to the West Indies at home for the first (but definitely not the last) time; the football team lost 1–0 to the United States in the World Cup, a competition British teams had previously spurned as trivial; and, as would become the custom, all the British players crashed out of Wimbledon. All this was reported in terms of great restraint, partly because the *Mirror* was still restricted to twelve pages and partly, perhaps, because one of Bartholomew's quirks was that he was notoriously anti-sport and did his utmost to restrict its coverage in the *Mirror*.

Other trivia of national life were given as much scope as the space allowed: a dentist in Ealing refused to treat men without ties and women wearing slacks; there were demands for nude sunbathing in the national parks; a councillor in Bognor Regis complained that the resort was being ruined by fat women from Bermondsey in comic hats (Bermondsey, egged on by the *Mirror*, was furious); Southport Highways Committee deducted 3s 6d from the wages of James Clarkson, a thirty-five-year-old workman, for time he spent rescuing a man on a sandbank; and a boy in Glamorgan committed suicide because his pet rabbit's babies all died. There were 246 cases of indecency and assault reported in one year against children who asked adults to take them in to see 'A' films, which under-sixteens were not allowed to attend on their own.[33]

Clippies – women bus conductors – were in the paper a lot in 1951. In Cardiff it was alleged that they broke up drivers' marriages; in Stockton the local Transport and General Workers' Union insisted they were not temptresses; in Birkenhead twelve of them were recruited but were unable to work because the male conductors threatened to go on strike. In December 1950 dustmen went on strike because one of their number was sacked for harassing a woman who refused to give him a Christmas box. That was also in Birkenhead. Possibly there was a lot of this sort of thing already going on in Merseyside. There was certainly a lot of it in the *Mirror*, which reinforces Henry Fairlie's point about its truly national character.

In Paris, women were barred from judging a Most Handsome Man in the World competition. 'Women are unreliable,' said the organizer, 'because they get very disturbed by a mass display of masculine beauty. They forget to observe the technical Greek points of muscular perfection.' Men may or may not have been disturbed by the pictures the *Mirror* printed. The world's most exciting woman was deemed to be Fernanda Mantel, The Girl With A Thousand Freckles, though there was also The Girl With Perfect Legs, Hollywood actress Julia Vogel, and Dany Dauberson, The Girl With The Most Shapely Shoulders in the World ('shapely' was a much-used word in the *Mirror* of the 1950s). Sub-editors invented these titles as though they were formal offices, like Lord Privy Seal or President of the Board of Trade. The office-holders tended to be portrayed with breasts prominent and uplifted, but firmly strapped in.

Other attitudes were even further removed from those of modern tabloids. As early as 1949 the *Mirror* had attacked the developing system of apartheid in South Africa as 'harsh and immoral'; but in 1951 it was still possible for Cassandra, whose feelings (or reflexes) were more reliably liberal than most, to tell without inhibition the story of the 'darkie' stealing chickens who hears the owner pass by with a shotgun:

'Who's there?'
'There's nobody here but us chickens.'

In May 1951 the price of the *Mirror* rose, after more than thirty years at a penny, to a penny-ha'penny. The penny press, which had succeeded the ha'penny press started by Northcliffe, was now gone for ever.

In February 1952 George VI died:

HIS VALET FOUND THE
KING DEAD
He called softly to his master – but there
was no answer.

The *Mirror* did not produce the black-ruled columns of old but its coverage was warm and respectful. 'His strength was not brilliance or power,' wrote Cassandra. 'It was stronger than that. It was simplicity, goodness and a sense of duty.' For the funeral the paper switched to a purple-lettered title-piece above the famous picture of the three queens (the King's mother, wife and daughter) in mourning. This time, however, Queen Alexandra was not around to allow the *Mirror* to use a shot of the King in the coffin, and no one would have been in the business of snatching one.

But it is 1953 when one senses the *Mirror* entering its pomp. There was enough paper now for editions of sixteen pages and much bigger headlines. With Cudlipp in control and Nener editing the paper, the headlines also became more direct (HIS VALET FOUND THE KING DEAD might not have passed muster a year later). There was a sense of a presiding genius projecting the news, and he, all the evidence suggests, was indeed Cudlipp. On 22 January, a week before Bolam quietly resigned, this dominated the paper:

CHALLENGE TO THE
GOVERNMENT ON
SMOKING

ANSWER THIS QUESTION
The Daily Mirror challenges the
Government to find an answer to this
question: What is the truth about smoking as the cause of lung cancer?

There was no blame attached to the tobacco industry, the *Mirror* added, with an eye on its lawyers. Ordinary news would be projected with the same vigour.

DEATH LAPS GENTLY ON A SILENT ICE-COLD ISLE

said the headline above a report by Elizabeth Hickson from Canvey Island on 3 February, after the East Coast floods. 'A parrot squawked on top of a wardrobe; in the next room its owner lay dead.' On the twentieth, there was a page 1 leader on Korea, headed simply

DANGER!

The *Mirror*'s pin-ups were getting a little bigger too. Sal McClosky, a Las Vegas dancer, swung her legs, fishnet tights and all, over the whole of page 9 one day. A standard pose developed in which starlets stood with their arms on the back of their heads, giving readers a glimpse of full-frontal shaven armpit. Another day there was Harriet Andersson, 'a sultry, smouldering temptress', with her blouse off-the-shoulder and almost off-everything-else. But Cudlipp was never to repeat what he did once at the *Sunday Pictorial* and bare anyone's breasts, however demurely.

The *Mirror*'s gestures were also getting more expansive; newspapers were no longer universal providers of insurance, and they were happy to let the football pools companies hand out all the jackpots. But the *Mirror* could be relied on for the occasional display of big-heartedness. When the Sheffield Wednesday footballer Derek Dooley lost a leg, and thus had his career very publicly ended, the *Mirror* offered him the post of 'sports adviser'. When a young Canvey Island bus conductor and his teenage bride lost their home in the floods, the *Mirror* invited them to have their honeymoon in a Park Lane hotel. 'I thought I was dreaming,' said Pat Larter, 16.

This sort of fairy-godmothery, in which the rich man's castle would be temporarily invaded by the poor man at the gate, with the *Mirror* footing the bill, was a recurring feature. Donald Zec is particularly fond of the story that began with R. A. Butler making a speech as Chancellor of the Exchequer containing the warning: 'We must not drop back into easy evenings of port and over-ripe pheasant.' Cudlipp, sharp as ever, ordered Zec to round up a dozen 'ordinary' people that afternoon to have just such an easy evening. Zec booked a room at the Savoy easily enough; his party-piece account of his tour of London streets to find a dozen working men to join him is a Fleet Street classic.

'I wonder whether you'd care to have dinner with me at the Savoy Hotel?' he went round asking, getting responses like 'Gitthatovit.' 'You feelin' all right, mate?' and ''Ere, can you take advice? I advise you to piss off.'

Eventually a friend of his in Wembley combined with her greengrocer and produced a dozen candidates. It made a splendid *Mirror* feature, told with Zec's customary gusto. 'Blimey, don't arf pong,' they said when the pheasant was produced.

The *Mirror* enjoyed similar stunts, like a charladies' ball and an alternative debutantes' ball for factory girls. But is it possible to detect here a cloud, as yet no bigger than a man's hand, which was eventually to build into a storm big enough to destroy the paper's grip on its market? It was not just Butler whose tastes were far removed from those of the average *Mirror* reader; the paper was run by people who were far more likely to dine at the Savoy than in Joe's Caff. Eventually, it would show. But there was a lot of fun to be had in the meantime.

Cecil King's equivalent of Christiansen's Man on the Rhyl Promenade was the wife of a Sheffield bus conductor. Stories had to be judged on the appeal they might have for her, which would explain the obsession with the behaviour of clippies. In 1954 the *Mirror* introduced a new name who was to touch the lives of more bus conductors' wives than any journalist in history:

INTRODUCING MARJORIE PROOPS
WHO SAYS HALLO!
THIS MORNING IN A
SPARKLING NEW COLUMN FOR WOMEN

Funny the way, when a marriage breaks up, it's so often the little things that bring it to an end . . . not the sordid infidelities or the harsh cruelties or the squalid, searing scenes.

This week, a couple finally parted after twelve years of marriage over a dish of macaroni cheese. She'd cooked it. He let it get cold while he talked on the telephone. That dish of macaroni was the last soggy straw. If only husbands would realise how painful and insulting is indifference to efforts over a hot stove there would, perhaps, be fewer divorces.

There would be many more divorces over the years ahead, but many people would be nursed through them by Marje. She had originally been hired by Cudlipp in 1939 as a fashion artist, and had developed into a columnist in women's magazines and the *Daily Herald*, where she had been told off by the editor, Hugh Cudlipp's elder brother Percy, when she wrote that there were no frilly knickers in the Labour Party. 'You've got to watch it, Marjorie, you're a sexy writer.' The *Mirror* was less inhibited, though she did not take her agony-aunt column out of the magazines and into the newspaper until 1971. But she touched on subjects that no one else did.

XIII

On 24 November 1953, Winston Churchill threw away his copy of the *Daily Mirror* at 10 Downing Street with a gesture of disgust. 'They want Prince Charles to mix with working people. I suppose they would have a ballot, and each day the successful twelve would come to the Palace. I wish we could buy that rag. It is doing so much harm.'[34] It was certainly irritating the PM. SHOULD CHURCHILL RETIRE? the *Mirror* had asked that June, saying he was 'fagged out' at a time when the country needed virile leadership in foreign affairs. This was hardly a party political point, since Labour was still led by Attlee, who was seventy; but it rapidly became the dominant theme of the *Mirror*'s political coverage.

It had been there in an undertone for a long time. When Lloyd George announced his retirement from politics in 1944, aged eighty-one, the *Mirror* said it should be an example to other politicians in their dotage. In the mid-1950s, when party politics was quiescent, it became the one drum the *Mirror* found itself able to beat with any conviction. 'Sir Winston is 79,' said a *Mirror* leader on 1 April 1954. 'Old and tired, he mouths comfortless words in the twilight of his career. His battles are past. He has borne his burden too long. THIS IS THE GIANT IN DECAY.'

By the time of the 1955 election Churchill had retired, and in the contest between fifty-seven-year-old Eden and Attlee, the *Mirror* supported Labour only tepidly.

EVERY VOTE FOR LABOUR WILL HELP TO KEEP THE TORIES TAME

and

DON'T LET THE TORIES CHEAT OUR CHILDREN

were the feeble rallying cries. But there was also criticism of the presence of Labour leaders like Attlee, 'born two years before the invention of the gas mantle', Herbert Morrison (67), Emmanuel Shinwell (70) and Chuter Ede (72). In contrast it commended men like Gaitskell (48), Harold Wilson (39), James Callaghan (43), George Brown (40) and, on the Tory side, Iain Macleod, 'the lively Minister of Health', Reginald Maudling, 'an up-and-coming 38' and Sir Edward Boyle, only 31.

Supposedly, Attlee was perfectly aware of the passing years, which is why he was determined to stay on long enough to ensure that Morrison, whom he detested, would be too old to replace him. 'THIS IS NOT A PARTY ISSUE' shouted the *Mirror*. Indeed it was not; there were few party issues in 1955, which is one reason the *Mirror* had to do so much shouting in capital letters. 'WE ARE LIVING IN THE FASTEST, YOUNGEST AGE IN THE HISTORY OF MANKIND. Let's speed things up in politics, too.'

The *Mirror*'s coverage is given added piquancy by the knowledge that Nener was in fact a Tory. But it was hard to offer compelling reasons for voting Labour in 1955. WHO IS TO BLAME? asked the *Mirror* on 28 May, two days after the poll. The answer was that the Labour leaders were TOO OLD, TOO TIRED, TOO WEAK; the Labour movement was BAFFLED, BEWILDERED and BETRAYED by internal feuds; and its organization was RUSTY, INEFFICIENT, pathetically INFERIOR to the slick Tory machine.

XIV

Labour's decline still made no difference to the *Mirror*. That same day's paper carried Cecil King's annual report as chairman, announcing that the circulation lead over the *Express* had almost doubled to 656,000. Only lower down did it mention the inconvenient fact that trading profit had declined, due to higher freight charges and wage costs. King might also have mentioned the prognosis for the following year, which was certain to include a very sharp fall in profits.

How, one might wonder, did the *Mirror* cover the story when Churchill did finally give way and retire? We shall never know the answer. Churchill left Downing Street in April 1955, in the midst of a twenty-six-day stoppage when all the national papers ceased publication. The issue was a demand for a pay increase of just under £3 a week by 700 members of the electricians' and engineers' unions. Only the provincial morning papers kept going, which helped bring the *Manchester Guardian* to a wider audience, before the customary fudged settlement brought everyone back to work.

'OH, HOW I MISSED THE STRIPS,' SAYS THE DUKE

according to a post-strike headline quoting the Duke of Edinburgh. The quote beneath it actually reported him as saying 'I must confess I only really missed the strip cartoons,' which did not amount to quite the same thing.

Fleet Street was about to reap the industrial relations whirlwind from a breeze sown by Northcliffe and enthusiastically fertilized by Beaverbrook. Northcliffe believed that his staff deserved to be paid well, and from the start increased wages to lift the business out of the old Grub Street ways. Beaverbrook increased wages too, at least partly in the belief that it would help bankrupt his rivals, many of whom were now struggling.

The *Express* and the *Mirror* both appeared fireproof. On 22 September 1955 the *Mirror* gleefully reported the *Financial World*'s description of itself as 'the most phenomenally successful newspaper in the Empire'. But the enemy was massing silently beyond the frontiers. That very night commercial television began in the London area. Clifford Davis, the *Mirror*'s TV critic, reported next morning: 'After a stuffy forty-five minute start, with *dull* speeches from the Guildhall, the new-style TV got under way with a slick, fast-moving evening of entertainment.' It included Britain's first £1,000-a-minute advert.

The *Mirror* dwarfed news of ITV's beginnings with a report on the BBC's counter-coup – the death, by burning, of Grace Archer, wife of young Phil Archer, in the eponymous and everlasting radio soap opera – and a plug for its own star sports writer, Peter Wilson, The Man They Cannot Gag. But slick, fast-moving evenings of entertainment represented the future. Newspapers' virtual monopoly on advertising was now over; and the end of the last vestiges of newsprint rationing completely changed the relationship between supply and demand. The weaker papers began to suffer at once. The Manchester-based *Daily Dispatch* closed that very week, merging with the *News Chronicle*, which swallowed its 463,000 circulation with barely a gulp.

In 1956 the *Mirror* found an issue and regained a little political self-confidence. The Suez invasion brought forth its biggest headlines yet. It was, as the *Mirror* insisted, day after day, Eden's war. Within a fortnight it was demanding his resignation; within two months it got its way. But there were matters of even more pressing concern to the young readers whom the *Mirror* was so keen to attract. These were summed up on 19 December in the headline over Marje Proops's column:

WHAT A YEAR – FOR THE BOSOM BRIGADE

There was, for instance, Jayne Mansfield (40–22–35), 'The Bustaceous Blonde of Broadway'; also Diana Dors, Marilyn Monroe, Anita Ekberg (39½"); and Sabrina, also 39½", who stopped the traffic in Sheffield when she was there to open a shop. 'Would 4,000 people go wild to see a girl of more modest proportions open a shop?' asked Marje. 'I think not. In fact, I do not think a girl of more modest proportions would ever be invited to open a shop ... Can you recall any outstanding woman of science, of politics, of art or music or valour, or any woman, apart from Rose Heilbron,[35] who have distinguished themselves in this year of feminine disgrace – 1956? I can't.'

All these mammaries were displayed prominently, occasionally plungingly, but always properly covered up, according to the conventions of the time. And the *Mirror* was very knowing about the game it was playing with the film stars' publicists: Ekberg was THE BORE WITH THE BUST when she failed to turn up at a party held in her honour. Donald Zec became very world-weary when obliged to report Diana Dors's love life:

The tear-stained gap between Diana Dors and her husband Dennis ('The Menace') Hamilton gets smaller and smaller. They spent yesterday, the second day in Britain of their much-proclaimed parting, just like the first, together . . . This must seem like the strangest estrangement ever . . . so Mr Hamilton was asked: 'Does this mean a happy ending?' He shrugged and replied: 'Who knows?' They ought to decide pretty fast before their ever-lovin' public begins to ask: 'WHO CARES?'

Modern popular papers have lost the art of reporting trivia with a dash of vinegar instead of going to the extremes of either sugar or vitriol.

But the *Mirror* of the late fifties seemed in tune with the times. The young people about whom the paper made so much fuss were rebelling very gently: jiving to Bill Haley and the Comets, mooching about in espresso bars, perhaps voting Labour. It threw itself into Bill Haley's tour of Britain under the headline

WE'RE GOING TO ROCK AROUND THE CLOCK!

offering free tickets and free records, and drew 50,000 entries. In 1959 Sydney Jacobson, the *Mirror*'s political editor, was able to file the ultimate *Mirror* story from Leningrad on the Labour leader's tour of the Soviet Union:

GAITSKELL MEETS A BOOGIE-WOOGIE FAN

Before the election in October 1959 it was able to cry:

GIVE THEM THE VOTE AT 18

and announce that the paper's greatest contribution to the campaign would be to LET YOUTH SHOUT ITS HEAD OFF. The *Mirror* certainly managed, as it had not in 1955, to shout its own head off:

LABOUR NOW EXPECTS VICTORY

DON'T KNOWS SWINGING TO LABOUR

THE TIME HAS COME FOR THE TORIES TO GO!

But alas:

IT'S THE TORIES BACK AGAIN
By Sydney Jacobson
The Tories are back. And with a bigger majority.

Four days later the *Mirror* dropped its 'Forward with the People' slogan. The Labour politician Richard Crossman lost his column. Jane sailed off into the sunset. They did not, however, touch the newest cartoon symbol of the *Mirror*, the cloth-capped layabout Andy Capp, who would be syndicated all over the world, though he might have been regarded as dated and stereotyped even in 1959. All this had apparently been decided at a conference at lunchtime on election day itself and not as a response to the results. On the Monday the paper promised 'NEW ideas. New features. New contents. New writers' and ran Tommy Steele's life story instead of a leader column.

But the election was decided on the tiniest swing of the pendulum – hardly more than 1 per cent. There were still more than twelve million people who voted Labour; and of the 4.5 million buying the *Mirror*, a large percentage, as we have seen, neither knew nor cared about the paper's politics. The *Mirror* was right to keep reinventing itself. But it drew the wrong conclusion from the 1959 election, and in the end the results would be catastrophic.

XV

On 8 March 1960 the *Daily Mirror* unveiled (as well as model girl Leonie Green in a mink bikini) a new columnist. This was Derek Dale, with a title no one had used before: the *Daily Mirror* City Editor.

Welcome to the world of money. What's that? You always thought stocks and shares a stuffy subject?

You've always thought the City was populated by pin-stripe trousers, toppers and old school ties? Don't you believe it.

THERE IS NO MORE FASCINATING PROCESS IN THE WORLD THAN TURNING A PENNY INTO TWOPENCE.

And as City Editor of the *Daily Mirror* it will be my job to help you.

In a sense, Dale was already too late: in that very first column he warned that share prices, which had doubled in two years, were running out of steam; and he was too early for the great boom in working-class capitalism, which was more than two decades away. But the tone of those first four paragraphs was very telling. It needs to be read in the kind of voice used in that era on Children's Hour, or by actors playing doctors in adverts for patent medicines: caring, decent and honourable, but didactic to the point of being patronizing.

On the same day a new strip cartoon appeared, featuring Joe and Prue Hope, who were trying to keep up with the Joneses upstairs. This was transparently part of the same strategy. It did not last long: humour cannot be manufactured to order.

Pin-ups ancient and modern: the *Daily Mirror*, 4 May 1908, showing Miss Ivy Lilian Close, winner of the Mirror Beauty Contest, as exhibited in the Royal Academy by Mr Arthur Hacker; *The Sun*, 17 November 1970, showing Miss Stephanie Rahn, who inaugurated the tradition of topless Page Three Girls.

Faces of the *Daily Mail*: Lord Northcliffe *(above)* as drawn by Spy in his gilded youth, and as photographed in his corpulent middle age; his brother, the first Lord Rothermere *(below left)*; and the first edition of the paper – 'cheap without the appearance of cheapness'.

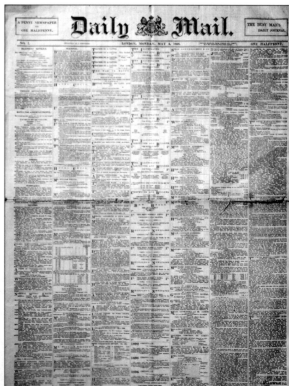

Selling the news: *(above)* news vendors of 1893; *(below)* a news stand set up for an *Observer* photographer in 1961 to show all the publications controlled by the *Daily Mirror* after the merger that produced the International Publishing Corporation.

Faces of the *Daily Express*: fallible prophets *(above left)* Ralph D. Blumenfeld and *(above right)* Lord Beaverbrook (speaking in 1941); *(below)* the master technician Arthur Christiansen, shown playing himself in the 1962 film *The Day the Earth Caught Fire*.

Opposite:
The calm and the storm: the *News of the World* sub-editors' room on a Saturday afternoon, 18 April 1953, when the circulation was above eight million. On the left at the back is the editor, Arthur Waters. C. J. 'Tiny' Lear, then chief sub-editor and later editor himself, is at the head of the table; *(below)* the scene at Wapping on 15 March 1986 when demonstrators stormed the barricades round the works where Rupert Murdoch was producing the *News of the World* and his other papers without the traditional print unions.

Tabloid allies: *(above)* Cecil King, chairman of International Publishing Corporation, owners of the *Daily Mirror*, with Hugh Cudlipp, his successor as chairman and the paper's presiding genius; *(below)* the men who plotted the *Mirror*'s downfall, Larry Lamb, on the left, and his young boss Rupert Murdoch in 1969; *(right)* Kelvin MacKenzie, Lamb's successor, pictured when he left the Murdoch empire in 1993.

Two different wars: *(above)* Strube of the *Daily Express* in 1933 on
the effects of the newspapers' own private war; *(below)* Jane, the
Daily Mirror's sex symbol, at the end of the Second World War.

Royal coverage ancient and modern: the *Daily Mirror*'s loyal coverage of Coronation Day (this edition of the paper sold more than any other British daily in history) and the *News of the World* in 1995.

After 1961, King and Cudlipp also had responsibility for the *Daily Herald* (later *The Sun*: see Part Six) and they had to devise a response to the changing times. Unfortunately, they misread them. They bought a thesis wholesale from an academic, Dr Mark Abrams, based on the theory of 'embourgeoisement', namely the claim that people were moving away from their working-class roots. It was the application of this idea to newspapers, which Abrams suggested should also move up-market, that was to prove so misguided. In 1967 Cecil King wrote that Abrams's findings were in accord with everyone's personal experience of a changing society: 'that popular newspapers will follow their present course of becoming increasingly intelligent and less ideological.'[36] King was to be right about the ideology part, anyway.

The capital letters in the third paragraph of Derek Dale's opening lecture to the masses were typical of the paper at the time. Emphasis was the keynote of the *Mirror* of the 1960s; it may have been a substitute for empathy. This was the era of the Shock Issue, when the *Mirror*, at Cudlipp's direction, would give over huge chunks of a day's paper to a sub-topical subject that the *Mirror* wished to tell its readers was IMPORTANT. These started as early as 1955 when THE ROBOT REVOLUTION took over the whole of the front page:

LESS DRUDGERY FOR ALL
IF WE MASTER THE
ROBOTS

There is a word creeping into the language called A-U-T-O-M-A-T-I-O-N . . .

It can mean a four-day-week, bigger pay packets, more leisure, higher living standards, an end to the smoky slums.

OR

It can mean misery. If the march of the robots gets out of hand it can mean unemployment for millions.

Within a month in the spring of 1960 *Mirror* readers were given a Shock Issue on neglected children

THE HIDDEN HORROR

and another entitled

SPRING IN THE SLUMS OF BRITAIN

This was also the year of the classic *Mirror* front page aimed at the Soviet leader Mr Khrushchev:

> **MR K!**
> (If you will pardon an olde English phrase)
>   DON'T BE SO BLOODY RUDE!
> PS Who do you think you are? Stalin?

And by now even W. G. E. Rump of Ruislip, who had objected so vigorously to the same word in a far less prominent position in 1949, had probably given up the battle. This was undeniably great, startling journalism. And readers need to be startled. But the trick of journalism – easier in theory than practice – is to put together a product with which readers feel comfortable without ever being lulled into boredom. I am not sure the Shock Issues helped this process. This may be hindsight. The *Mirror* moved closer to five million sales. And most of the time it allowed its readers to have their fun, like an indulgent nursery teacher, who only very occasionally made the children gather round and listen to something important.

WHICH OF THESE SEVEN IS <u>YOUR</u> DREAMCASTER?

asked Marje Proops, above seven pictures of TV newscasters, knowing that readers were not good at concentrating on anything serious, even on telly. Readers voted for Huw Thomas of ITN ahead of Kenneth Kendall of the BBC. 'You never see Huw with a scruffy shirt,' wrote a mother of five. 'I bet *he* never slops around the house with his braces hanging down.' Not all the fun was wholly tasteful. A pin-up of a busty woman in fishnet tights turned out to be 'television star Joan Savage, 25, in hospital last night with kidney trouble'. In 1962 there was this:

> **IT'S LOVE IN THE SUN**
> *By Amy Landreth*
> From the age of 16 onwards, the Italian man's life is one long game of love.
>   Every woman, except the very old, is subjected to his calculated, up-and-down stare. In crowded buses, things sometimes happen that would bring a slap on the face from girls in other countries . . .

This bog-standard piece on Latin Romeos has probably been repeated, with minor variations, in every tabloid newspaper since the earliest beginnings of mass tourism. On this occasion, however, it was part of a four-page special on Common Market countries, coinciding with the Macmillan Government's application for membership, and appeared under the main heading

BUON GIORNO, EVERYBODY

The whiff of the lecture theatre was starting to get just a little too pervasive.

XVI

Around this period a *Daily Mirror* photographer gatecrashed a posh function and, when challenged, mumbled that he was from 'the paper of the times', hoping only the last two words would be heard and he would be allowed to stay. He was kicked out anyway. And there was growing evidence that the *Mirror* was no longer quite so in touch with the times as it liked to believe. On 17 April 1960 the American singer Eddie Cochran, who had the hit singles 'Summertime Blues' and 'C'mon Everybody', was killed in a car crash. We may presume that the *Mirror* office, like any other, divided into those who were stunned by the news and those who had never heard of Eddie Cochran. It dominated the front page next day, but under the headline

'ROCK' STAR DIES IN CRASH

The quote marks are significant. They meant the *Mirror* was not yet at ease with the word 'rock'. And this unease was not about to diminish. The next few years would bring a revolution in attitudes: popular music was to be the catalyst and teenagers would be the leaders. Here was the paper that prided itself on being the paper of young people – LET YOUTH SHOUT ITS HEAD OFF. Youth did just that in the 1960s, but the *Mirror* never really came to terms with the noise.

In 1962, when the paper began a series entitled 'The Go-Getters', the first subject was exciting Kenneth Sampson, a supermarket chief who was actually forty-one and did not look a day over sixty. The *Mirror* did have a pop music writer, Patrick Doncaster – 'The *Mirror*'s DJ' – though his picture-byline, which in this context was more important than how he really looked, made him appear rather like Dr Beeching, a tubby, moustachioed and deeply unpopular man who was engaged in the task of closing down the nation's railways.

The tone of the *Mirror*'s coverage of what was, in effect, the story of the decade was much like that adopted by the BBC, whose pathetic attempts at covering popular music in the early 1960s are vivid in the memory of anyone who grew up in that era. Agreements with the Musicians' Union meant that only a limited amount of 'needle-time' was allowed, and so the Light Programme would play embarrassing ersatz versions of chart hits sung by in-house artistes. Politically, this was not the kind of thing the *Mirror* was inclined to oppose, and its reporting was very Light Programme.

'Maybe we should start calling it LiverPOP,' burbled Doncaster after Billy J. Kramer and the Dakotas joined the Beatles and Gerry and the Pacemakers in the *Mirror*'s Pop 30 early in 1963. 'Liverpool, Lancashire, that is – gateway to the hit charts.' That October the Beatles made it on to the ITV programme *Sunday Night at the London Palladium*, the very summit of fame in early sixties Britain. 'The Beatles seemed a very cute bunch,' wrote Clifford Davis, the TV critic. 'One shake of their monk-like hair-dos had the girls screaming with the same fervour as the Palladium showered squeaks and yells, a few years back, on Johnnie Ray and Frankie Laine.' Very cute? The *Mirror* was reporting the Beatles as though they had come from another galaxy: these are friendly aliens, the paper seemed to be saying, but aliens nonetheless.

The *Mirror* was no more comfortable with developments in even more mainstream culture. The TV series *Z Cars*, set on Merseyside, land of the clippie-temptresses, depicted policemen who were rougher diamonds than Dixon of Dock Green, the genial old bobby played by Jack Warner who had dominated the screens in the 1950s. Davis's colleague, Richard Sear, was horrified at the details being shown so early in the evening:

> . . . a young girl cowering in a wood with her thighs exposed. Another teenager was dragged along by her attacker in a horrible way. On top of this, and as a sub-plot, a hospital nurse opened the programme by taking her clothes off in a bedroom to introduce a 'Peeping Tom' theme. This smacked of sensationalism.

Hang about. Wasn't the *Mirror* meant to be a sensationalist newspaper? 'Sensationalism does not mean distorting the truth. It means the vivid and dramatic presentation of events so as to give them a forceful impact, etc. etc. . . .' Was everyone forgetting that?

Davis's report on the Beatles was published on 14 October 1963, the very day the *Mirror* began a series of Shock Issues for what it called OLD FOLKS WEEK. This highlighted the plight of people like Jimmy Dunn, 65, who lay dead for six months in his room in Liverpool and was only discovered because some housebreakers smashed his window to rob his gas meter, and John Cummings, 86, who said 'There isn't anyone on earth who cares whether I live or die.'

'The trouble with the Old Folk,' concluded the *Mirror*, 'is that they are not "with-it" people.' In fact, it was to be Old Folks' Week in a way the *Mirror* had not anticipated. After several days of what the paper called

THE GREAT TORY FARCE

and

UNHOLY DEADLOCK

the fourteenth Earl of Home, 60, to be known after he renounced his peerage as Sir Alec Douglas-Home, emerged as the new leader of the Conservative Party and Prime Minister in succession to the ailing Harold Macmillan. Home was a throwback: the last Etonian to become Prime Minister, the last from the House of Lords, the last to be chosen by mysterious processes controlled by the outgoing leader and not by the party or its MPs. Though he had been Foreign Secretary, he was little known to readers of the *Daily Mirror*. It was an open goal for a newspaper like this one.

BRAND X IS THE BOSS
Page One Comment

A man without a face has been smuggled into No. 10 Downing Street and juggled into position as Premier-designate of Great Britain . . . a cipher, a man existing in the imagination of the posher members of the Tory hierarchy and a handful of aristocratic, knickerbockered, pheasant-shooting cronies.

A nice chap and a polite peer.

But Caligula's appointment of his horse as a consul was an act of prudent statesmanship compared with this gesture of sickbed levity by Mr. Macmillan.

And the circulation kept going up: after a decade stuck at just over four and a half million, the figures climbed from the second half of 1963 to peak at 5,282,137 in the second half of 1967. And no wonder. Who would have wanted to be without a newspaper in 1963?

KENNEDY ASSASSINATED

STORM OVER RACHMAN

MAIL TRAIN – THE
BIGGEST ROBBERY EVER

GAITSKELL DIES

PROFUMO QUITS

and, as the *Mirror* was able to put all over the front page on 13 June 1963:

SMELL OF CORRUPTION AND EVIL PRACTICES IN
HIGH PLACES – By a bishop

Politically, the flow was all with the *Mirror*. The country was moving against Sir Alec Douglas-Home and his knickerbockered pheasant-shooting cronies. It was about to vote, in two successive general elections, for the *Mirror's* idea of vigorous youth, represented by Harold Wilson, forty-eight when he became Prime Minister in October 1964. The day before the election there was a special Election Shock Issue:

IS THIS THE PROMISED LAND?

above a picture of 'a backyard . . . six feet by nine feet. Washday in Sampson Street, Liverpool; 1964. No hot water. No bathroom. Just one of 600,000 slums in the Tories' "affluent society".'

LET'S ALL VOTE TODAY AND VOTE FOR OUR FUTURE

shouted the next day's *Mirror*. It remains hard to believe that so many people failed to get the message, and that Labour won by only four seats. The *Mirror's* computer – 'Ringo' – was surprised, anyway: midway through election night it was predicting a majority of forty-eight.

The 600,000 slums were indeed demolished; unfortunately they were replaced by high-rise blocks with urine in the lifts, where people didn't know their neighbours and would recall six-by-nine backyards with undying affection. It was, politically, a time of blighted hopes, of rhetoric outrunning reality, and the *Mirror* rapidly found itself in a far less cosy position than when it had the increasingly easy targets of Eden, Macmillan and Douglas-Home to fire at.

Often, the *Mirror* would find itself acting as a sort of prime ministerial bodyguard against enemies who were the *Mirror's* own readers: 'Futile! Savage! Insane! The go-slow railway footplatemen are putting a noose round their own necks.' At other times it was acting as candid but exasperated friend: 'It is not only the pound that has been devalued,' the paper editorialized after the central plank of Wilson's economic policy collapsed in November 1967, 'it is also the integrity of the Government. And there is so little good will left to squander.'

The Government's incoherence and unpopularity led to dramatic events inside the *Mirror*. In the spring of 1968 Cecil King, as chairman, took over the front page to say

ENOUGH IS ENOUGH

and to demand that Wilson should go and be replaced by a coalition. Privately, he had tried to gather support for something very like a *coup d'état*. Enough was indeed enough, but not in the way King anticipated. He was himself deposed by a boardroom coup and replaced by Cudlipp, in much the same way that King had replaced Bartholomew seventeen years earlier. Politically, the *Mirror* resumed its former uneasy course. Cudlipp now had a huge range of responsibilities. The editor, Lee Howard, was an even more remote figure, hardly ever seen outside his office, though those who knew him well admired both his bravery in wartime and his phenomenal alcoholic capacity. The paper needed firmer leadership to keep abreast of events. Don Short replaced Patrick Doncaster as pop columnist, but he was soon floundering too. In November 1968 he wrote:

> Count me out of this scene. I've just been labelled square by Mick Jagger. But if you can understand, appreciate and come to love the Rolling Stones' new LP [*Beggars Banquet*] . . . then you are enrolled as a member of today's new in-set . . . P.S. Perhaps you can let me know about the sleeve too. I'll be glad if someone can tell me what it's all about.

The *Mirror* had not suddenly become a bad newspaper; very far from it. It did not lose its technical excellence. It did not lose its newsgathering skill. It did not lose its panache. It did not lose its moral bearings. When the Moors Murderers, Ian Brady and Myra Hindley, were tried in 1966, a particularly harrowing tape was played in evidence: 'The *Daily Mirror*, with its readership of 15,000,000 souls, has a special responsibility. We are reporting the case, but not at undue length and not in undue detail.' The *Daily Express* was taking the same line; *The Times* was printing much more, and the *Mirror* was content that it should.

> Barristers and judges read it to assess
> with what skill and prudence their col-
> leagues are conducting their advocacy
> and deliberations ... The *Mirror* rec-
> ommends *The Times*, price sixpence, to
> any readers of the *Mirror* and *Express*
> who feel cheated of salacious detail we
> prefer not to print.

This is not a line the paper might have been free to take at a time of more heightened competition. But no one expected competition.

It was not just the footplatemen who were Futile! Savage! Insane! Fleet Street unions were making normal managerial cost control close to impossible, and it was hard to imagine anyone trying to start a new national newspaper.

The great advantage the *Mirror* had as a pro-Government newspaper was privileged access. But that also meant it was forced into a cul-de-sac. It was tied to Harold Wilson's failures. In the wake of his second, and this time overwhelming, election victory in 1966, Wilson gave the *Mirror* an exclusive interview:

WE'RE ALL IN 'THE ESTABLISHMENT' NOW

*By John Beavan, Political Editor of
the Daily Mirror*

What Wilson and Beavan were trying to say was that under Labour there would be equality of opportunity. Hindsight lends it all a certain irony. Beavan was created Baron Ardwick of Barnes in 1970; Cudlipp was created Baron Cudlipp of Aldingbourne in 1974; Sydney Jacobson became Baron Jacobson of St Albans in 1975, the same year that Ted Castle – another *Mirror* executive and husband of the more famous Barbara – became Baron Castle of Islington.

Influenced by Abrams, the *Mirror* believed that its readers shared its senior editors' upward mobility. Its Mirrorscope feature explained the world in simple terms. It began an up-market gossip column, by Tony Miles, with acute, if lengthy, paragraphs. In 1969, at enormous expense, it began its own colour magazine whose only flaw might have been that it was ahead of its time. But consider the hubris that surrounded its beginnings. The *Mirror* took a full-page advert in *The Observer* that was in effect a report of the magazine's launch meeting, in front of an audience of opinion-formers and potential advertisers at the Festival Hall. The *Mirror*, it quoted Cudlipp as saying, was becoming 'the first quality popular paper. The *Mirror* realises that people have wider interests. Television has educated them – it's not all just cowboys.' The menu at this launch was champagne and bangers. And at the bottom of the page was the paper's most recognizable symbol, Andy Capp. 'Blimey,' he was saying, 'Not a Beer in the Place – I'm off.' Many a true word. Capp himself was still with the paper in 1996, perhaps its last link with the 1950s. But the real-life Capps were indeed off, as soon as an alternative presented itself.

A few years earlier, the *Mirror* had printed one of its most daring pin-ups yet, a picture of Carroll Baker, the then slightly ageing star of *Baby Doll*, wearing what it called 'about as near as you can get to a topless dress without risking arrest', with just enough strategic camouflage over her nipples for newspaper decency *circa* 1964. 'It seems a shame to hide your figure,' she said. 'It does not go on for ever.' The same goes for a brilliant circulation figure – as the *Mirror* was about to discover.

PART FIVE

'Something Appealing, Something Appalling'
The Role of the *News of the World*

Prologue

On 15 October 1978 the following appeared on page 3 of the *News of the World*, then already owned by Rupert Murdoch but not yet turned into a tabloid:

IF YOU GO DOWN TO THE WOODS TODAY, YOU'RE SURE OF A BIG SURPRISE

By Tina Dalgleish

It all began when maths teacher Arnold Lewis decided to organise a naughty party in the woods.

He put an advertisement in a contact magazine, saying: 'Join our Welsh Hills picnic party for remote rural rambles and shining summer scenes. Pub Social meeting first.'

The *News of the World* decided to check out what might be in store for people answering the advert . . .

Five people eventually turned up: Mr Lewis himself, a couple called Alan and Maggie, and the representatives of the *News of the World*. Mr Lewis had been expecting about thirty. Eventually, they made their way to his caravan, leaving a note for any latecomers saying it was 3.8 miles up the road:

. . . As soon as we entered the caravan he offered us all a glass of British sherry.

On the table was a plate of chocolate-covered biscuits.

Pornographic magazines were laid out on another small table. Contact magazines were propped up above the windows, and an open drawer revealed neatly-arranged contraceptives.

We asked Mr Lewis where his wife was. He told us she was not part of his swinging activities. 'She doesn't know I do this sort of thing.'

What did his wife think he was doing at the weekend? 'Motor rallying,' he replied with a smile. But he confided that he wished she were in on it with him . . .

. . . Maggie assured us that emotion did not enter into wife-swapping. 'I wouldn't want to get emotionally involved with anyone else,' she said.

Mr Lewis agreed. 'It's a physical pleasure and not an emotional one,' he said. 'Nothing funny has ever happened to me. All I've met is frightfully nice people.'

Until then, anyway.

As we had made it clear we were not going to join them, we got up to leave. But they did not give up so easily.

> They began to undress and Maggie
> beckoned Arnold to join her and Alan
> on the bed.
>   'Stay and watch us,' they suggested.
> We declined their offer and left them
> to it.

Every detail of the story is poignant: the British sherry, the maths teacher's precision in the 3.8 miles, the wistfulness about his wife. But not nearly as poignant as what happened next. The morning that report was published, Arnold Lewis's body was found in his car. He had killed himself by inhaling carbon monoxide from the exhaust. He was fifty-two. He had not seen the report but Miss Dalgleish had called him two days earlier, in keeping with the paper's practice, to inform him that it was due to appear.

At the inquest, counsel read Mr Lewis's suicide note and asked Miss Dalgleish: 'Does that not upset you?'

'No, not really. I can see that it might upset his wife but it doesn't upset me.'

Looking back in an interview in 1995, the paper's then editor, Bernard Shrimsley, was more tortured:

> He was dead before the newspaper appeared, so it might be that he thought it would be worse than it was, that there were things known to him that were not known to the *News of the World*.
>
> The *pro bono* arguments are there and were well-rehearsed at the time: this magazine could fall into anyone's hands and you don't know what the outcome will be: death, violence, disease. You don't think parents would wish their children to be taught by someone who behaved in this way. If we'd known what the result would be we wouldn't have done it.
>
> 'Did you lose sleep over it?'
>
> 'I still do.'[1]

I

Throughout the nineteenth century British Sunday newspapers thrived and grew stronger with precisely the agenda of 'carnal business' that George Crabbe noted in 1785, and bothered less and less to 'veil with seeming grace the guile within'.

And yet the British Sunday was growing stricter and stricter. Among educated people in Europe it was already proverbial for its dullness. Clergymen and Sunday School teachers had growing success in imposing their standards throughout society: 'They undermined the festal Sunday tradition in accordance with which the lower classes already cleaned and dressed themselves on Sundays. They wanted a day of abstention, whereas the workers kept a holiday, a feast not a fast ... The Sabbatarian standards of the Victorian Sunday were essentially middle-class phenomena.'[2]

In 1899, when Lord Northcliffe began the *Sunday Daily Mail,* and his main daily rivals introduced a *Sunday Daily Telegraph,* they were howled out of business within two months by a furious outcry from the religious lobby.[3] Yet the existing Sunday papers, far more salacious than anything either Northcliffe or the *Telegraph*'s owners would ever have produced, were allowed to carry on with only occasional, and mostly local, hindrance.

There were parliamentary Bills to suppress Sunday papers in 1799 and 1820. But when the Bishop of London, Charles Blomfield, called the Sunday newsrooms whose papers were available 'a sort of moral dram-shop where doses of the most deleterious poison are imbibed by thousands of persons',[4] no one did anything. The Sunday papers became a sort of refuge, a balmy haven of comfortable moral sloppiness away from the cold winds of evangelical fervour blowing outside. It was a classic British compromise, and the papers were tolerated by the authorities in the way that prostitution was tolerated: 'These papers were, so to speak, journalistic *filles de joie* who, by the sacrifice of their own reputation, safeguarded the vestal innocence of the responsible sheets.'[5]

For almost the whole of the past hundred years the blowsiest of those tarts, the *News of the World,* has been the biggest-selling Sunday paper. Daily papers have risen and fallen; journalism has changed beyond recognition; the world itself has changed beyond recognition; the *News of the World*'s role in society, as chronicler of its sexual and criminal underside, has altered less than almost anything else. Indeed, for the past two decades, its sister paper *The Sun* has been Britain's largest-selling daily paper. Thus the attitudes that were once confined to an isolated tributary of journalism have become the surging current of the river itself. It marks a massive change from the days of Northcliffe, Beaverbrook and Cudlipp. And to understand how it happened it is necessary to go back to the source.

II

Some time about the year 1891 *Lloyd's Weekly News* had a huge poster on prominent hoardings. This depicted a yacht race, with a buoy labelled 'The Million Mark'. A splendid craft with the word Lloyd's on the mainsail was rounding the buoy while a string of boats representing other Sunday newspapers straggled far behind. The *News of the World* was not even in the picture. It was beyond the horizon: listing heavily, presumed more-or-less sunk.

The paper which had been awaited so avidly when it arrived at the station at Neath, and hundreds of similar places, with news of the Crimean War, subsequently fell on terrible times. In 1855 the *News of the World*'s founder, John Browne Bell, died, and his son J. W. Bell – apparently through sheer diffidence – could not bring himself to follow his rivals and cut the price to a penny when stamp duty was abolished. He believed he held the paper in trust for his brothers and did not dare take a calculated business risk. And so, over the next twenty-five years, the audience dwindled away, and by the time his own sons, the fourth generation of newspaper Bells, took control in 1880 and finally did reduce the price, sales were down to about 30,000, far behind the opposition.

The formula, however, had not changed a jot:

SHOCKING PARRICIDE IN ILKESTON

ATROCIOUS CHILD MURDER IN WORCESTERSHIRE

HORRIBLE TRAGEDY NEAR UXBRIDGE

EXTRAORDINARY OUTRAGE ON A YOUNG WOMAN

Louisa Hearne, a housemaid to a lady in Shacklewell stated: 'I was cleaning the doorsteps, when the prisoner, whom I never saw before, came suddenly behind me, and tossed my clothes completely over my head.' Constable Aylyn asked him why he did it and he said 'Because I like.' A month's hard labour.

That was in 1861. The paper was also fascinated, as it always has been, with things that were not quite as they seemed:

THE WOMAN IN MAN'S CLOTHING

Mary Newell, a servant wearing her master's clothes, with her hair cropped short and smoking cigars, courted a young woman as her sweetheart . . . It was not madness nor felony, but a case of diseased mind. Eighteen months.

A MAN IN WOMAN'S CLOTHING

Richard King, 18, was charged with disorderly conduct, and causing a mob to assemble in Chalton Street, Euston Road . . . The defendant was fully dressed in woman's clothes, with chignon. He said it was for a lark to amuse his sisters. He had been at sea for five years and taken a drop too much. Five shillings fine.

The paper always had its own priorities. The arrest of Charles Dickens, 30, 'of respectable appearance', who was sentenced to one month's imprisonment in 1881 as a rogue and vagabond, was given about 450 words; the death of another, to most people rather more famous, Charles Dickens, eleven years earlier, got forty-five words.

The death of John Owen, alias Jones, better known as the Denham Murderer, who killed seven members of the same family, was infinitely more interesting. Public executions had just been abolished, but reporters were still allowed into the jail to observe the closing moments:

He ate his breakfast heartily, and spent the remainder of the morning in joking. At three minutes to eight the bell began to toll, and he was brought from the cell by two warders . . . When the culprit came in sight of the gallows it seemed to absorb his whole curiosity, and after surveying it for a moment he attempted to go up two steps at a time, but at the request of the warders he walked up in a more orderly manner. Calcraft [the hangman] then placed him on the drop, put the rope round his neck and the white cap over his face. The culprit asked to be allowed to make a statement . . . Calcraft lifted the cap above his mouth. The culprit then said: 'My friends, I am going to die for the murder of Charles — what's his name? I forget. Oh! Charles Marshall; but I am innocent.' He then turned round again, and put his feet close together to be pinioned. Calcraft at once strapped them, immediately walked off, and drew the bolt . . .

Not everything was quite so melancholy. On page 1 there was always a selection of jokes from *Punch*:

> THE DEAR DEPARTED – Venison.
>
> STOCK EXCHANGE SENTIMENT –
> No Bonds of Affection so true, so dear,
> so lasting as Treasury Bonds!
>
> A COOL RECEPTION – Being pelted
> with snowballs.

On second thoughts, the details of the execution were perhaps a little less gruesome than the jokes. By the 1880s the paper also carried a 'Correspondence' column, in which the paper gave answers to its readers, without giving any clue as to the nature of the question. This gives rise to fascinating speculation on the possibilities:

> T.R.D.: Not under 16 years of age.
>
> A CONSTANT READER: An exclamation denoting surprise or disapprobation, with some degree of contempt.
>
> A THIRTEEN YEARS' SUBSCRIBER: You must mean *Sexangle*, which is a figure having six angles.

As opposed to a sex angle, which is what, even in those days, the *News of the World* searched for tirelessly.

Since 1857 divorce had been possible in the courts without requiring a special Act of Parliament, and there the veneer of Victorian decorum would be stripped ruthlessly away day after day for the delight of Sunday paper readers. One week there was the master of the *Lusitania*, Captain Powell, denying that anything wrong had occurred between him and a Mrs Furrell; he said he had done no more for her than he would for any lady passenger on board his ship. Another week there was Francis William Robins, formerly a lieutenant, denying that he had ever taken liberties with a servant. As was usual, the evidence was reported in indirect speech, in a sort of shorthand, as though the paper was conscious that its readers, like the judge, had heard this sort of thing a great number of times before:

> He never recollected calling his wife an idiot. He never threw cold water over her when she was in bed. He denied that he ever pinched his wife or dragged her by the hair. He was never guilty of cruelty towards her. If he got into the

> bed of Mlle. Jumeau it was without his
> knowledge. He never took up the poker
> to his wife in Nice. There were no pokers
> on the Continent . . .

News of the World readers would, I think, have known what to make of a man who knew whether or not there were pokers on the Continent, but not whose bed he was getting into. They would also have had their opinion on the case of *Dunn v. Dunn and Wall,* in February 1888, in which Richard Dunn, a bookmaker, of Haverstock Hill, was alleging adultery between his wife and a Mr Harry Wall:

> Ann Lavender, housemaid, said she received instructions not to go into the room when Mr Wall was there. But she went into the dining room and saw Mrs Dunn and young Mr Wall lying on the couch and they had blankets round them. How was Mrs Dunn dressed? She had her night-dress on and her dressing gown over it. How was Mr Wall dressed? He was partly dressed. Had he gone to bed with his 'tail-coat' on? He had no coat on. She then took some soda and milk to her bedroom and saw Mr Wall there. How did you see this? I suspected it, and looked through the keyhole . . .

The problem for the *News of the World* was that its rivals were doing this sort of thing just as well, and more cheaply. *Lloyd's Weekly News,* for instance, was far more enterprising. In 1885 when W. T. Stead of the *Pall Mall Gazette* went to jail for abducting a girl to prove the existence of the white slave trade, *Lloyd's* found the girl and bought her story. In 1885, when John Lee of Babbacombe – 'The Man They Couldn't Hang' – had to be released because the gallows failed to work three times running, he was besieged by reporters with offers for his story and promises of money; *Lloyd's* won, because its reporter produced not a promise but a bag of 300 gold sovereigns. Even the most dramatic running story of 1888:

ANOTHER BRUTAL MURDER IN THE EAST END.

HORRIBLE DISCOVERY.

A WOMAN DISEMBOWELLED.

COMPLETE PANIC IN THE DISTRICT.

failed to make much difference. Indeed, *The People,* later to become the *News of the World*'s most potent rival, but then a new and struggling Conservative Party paper, achieved its greatest early triumph when its proprietor, W. T. Madge, had a Saturday night tip-off about one of the Jack the Ripper murders, took a cab to the East End at once and continued printing all day with his exclusive report. The *News of the World* did have a brief rise in circulation in 1881 when Pegasus, the racing tipster, successfully gave Foxhall for both legs of the Autumn Double, the Cambridgeshire and the Cesarewitch. But by 1891 the Bells were in terminal trouble.

They sold out to Lascelles Carr, proprietor of the *Western Mail*, a Tory paper that was highly successful in non-Tory Wales. Carr was also the inventor of a gun that did not shoot straight, based on the principle that the human arm was crooked, a useful intellectual principle on which to base the management of the *News of the World*. The Carr family would be the owners for the next eighty years; and Lascelles Carr immediately installed his nephew, Emsley Carr, as editor, a job he would hold for the next fifty of them. He then brought in his lawyer, George Riddell, who gradually took over effective control of the organization. The Carrs at once beefed up the whole operation. The *News of the World*, however, remained the *News of the World*.

III

When Emsley Carr first walked into the paper's decrepit offices in Whitefriars he was shocked by what he saw on his desk: piles of lurid copy sent in by freelance journalists – who knew which stories to submit to the daily papers and which to hold back for Sunday – from all round the country. 'It seemed', he wrote many years later, 'as though the whole world had vomited murders and suicides on one particular day.'[6]

But he did not change the system; the journalistic principles, if that is the word, of the *News of the World* did not change. Instead the paper was modernized, 'not without some loss of sedateness', in the splendid phrase of one contemporary critic.[7] Its design was revamped. It had a banner that was very often a slogan rather than a headline across the front page:

NO OTHER NEWSPAPER GIVES SO MUCH
CRICKET AND SPORT.

and a cartoon and news below that. Indeed, its appearance was not dissimilar to the popular look that Northcliffe tried and specifically rejected for the *Daily Mail* when he opted for something that did look sedate.

Meanwhile, Riddell reorganized the business. There was a huge market out there to be won. And he won it, giving the paper a sense of purpose and enterprise which it has never lost, though the yachts that were once so far ahead – *Lloyd's, Reynolds's,* the *Sunday Referee,* the *Weekly Dispatch,* the

Sunday Chronicle – have long since rusted at the bottom of the ocean. In 1850 only one Briton in twenty bought a Sunday paper, even if many more read it, or had it read to them, second-, third- or eighteenth-hand. By 1900 the figure was to be one in five, thanks to a generation that was more literate and did have at least the odd couple of ha'pennies, if not much more than that, to rub together and buy one newspaper a week.

Riddell is a forgotten figure now. But not only did he play golf with Lloyd George – especially at Walton Heath, the course the *News of the World* came to own; he even bought him a house. He became a knight and then a peer, as Lloyd George's chums tended to do, and he acted as press liaison officer at a succession of peace conferences after the First World War. His published diaries for 1908 to 1914 are full of high-level hobnobbing and passing political intrigues.[8] In 238 pages there is only one reference to the *News of the World*; otherwise there is no clue that the writer was mixing with the great figures of the day not because of his own merits, but because he happened to be chairman of a grubby but by then huge-selling newspaper. Riddell certainly had the lunacies of a traditional newspaper proprietor: he was obsessed with germs; he swore vigorously in any company; he was thought to slip away for secret elocution lessons to get rid of his Cockney accent; and he wandered round the office in a shabby tweed suit at a time when everyone else in Fleet Street was wearing frock coat and top hat.

But most observers gave him the credit for the *News of the World*'s revival. He devoted as much attention to detail as the *News of the World*'s court reporters did, and his Saturday nights were spent not at fashionable dinner-parties but wandering around London termini handing out half-crowns to porters whose job it was to get the newspaper parcels on to the trains. He reorganized the paper's entire distribution system, getting round the opposition of the trade and the Sunday Observance lobby by hiring agents in every village in the country, a more dynamic variant of the ploy pursued by John Browne Bell when the paper started. Riddell and Carr would bring out editions as early as Thursday or as late as Sunday night if the news warranted it.

The editorial staff at first consisted only of Carr and his assistant, R. Power Berrey, known as Bob, a charming Irishman who would bribe the Scotland Yard duty inspector every Saturday with a bottle of whisky. For decades afterwards, the paper had a special relationship with the police.

The formula worked. The court cases remained, but they were now often illustrated by jaunty little line-drawings (usually by Ned Smythe) of the participants – men with droopy moustaches, women with absurd hats, most of them with raging libidos – and were more tautly and often tartly written; one suspects Carr was a good enough editor not to be distracted by the fact that the penny-a-line freelances sent in their copy closely spaced to discourage anyone from cutting and rewriting it. Sometimes the judges would be desperate to get themselves in the paper:

> Counsel: The courtship went on for two
> years and during that time the defendant
> seemed to have treated her pretty hand-
> somely. He took her to Blackpool, Llan-
> dudno and the Isle of Man.
>
> His Honour: I have always understood
> those were fatal places.

This was a breach of promise case. These went on all the time in the 1890s and their splendid idiocies filled the paper.

A FICKLE SWAIN AND HIS JILTED SWEETHEART.

HE WAS SHY AND RESERVED BUT A JILT.

and, best of all:

A HYPOCRITICAL HUMBUG.

This case, from 1896, concerned a preacher from Shropshire: 'He talked religion to her and took her to religious meetings and ultimately he seduced her.' This was almost as good as 'ANOTHER Roman Catholic priest'. In a hundred years the *News of the World* has never lost its taste for exposing mucky ministers.

And there were still the divorce courts. Many of these would be given in brief in a column entitled something like CUPID'S FAILURES or MATRIMONIAL MISERY. Below this would be sub-headings like:

ELOPED WITH A FRIEND.

A PUBLICAN'S MISCONDUCT.

SEEN THROUGH A KEYHOLE.

THE COMMANDER'S EXCUSE.

(The excuse was that sailors were not, the commander supposed, the best judges of what constitutes a prudent marriage.)

Upper-class divorces, of course, got far more space. For instance, there was the case of the Earl and the Countess of Cowley in 1897, in which the Earl confessed under cross-examination to 'having taken a woman of a certain class to a West End hotel . . . misconduct in a railway carriage . . . frequent visits to a house in Warwick Street' and the following week, for good measure, 'adultery with a woman at Brighton'. How could he have forgotten Brighton? If there were no peers involved, there were always the vicars, such as the Revd. A. B. Winnifrith, curate of Dalwood, Devon, sued as co-respondent by the village miller, Mr Hern.

> Mr Hern, in his evidence, said his wife was fond of music, and met Mr Winnifrith at parish concerts. He was surprised when he saw the curate with his arm round her waist and her head resting on his breast, but still 'he didn't think there was any harm in it.' His wife told him Mr Winnifrith had the earache or toothache or something of the sort, and had no one to look after him.

Mr Winnifrith's charwoman then gave evidence.

> Mrs Mary Mears, residing at Dalwood, said she had never seen actual impropriety, but had seen Mr Winnifrith kiss Mrs Hern many times and Mrs Hern kiss him. She had seen them sitting down very comfortably in the armchair together, and on the sofa, and also on the hearthrug. She had also seen Mr Winnifrith unlace Mrs Hern's boots and put her slippers on. Did you speak to him about it? Yes; we had many words about it. I told him that if I was in Mr Hern's place I would put him in the millstream and I would horsewhip her and tie her up.

Decree nisi with costs that time; custody of the children to Mr Hern and quite right too, everyone would have thought.

The routine court reports were now often informal, to the point of being rather jolly.

> 'Oh, it was such fun!' Frederick Hall, 21, a box-cutter, laughed ever so when he thought about the practical joke he was going to play on the Metropolitan Fire Brigade . . . It is so funny to go and break the glass on a fire alarm and it is still funnier to run away when you've done it, and grin round a safe corner . . . Frederick Hall broke the glass all right, but his joke broke at the same time, and when the engine did arrive the firemen found the joker in the safe custody of Police Constable Campling. Five pounds or one month.

> Walter John Collett is a boy calculated to bring grey hairs in sorrow to the grave . . . last week he was up at Bow Street charged with stealing a cabman's whip, and now he has added to his crimes by embezzling £2 from Messrs Pearce and Plenty, who in a moment of misplaced confidence engaged him as cash boy – Mr Vaughan [the magistrate] has transferred the lad to the ministrations of the prison chaplain, who will try his best for three months to come.

Riddell always liked to claim, if upbraided about the quality of his news-paper by one of his smart friends, that it was actually a very moral paper, because it gave the punishment as well as the crime; ever since, this has been echoed by its defenders, which has usually meant people on the payroll. But the *News of the World* of the 1890s was a very fine paper indeed. All the news of the week, indeed the news of the world, was in it somewhere. For instance, the death of Gladstone – on a Thursday – filled two inside pages; all the important deaths of the week would be conscientiously listed, sometimes under headings like

THE REAPER BUSY.

WELL-KNOWN MEN REMOVED FROM OUR MIDST.

The reporting was not always distinguished, and some of the war coverage in 1898, as interpreted by deskbound warriors, established a tradition for *The Sun* to live up to almost a century later:

GORDON AVENGED

GREAT BATTLE IN THE
SOUDAN

Twice again have the Dervishes been
beaten, and this time their loss has been
heavier than ever. It was only after a deal
of coaxing that Mahmoud's men could
be got into the open, and when this was
effected on Tuesday, Fuzzy-wuzzy's
courage oozed out of his finger-tips.

But, during the Spanish–American War that same year, the paper promised a special pink Sunday edition if there was any news, and its remarks on the behaviour of the American press at the time were nicely sardonic: 'The *New York Herald* has been printing daily articles dated on board the flagship *New York* . . . this, in view of the fact that Admiral Sampson compelled all newspaper correspondents to leave the fleet a week ago, seemed somewhat startling.' The paper got its own exclusives, too: it brought out a special edition with its on-the-spot coverage of the murder in December 1897 of the star actor William Terriss at the stage door of the Adelphi. Someone who read only the *News of the World* might end up with a rather strange sense of priorities, but they would not miss anything important. It was easy to believe, as Berrey claimed, that grizzled hunters in the Far West of Canada could reach a remote hut at nightfall and find an old copy neatly folded under a stone so that they could read of home by candlelight and then save it for the next passer-by.[9]

Riddell had all Northcliffe's flair for stunts: treasure hunts, football prediction games and a Popular Barmaids Competition, which led the paper to be called the Barmaids' Bible. But he also had some interesting sidelines. He was known as a particularly ruthless landlord and property developer ('I can't afford mercy,' he was quoted as saying), and one of his specialities was buying and selling music-hall sites. In 1898 the *News of the World* began publishing a music-hall song every week, so readers could play them at home or down their local. It was a tradition that lasted, changing with the years, until 1942, long after the halls had been superseded by radio and the cinema. A piano was installed in the office so that artists like Marie Lloyd and George Robey could come in and try their new numbers.[10] The first was 'Our Lodger's Such a Nice Young Man', as sung by Vesta Victoria, a ditty whose story-line

> He made himself at home before he's been here a day
> He kissed mamma and all of us, 'cos papa was away . . .

was entirely in line with the rest of the *News of the World*'s contents. It was rapidly followed by such numbers as George D'Albert's 'The Curate':

> First he appeared as a curate – such a very, very good young man.
> And then disappeared with a large amount of cash – this very, very good
>   young man.
> Next he appeared with a full-grown beard, and some officers of law were
>   on his track –
> So now he's appearing at a well-known jail,
> With some pretty little arrows on his back.

and Ellaline Terriss's 'I Love You, My Love, I Do':

> Now believe me what I say is true;
> Don't you think I'm getting silly,
> When I say you is my lily
> 'Caze I love yer, my love, I do.

which is probably roughly what Mr John George Cuthbertson, retired licensed victualler of Wanstead, whose case was reported the day those words appeared – 15 May 1898 – told Miss Alice Evans when he took her to the bar at the Hotel Cecil. Later, however, Mr Cuthbertson decided that Miss Evans was not a suitable wife for him. Miss Evans told the court that Mr

Cuthbertson was no gentleman, but only a cad. £1,000 damages for breach of promise. Next case.

IV

And the formula was extraordinarily successful. The *News of the World* gained on the yachts in the *Lloyd's* adverts as if it were a speedboat.

Its methods were apparently unaffected by the revolution Northcliffe had wrought in daily journalism after 1896. After the closure of the *Sunday Daily Mail*, Northcliffe did then get into the game by buying the *Weekly Dispatch*. But he did not understand that the rules on Sunday were different. Kennedy Jones told him what had to be done:

> They lie in bed and read till the public-houses open. They want their Sunday paper to give them the same kind of titillation that well-to-do people get from novels about divorce, murder, seduction, forgery. Fill it with crime, not excluding the unmentionable sort, and it will sell like hot cakes.
>
> But Alf [i.e. Northcliffe] says No; he will not adopt such means. Sport, he agrees, shall bulk largely . . . but salaciousness he will not have. He will persuade the manual workers to like other features that he will introduce.[11]

Of course, he failed. The *Sunday Dispatch* (as it became) is remembered only for the huge leap in circulation it took when it serialized the risqué novel *Forever Amber* after the Second World War; and it lasted little more than a decade after that.

The Boer War took up a lot of space in the *News of the World*, but not enough to prevent three pages out of twelve in March 1901 being devoted to the trial of Herbert John Bennett, who murdered his wife on the beach at Yarmouth. The paper's correspondents would peruse the court lists for the weeks ahead and analyse them like connoisseurs. When the July Sessions opened at the Old Bailey in 1898 it summarized the list of prospective cases like the football results: housebreaking two; libel two; fraudulent bankruptcy one; throwing corrosive fluid one; bigamy three; forging bank notes one; uttering counterfeit coin six; embezzlement three; forgery five; letter-stealing two; murder two; throwing missiles on the railway one; burglary six; robbery with violence eighteen. There was a lot of that about even then, and the court reporters began editorializing:

LONDON ROUGHS.

MORE OF THEM SENT TO HARD LABOUR.

'THE REIGN OF TERROR' IN SOUTH LONDON.

. . . It is said that the Southwark and Lambeth magistrates have determined, by inflicting heavy sentences, to put down the ruffianism which exists in that part of South London, but the sentences on some of the 'Hooligans' convicted of violence this week do not confirm that. Several of the sentences this week were altogether inadequate, and the magistrates should alter this state of affairs at once. Something with 'boiling oil in it' is what the 'Hooligans' want . . .

This was and is not a conventional way of writing court reports, but the nature of the *News of the World*'s subject-matter meant that it had to be an accurate newspaper. All the paper needed was humanity to behave in its customary argumentative fashion, and it would set down the facts. Should people show any signs of living in harmony, as they briefly did in June 1901, it was in trouble:

There is a singular absence of vitality in the breach of promise actions set down for hearing this term. Out of a total of nine or ten, four have already been withdrawn, settled or undefended. This week the sixth on the list was opened with a fair promise of lasting a few hours, but the plaintiff's counsel had barely reached the interesting part of the story when an agreement was suddenly come to . . .

But at other times the paper would be in a state of almost childlike excitement about such matters. When it received the official list for the Hilary Sittings of the Divorce Court in 1906 it salivated as if reporting the FA Cup draw:

In the defended list is the petition of Albert Edward Smith, for restitution of conjugal rights. This case will revive an interesting Midland romance — a story of secret love making, between a lady belonging to a well-known and wealthy Leicester family, and her brother's coachman, which culmi- nated in a runaway marriage at Bolton, the 'spiriting away' of the bride by her relatives two days after the wedding, and a sensational law suit at Leicester Assizes . . . The facts disclosed at the trial were of a MOST ROMANTIC CHARACTER.

The paper even made stars of some of the judges. Five years after her song began the paper's music-hall tradition, Vesta Victoria's own private life was bared in the paper. In her case, it was not a lodger, but her husband and a young lady at Westcliff-on-Sea. 'It may be my ignorance, but what do you do?' Mr Justice Buckmill, almost certainly hamming it up something rotten, asked Miss Victoria. 'I sing and dance, my Lord,' replied one of the most famous women in the country. Then there was Mr Justice McCardie, the bachelor judge, who virtually turned into a member of the *News of the World* repertory company, having made his debut when he was cross-examining a witness in a dispute between rival corset-makers:

> The Lord Chief Justice suggested that the questions were irrelevant as counsel must, he supposed, know all about it — Mr McCardie remarked that he was not married, a confession which caused roars of laughter, in which his lordship joined.

Occasionally, the paper did venture a political opinion, usually of what might be called a right-wing nature: it opposed the introduction of old age pensions in 1908 on the grounds that they were unfair to the thrifty. But one senses — and this has never changed — that the politics was there only for form's sake: it did not look as though it was meant to be read. Such matters were never allowed to interfere with the main business of the paper, which was sometimes only tangential to conventional journalism. The most important development of the Edwardian era was probably the introduction of what came to be known as the Golden Column:

UNCLAIMED MONEY.

THIS COLUMN MAY BRING YOU A FORTUNE.

> Among numerous persons wanted for 'SOMETHING TO THEIR ADVANTAGE' are Samuel and Francis Sneade, who left for America fifty years ago; John Viccars, who was a soldier in 1840; William Pridham, of Exeter in 1831; Amanda S. Jenkins, last heard of as a pianist at a hotel in Yorkshire; and Henry Shaw, who wore a shade over one eye.

The chances of William Pridham turning up to claim his money after seventy-five years must have been pretty remote. But the column had the appeal of the football pools or the National Lottery, because you never knew, did you, and who knows whatever became of that long-lost uncle. Solicitors regularly used the column to sort out probate matters, and it did score hundreds of hits — possibly even with hunters in the Far West of Canada, reading an old copy of the paper in a hut by candlelight.

Year by year the circulation rose. In 1903 it was claiming rather modestly:

THERE ARE ONLY THREE NEWSPAPERS IN THE UNITED
KINGDOM WITH AS <u>LARGE</u> A CIRCULATION AS
THE 'NEWS OF THE WORLD'.

In 1912 its circulation was over two million; in 1918 2,750,000 and then
three million:

LARGEST CIRCULATION IN THE WORLD.

King Edward VII died, the *Titanic* sank, the Empire marched to bloody
war. These events were recorded dutifully, if necessary in great detail. But
they were somehow secondary. Reading old copies of the *News of the World*
there is no sense of the years hurrying by, as there is reading old copies of
the *Daily Mail*, say. Daily papers thrive on the new and the startling. The
News of the World thrived on the things that had existed since Adam, but
could startle nonetheless. The paper's lifeblood was not the obviously
extraordinary but what lurked behind the very ordinary. It did not open a
window on the world so much as twitch back the lace curtains on its
homes and bedrooms. Nothing was beneath its notice. In 1906 the Lord
Chief Justice upheld an award of £85 to Elizabeth Smellie, an entertainer
who got phlebitis because the theatre laundry failed to do its job properly.
The headline was:

A CHORUS GIRL'S TIGHTS:
JUDGES SAY THEY MUST BE
WELL-AIRED.

And who could disagree with that?

V

There was something else: pigeons. If the *News of the World* and pigeon
racing conjure up similar images, it is no accident. The 'Pigeon Notes' were
a feature long before the First World War, and deep within the grey, densely
packed column serious allegations sometimes lurked – 'Some ugly rumours
are rife relative to certain races in the Northern district.'
   After war broke out the authorities decided to recruit thousands of pigeons.
And who better to provide them? The *News of the World* pigeon editor, A. H.

Osman, was made head of the Pigeon Service, with the rank of colonel. And from where he sat, anyway, the war was a triumph, as he reported on 17 November 1918, the Sunday after Armistice Day:

THE PIGEON WORLD.

How bleak was the outlook for us pigeon men at the commencement of the war. How bright it is now. At first our pigeons were treated as spies, and we got orders to intern them. Then the railways refused to carry them, and the police visited our lofts . . . Only a short time after it was found our men on the coasts could render splendid work with the birds and they did it . . . Needless to say the *News of the World* helped splendidly . . .

VI

DOPE AFTER BALL.

REVELATIONS AT INQUEST ON ACTRESS.

TRAFFIC IN COCAINE.

There has rarely been such drama as that which the death of Billie Carleton has brought to light. It is a lurid drama of a gay life, a feverish search for excitement, a descent from fun to debauchery, and a dismal death.

Billie, a beautiful, greatly-admired girl of 22, on the highway to a brilliant career, died from cocaine poisoning a few hours after she had returned from the famous Victory Ball at the Albert Hall . . .

The Coroner's inquiry has revealed a state of things almost unbelievable. Young women and men have confessed to being drug-takers — the drugs indulged in being cocaine (chiefly) and heroin . . . In the West End of London in the quiet seclusion of luxury flats, the 'most disgusting orgies' take place. Men and women, the former in pyjamas, the latter in chiffon nightdresses, recline in a circle of soft cushions, and pass from hand to hand and mouth to mouth the opium pipe . . .

Mrs Lo Ping You, Scottish wife of a Chinaman of Limehouse Causeway, described as 'high priestess of these unholy rites' was jailed for five years.

Now, when might this have been? Last week? Last year? This kind of story is an enduring *News of the World* classic. The only clues are in the tiny details: the opium pipe, the pyjamas and chiffon nightdresses as emblems of depravity, the Limehouse Chinaman, an old-fashioned sort of villain, and –

the real giveaway – the Victory Ball. It appeared in the paper on 5 January 1919, less than two months after the end of the First World War.

There had been a headline reading:

ORGIES OF WILD WOMEN.

in March 1912 but this, disappointingly, was merely a reference to the latest Suffragist outrages. Reports of the more exciting sort of orgy seem to have been a post-war development. Since the *News of the World*, alone among the papers, took its tone primarily from what happened in the courts, one may take this to be a genuine reflection of a change in society rather than just a change in journalistic fashion. Those members of the younger generation who had somehow survived the war were in a mood that could range from forced jollity to nihilism.

The apparently rock-like society of Britain had been shaken loose by the war, and the *News of the World*, which had specialized in writing about whatever crawled beneath the placid surface, now found itself almost spoiled for choice. The price was increased – to a penny ha'penny, just as the old ha'penny dailies were going up to the *News of the World*'s old price of a penny. But the headlines were blacker; it was easier to use photographs, which mostly seemed to be of women in cloche hats who had done something wicked; and the raw material was super-abundant. When the Divorce Court correspondent got the list for the new session in March 1919, he was audibly rubbing his hands with excitement:

NEW DIVORCE LIST.

STAGE AND SOCIETY IN
SUITS TO BE HEARD.

There is a never-ending stream of matrimonial troubles ahead . . .

Actually, he was wrong – in the sense he meant. After seven years, the stream was to dry up for ever. As the divorce rate rose, too many influential members of society found it was their troubles which were being dragged through the newspapers, and they were getting tired of it. On 15 December 1926 the Judicial Proceedings (Regulation of Reports) Act received the Royal Assent. This forbade the reporting of anything but the barest details of divorce cases. Moreover, 'indecent medical, surgical and physiological details calculated to injure public morals' were specifically barred.

The Bill had passed through both Houses with little dissent. Sir Evelyn Cecil (Cons., Aston) said the papers that printed these cases went to India, where they did great harm.[12] Lord Burnham, the proprietor of the *Daily Telegraph*, said the existing situation was unjust because people of means went to the Divorce Court whereas the poor were more likely merely to get separation orders from the magistrates' courts where the case would not be reported. This, he said, gave 'an oblique view, I believe, of the standard of sexual morality that prevails among the well-to-do people of this country'.[13] It's the same the 'ole world over, it's the rich wot gets the blame.

It was thought at the time this might be the end of the *News of the World*. But it was reported that among those who calmly voted for the Bill in the House of Lords was the paper's chairman, Lord Riddell. The water from society's dirty washing was still going to find its way into the public domain; it merely had to find new channels.

Between 1919 and 1926, however, the stream was in full, glorious spate, from the post-war case of *Everitt* v. *Everitt* –

> ... A nurse went into the boudoir without knocking and found Dr Wheatley, the co-respondent, and Mrs Everitt sitting opposite on a stool in front of the fire. Mrs Everitt was in her combinations and dressing gown ...

– to the case in 1926 headlined:

MR FRUITY'S LETTERS

Modern slang plentifully besprinkled the cross-suit for divorce between a young couple, whose marriage was only six years ago. The judge, Mr Justice Hill, frankly puzzled, had to ask for explanations for some words, remarking: 'I am afraid we older people find it difficult to keep pace with the latest slang.' He was informed that 'blotto' meant getting drunk, 'a pretty misty night' would stand for a cheery evening and 'pessers' signified a little pessimistic ... The parties in the case called each other by nicknames, the wife being known as The Rat and the husband as Mr Fruity.

For divorce reporters, it was an Indian summer; in another sphere of the newspaper's operations, the most golden of all harvests was about to be reaped. Looking back from 1946, Orwell wrote his most famous essay:

It is Sunday afternoon, preferably before the war. The wife is already asleep in the armchair, and the children have been sent out for a nice long walk. You put your feet up on the sofa, settle your spectacles on your nose and open the *News of the World*. Roast beef and Yorkshire, or roast pork and apple sauce, followed up by suet pudding and driven home, as it were, by a cup of mahogany-brown tea, have put you in just the right mood. Your pipe is drawing sweetly, the sofa cushions are soft underneath you, the fire is well alight, the air is warm and stagnant. In these blissful circumstances, what is it that you want to read about?

Naturally, about a murder.[14]

He might have been thinking back nostalgically to 1922, the year when Armstrong the Hay-on-Wye solicitor was hanged for poisoning his wife and attempting to poison his business rival. It remains the classic British murder for the mousiness of the villain, the respectability of the ambience and, of course, the lingering possibility that he might have been innocent all along.

Armstrong was not even in the news on 22 October, the day that produced what may have been the all-time classic edition of the *News of the World*. Everything else was there, including the committal hearing for the Thompson and Bywaters case, another of the great British murders.

RECTOR'S LOVE SECRET.

SECRETS OF A GRAVE.

WHITE SLAVE CHARGE.

TEA-SHOP SUICIDE.

MOTHER OF 14 ADMITS BIGAMY.

ACTOR DEPRIVED OF HIS FREEDOM.

This last did not mean he went to jail; it meant he had his decree nisi rescinded, because the King's Proctor, the official empowered to intervene in these matters, discovered he had had secret love affairs of his own.

And there was, somehow, still room for the news that Liverpool remained at the top of the First Division, and that Lloyd George had been deposed as Prime Minister. Despite Riddell's friendship with him, the leader column discussed the matter in the bland terms normally associated with local newspapers and specifically designed not to upset readers. 'The times demand sure insight and unfaltering courage in treading the path dictated by necessity.' Well, when on earth don't they?

Most *News of the World* readers, we may safely assume, were not spending their time at luxury cocaine parties or patronizing Violet Fawdon, the woman known to police in Piccadilly as The Dope Fiend Queen. Before the war the paper had specialized in printing pictures of large family groups; in June 1919 the wife of Reginald Bezzant, the circulation manager, dreamed up the idea of singling out mothers with ten or more children – 'What of the dear, patient soul, whose daily round and common task is a labour of unselfish love for the large family of children growing up around her? For her, no decorations and high orders; yet, in spite of all, a queen in a citadel of loving subjects.' They were invited to apply for blue-and-white willow pattern trays. There were 33,000 applications in the first month. It is not known whether the bigamous mother of fourteen was among them. The search unearthed Mrs Mary Jonas of Chester, who had thirty-three children – mostly twins – and a woman in Naples was reported to have sixty-two. No wonder newspaper circulations were rising.

This, the *News of the World* was continually saying, is deep down a family newspaper. For those whose sexual activities were of a, shall we say, less regular and more venturesome nature, it had its own code. The seventeen-year-old girl allegedly sold into prostitution, aka the white slave trade ('She ought to go very well on the 'Dilly,' said her abductor) had never had sex with anyone. But she did admit being intimate. People were molested, never raped. And they had their clothing disarranged. This quaint form of linguistics was to last long after the Second World War. It was all part of the elaborate pretence that the *News of the World* was not really a mucky newspaper. It was, as the enamel plates stuck on newsagents' walls all over Britain proclaimed, the Good Old News of the World, with the £1,000 Must-be-Won Good Old Football Competition, £1,000 Crossword Competition and the Frock Competition. In this readers had to pick the best six out of a dozen Selfridges frocks, bathing costumes or not particularly negligible negligés, in which the models all looked about as erotic as they might in the old Bile Beans adverts. There was A. C. MacLaren, the former England captain, writing on cricket. There would be the life story of perhaps Edgar Wallace or the actor Seymour Hicks. There was still a song every week, and a serial.

Meantime, the judges and police regarded it as very close to being their trade paper. The transactions between the police and reporters would take place in private, but the more demonstrative judges clearly acted up to get their names in print. Chief among these was the bachelor judge, Mr Justice McCardie. Week after week he would come out with something pithy after hearing a breach of promise case. On 21 March 1926 he said Mr Nathan Sellar of Shadwell, by breaking off his engagement with Miss Cissie Cohen, had done her a favour by saving both of them from an unhappy marriage. The following week, in a similar case, he compared the jury's task 'to that of the assessor in an Eastern slave market'. In April he listed the qualities required to secure married bliss: 'the spirit of forgiveness, the spirit of kindness, the spirit of compromise and the spirit of patience'. Said counsel, Mr Norman Birkett, drily: 'Your lordship speaks with great plausibility on these matters.'

VII

In January 1933 the *News of the World* began running a series of a dozen stories, bought at vast expense and given huge prominence. They were about an innocent girl being seduced by a wicked squire, a girl snatched from the gallows and The Man Who Married a Maniac.

All these subjects were of course the very stuff of the paper's news columns. But they were, on this occasion, *Tess of the D'Urbervilles*, *Adam Bede* and *Jane Eyre*, three of The World's Greatest Stories (rather than the *News of the World*'s greatest stories). Twelve of these had been rewritten under the by-line Winston S. Churchill, who, for a fee of £2,000 for the series,[15] got his assistant Eddie Marsh to boil the books down before he rewrote them with what the blurb called his 'graphic, virile and dramatic pen' – which was fair comment. 'There in the darkness and the silence, under the ancient oaks and yews, he had his will of her.' Hardy's original was subtler and more allusive, but the Churchill version may well have done more to make ordinary British people actually *read* literature than the sets of Dickens which Fleet Street was throwing around in the early thirties. He was also to contribute Great Men of Our Time and Great Events of Our Time; and even, in 1939, The Great Offices of State. Churchill was, notoriously, under-employed at this time – and rather hard up.

The *News of the World* did have to try a little harder as the competition intensified. It was forced to hand out insurance and free gifts to match *The People*, but it waited several years before doing so.[16] When it did join in, it did so with a vengeance and vengefully: it had up to 1,000 canvassers out at a time and opened a couple of shops in the provinces giving away gifts to anyone who brought in the heading from that week's paper. Riddell was every bit as furious with J. S. Elias, chairman of *The People* and the *Daily Herald*, as Beaverbrook was, and told him: 'I'm quite ready to break myself – after you.'[17]

The paper also became more conscious of the need to keep up with the news; early editions on 8 March 1931 had

LATE NEWS: ROUSE HAS CONFESSED

rubber-stamped by hand on top of page 1. Rouse was the Northamptonshire blazing-car murderer, later hanged. Actually, he hadn't confessed. But, as we have seen, newspapers were becoming more casual about details like that.

There was also an increasing urge to tell people at the start that, if they read on, they would find something to entertain them, instead of printing the news in grey columns, knowing that the readers took them on trust. Trials now tended to be 'amazing', developments 'sensational' and stories 'extraordinary'. 'Scenes unparalleled in the history of the Old Bailey' were enacted on a regular basis.

Circulation just kept rising: up to 3,350,000 by 1933, 3,750,000 by 1938, four million by 1939. While Emsley Carr was alive, wrote one of his successors, there was never a ripple on the surface. Journalists never left the *News of the World*, except to retire or die.[18] There was a quiet assurance about the place. In 1927 work began on what then seemed like a smart new building in Bouverie Street, just off Fleet Street. It opened in 1930.

It was becoming a slightly more political newspaper, and at times there seemed to be a conscious attempt to ape the *Daily Express*'s absurd optimism. A cartoon figure called Dismal Jimmy appeared, who would moan about the economy only to be overwhelmed by the truth about British expansion and prosperity. Often, during some very bleak years, the paper's lead story might be an excitingly upbeat interview with, say, the Minister for Agriculture. As with the *Express*, it was not clear whether anyone was really meant to read this stuff. It was a top-dressing; underneath, everything was as earthy as ever, despite the loss of copy from the Divorce Court.

For the first time a star by-lined reporter emerged from the anonymous ranks. This was Norman Rae, the crime correspondent, whose presence on a story always terrified the other reporters, since his contacts were unrivalled and the more publicity-wise detectives liked to save up some golden nugget for the Sunday papers. One of Rae's early triumphs was securing the confession of the double murderer, Dr Buck Ruxton, hanged in 1936.

Meanwhile, the paper continued to be filled with the smaller tragedies and, occasionally, comedies of life. Take 1933: in Ipswich, a man was shot dead with his own gun by his four-year-old son, who had picked it up to show his mum he could fire it; two men were drowned in Salford trying to rescue a kitten from the river (the kitten, naturally, escaped unharmed); even under the new law, the paper was able to announce the fact that the Divorce Court refused to grant Mr Renshaw of Salford or Mrs Renshaw a divorce, though he was convinced she was carrying on with a vicar and she accused him of cruelty; it did not explain what on earth they were supposed to do next – kiss and make up?

Twenty-seven people, mostly chefs and waiters, were jailed, for up to sixteen months, for being involved in 'the exhibition of lewd and scandalous performances to the manifest corruption of the King's subjects'. This followed a police raid on what the Recorder, Sir Ernest Wild KC, called 'a sodomitical haunt' in Holland Park. There were forty-six men dancing there at the time and six women. 'What kind of fun can there be in a dance like this?' asked Sir Ernest. 'I don't know, perhaps I'm old-fashioned.'

And Mr Justice McCardie, the garrulous bachelor judge, shot himself dead, aged sixty-three. The verdict was 'suicide while the balance of the mind was disturbed'.

One of the stars had gone, but the show went on. Pin-ups began to appear, of a particularly unsexy sort. Although Churchill was its highest-paid contributor, the *News of the World* was as dazzled by the chimera of Munich as anyone else: 'Glorious statesmanship . . . Europe has been made safe to live in for a generation,' it drooled on 2 October 1938. Six months later, after the march into Prague, it was reporting Chamberlain's question: 'Can there be faith in any future assurance from Germany?' 'To ask the question is to answer it,' said the leader column gloomily. 'Faith there can be none.'

On 3 September 1939, the day war broke out, the most telling comment was in the relatively new horoscope column. This week's advice to all people born under Pisces, which included Chamberlain, was: 'Repay people in their own kind.' The song the following week was the cloying 'Be Optimistic', by Walter Bullock and Harold Spina, as sung by Shirley Temple:

> Be optimistic, don't you be a mourner,
> Brighten up that corner and smile.
> Don't wear a long face, it's never in style.
> Be optimistic and smile.

VIII

On 1 May 1941, at the grim height of the war, the *News of the World* held a lunch for 150 people at the Dorchester Hotel to celebrate Sir Emsley Carr's fifty years as editor of the paper. Cecil King of the *Daily Mirror* was among those present. 'What a moment to celebrate such a trivial event!' he wrote in his diary. 'After all, at all relevant periods, the editor-in-chief was Lord Riddell, as we all knew.' However, many of the major figures were present, including Churchill, who apparently had five years left to run on his contract with the paper.

Carr was to die later that year, aged seventy-four; Riddell had died seven years earlier. The new editor was Percy Davies, a qualified barrister who had been Carr's deputy, so nothing much changed. The paper was cut back to eight pages, and there was not much room, but everything still had its place:

REBUKE FOR GAOLED CURATE

BOGUS CAPTAIN EXPOSED

JUDGE SAYS HUSBAND ACTED AS 'CAD'

'QUIET LITTLE MAN' HAD A PAST

'GREATEST BATTLE IN WORLD HISTORY'

– which was not necessarily an exaggeration; this was Stalingrad.

In 1942 Professor John Hilton, who had been one of the most reassuring broadcasting voices in the 1930s, began his own advice bureau, which was more formal than Garry Allighan's column in the *Daily Mirror*, but infinitely longer-lasting. Hilton died the following year, but the bureau continued under his name as a free service until 1974; it received more than four million enquiries and replied to them all.

IX

There is a Fleet Street anecdote/story/legend that just after the war the *News of the World* did some market research. The vast majority of readers all said they were not interested in the sex stories. So they were dropped. This lasted two weeks. Then the editor was sacked.

If true – and, frankly, it's too good a story to be spoiled by checking – it must have happened in 1947, when Robert Skelton was fired, barely a year after being hired as editor from the *Daily Telegraph*. This was a rare exception. Normally, editors of the *News of the World* were carried out rather than either walking out or being pushed – Carr, Davies and Arthur Waters, Skelton's successor, all died in office. Then the deputy took over. This was the most successful newspaper on earth. What kind of idiot would tamper with it?

Between January and June 1950 the circulation of the *News of the World* was officially computed at 8,433,917. The peak is believed to have been reached in June itself, at round about eight and a half million. This figure is unparalleled in the history of British journalism; moreover, emerging from the war with the circulation above seven million, the paper remained above eight million for six years between 1949 and 1954. This means that through-out this period one in every two households in Britain had a copy.

If such numbers have been approached anywhere in the world, it can only have been in Japan, Communist China or the old Soviet Union, where readers were not necessarily spoiled for choice. In Britain in 1950 there were at least ten Sunday papers with a national circulation, and both the *Sunday Pictorial* and *The People* sold more than five million. Since the papers only cost tuppence and were restricted – to ten pages for the broadsheets – by paper rationing, clearly many people bought more than one.

The *News of the World* was now on its third editor since Carr, an old hand called Arthur Waters. Very little had changed. Waters sat in his office drinking tea – mahogany-brown, one trusts – out of a chipped mug and on a Saturday night would leave long before the deadlines for the later editions to count the takings at his wife's pub. He was also a notoriously mean editor, not that anyone on the paper had ever been profligate.

'Let me see now, how much do you earn?' he said to a young reporter who had just done a story brilliantly.

'£4 a week, sir,' said the lad expectantly.

'Oh, I *am* glad.'[19]

There were only a handful of by-lined writers, none of them worth reading for their own sake. The supposedly serious articles on the leader page often seemed to have a touch of desperation:

BRITAIN CAN STILL DO IT:

OUR JETPLANES ARE THE
WONDER OF THE WORLD

By Lord Brabazon of Tara

The appeal was the same as it had always been: the old Adam and, indeed, the old Eve, though, just occasionally, there was a modern twist:

BIKINI GIRLS TELL 'WHY I
LIKE TO WEAR IT'

For the second time this year 24-year-old Mrs Yvonne Goodman made an unsuc-cessful attempt yesterday to swim in a Hampstead Heath pond in her home-made 'bikini' costume ... She was stopped by a keeper who said: 'Your costume does not conform to the regu-lations. You must put your clothes on at once. You cannot swim in that costume.'

This was undoubtedly true, because there was a picture of Mrs Goodman being stopped by a man in a bowler hat. If the man in the bowler hat had been unaccountably absent, doubtless the photographer and Mrs Goodman would have circled the pond several times to make sure of attracting his attention. Underneath this item was her first-person story:

TO ME THE SUN IS LIFE
BY THE GIRL IN THE
'BRIEF'

'It's time these Victorian ideas of not showing one's body were done away with for good and people's eyes opened to the fact that there is no better feeling than exposing the body to the sun. To me the sun is life and the body needs it . . . I know a lot of other girls would like to wear a costume similar to mine, but they haven't the courage to do so.'

Other things went on, as they always had:

15-YEAR-OLD GIRL MADE A
SECRET OF HER AGE –
'WORE MAKE-UP'

A 15-year-old girl told Mr Justice Jones at Chester Assizes that she did not like anyone to know her age. Asked why she had told a bricklayer's apprentice she was 19, she made no reply. The apprentice, Charles Henry Croft, aged 21, was found not guilty of an offence against her . . . Croft suggested intimacy, Mr W. L. Mars-Jones, prosecuting, alleged, and it occurred twice.

Did he actually say: 'Would you like intimacy?' Perhaps, if he had grown up in a household in the *News of the World* half of the country, he did exactly that.

If the murders were not of the old quality, it may have been because would-be poisoners were not now finishing off their victims. The paper of 18 June 1950 reported that a sixty-three-year-old man put potassium cyanide and barium chloride in his wife's bedtime milk powder; they had been married forty-one years. He told her: 'I will give you something, going with Sid.' He told police: 'She bought herself a new costume, and some new silk nightdresses. What does she want with things like that at her age?' She survived; it is not known what happened to the marriage. Just before that, a forty-one-year-old bespectacled chemist's clerk had put arsenic in his aunt's sugar bowl. She lived too. When there was a murder, the *News of the World* was still *the* paper: Norman Rae's greatest triumph was getting John George Haigh's admission, in 1949, that he had murdered nine people and drunk their blood:[20]

HAIGH'S SENSATIONAL
CONFESSION

'. . . I first acquired the taste in childhood
when my hand was smacked with a hair-
brush. The sharp bristles drew blood. I
thought I should die. I licked it off, and
found it an agreeable sensation . . .'

In August 1951 a nineteen-year-old Nottingham youth, Herbert Leonard Mills, rang the paper to say he had found the body of a murdered woman, Mabel Tattershaw, in an orchard, which provided a dramatic front-page splash:

THE VOICE ON THE PHONE SAID:
'I'VE FOUND A BODY –
IT LOOKS LIKE MURDER'

Well, Mills could hardly have been wrong about that since, as became clear over succeeding weeks, he had strangled her. The reporters had been suspicious all along; he said he had been in the orchard reading Shelley, which was obviously suspicious behaviour. Why wasn't he out being intimate, like everyone else?

Arthur Waters died in 1953, and again the deputy moved up: Reg Cudlipp, elder brother of Hugh, who was already running the Mirror Group, and younger brother of Percy, editor of the *Evening Standard*. Cudlipp was said to have been a master of detail but reluctant to delegate. He certainly changed very little. Circulation was falling, but then it could hardly do anything else. Indeed, it needed to fall a little. With paper rationing easing, the papers had to get bigger; and to print eight million extra *News of the World*-size broadsheets cost more than could possibly be recouped from advertisers. It was a strange problem. But the fall was far too precipitate. The figures went below eight million in 1955, below seven million in 1958, below 6.5 million in 1959. Its two rivals, meanwhile, the *Sunday Pictorial* and *The People*, were both rock-steady at round about five million throughout the 1950s.

But in the 1950s the *News of the World* seemed like one of the nation's great unchanging institutions, almost a dignified part of the constitution –

the Pornographer Royal, perhaps – in an era when nothing much seemed
to be changing. Occasionally, the old themes would have a contemporary
resonance:

> To gain the interest of a schoolgirl, a
> man posed as an agent of a film company
> and offered to give her a screen test,
> alleged Mr J. C. Phipps, prosecuting, in
> a case at Greenwich . . .

The song, however, remained very much the same.

X

IT'S DORS

IT'S DYNAMITE

WILD AND WICKED

> I first noticed I was different from other
> girls at school in Swindon. I had more
> bulges. Buttons tended to pop off my
> gym costume. I used to pose in front of
> the mirror at 12, imagining myself a film
> star. Admiring my body.
> Boys noticed it too . . .

Reg Cudlipp left the paper at the end of 1959. Again the deputy took over.
This one, Stafford Somerfield, decided to change the act: 'On my first day
in the editor's chair I called the staff together and said: "What the hell are
we going to do about the circulation? It's going down the drain. It's still the
largest, but won't continue so if we go on like this. We want a series of articles
that will make your hair curl. We haven't had one for years." '[21]

And, indeed, even allowing for Somerfield's vanity, which appears to have
been considerable, he did change the paper faster than anyone in seventy
years: and the circulation did steady. *The People*, under the lively editorships
of Harry Ainsworth and Sam Campbell, had long specialized in major investigations, exposés and buy-ups, though it tended to concentrate on crime rather
than sex. Now the *News of the World* joined in; and the Diana Dors story
was just the start:

THE PICTURE THEY TRIED TO BAN

The word 'ban' was stuck strategically over Miss Dors's right nipple. She was
paid £35,000 for a two-month series. The hidden cost was that the army of
bien-pensant tut-tutters, headed by the Press Council, now focused on the

News of the World. On a television programme called *The Editors,* Somerfield was questioned by the young Liberal MP, Jeremy Thorpe.

Thorpe: Do you agree with the stricture of the Press Council that the conduct of your paper in regard to the Diana Dors articles allowed standards to be debased and, I quote, to a level which was a disgrace to British journalism? Would you say that was part of your job of useful instruction or of valuable adult amusement?

Somerfield: The Press Council were quite out of step in saying that. They were trying to exercise control on the contents of a newspaper. That's not their job at all. Their task should be to control behaviour. That is something they have lost sight of. Of course I don't agree with what they're saying. The Diana Dors story was fascinating; instead of the usual six and a half million people buying the paper, many thousands more read it. Who is to say they were wrong?

Thorpe: Let me get down to some phrases. 'As I hit the floor my coat burst open revealing my naked body to our guests.' Now, what sort of principle of journalism do you feel you are enhancing by printing that sort of thing? Would you say that this was one of the more important contributions of which you are particularly proud as a journalist?

Somerfield: I'm proud of the paper as a whole.

Thorpe: Could you answer the question?

Somerfield: I'm not in the witness box, Mr Thorpe.

Nor, nineteen years later, would Jeremy Thorpe go into the witness box when he was charged with attempted murder. But that's another story. Thorpe went on to point out a picture of three near-naked Malayan ladies . . .

Somerfield: You have not gone through the paper fairly. You have said nothing about a report on the war in the Congo, an article by the Archbishop of Canterbury, and another on cancer research.

It says something either about Somerfield's gameness or, more likely, about his thick-skinned pomposity, that he reprinted this pathetic performance in his autobiography.[22] Later editors in his position would be more inclined to state the truth, namely that they are paid to sell newspapers, not indulge in 'useful instruction' – to tickle the public, not to teach them – or, alternatively, they would avoid appearing on such programmes at all.

There was a deal of humbug on both sides in this argument, and it was at this time that the *News of the World* acquired the tone of hysterical hypocrisy that was to replace its old measured prurience. This was one of the first examples, on 15 November 1959:

COMING OVER – A FLOOD OF HORROR FROM AMERICA

A GRAHAM STANFORD INVESTIGATION

Fantastic details were revealed to me yesterday of a high-powered American plan to flood Britain with cut-price sex novels, blood-chilling adventure magazines and near-horror comics. One of my informants, in a searching all-angle probe of the position, was the chief of a well-known firm of British pocket-book publishers.

'Just look at this stuff,' the publisher said disgustedly as he threw an assortment of jacket covers across the table . . .

I inspected the garish, gaudy jackets and studied their titles – 'I Live to Love', 'Mr Madam, the Story of a Ponce', 'The Naked Lovers', 'Sex on Tap', 'The Last Virgin' . . .

And on 13 March 1960, another:

THIS STARK REPORT MUST BE PRINTED

From Victor Wyeth. Winchester, Saturday.

This is the most distressing and appalling story I have had to write in 40 years of reporting on the raw facts of life as revealed daily in the magistrates' and assize courts. It is a dreadful and damning indictment of the behaviour of what, one fears, is a grievously large and growing section of our young people.

In the calendar of the Hampshire Assizes and General Gaol Delivery being held at the Castle no fewer than 32 of the 73 prisoners were indicted on sexual offences . . . 27 for having unlawful sexual

intercourse with girls under the age of 16. It is the highest number of such cases that I have ever come across in one assize calendar.

For three days I have listened to the wretched, sordid details of these boy-girl 'associations' . . . Most of them pleaded guilty and expressed their shame and regret. But in almost every instance it became evident that the girl concerned was just as bad as the boy. And in some cases worse.

Did Victor Wyeth write that with a straight face? What were all those unspecified 'offences' that the *News of the World* had been reporting all those years? But there were a lot of what the paper kept calling World Scoops, achieved by the simple technique of spending money. Diana Dors was followed by the prison escapologist Alfie Hinds, Maurice Chevalier, the Shah of Iran – and Brigitte Bardot:

THE BB STORY

By Gerard Fairlie

> Slim and strong; glamorous to watch;
> dangerous to touch; Brigitte the panther
> . . . 'I must have my secrets like any
> other girl.'

In other words, she has not been quite as forthcoming in return for her fee as button-popping Diana Dors.

Somerfield's next upping of the journalistic ante came in the febrile summer of 1963, when the *News of the World* paid £23,000 to Christine Keeler, the prostitute who had an affair with the War Minister, John Profumo:

CONFESSIONS OF CHRISTINE – BY THE GIRL WHO IS ROCKING THE GOVERNMENT

> . . . It was the third time that he came
> round. I didn't anticipate what was going
> to happen. We started talking and laugh-
> ing as usual, then suddenly we both
> stopped. It was one of those electric,
> potent silences – then without a word we
> were embracing, and he was kissing me,
> and I was returning his kisses with
> everything that I suddenly felt for him.

The Press Council's opinion of this was published four months later, on 6 October, at the bottom of page 11: 'The action of the *News of the World* in paying £23,000 for the confessions of Keeler and publishing in these articles details of her sordid life story was particularly damaging to the morals of young people. By thus exploiting vice and sex for commercial reward the *News of the World* has done a disservice both to public welfare and to the Press.'

Somerfield's response was in bold type on page 1.

> The Christine Keeler story is news. No newspaper has failed to recognise this. The only difference between the *News of the World* and other newspapers is that we were the first to publish material with an authentic basis. In order to provide the facts we had to pay . . . Does anyone suggest the Christine Keeler story should have been suppressed? . . . A prodigious and mounting readership tacitly acknowledges the rightness of the course we have followed.

This was rather more robust than his defence of the Dors story. And it is hard to see the moral justification for not letting Christine Keeler tell her story. For better or worse, British society was moving on, a point Somerfield, with a popular journalist's instinct, had grasped. It was a point the *Daily Mirror*, at that time the leading daily paper, failed to grasp adequately, with far-reaching consequences.

The *News of the World* was never again to sell eight or even seven million copies every Sunday, or, after 1972, six million. But it continued to dominate its market – even though some of its traditional practices were being cramped by the opinions of the non-*News of the World*-reading classes. In 1962 reporting restrictions were imposed on committal hearings, cutting off one source of court copy; the decision to pay £1,000 in 1965 to David Smith, chief prosecution witness in the Moors Murders trial, was widely condemned and only half-heartedly defended, and such payments were more or less outlawed (though they resurfaced in the Rosemary West trial of 1995, when the competitive pressures again outweighed moral ones).

The emphasis now was on investigations – some legitimate, worthy and public-spirited exposés of villainy: doctors who prescribed heroin, dodgy agencies offering bogus diplomas, conmen fleecing housewives with get-rich-quick schemes – some not:

SEX IN THE SUBURBS

THE MARRIAGE CHEATERS –
A SIX-MONTH INVESTIGATION

But, whenever it was legally possible, the paper still, throughout the 1960s, found room on its capacious broadsheet pages for the old faithfuls. Even here, though, the news could now be a little different, as with these two stories, both from 14 January 1968:

HOW TIMES CHANGE – BY A JUDGE

Awarding a husband £50 damages instead of the £500 he claimed, a Judge in the Divorce Court said the case of the virtuous wife who was seduced by a wicked lover was a social situation which had wholly disappeared.

Nowadays things did not happen that way, observed Mr Justice Ormerod.

'I think it extremely distasteful,' he went on, 'to have to assess damages against a man without any particular responsibility for the breakdown of a marriage, except that he happened to be the man that the wife met and liked.'

**TEMPTED BY HER
MINI-SKIRT**
There was something about the long
smooth stretch of leg showing under the
shop girl's mini-skirt. He touched her on
the leg . . . Assault. Fined £30.

XI

There is a story that some economic organization declared the *News of the World* in the 1960s to be the worst-run company in Europe. It was certainly idiosyncratically run, the early part of the week being dominated by enormous benders in which the leading actor was the chairman: Sir Emsley Carr's son, Sir William Carr, generally known as 'Pissy Billy'.

The most enduring Pissy Billy anecdote concerns an uproarious binge in the midst of which he got agitated about something and demanded to speak to the Prime Minister, then Sir Alec Douglas-Home. Since the *News of the World* was the country's biggest-selling paper and because the Profumo Affair was fresh in everyone's mind and no one was quite sure what new scandal the papers might have uncovered, requests for an audience from Sir William were not dismissed lightly. One was arranged at Downing Street at eleven o'clock the next morning.

By that time, however, Sir William had sobered up and had not the slightest idea what it was he wanted to tell Sir Alec in the first place. So when the Prime Minister asked 'Well, gentlemen, what can I do for you?' he sat there in total silence while his companion (believed to be Mark Chapman-Walker, the managing director) desperately played for time by saying they were very concerned about Nyasaland or the economy or something. Finally, Sir Alec changed the subject: 'Would you like a drink, perhaps?' at which point Sir William at long last broke his silence. 'Gin and tonic,' he said.

The organization was wrought in his image. No one was paid very much, but they did not have to work very hard either. Every Monday the staff had the freedom of the course at Walton Heath; every Saturday, between editions, they would be given dinner at a Fleet Street restaurant; every year they would be invited to the paper's traditional Leg o' Mutton Supper, a monumental booze-up even by Fleet Street standards, and to an annual garden party at the proprietor's country home (wives invited, but not girlfriends). Here the butler would call out each guest's name, upon which he would walk the length of the hall, feet echoing, to be presented to Lady Carr before a manservant poured him a treble of whatever he fancied. It was said he made the measures extra-large to spite Sir William, whom he loathed.

The *News of the World* was making money still. But for whom? The Carr family still held most of the shares, with the majority split between Sir William and his cousin, Professor Derek Jackson. (Under other circumstances, Jackson might have found himself in the *News of the World* – he had just married his sixth wife.) Carr had never interfered in the editorial content; Somerfield was allowed to get on with it. It was a happy, old-fashioned arrangement for what was still a happy, old-fashioned paper. Jackson had never played any active part at all, and in 1968 he decided to sell. Carr did not have the money to buy him out, certainly not enough as rumours spread and the share price went up. The rumours then took the substantial corporeal shape of Robert Maxwell, at that point Labour MP for Buckingham. Maxwell already had Jackson's shares and now, to gain control, he bid 37s 6d for shares that had previously been trading for 28s.

Carr was already a sick man, and his health was not improved by developments. All millionaires who profess to be socialists are distrusted; this one rightly so. The print unions took against Maxwell, and on 20 October 1968 Somerfield denounced him in an extraordinarily malignant front-page article:

THE BATTLE FOR YOUR NEWSPAPER –
By The Editor

... Why do I think it would not be a good thing for Mr Maxwell, formerly Jan Ludwig Hoch, to gain control of this newspaper which, I know, has your respect, loyalty and affection – a newspaper which is as British as roast beef and Yorkshire pudding ... This is a British newspaper run by British people ...

Somerfield also made the point, a more reasonable one on the face of it, that Maxwell was a 'Socialist MP' and the paper would thus lose its independence, an argument which would have been valid if anyone could ever have remembered the *News of the World* having a political opinion. Bernard Levin said that closer to Somerfield's heart than roast beef and Yorkshire were rape, indecent assault, incest, buggery and the disarrangement of young ladies' underclothing in darkened railway carriages.[23]

British newspaper takeovers are characterized by those involved always preferring the devil they do not know to the one they do: very often a search goes on to find a buyer who does not own a paper already – and is therefore less likely to merge the operations – and is not known to have the dictatorial or eccentric habits of the existing proprietors. Everyone knew enough about Maxwell to know they disliked him, though not enough to know quite why – hence Somerfield's flailing xenophobic attack. They knew very little about the young man who emerged as an alternative.

Rupert Murdoch flew into London the morning Somerfield's roast beef and Yorkshire piece appeared. A deal was put together which was widely believed to have involved the *News of the World* buying its own shares to fight off Maxwell, which was against City rules. Gradually, a deal was stitched together, and Maxwell was stitched up. On 5 January 1969 the paper announced that the shareholders had reached agreement with News Ltd of Australia, a bland-enough sounding organization, and that the paper would continue 'INDEPENDENT AND FREE to serve the greatest readership in the world'. Doubtless the man who had saved them from Maxwell seemed very pleasant: as British as kangaroos and Sydney Harbour Bridge, which was British enough. No one took much notice of Murdoch's answer, when asked if he was going to interfere in the paper: 'I did not come all this way not to interfere.'

There emerged what Carr, in his sickness, innocence and perhaps alco-holic stupor, believed to be a partnership, with him as chairman and Murdoch as chief executive. That lasted three months. Then Murdoch went down to Carr's house to get his resignation. In May 1969, when Somerfield was away, Murdoch went in and made changes to that week's paper, including the removal of the leader page. Somerfield went into full high-horse mode: arriving back on the editorial floor, he stood there – an imposing man, looking rather like an old actor-manager – and said loudly: 'Somebody's been messing about with my newspaper.' Then he went downstairs and changed everything back. He followed this with an absurd and fatal memo to Murdoch about the ethics of editorial independence. 'I could not believe it,' he wrote in his autobiography. 'The leader page was a most vital page of the paper. In it were the serious views of the key writers of the day; this was the page that was quoted the world over . . .'[24]

This, of course, was a load of nonsense. The leader page was the paper's fig-leaf of respectability, on which, when there were no drum-beating Britain is Best pieces, politicians' assistants wrote dull articles in their boss's name that hardly anyone read, but which made the politician think he was communicating with half the electorate. It remains just that. Even Rupert Murdoch, in the end, has had need of fig-leaves.

The battle between Murdoch and Somerfield simmered for the next nine months, before it ended as these battles always would. Somerfield would not resign, so he was fired, with an £80,000 pay-off, which was enormous for 1970. He went off to breed pedigree dogs and write a column for *Dog World*. Not a word of the dispute appeared in the *News of the World*. When he died, in early 1995, he rated one paragraph. Yet no one, Riddell and Emsley Carr aside, has done more to make the paper what it is. If the *News of the World* does not think that is an achievement, who does? Somerfield told the *Evening Standard*: 'Perhaps I've been too nice.' Murdoch had a different interpretation: 'He was too nasty, even for me.'

It is a moot point whether the paper was to get nicer or nastier under the new regime. But it was about to acquire a little sister, which would change the face of British journalism for ever.

PART SIX

'This Is It, Folks!'
The Sun Era

Prologue

It is time to return to the thoughts of Ralph D. Blumenfeld, former editor of the *Daily Express*, the man who predicted that there was no future in aviation, commuting or mechanical printing, and insisted that firemen would always yell 'Hi! Yi!' on their way to fires. By 1933 he had retired and turned his mind to the future of the press and how it might look fifty years ahead, in the then barely imaginable year of 1983.

'The actual interests of the great majority of people will run in more or less the same directions as they do now,' Blumenfeld began, reasonably enough.

> The difference will be in the keener intelligence with which they will pursue their interests, and the greater knowledge and maturer judgment they will bring to bear on the problems of life and the questions of the day . . .
>
> It will no longer be necessary for the popular newspaper to give its news and critical commentaries in disjointed snippets . . . its reports and articles will have more 'body' than at present . . . 'Gossip' columns will figure as largely in the newspapers as they have done in those of the past. I think, however, that in years to come the Press will use this feature more scrupulously, and certainly with more taste than has been the tendency of late. Public opinion will probably insist on a higher code in this respect . . .
>
> I believe that as newspapers continue to grow in intelligence and vision, and evince greater circumspection in regard to what are colloquially termed 'stunts' . . . [they] will become increasingly recognised as indispensable adjuncts to the family life, and as guides, counsellors and family friends.[1]

Good old R.D.B.! More 'body' indeed! At least he was right about that. There are definitely parts of the body that were never in the newspaper in his day. Hi! Yi!

But anyone reading Blumenfeld in the late 1960s might have imagined the whole of his thesis was going to be proved right. Newspapers were working on the basis that their readers had keener intelligence and maturer judgement. Around that time Leslie Sellers, production editor of the *Daily Mail*, wrote a couple of books that came to be recognized as bibles for aspiring reporters and sub-editors. In one of them he wrote a simple A to Z guide to journalism. Under 'I' he wrote the following:

> INTRUSION into privacy and private grief is now mainly confined to the occasional television programme . . . Newspapers are the goodies now – perhaps sometimes too goody for their own good. Many times stories and pictures are unused by newspapers because they show public figures, perhaps caught in an off moment, in an unseemly or ridiculous light. This is partly the result of the growing influence of the Press Council but more because of a greater sense of responsibility.[2]

What a period piece that now seems. In the last quarter of the popular press's first century, there was a spectacular change. At the root of it was one man with a very keen intelligence whose sense of responsibility is more open to dispute: Rupert Murdoch.

I

In the late 1960s and early 1970s there was an Australian cartoon character, invented by Barry Humphries, called Barry Mackenzie, whose adventures appeared fortnightly in *Private Eye* and who rapidly became established as the archetype of the amiable, boozy, thick Ocker. In the film version Mackenzie arrives at Heathrow, asks the taxi driver for Earl's Court and is taken via Stonehenge and the seaside, while the meter goes berserk.

A large number of people in Fleet Street at the time envisaged Rupert Murdoch as Barry Mackenzie made flesh, most particularly the print workers, some of whom did indeed drive taxis in their ample spare time and generally managed to go through life with the meter running. The British, having gained their cartoon view of Australia as a place of kangaroos and piss-artists largely from the popular press, did not realize that it is a country that has an Establishment like any other, still less that their new master sprang from the very heart of it.

Keith Rupert Murdoch was born in 1931, the son of Sir Keith Murdoch, the reporter who broke the story of Allied incompetence at Gallipoli and rose to become editor of the *Melbourne Herald* and managing director of the *Herald and Weekly Times*, Australia's most powerful newspaper group. He was friendly with, and influenced by, Lord Northcliffe. As the years went by he was sometimes known as Lord Southcliffe.

Sir Keith was forty-five when his only son was born, after one daughter and before two more. Young Rupert was variously described as shy, gentle, thoughtful, ordinary, cocksure and a fidget. His father was remote and strict in some accounts,[3] affectionate and indulgent according to others.[4] As a child, Rupert collected manure from the paddocks round his country home and sold it to neighbouring old ladies. At school he was known as a left-winger, who would take debating positions far removed from those espoused by his father's conservative newspapers. When he came to England to take up a place at Oxford he had a bust of Lenin on his mantelpiece, though he did spend more time at casinos than is customary for student Communists. Just before he took his finals his father died, leaving him one small newspaper that he owned personally, the *Adelaide News.* After six months as a junior sub-editor on the *Daily Express* – his father was also a friend of Lord Beaverbrook – Rupert Murdoch went back to Australia, aged twenty-two, to take up his inheritance.

At the *News* he indulged a forceful left-wing editor and old family friend, Rohan Rivett, particularly in a campaign against the execution of an Aborigine, Rupert Max Stuart, on a dubious murder charge. Stuart was reprieved, but the campaign did the paper little good with advertisers and readers. Weeks later, Rivett was curtly fired.

From his niche, Murdoch expanded. The Fairfax group, which controlled both evening papers in Sydney, *The Sun* and the struggling *Daily Mirror,* allowed Murdoch to buy the *Mirror* cheaply. They did not want to close it, which would have led to criticism; anyway, they did not take the Boy Publisher very seriously. Like the water going down the plughole, everything was the wrong way round in Australia: Murdoch had the *Daily Mirror* and the enemy was *The Sun,* but the down-market tabloid battle which ensued was, in its rough, small-world, Australian way, a microcosm of the war that was to follow on the far side of the planet, even down to the detail of Murdoch being handed the paper cheaply. It was a war with at least one fatality, thus prefiguring the case of Arnold Lewis, the *News of the World*'s victim. According to Murdoch's most sympathetic biographer:

> There was one series on sexual antics in a Sydney school, which led to such headlines as WE HAVE SCHOOLGIRL'S ORGY DIARY. The *Mirror* then reported that one schoolboy had been suspended. Soon afterwards the boy was found hanging from a clothesline, but the *Mirror* did not report that. The girl who wrote the diary was found to be a virgin; her diary was all hallucination. It was the *Mirror* which had driven the boy to suicide.[5]

Murdoch also started Australia's first national paper, *The Australian,* which – at first, anyway – was a liberal and up-market broadsheet. By the time he acquired the *News of the World* he was a very, very big and predatory fish in the confined newspaper pond of Australia. It was not his fault that hardly anyone in Britain knew anything about him.

II

When Rupert Murdoch entered Fleet Street, it was as if a gunslinger had smashed open the swing doors of a Dodge City saloon and found himself staring into the snug bar of an English country pub. Everyone looked up briefly, then tried to go back to their pints.

In 1969 there were eight general national newspapers.[6] At the top end of the market *The Times*, now owned by the Canadian magnate Lord Thomson, had modernized itself, putting news on the front page and beginning its long descent from journalistic Olympus. It was increasingly under pressure from *The Guardian*, which had gradually shed its Mancunian roots and become a fully fledged national paper, winning growing circulation and reputation as an unstuffy alternative. Both struggled to make money, and in 1966 they almost merged.

The *Daily Telegraph*, with its safely conservative politics and approach to journalism, its capacious news and sporting columns and its uncomplicated crossword, retained the loyalty of the Pony Club classes and a sale close to a million and a half, more than twice as many as its two rivals put together. In the 1950s it had reported that Elizabeth Taylor had arrived at London and told journalists: 'I'm feeling like a million dollars (£357,000).'[7] It had not loosened up much since.

In the middle there was, above all, the *Daily Express*. After 1949 its sales figures were always behind those of the *Daily Mirror*. But it remained an extraordinarily rich, powerful and successful newspaper. Beaverbrook was a slightly more mellow figure in his later years, though he had one last hurrah in his campaign to keep Britain out of the Common Market. He walked in Hyde Park almost every morning with Christiansen's successor as editor, Ted Pickering, but they discussed art as much as politics.[8] The *Express*'s six-monthly sales figures were permanently above four million from 1949 until 1964, which happened to be the year Beaverbrook died. The fact that they slipped at that precise moment was probably a coincidence. The fact that they kept slipping ever after – below three million in 1975, below two million in 1984, below 1.3 million in 1995 – was not.

In 1969, however, under Beaverbrook's son Sir Max Aitken, the *Express* was still selling twice as many copies as the *Daily Mail* under the second

Lord Rothermere, even though, in 1960, the *Mail* had swallowed the *News Chronicle*. The second-generation proprietor of that liberal and humanitarian paper, Laurence Cadbury, had reacted to a financial crisis that could almost certainly have been ridden out at the price of a few reasonable economies by closing it down without warning. Its 1.1 million circulation was sold off to the Tory *Daily Mail* and its principles down the river; its employees were thrown on to the street. Some journalists began boycotting Cadbury's chocolate in protest.

A couple of years earlier there had been talk of a merger with the *Daily Herald*, which would have created a left-of-centre mid-market paper with a probable circulation close to three million. Had this happened, the *Daily Mail* might have gone under, and the political balance of Fleet Street, perhaps of the country, would have been transformed. Instead the *News Chronicle* it was that died, of 'a simple thrombosis', said James Cameron, its most distinguished writer, 'defined as when an active circulation is impeded by clots'.[9]

At the bottom there were just two tabloid papers: the *Daily Mirror*, whose sale was nudging and sometimes surpassing five million a day (plus another half-million for its Scottish sister, the *Daily Record*), and the *Daily Sketch*, below 900,000 and sinking slowly towards oblivion. The *Sketch* merged with the *Mail* in 1971. That left just seven papers, and it was quite reasonable to speculate that the figure would soon go down to two or three, as in New York or Sydney.

The national press was being eaten from the outside by its most ferocious predator, commercial television, and gnawed at from within by the demands of the print unions, whose members were already being paid phenomenally well for the work they did, and the work they did not do, as a result of a series of bizarre agreements and Byzantine working practices, connived at by managements in the hope of a quiet life and uninterrupted production.

There was, however, still one more newspaper, just about. This was *The Sun*. It had emerged in 1964, pale and watery, as the successor to the *Daily Herald*, organ of the trade union movement and the paper that had begun the circulation battles of the 1930s. Like all the aggressors of that decade, the *Herald* had ultimately been defeated. It achieved the two million circulation it sought, but in the 1940s, as the *Mirror* headed towards four and five million, that no longer looked such a magic number. In the 1950s, when even the class war had taken a more pacific turn, the *Herald*'s figures dipped further. In 1961, its owner Odhams Press was sold to the *Daily Mirror*, whose chairman Cecil King gleefully acquired its vast collection of magazines, its successful Sunday paper *The People* and, with rather less glee, the *Daily Herald*.

Even King's editorial genius, Hugh Cudlipp, did not know what to do with the *Herald*. The Labour Party, under Harold Wilson, was starting to edge away from the unions, which were beginning to become increasingly unpopular except among those groups of workers which at any given time were trying to get a pay rise. No sane company wanted a newspaper that could not even criticize the union movement. But the huge conglomeration King now controlled, under the suitably grand title of the International Publishing Corporation, pledged when they bought Odhams that the *Herald* would not be merged with the *Mirror*.

Instead, King and Cudlipp decided to transform, rename and relaunch the *Daily Herald*. Once again they were influenced by Dr Mark Abrams, the market researcher who brought a statistical dimension to what might be called Blumenfeldism: the belief that people wanted more intelligent and mature newspapers. Whether or not they wanted them, they told market researchers they did; they didn't tell strangers with clipboards that they wanted breasts on page 3.

Thus the *Herald* died and *The Sun* was born. One member of its staff recalls sitting in Cudlipp's garden on a hot day in the summer of 1964 and being told that the new paper would be aimed at 'a middle-class couple, aged 28 with two children, and living in Reading.' A few such families must have existed; maybe they bought the paper.

The *Sun* that existed between its launch in September 1964 and its takeover by Rupert Murdoch in November 1969 is usually remembered as a terrible paper. This is not entirely fair. It was a handy size, slightly smaller than a conventional broadsheet but big enough to project news and pictures well – what is known in the trade, non-pejoratively, as a bastard tabloid. It had some excellent writers, such as Clement Freud on sport and Nancy Banks-Smith on television. Its women's pages, Pacesetters, were greatly admired. It looked quite handsome, if a little full of sixties gimmickry. On a good day one might think it had that formula for undemanding but not wholly unintelligent modern, middle-market, middle-class journalism that the *Daily Mail* was to make its own in the next decade.

Unfortunately, there were not that many good days. Before Day One Sam Campbell, the editor of *The People*, is said to have offered the editor, the old *Mirror* hand Sydney Jacobson, one of the investigative exclusives in which he specialized, just to get the paper off to a flying start. He was rebuffed. *The Sun* preferred to lead its very first edition with

GOOD MORNING! IT'S TIME FOR A NEW NEWSPAPER

This did not offer a compelling reason for anyone to buy the paper on Day Two. The opening gimmick was that all the pubs with the word Sun in their names were to give away free beer, provided by IPC. This went wrong too.

One version is that each pub only got a small barrel, and so irritated everyone by running out. Some of the paper's staff went round the corner from the offices to The Sun Tavern in Long Acre and reported that it was disgusting stuff anyway.

The major problem with the paper was that it was so half-hearted. The *Mirror* management had pledged to keep it alive until the end of the 1960s, but it soon became apparent to the reporters that they did not intend to do anything more. There was a plan – another if only – to take *The Sun* down-market while letting the *Mirror* gradually float upwards in the hope of catching nice 28-year-olds in Reading. 'King was keen on it,' said Cudlipp. 'I wasn't. We didn't.' The *Mirror* could not allow anything to detract from the product that paid for everything else, so *The Sun* suffered from chronic under-investment. 'King's cross', people called it.

It was a breathtaking decade, full of news and excitement. *Sun* readers, however, may not have been entirely aware of this. The staff complained that when there was a big story, as there often was, the paper's executives were nowhere to be seen. One or two of them seem to have fitted into the spirit of the decade in the sense that they spent a good proportion of it out of their skulls. *The Sun* steadily lost both readers and money. As the 1960s ended and the *Mirror*'s obligation to keep it alive began to run out, Cudlipp – who had become chairman of IPC when King was ousted in a boardroom coup in 1968 – was delighted to find two mugs keen to take it off his hands.

The first was Robert Maxwell, who made a list of prior demands from the unions and was rejected. The second was Rupert Murdoch, who had bought the *News of the World* a few months earlier and wanted a daily paper to share the overheads. He had already tried and failed to buy the *Sketch*. Cudlipp sold him *The Sun* for well under £1 million, which soon became *The Sun*'s weekly profits. It is remembered as one of the greatest of all Fleet Street misjudgements, the precise repetition of what had occurred when Murdoch picked up the *Mirror* in Sydney.

The *Mirror* dare not close *The Sun*. 'If I'd closed it,' said Cudlipp, 'the unions . . . would have closed down the whole of IPC's vast publishing empire. Women's magazines would have vanished from the bookstalls, ninety-two trade and technical newspapers would have closed down, four national newspapers. And for a considerable period. The cost of that would have been astronomical.'[10] And, as in Sydney, Murdoch was still not regarded that seriously. But it was clear that if no one sold him an existing daily paper he was going to start one. The name would have been different; the phenomenon would have been the same.

III

The readers of the *News of the World* probably noticed nothing after the Murdoch takeover. His first major venture out of the journalistic ordinary sprang from an idea by Stafford Somerfield, the editor with whom he was feuding, and came straight out of the paper's recent history. It acquired a rehashed version of Christine Keeler's memoirs. On 28 September 1969, the day the price of the paper – which had been rising in old-penny leaps throughout the 1960s – went up to eight old pence, the memoirs began again:

THE STORY THEY DON'T WANT YOU TO READ

Inflation did not affect Christine Keeler. What was worth £23,000 six years earlier now cost only £21,000. There were a few new tit-bits, but she was now very old news. This added to Establishment anger at the revival, because John Profumo had spent the intervening years working for charity, and there was a widespread feeling that he had suffered enough.

The serial was not even a massive success: circulation rose by 100,000, only one and a half per cent, and when readers were asked with an enormous flourish: 'Should you be allowed to read the Keeler story?' the paper was obliged to report, very much more discreetly, that only six out of ten said they should. Murdoch made the mistake of trying to defend the decision on television against the young, thrusting interviewer David Frost and came off worst. He learned.

The staff of the *News of the World*, though, soon discovered that their new master was not a cartoon Aussie. The alcoholic haze that enveloped the place under Pissy Billy began to lift; Murdoch began work early and expected others to do the same. He is reputed to have arrived at Walton Heath Golf Club, which came his way with the newspaper, marched briskly up the first fairway and back down the eighteenth, and promptly sold the place. A curious pattern began to emerge in Murdoch's methods. He would not tolerate for a moment Somerfield's sacerdotal incantation of an editor's holy rights and responsibilities; he could do what he liked when he liked with the newspapers he owned. Having made his point, he had little wish to interfere once they were being run smoothly, i.e. profitably, and by editors who did not presume they were acting as free agents.

His staff rapidly became aware that he understood the technicalities of newspapers. The *News of the World* printers told him it was impossible to produce a tabloid paper on their presses. Murdoch said that was nonsense. All they needed were the crusher bars, which would have been supplied with the equipment. There was a lot of head-shaking. Murdoch then jumped on to a chair, found a dirty old box on top of a press and emerged with one of the bars, wrapped in sacking. For those present, it was an electrifying moment.

Dummy issues are considered as crucial to new newspapers as rehearsals to a play. This is not a novel technique: remember that Northcliffe went through dozens before the *Daily Mail* started in 1896. Murdoch's *Sun* went to the opposite extreme. It had to. On the Friday night, 14 November 1969, the last of the old *Sun*, no. 1,604, rolled off the presses while a kilted piper played a lament. On the Monday morning the new *Sun* was due to start. Murdoch could have waited, recruited his staff at leisure, and prepared properly. But the existing *Sun* readership would have gone off elsewhere. He chose to start at once.

In the second-last edition of the old *Sun*, Nancy Banks-Smith had written what might be described as a TV-crit-à-clef saying farewell to a worthy but failed soap opera called *The Newcomers*: 'It was a Serial with a Social Conscience . . . Ever attempting to enlighten our darkness in depth. On income tax or how to build a bungalow . . . it was an honest, hard-up, unsensational serial which never quite ignited. Nor drew the juicy multi-million circulation of some. God bless it and all who sank in it.' The paper's final leader column talked earnestly about the paper's campaigns against starvation in Biafra and torture in Greece, while the new proprietor was given space on the front page to talk about how the new paper would be 'the paper that CARES . . . about truth, beauty and justice'. This was in line with what Murdoch had been saying for months. The *News of the World* had quoted him on 26 October in what may have been the first of Murdoch's commercial cross-promotions, in Britain anyway: 'It will be an honest and straightforward newspaper with strong convictions.'

The most accurate interpretation of all this had already come in *Private Eye*: 'Mr Rupert "the Dirty Digger" Murdoch has said publicly that he thinks *The Sun* "should be brightened up a little". In private he expresses himself more forthrightly: "I want a tearaway paper with a lot of tit . . ."'[11] At a meeting of the staff, Murdoch told them the three elements that were going to sell the paper: 'Sex, sport and contests.'

That aside, Murdoch appears to have given very little instruction about the kind of paper he wanted. He found an editor, Larry Lamb, and a deputy, Bernard Shrimsley, both of them former *Mirror* executives whose promotion routes were blocked. Lamb had been a grammar-school boy from Fitzwilliam, the pit village that spawned Geoffrey Boycott, and he was a similarly gifted but chippy sort of Yorkshireman. He had worked at Brighouse Town Hall

rather than going to university before joining a local paper and slowly estab-
lishing himself as a skilful newspaper technician. All of them agreed, more
or less instinctively, that what was needed was a paper that recaptured the
Mirror's old sense of excitement. No one seemed to have firm ideas on how
that was going to be done.

Vic Giles, the designer, sat down on the Saturday morning and began
mapping out pages using the new typeface that had only just arrived from
America. In the largest size there were only three metal Es so, as someone
remarked, there had better not be any headlines about the Bee Gees. Luckily,
they had a story: involving an obscure racing trainer who admitted a bit of
hanky-panky, it ran under the headline:

HORSE DOPE SENSATION

Well, it was better than GOOD MORNING!

The chaos of that weekend has been well documented: the reams of worthy
stories submitted by reporters from the old *Sun* who still imagined the paper
might care about Biafra and Greece; the fact that the phones arrived only
just in time after Lamb pleaded with the Postmaster-General, John Stone-
house; the overcrowding and confusion in the office; the sports desk secretary
telling some bloke to move the furniture, not realizing he was the proprietor;
union officials demanding that Mrs Murdoch be made an honorary member
before she be allowed to touch the button ceremonially to start the presses;
the fact that when she did press the button the damned things wouldn't start
properly anyway; the paper limping off the presses three hours late; Mrs
Murdoch suggesting that perhaps she and her husband ought to go straight
back to Australia; the paper failing to arrive in the north of England until
mid-morning but getting safely into the *Mirror* offices, where Cudlipp
chortled that there was nothing to worry about . . .[12]

But one button worked right from the start. On that Monday morning,
Murdoch found, without fumbling, the British public's funny bones and
erogenous zones. He has never let go. Never has the old rhyme been more
apposite.

> Tickle the public, make 'em grin,
> The more you tickle, the more you'll win;
> Teach the public, you'll never get rich,
> You'll live like a beggar and die in a ditch.

IV

Just below the red seal saying *The Sun* was the slogan dropped by the *Mirror* in 1959: Forward With The People. In some editions, it crept up into the red background, creating a maroon smudge. Much of the paper was ripped off from the *Mirror*: 'Liveliest Letters' instead of 'Live Letters'; on the first Saturday there was a column by Robert Connor, Cassandra's son; among the cartoons there was Wack, who was a younger version of Andy Capp, and instead of the hunk spaceman Garth, there was Scarth, a bare-breasted spacewoman operating in the year 2170.

Scarth's were the only breasts in the first paper. Page 3 did have a pin-up – 'Swedish charmer Ulla Lindstrom . . . She's just the sort of gorgeous blonde you hope will smile at you on a dull back-to-work Monday morning.' But she was actually displaying less flesh than the average blonde one did meet on a Monday morning in the mini-skirted year of 1969. The following day there was a photo of a topless girl: Uschi Obermeier, who was shown on the centre pages amid the vague pretence that here was a news story: she was a £100-a-day model who preferred to live in a Berlin squat. And on the second Tuesday Gunila Wall's nipples were decidedly visible through a wet T-shirt. But the stylized, breast-centred, Page Three pin-up did not yet exist.

Nonetheless, sex pervaded the paper. On Day One *The Sun* began serializing Jacqueline Susann's new steam-pot novel *The Love Machine*. The first Pacesetters page in the tabloid *Sun* had a feature entitled 'Undies for Undressing'. And the fourth issue had a front-page story headlined

MEN ARE BETTER LOVERS IN THE MORNING – OFFICIAL

These sorts of stories would become staples of tabloid journalism, often picked up from obscure medical journals or market research documents. At the time it was revolutionary. News was meant to be news. And even Lamb was not entirely convinced by the discovery: the story was dwarfed by a *Mirror*-style Page One Comment about solicitors overcharging for conveyancing.

But after only a week the paper began editorializing on sex: 'The Permissive Society is not an opinion. It is a fact . . . *The Sun* is on the side of youth. It will never think what is prim must be proper. It will never accept a code without reason. It will never urge others to do so. **It believes the only real crime is to hurt people.**' How very 1960s. And, very soon, the young paper's hormones were absolutely raging.

GIRLS, DON'T BE CAUGHT BENDING

A personal letter from a college principal to 400 teenage girl students warns them of the dangers of bending over in a mini-skirt.

The sight of exposed bottoms is proving too distracting for male students and lecturers at Elms Technical College, Stoke-on-Trent.

SEX IS A PLEASURE – EVEN FOR CHELSEA PENSIONERS

MINISTER UNCOVERS A WIFE-SWAPPING CLUB

A Methodist minister, it must be stressed, in Consett, County Durham.

STRIPPER AT THE TEACH-IN ON SEX SHOCKS CITY'S MAYOR

LADIES OF THE W.I. STRIP FOR PANTIE PANTO

HOW TO BE IRRESISTIBLE: Six easy lessons on how to win with women

And so on. The journalists were giving Murdoch the first of the three elements he wanted: sex. And contests there were – endlessly. The sport was an interesting case. Theoretically, the paper had no chance. With no Manchester printing, it had absurdly early deadlines and for about a third of the country was unable to provide a basic service of evening football results and match reports. Instead the sports editor Frank Nicklin filled the paper with ghosted columns, some churned out by put-upon hacks under the names of highly paid stars, some given a regional flavour. They were so popular that when deadlines did improve and there was more live match reporting in the paper, people screamed to have the old stuff back.

The whole paper seemed blessed from the start, even in the most traditional way imaginable: the racing tipster Templegate started picking winners from Day One and on Day Four got ten up out of thirteen. *The Sun* was being talked about; people wanted to see it, and if it was slightly elusive because the distribution was so haywire, that merely added to its appeal.

'This is an old way to create a new paper. Sex and sensation . . .' sniffed a *Times* leader-writer dismissively after scanning the first issue, little dreaming that in less than a dozen years he and his ilk would become a minor outpost of the empire of *The Sun*. He then went on to consider the use of language in Nicklin's opening address to the readers of his sports pages:

THIS IS IT, FOLKS

'It would be interesting to know,' said *The Times*, 'whom, except for his readers, Mr Nicklin would address as "folks". Would he call his colleagues in the office "folks"?' Nicklin sent a cheery riposte, which was probably the first letter to be published in *The Times* beginning 'Dear Folks'.

But within a few weeks the media columnist Sheila Black was writing in the *Financial Times* that *The Sun* had 'a soaraway, crest-of-the-wave feeling'. Sheila Black happened to be married to Lee Howard, editor of the *Mirror*. It was typical of the new paper's jackdaw qualities that 'soaraway' was seized upon as a catchphrase, as was 'folks'.

Larry Lamb would wander round the office, and whisper into Vic Giles's ears the latest sales figures: 1.2 million, 1.4 million, 1.5 million . . . UP, UP, UP, as the paper announced after just three months. Within a year Graham King, the promotions director – another Australian, and author of a book on the French novelist Zola (Strewth, as Barry Mackenzie would have said) – had evolved the breathless style of TV ads using the actor Christopher Timothy getting as many words as he could into thirty seconds of Sunday night prime time to promote whatever the theme was for that particular week: Pony Week, Laugh Week, Fishing Week, Doggy Week, Down Under Week. Ooh la la Week offered free weekends in Paris, for instance – and half-price French knickers. The Independent Television Authority were unhappy about the knickers, but not nearly as unhappy as they were about Pussy Week.

This was not *The Sun* of the 1980s. It was 'free from nastiness', Lamb insisted later.[13] 'It was almost innocent,' according to Bernard Shrimsley. 'We were a bit naughty, a bit cheeky. We weren't being filthy.'[14] When the sports editor tried to put in a headline related to the Football Association saying

SWEET F.A.

Lamb objected, saying: 'We all know what that means.'

The success of the formula was evident long before the paper's first birthday, when the paper announced the presents it was giving its readers:

WIN The holiday of a lifetime

WIN A piece of Tom Jones and Engelbert Humperdinck

AND THAT'S NOT ALL!

SUPERDAY! The birthday suit girl. Page Three

Before readers could receive anything there was a little speech:

> From time to time some self-appointed
> critic stamps his tiny foot and declares
> that *The Sun* is obsessed with sex. It is
> not *The Sun*, but the critics, who are
> obsessed. *The Sun*, like most of its
> readers, likes pretty girls. And if they
> are as pretty as today's Birthday Suit
> girl, 20-year-old Stephanie Rahn of
> Munich, who cares whether they are
> dressed or not?

And there she was: sitting in the woods, elbows on her knees, arms caressing her shoulder, left nipple erect. Funny how the Germans are always the first to strip off.

V

Murdoch told Larry Lamb he expected *The Sun* to pass the *Mirror* in five years; Lamb, nervously, said ten. It took eight and a half on the official ABC six-monthly figures, until the first half of 1978, though *The Sun* reckoned the change actually came late in 1977. *The Sun*'s circulation had gone past two million in 1971, past three million in 1973, and the graphs crossed just under the four million mark.

The Sun's rise was unprecedented in newspaper history, but the *Mirror*'s fall was not catastrophic. It was just that they seemed entirely unable to evolve a coherent response. Cudlipp was said to have banned the subject in his hearing before he retired in 1973. He became fatalistic: 'A hand reaches out from the grave to all successful empires at some time or other,' he said in 1995. 'The *Daily Mirror* did not wish, certainly in my time, to compete with the tit and bum policy ... However, that was the situation. And now *The Sun* has the top sale. Good luck to it.'

It was five years before anyone overtly began to take a different line. Derek Jameson, then the *Mirror*'s northern editor, tentatively began to steal the idea of Page Three girls (buying cheaply from the freelance photographers the shots *The Sun* rejected), using them in the Manchester edition of the paper and, so he claimed, starting to reduce the slide in circulation. He reported an exchange with Tony Miles, Cudlipp's successor as editorial director.

'What are you doing putting nudes in the *Daily Mirror*?'

'OK, Tony,' replied Jameson. 'If you don't mind *The Sun* overtaking the *Mirror* in the north, then we'll stop printing nudes.'

'Well, I'm not saying that, am I, cock?'[15]

It was not clear what Miles *was* saying. If the *Mirror* announced a new idea for the following week, *The Sun*, much nimbler in its decision-making, would often just pinch the idea: when the *Mirror* trailed a sporting 'Where Are They Now?' series for the following week, Nicklin got his chums at the Hayter's sports agency to bash out a bigger version over the weekend. The *Mirror* could not respond as fast because the set-up was so much more bureaucratic. Not until 1976 did the paper even appear to confront the problem when Mike Molloy, now the editor, was talking to the safely neutral figure of a *New York Times* reporter: 'The *Mirror* had a middle-aged image,' he said. 'People who worked for it had got older. They were either too frightened or unable to change the formula. Well, we're doing it now.'[16]

But it never really worked, even then. The *Mirror* tried nudes, then stopped. It ceased trying to be intelligent and, in the process, ceased to be itself. It could never be as economic because it was so overstaffed, and in the political climate of the 1970s it was not possible for a paper so strongly allied to the Labour Party to deal with the situation. The *Mirror* could no longer be anti-Establishment, because all those peers on its payroll or pension roll now *were* the Establishment. In 1970, *The Sun* had called for the honours list to be abolished.

The Sun never lost the raucous confidence it displayed from the very first day. Slowly the idea of the topless pin-up became firmly established, though it was the mid-seventies before it became compulsory in all circumstances except the direst national emergency. Between 1972 and 1975 Lamb handed over the editorship to Shrimsley and became the group's editorial director; the paper never missed a beat, though Shrimsley was perhaps a little more concerned with the details of design and a little less with the actual size of the girls' breasts (he is reputed to have once pencilled the instruction: 'Make nipples less fantastic' on a picture).

Sun reporters still covered news stories in the old-fashioned way, even foreign news stories. But by 1977, when 'Forward With The People' had finally disappeared from page 1, it was possible to detect the paper freeing itself from more of the old newspaper conventions. It began not merely to report the salacious stories but to splash them on the front page:

BLACK BRA BAN ON SCHOOL LOLITAS

VICAR QUITS FOR LOVE OF NURSE

RAPE JUDGE AND A MR X

This process was helped by the appearance on the scene of Joyce McKinney, a beauty accused of kidnapping a Mormon missionary out of sexual obsession who announced that she loved him so much she 'could have skied down

Mount Everest in the nude with a carnation up my nose.' (That's what the papers said, anyway.) In the face of stories like this, it was difficult for any journalist to contend that the paper should be concentrating on the latest negotiations between European agriculture ministers.

VI

'Apparently,' said Cecil King witheringly, when Murdoch took over the *News of the World*, 'it will give him greater standing in Australia.' But the advent of *The Sun* had a curious effect. News of the screws was now available in *The Sun* every morning and Sunday was no longer special. Circulation fell spectacularly, from 6.4 million at the start of 1970 to the merest fraction over four million by 1983. Its rivals, the *Sunday Mirror* and *The People*, fell almost as rapidly as the *News of the World* and its position as market leader on Sundays was never threatened, but for a few months in the early 1980s *The Sun* overhauled it as the biggest-selling paper in the country and the English-speaking world.

Bernard Shrimsley, editor of the *News of the World* between 1975 and 1980, begged Murdoch to turn it into a tabloid. But he refused. It was as though he was in awe of the institution. Bare breasts crept into the *News of the World* much more slowly and coyly than they did into *The Sun*. In its hypocrisy, though, the paper was more shameless than ever:

THIS TV SHOCKER IS THE WORST EVER

By Weston Taylor

A programme which goes further than anything I have ever seen on TV is to be screened on Thursday night.

Millions of viewers will find its frankness offensive. ITV should brace itself for a wave of protest.

The programme is a documentary about the weird underground film-maker Andy Warhol.

In it pretty young women use four-letter words frequently and talk about all types of sexual activity.

This appeared on 14 January 1973, on a front page which also contained:

DOUBLE LIFE OF A TOPLESS DANCER

STAR FACES STRIP CHARGE

BANK GIRL IS THE NUDE OF THE MONTH

PARTY KILLER BURIED NUDE VICTIM

And it was the prelude to a spectacular run of splash stories. On the five Sundays from 28 January to 25 February 1973, the major news stories of the week were:

SCANDAL OF THE SEX SHOW BOOM

HOLY MAN LURES GIRL INTO SEX TRAP

SHOCK RISE IN SEX CRIMES

ORGY GIRL MURDER SENSATION

DIAL-DATE GIRLS IN SEX SHOCK

Perhaps no paper in the history of popular journalism has ever had a streak like that, though it ended with a dull thud on 4 March:

**WHAT'S WRONG WITH
LABOUR?**

By Lord George-Brown

The word 'sex' appeared in nine of the *News of the World*'s main headlines in 1973, 'vice' in three, 'strip' in two and 'love' in two – but only in connection with 'nest' and 'raft'.

Journalistically, the paper had its legitimate triumphs in the 1970s. In 1971 it exposed the 'payola' scandal at the BBC: record-pluggers used cash and sexual favours to get their discs played on Radio One – an abuse of the broadcasting monopoly that Rupert Murdoch would have relished exposing even more enthusiastically twenty years later when his television channels were in direct opposition to the Corporation. In 1973 the paper got the story of the prostitute, Norma Levy, who slept with a junior defence minister and provided an engaging if lower-key reprise of the Profumo Affair. In 1978 it infiltrated a paedophile organization.

Bernard Shrimsley was wont to hum a snatch from A *Funny Thing Happened on the Way to the Forum* as he wandered round the 'stone', where the metal type, before new technology arrived, was hammered into a newspaper page: 'Something appealing, Something appalling, Something for everyone, It's comedy tonight.' Which was a fair summary, except for anyone unfortunate enough to get in the paper's way. Sometimes it all got very complicated:

THE NIGHT A SERGEANT WENT UPSTAIRS
WITH HIS WIFE'S VIRGIN TWIN SISTER

HUSBAND CHANGES SEX TO KEEP LESBIAN
WIFE WHO FELL FOR A NANNY

THE DOCTOR, THE DEVIL AND THE
TOPLESS GO-GO GIRL

and, in newspaper folklore, most famously:

NUDIST WELFARE MAN'S MODEL WIFE
FELL FOR THE CHINESE HYPNOTIST FROM
THE CO-OP BACON FACTORY

All human life was there, all right. But then it was there every morning in *The Sun* as well. It was creating a bit of a problem.

VII

By the mid-1970s Murdoch was moving on. In 1973 he bought his first US paper, in San Antonio, Texas. In 1976 he bought the *New York Post*, taking a liberal, much-liked but little-read newspaper down to what many Americans regarded as the journalistic gutter. They had become very fastidious in these matters, and as likely to be horrified on a trip to Europe by first sighting *The Sun* as by their first sight of a Turkish toilet.

American daily papers, once the epitome of journalistic excess, a crucial influence on both Northcliffe's *Mail* and Bartholomew's *Mirror*, were now as respectable and as drearily written as the grey-prose Fleet Street papers of the 1890s, whose cosy world was destroyed by Northcliffe. Murdoch did not have the same effect on the American press. He started a few local circulation wars before his attention was caught by the electronic media, which is another story. In truth, his *Post* was always more like the *Daily Mail* than *The Sun*, but that did not stop the American Establishment being shocked by it. At a party, Murdoch is supposed to have chided a director of Bloomingdale's for not advertising in the *Post*. 'But Rupert,' he replied, 'your readers are my shoplifters.'

Over much of America, not only the shoplifting classes but the working classes too were ceasing to read daily papers at all. Whatever else *The Sun* may have done, it ensured that the habit of daily newspaper reading, which had slowly developed over the past century, remained ingrained throughout British society.

There was another reason for Murdoch to be elsewhere. On 29 December 1969, six weeks after *The Sun*'s launch, Muriel McKay, the wife of Alick McKay, Murdoch's deputy chairman, was kidnapped from her home in Wimbledon by two Trinidadian brothers, the Hoseins, who were ultimately convicted of her murder. Her body was never found. At the time the Murdochs were in Australia and McKay was using the boss's Rolls-Royce; the brothers apparently believed Mrs McKay was actually Anna Murdoch. They were not caught for eight months and during that period police advised the Murdoch family to stay in Australia. It was said, in any case, that London society did not appeal to the Murdochs and vice versa. The kidnap did not improve Mrs Murdoch's enthusiasm for living in Britain.

This meant that Murdoch was less of an activist proprietor than he might have been. When Murdoch was asked about *The Sun*, he was inclined to say: 'It's not my paper, it's Larry's.'[17] He endorsed its general direction, occasionally made suggestions, sometimes shuffled the managerial team, decided when to invest money in TV advertising. Murdoch was on the phone to Lamb all the time, especially in the early days, often without regard to the time of day. But he did not bombard his editors with daily instructions about what should or should not be the main story, like Northcliffe or Beaverbrook. He was more often wise after the event.

Once during his time as editor Shrimsley got a call from Murdoch suggesting the paper should call for the withdrawal of British troops from Northern Ireland. Shrimsley thought that would be immoral, argued his case, and Murdoch backed off, which is one telling detail. But not before he had advanced his major argument: 'It would be popular,' he said.

It would be popular! It is a line to bear in mind when one considers the twists and turns of the paper's political direction. There were six general elections in the first two decades of Murdoch's *Sun*. Not once did it oppose the party which looked as though it was going to win. In 1970 it endorsed the Labour Party, which was expected to retain power under Harold Wilson – not as slavishly as the *Daily Herald* would have done, nor even as full-heartedly as the old *Sun*, but firmly enough: 'THE SUN WOULD VOTE LABOUR. Not because the Government has been a scintillating success. But because, all things considered, we think that Harold Wilson has the better team.' To general surprise, Wilson lost. In February 1974, when Wilson's conqueror Ted Heath called an election to enquire who should run the country, the Government or the striking miners, *The Sun* endorsed the view of the opinion polls that Heath should: 'Ted's Tories look the better bet . . . Mr Wilson is incapable of inspiring the sense of national pride and purpose which alone can save us.' Again there was an upset. Heath lost, though so narrowly that Wilson had to call another election seven months later.

This time *The Sun* was thoroughly confused: 'The best answer is to vote for the candidates you would like to see in a Government of all parties.' The country got a Labour Government again, with just enough of a majority to linger on in office, under Wilson and then Jim Callaghan, until May 1979.

The paper's indecisiveness meant its readers probably got more balanced election coverage than those of any mass-circulation paper in British history. They just did not get much of it. The last week of January 1974, with the country in the grip of the three-day week and Heath preparing to go to the polls, was Laugh Week in *The Sun*. However, the paper was edging towards a different approach. And in the late 1970s the new leader of the Conservative Party began to appear regularly in Larry Lamb's office of an evening for chats and glasses of whisky.

The two most detailed histories of *The Sun* differ slightly in their interpretations of the change that occurred. 'Rupert and I both began to feel that socialism was not the answer to anything,' wrote Lamb years later. 'In particular, I began to sense, in the words of Labour's former deputy premier, George Brown, that it wasn't so much a question of my leaving the Labour Party as the Labour Party leaving me.'[18] The paper's chroniclers thought he might have been more influenced by the courtship sessions in his office:

> When the meetings warmed up she would slump into an armchair, cross her legs demurely and gently flex her ankle, allowing her shoe to dangle from the tip of her toe. Lamb assumed a commanding but relaxed position, informally resting his backside on his desk. When the hacks asked questions Mrs Thatcher would answer inconclusively, or descend into deep and puzzled thought aided by more shoe-dangling. Finally she would turn her eyes upwards towards Lamb and in a quiet, concerned voice ask: 'What do you think, Larry?' Lamb would puff up with pride and begin pompously expounding his thoughts on the country's problems. As he droned on Mrs Thatcher would nod steadily, mustering as much rapt attention as the whisky would allow. 'You know, that's marvellous,' she would say finally. 'If only I had people like you who really know how to communicate. Absolutely marvellous.'[19]

Everyone had by now happily forgotten that it was *The Sun* which had gleefully popularized the phrase 'Maggie Thatcher – Milk Snatcher' when she had abolished free school milk as an economy measure during her stint as Heath's Education Secretary.

Larry Lamb had come a long way from Brighouse. He was a rich man who enjoyed the good life. It was hard to see what he imagined the Callaghan Government had to do with socialism, but it was perfectly reasonable for him to be attracted personally by the tax-cutting agenda proposed by Mrs

Thatcher. His proprietor no longer had a bust of Lenin in his room, either. He was a global businessman. But this was perhaps a minor detail; he wanted to back the winners and this time it was easier to judge who they might be. Had their newspaper merely mumbled an endorsement of the Conservative Party on an inside page the day before the election, it would probably have been as uninfluential as it was in 1970 and 1974.

But by the end of the decade *The Sun* found itself in step with the mood of the country with almost the same certainty of touch that the *Mirror* had displayed in 1945. The editor understood the journalistic problem – 'Politics don't sell newspapers, but they cannot be sold without them'[20] – and he had Cudlipp's intuitive grasp of how a paper can exercise its subsidiary function of influencing events.

Callaghan was expected to call an election in October 1978, when the opinion polls suggested the gap between the parties was very narrow. The polls, however, had not done well at the previous three elections. He chose to wait. But as autumn turned into a cold winter, the fragile pact between the unions and the Labour Party fell to pieces. So did the Prime Minister's political judgement. Early in January 1979 he went to a conference of Western leaders which happened to be held on the French Caribbean island of Guadeloupe. It must have seemed a good idea at the time. While he was away, being pictured in a fetching beach shirt, there was a series of public service strikes and *The Sun* was running these headlines:

2 January   CARRY ON SHIVERING!

3 January   SIBERIA SOCKS IT TO BRR-BRR BRITAIN

4 January   BRRR! IT'S GOING TO GET WORSE!

5 January   SHOPPING PANIC – AIRPORT CHAOS

8 January   MILES OF MISERY

This was a reference to the petrol queues, which had now been added to the airport, rail and lorry strikes. Two days later Callaghan arrived back at Heathrow and was asked by reporters what he planned to do about the 'mounting chaos'.

'That's a judgement you are making. I don't think other people would share the view there is mounting chaos . . . as regards domestic affairs, I'm trying to raise your eyes a little because, believe me, there are other issues in the world as well.'

The headline Lamb put on this was:

CRISIS? WHAT CRISIS?

It was not a quote. *The Sun* did not pretend that it was. But it was a brilliant summary of Callaghan's tone. And it has passed into the language.

On election day, 3 May 1979, *The Sun* published a three-page comment, welded together by Lamb, headed

VOTE TORY THIS TIME

This is D-Day. D for Decision. The first day of the rest of our lives.

The Sun today particularly wishes to address itself to the traditional supporters of the Labour Party and to those people who have not hitherto had the opportunity to vote in a General Election.

We are particularly well-qualified so to do . . .

Hang on a moment. Particularly (twice)? Hitherto? So to do? Are these tabloid newspaper constructions? Was this written by the man who came up with CRISIS? WHAT CRISIS? One can sense a newspaper nervously clearing its throat. There was reason to be nervous. The print workers sabotaged the typesetting, were forced to do it again – which meant, under Fleet Street's prevailing lunacy, that the perpetrators were paid double – and the paper was late. But *The Sun* had the winner this time, all right:

NUMBER TEN, MAGGIES DEN

was the headline on the Saturday morning. The following Wednesday, the paper printed twenty-six different nipples to give readers an opportunity to choose their favourite Page Three girl. But the pin-up *The Sun* was to love the best and the longest was now in power.

VIII

Margaret Thatcher was to have one rival for *The Sun*'s affections, and she was just moving into the readers' consciousness. She was unveiled on 8 September 1980:

HE'S IN LOVE AGAIN

Prince Charles has found love on the rebound.

He has fallen head over heels for beautiful Lady Diana Spencer, 19 years old and a perfect English rose. And last night friends were asking: Is it the real thing for Charles at last? For dishy Diana is acceptable in every way to the Queen and Prince Philip.

She is quiet-spoken, unassuming and has an impeccable background – the perfect qualities for the future queen.

Here, then, was the tabloid editor's promised land, inhabited by both Margaret Thatcher and Princess Di. It was a land which, like Moses, Larry Lamb was only to glimpse. By 1980, it had been more than a decade since he took over *The Sun*. He was past fifty rather than just forty. There was a feeling among Murdoch's associates that he had begun to get, in the splendid Australian phrase, rather up himself. The newer *Sun* reporters had no opinions on this subject since they hardly saw him. There was a special phone on the back-bench, the desk where the senior sub-editors sat, which only took calls from the editor. He had become as remote as Lee Howard. He was very interested in his fine wines.

Despite Lamb's suggestion in 1970, the Honours List had not been abolished. Indeed, with Mrs Thatcher in power, it began to be used more blatantly than for many years to reward those who had performed political favours. When the Birthday Honours were announced in June 1980, the headline

OWZAT!

proclaimed the news that Geoff Boycott had been awarded an OBE. This provided a convenient peg to mention, not too loudly, that Fitzwilliam's other famous son, Mr Larry Lamb, had been knighted for 'services to journalism'. That's what the citation said, anyway. Possibly Lamb believed it to be true. Everyone else knew that he had been knighted for his services to the Conservative Party. He had become a 'knight of the garter,' wrote Roy Hattersley, 'the exotic bra, the frilly knickers and the novelty suspender belt'.[21]

But *The Sun*, for the first time in its meteoric history, was in a little difficulty. Its daily sale in the second half of 1978 was a fraction under four million: 3,989,599. It would have been over four million but for the fact that on 2 November, it acquired a new rival.

This book is the story of newspapers run by people who understood the taste of a generation, who thrived for a time then were undone by newer, brasher, less inhibited competitors. It is like a biblical list of begattings. Thus *The Times* was superseded by the *Telegraph*, which was superseded by the *Mail*, which was superseded by the *Express*, which was superseded by the *Mirror*, which was superseded by *The Sun*. There was every reason to suppose that *The Sun* would one day suffer the same fate.

Its potential nemesis was something called the *Daily Star*, the creation of the Express Group. In 1977 Beaverbrook's son, Sir Max Aitken, tired, rather ill and short of cash for investment, had sold the *Express* to the conglomerate Trafalgar House. The firm's deputy chairman, a former contracts manager called Victor Matthews, took charge of the newspapers. 'Fleet Street', he said, 'is not overmanned, it is underworked.'[22] This was certainly true in the *Express*'s case; every year the daily print run was being cut by 100,000 because fewer people wanted to buy it. Thus the *Daily Star* came into being, with Derek Jameson, late of the *Mirror*, as editor-in-chief, printing in Manchester and concentrating on the north, where *The Sun* was still perceived as relatively weak, to utilize the *Express*'s spare capacity. What that meant was that Matthews had hundreds of workers he dare not sack doing very little. The new paper was a sort of make-work scheme, the strangest of all the side-effects of the industry's bizarre labour relations. There was not even the usual pretence of nobility.

'The *Daily Star*', said Jameson, 'will be all tits, bums, QPR and roll your own fags.' At least, that's what *The Observer* said he said: he denied it.[23] Indeed, he was hardly likely to mention QPR, a London football team, in connection with a northern-based paper. In fact, the *Daily Star* turned out to be rather more tits, bums, Manchester City and roll-your-own fags. It made *The Sun* appear highly sophisticated. Victor Matthews said he would probably not have it in his house, which may be a first for any newspaper proprietor. But the *Star* soon had something extra: it began to distribute bingo cards round the country and then printed numbers for people to check off. Bingo cards, in the early eighties, were to become to Fleet Street what Dickens novels were in the early thirties. *Star* readers would not have known who Dickens was.

In 1980 and early 1981 the *Sun*'s circulation fell: for a few weeks it may have fallen below the *Mirror*. It was time for Murdoch to play the traditional card of the worried proprietor, and change his editor. Had the *Star* not existed, the mantle might well have fallen on the assistant editor, Nick Lloyd – young, Oxford-educated, tabloid-minded, safe. Instead, Murdoch took a gamble.

IX

The history of the British popular press leads, if not exactly to a great man theory of history, and certainly not a good man theory of history, then at least to some sort of man-theory. The development of the papers has been a function of the human beings who shaped them: from Northcliffe, via Beaverbrook and Christiansen and Bartholomew and Cudlipp, to Murdoch, Lamb and Kelvin MacKenzie. Without any one of these people this would have been a very different book.

Kelvin MacKenzie was born in 1946. His parents were both journalists, on a weekly in south London. He was educated at Alleyn's School, Dulwich, and he apparently did pass an O-level: English Literature. His teachers thought he was thick. Had they been more perceptive they might have concluded that either he would become a popular newspaper editor or he would hang; and hanging, despite the best efforts of the newspaper MacKenzie edited, has not been reintroduced.

He began his journalism in south-east London at seventeen, starting on a local weekly, the *Kentish Mercury*. After a few days he had a drink with one of his colleagues, Pat Collins: 'I've sorted it out,' he said. 'They're all wankers here apart from you and me.' He soon joined a nearby news agency, Ferrari's, a traditional training ground for journalists destined for the rougher end of Fleet Street. Agencies like Ferrari's sell stories to newspapers; information equals money; and no is never a word that anyone wants to hear.

The unexpected development in his career was that he moved out of reporting into sub-editing. In journalism the profession splits into two roughly equal but in many ways opposite branches. Reporters go out on the road, have all the adventures associated with the profession, get their names in the paper and the expenses to match. Sometimes they become famous. Sub-editors work predictable hours, commute from the suburbs,[24] never go anywhere and hardly ever get any recognition. They tend to grumble a lot, especially about reporters. But – and the more down-market the paper the truer this is – they gather the power. Editors have more often moved up from the subs' table than from the reporters' room.

But they generally do so in a reasonably ordered progress, probably moving from paper to paper as opportunities occur, winning a reputation for competence, flair and nice-chapmanship – as Larry Lamb did. MacKenzie was different. He behaved obnoxiously. He is not an obnoxious man: as a young journalist, he was popular; he is capable of being very charming; he can be endearingly vulnerable. But the obnoxiousness turned into a relentless piece of performance art. He spent his time abusing anyone – reporters, colleagues, superiors – whose work did not match his own standards, in language that grew louder and coarser as the years went by. What made it possible is that his own standards were very high indeed. He had a natural, instinctive flair for turning raw information into highly readable stories on eye-catching pages. In 1973, he gravitated to *The Sun*, a paper where that sort of ability was truly appreciated. He knew at once he was in the right place.

When Murdoch was in need of journalists who could go and knock the stuffiness out of the *New York Post*, MacKenzie was a natural candidate, particularly as Lamb encouraged the move as a means of getting rid of someone it was easy to regard as a disruptive nuisance. Unfortunately for Lamb, MacKenzie enhanced his reputation on the *Post*. But his family did not settle in America, and Kelvin took a drop in status to come back and be deputy night editor of *The Sun*. Then the *Daily Express* offered him the job of night editor, a crucially responsible position. Murdoch was livid at the disloyalty, but when he scented the first hint of crisis at *The Sun*, he chose MacKenzie as his saviour. However, he did not formally announce the change at first, partly, perhaps, because there was still a small doubt in his mind, partly because the *Express* refused to release MacKenzie from his contract. A bizarre and almost certainly unique few weeks followed in which MacKenzie was racing between two offices running two competing newspapers. It would be impossible today, because now everyone has left Fleet Street the offices would be too far apart. It would have been impossible even then for anyone without MacKenzie's phenomenal energy.

It was going to take more than a few weeks of inspired night editing to revive the *Daily Express*. But at *The Sun* MacKenzie had a number of advantages. In May 1981 Murdoch reversed a previous price increase, reverting from the awkward and, at that time, slightly off-putting 12p to 10p. Secondly, he sanctioned a major investment in a bingo game that would easily surpass the *Daily Star*'s. The *Star* ran what it liked to call 'honest bingo', which anyone might win. The *Sun* game was more tightly controlled, ensuring that as many people as possible appeared to have a chance of winning as the week went on, while the paper knew that hardly any of them had a chance at all, as the numbers were predetermined. It was a far more effective circulation-builder.

This was also the year of the Royal Wedding: as *The Sun* had predicted, dishy Diana was about to become Princess Di. MacKenzie's flair, a price cut, bingo and Di – no proprietor in history had had such a combination. 'It's Sun-stoppable! It's Sun-beatable! Your super sell-out *Sun* sold 3,766,000 copies every day last month,' the front page yelled on 3 July. 'That was a fantastic 165,000 copies per day more than we sold in May.'

In June 1981 Di was on the front page ten times out of twenty-six; in July the figure was sixteen out of twenty-seven until she went away on honeymoon, which at that time put her off limits. From 9 June the bingo was there every day. Circulation went over four million. On 30 September *Sun* readers were told, on page 2, that Sir Larry Lamb had resigned as editor. He said, in the time-honoured phrase of the quietly paid-off: 'The time has come to seek new horizons.' That was as true for British journalism in general as it was for Larry Lamb. On 13 October *The Sun* carried its first truly Kelvinesque front page:

PAGE ONE OPINION

This morning *The Sun* presents the most odious man in Britain.

Take a bow, Mr Ken Livingstone, Socialist leader of the Greater London Council.

In just a few months since he appeared on the national scene, he has quickly become a joke.

Now no one can laugh at him any longer. The joke has turned sick, sour and obscene.

For Mr Livingstone steps forward as the defender and the apologist of the criminal, murderous activities of the IRA.

Livingstone wanted British troops removed from Northern Ireland. If *The Sun*'s proprietor remembered that he had once advocated taking the same position, he was keeping very quiet indeed.

X

Anecdotes about Kelvin MacKenzie cling to him, as they do to all the really great journalists. And they all seem to be true, or at least true enough in the journalistic era which he ushered in, in which newspaper truth and real truth moved further apart than ever before.

There was the time he fell back in his chair, and began screaming instructions from the horizontal, having heard someone shout 'The Queen's Dead'. It was some time before he could be persuaded that it was actually Steve McQueen who was dead. There was the incident during his *Express/Sun* period when he was bellowing down the phone an instruction that page 7 was 'absolute fucking crap' and the *Express* subs began rushing round trying to change it only to be told 'Not you, you useless cunts. I'm talking to the other load of useless cunts on the other fucking paper.' There was the time Tom Petrie, his news editor, began bashing his head against the wall by the lifts as MacKenzie arrived, saying he was giving himself a bollocking to save MacKenzie the bother.

It was a different editorial style from anything witnessed before: Arthur Christiansen crossed with Arthur Daley, perhaps. Some important journalists disappeared at once: for instance, Frank Nicklin, the sports editor. He and MacKenzie loathed each other.[25] Others gritted their teeth and survived. Some thrived on the sheer excitement MacKenzie generated, and discovered that if you stood up to him, and argued your corner, you won his respect.

But much more significant was the change in the paper itself. MacKenzie's *Sun* was at least as different from Lamb's *Sun* as that had been from the *Mirror*. Newspapers, as we have seen, have always been conduits for false-hoods. Before the twentieth century this was because their prime purpose was political propaganda; as the papers developed there were other factors.

First, since news can be defined as something that someone does not want printed, the best stories are inevitably caught as a terrier catches a rabbit down a dark hole. The nature of the process means some important bits may get left behind. Maybe the terrier chews off half the rabbit; maybe the reporter chews off half the truth. Secondly, reporters and sub-editors are fallible human beings working at speed. Thirdly, reporters work for money: either they are freelances selling stories for cash or they are staff writers desperate to keep their jobs. Hence the exercise of journalistic imagination; as we saw in the case of the *Express* and Filey Bay in 1902, not a new phenomenon. In times when competition is less intense, like the pre-*Daily Mail* 1890s, the pre-Murdoch 1950s and 1960s or the United States in the 1990s, it is easier for reporters to be more scrupulous. When papers are scrapping fiercely for every sale they can get, as in the 1930s and the 1980s, truth becomes a secondary consideration.

Fourthly, the process of newspaper production means the message gets distorted. A reporter may gather a set of facts from an interviewee. By the time he or she writes the story these will have been altered, perhaps through misunderstanding, perhaps because the reporter needs to harden up the facts and quotes to fit the demands of the paper. Then the sub-editor gets hold of the story and will make more changes, perhaps because the reporter has written with insufficient clarity, perhaps because, sitting in an office without the obligations that a reporter feels after meeting someone, the sub will decide that the account needs further hardening. To tickle the public, you tickle up the facts. So it goes. That's the game.

Wise people with no need to publicize themselves or their wares do not talk to the papers, most particularly popular ones. The *Mirror* is perhaps the best of all names for a newspaper because all papers are mirrors – but not conventional, accurate ones: they are the distorting mirrors of the seaside and the funfair. They record what is there, but the image comes out elongated or compressed. Under Kelvin MacKenzie, *The Sun* added an extra element to the distorting process. The facts had to be changed to suit the editor's idea of what was required, often to suit a headline he had already written.

No newspaper can survive by telling outright lies as a matter of habit. There is no point saying Manchester United have won when they have lost. But what a paper can do was summed up by the once-famous *Express* sports reporter Desmond Hackett: 'You'd get an idea and draw the facts towards it.' Thus it was on MacKenzie's *Sun*.

All the papers in this history have rattled and bent the bars that previously caged in newspaper techniques. MacKenzie did more than that: he smashed through them, and he was successful for a dozen years. Again, there are four main reasons. He had the support of his proprietor. His proprietor had a close relationship with a powerful and long-lasting Government, which valued *The Sun*'s political backing more than it deplored its journalistic excesses. The times were right: in the 1980s entrepreneurial freedom was in fashion; liberal intellectual tut-tutting was not. But the fourth reason was the most important. MacKenzie was a sort of genius. No other word will do.

XI

It is now probably the most famous headline ever written in Britain. Long, long ago it eclipsed the *Daily Express*'s Coronation masterpiece ALL THIS – AND EVEREST TOO! and any of the old *Mirror* screamers like MR K! DON'T BE SO BLOODY RUDE! It did not sum up the national mood like the Everest headline; it probably only summed up the mood among a few slightly unbalanced newspaper executives working late in Bouverie Street one night. But one word of Cockney slang has come to symbolize the journalism of a decade.

GOTCHA

It appeared on 4 May 1982 above the news that the Argentine warship *General Belgrano* had been torpedoed by the British, the first serious incident of the war between the two countries. It was a strange, strange time, unique in modern British history: the military dictatorship ruling Argentina had invaded the Falkland Islands, one of Britain's last remaining colonies – population 1,800 humans and a great many sheep – cold and windswept dots on the map, which the vast majority of *Sun* readers would never even have heard of a few weeks earlier.

National service had been abolished for more than two decades. Since that time Britain had become the most pacific of nations. There was the apparently interminable low-level conflict with the terrorists of the IRA. But ninety-something per cent of the population then under the age of forty had not only never marched to the sound of gunfire, they had never so much as held a rifle on a parade ground – including the editor of *The Sun*. Yet suddenly Britain was at war again.

It was a strange time in *The Sun* offices as well. The National Union of Journalists was in dispute with Rupert Murdoch's management, and on the night of 3 May the paper was being brought out by a dozen heads of department and other senior executives contractually obliged to continue working. Even in normal times, they would have felt as though they were manning a beleaguered garrison. There was, however, an extra person in the building. Because of the crisis with the union, Murdoch himself was there.

It was Wendy Henry, the pushy Woman's Editor, who first shouted the word Gotcha! round the office when the news came through over the agency teleprinters. It was MacKenzie who turned this instant reaction into a front page story. But as the evening wore on and further reports suggested that the entire crew of the *Belgrano* might have died, even MacKenzie took refuge in caution. For later editions the headline was changed to

DID 1,200 ARGIES DROWN?

Hardly anyone in London, where the last edition circulates, would have known about GOTCHA until it began to take its place in national folklore. But Murdoch knew about it. 'I wouldn't have pulled it if I were you,' he told MacKenzie. 'Seemed like a bloody good headline to me.'[26]

GOTCHA, wrote Robert Harris, was not an aberration. 'It was the logical culmination of *The Sun*'s coverage. It was the equivalent of ZAP! or POW! or – a headline which the *Sun* actually used later in the war – WALLOP! They were comic-book exclamations used by the *Sun* to describe a fantasy war which bore no resemblance to reality.'[27] Actually, it was not even original. *The Sun* had used precisely the same headline on its front page eight months earlier over a picture of the arrest of 'one of the underworld's most slippery villains, William "Billy Liar" Tobin'.

The Sun had been heading in this direction in the weeks leading up to the sinking of the *Belgrano*, with headlines like

STICK IT UP YOUR JUNTA!

(the promotions department turned this one into a T-shirt),

THE SUN SAYS KNICKERS TO ARGENTINA!

and

INVASION!

a report of the reinvasion of the outlying island of South Georgia, published before it had actually occurred.

The paper had popularized the word 'Argie', which until April had only existed as a piece of slang among the Falklanders. It had run a story, under Wendy Henry's by-line, that the first missile fired from the aircraft carrier HMS *Invincible* would carry the words 'Up Yours Galtieri' signed by its reporter on the ship, Tony Snow. It did not run a competition entitled

KILL AN ARGIE AND WIN A METRO!

That was a spoof in *Private Eye*. But the line between satire and *The Sun's* version of reality was now a great deal finer than the line between *The Sun's* reality and anyone else's.

After GOTCHA, *The Sun* turned on other parts of the media whose support for the war was less hysterical. Three days later, under the headline DARE CALL IT TREASON, the leader-writer Ronald Spark accused the *Daily Mirror* and *The Guardian* (as well as Peter Snow of the BBC) of being traitors.

> . . . *The Guardian*, with its pigmy circulation and absurd posturing, is perhaps not worth attention.
>
> The *Daily Mirror*, however, has pretensions as a mass-sale newspaper.
>
> What is it but treason for this timorous, whining publication to plead day after day for appeasing the Argentine dictators . . .

If it is possible to sum up accurately something as elusive as a national mood, then it was reflected neither by the *Mirror* and *The Guardian*, nor by *The Sun*. People were bewildered by a war for which they had been entirely unprepared, over islands which seemed so faraway and quaint. *The Sun* had not softened up its readers, as Northcliffe had before the First World War, by spending years fomenting nationalistic hatred. The last quarrel anyone had had with Argentina had been during a particularly bad-tempered quarterfinal in the 1966 World Cup; and the only Argentines most newspaper readers could have named before the war were Ossie Ardiles and Ricky Villa, two popular footballers who played for Tottenham, or perhaps – if they had seen the musical *Evita!* – the late Eva Peron.

But the British disliked the obvious stupidity, aggression and brutality of the Argentine invasion, accepted the principle that it had to be reversed, and admired the strong and principled way in which the Prime Minister, Margaret Thatcher, appeared to be going about the business. Had a thousand or so British sailors been killed by a torpedo – which might easily have happened – and the death toll among the British forces climbed above the population of the Falklands, opinion might have slid towards the *Mirror–Guardian* line.

But it did not. Mrs Thatcher was triumphant. A leader who until this point had been presiding, bossily, over a particularly painful economic recession and, according to the polls, was in danger of being usurped by an entirely new political party, the Social Democrats, now appeared as the personification of Britannia.

The Sun's war –

BLITZED!

WALLOP

THIS IS IT

CHARGE!

– was no one else's war. The *Daily Mirror* was right: *The Sun*'s coverage was 'coarse and demented'. There is no evidence that it sold newspapers: indeed, *The Sun*'s circulation dipped in the six months that included the Falklands conflict and was lower then than at any other time in the years 1981–4. In the 1980s, war sold fewer extra papers than bingo. Had Murdoch taken a different view of the GOTCHA headline on the night of 4 May, Kelvin MacKenzie might have been seeking new horizons there and then, and his editorship of *The Sun* might have been regarded as a failed experiment. But Murdoch approved of his editor: 'MacKenzie is what he is. He's out there, screaming and shouting, and he's good. Somehow it works.'[28]

No one has ever attempted a coherent defence of *The Sun*'s Falklands coverage. 'Look,' said Peter Stephens, the paper's editorial director, of Tony Snow's signed missile, 'we were tired. We just didn't have the time to sit around and have a sage discussion about the rights and wrongs of it.'[29] No one can defend the indefensible.

But Mrs Thatcher did not repudiate *The Sun*'s support. The previous year Murdoch had had his reward for the 1979 election. Unlike Lamb, he did not want a knighthood (indeed, in 1985 he became a US citizen to meet the requirements for ownership of American television stations). He settled for being allowed to buy *The Times* and the *Sunday Times* without reference to the Monopolies and Mergers Commission, a deal that sealed his position as the dominant figure of the British newspaper industry.

At the 1983 election, basking in post-Falklands popularity, Mrs Thatcher increased her majority from 43 to 143. Her victory was such a foregone conclusion, *The Sun* did not have to try all that hard on her behalf. It was more inclined to trumpet a bingo prize of £400,000 than news of an election that was not even a horse race. Mrs Thatcher's rivals for the paper's attentions were not the other party leaders but Koo Stark, Prince Andrew's actress girlfriend; Joan Collins, star of the American TV series *Dynasty*; and, as ever, Princess Di. Its election-day headline, all the same, was:

VOTE FOR MAGGIE
. . . More than any leader since Churchill was baying defiance at the Nazis,
she has captured the hearts, the minds
and the imagination of the nation . . .

If one remembers aright, this was not quite the national mood, and the Conservatives received less than 43 per cent of the votes. But against a badly split, ineptly led and increasingly left-wing Labour Party she was a certain winner. A strong leader with a huge majority ensured that for the next four years Britain would be governed in a manner closer to centralist absolutism than ever before. And dancing attendance on the Tsarina was her very own Rasputin of a newspaper.

XII

The best short guide to *The Sun*'s behaviour in the mid-1980s can be found in the recesses of *The Times Index*, one of the few publications now under Murdoch's control with no editorial slant of its own. Yet in the dry litany of stories about *The Times*'s new-found associate, one can almost sense the exasperation of an upright citizen listing the iniquities of a delinquent younger brother:

1983

SUN, The – Maltese PM awarded damages against, JAN 23; Press Council upholds comedian's complaint against, APR 25; report on trial ruled preju-dicial, MAY 11; Tony Benn considers suing over poll in Bristol East constituency, MAY 14; censured by Press Council over cartoon, JUNE 14; cricketer to be paid 'substantial damages', JULY 13; censured by Press

Council over made up world exclusive interview with widow of Falklands
VC, AUG 8 . . .

1984

SUN, The – Press Council upholds complaint about photograph of David
Niven, JAN 12; French protest over alleged anti-French campaign by,
JAN 26 . . . Press Council censures for printing picture of Brigitte Bardot,
APR 12, to be sued for contempt of court . . . actor wins damages . . .
complaint upheld . . . Press Council criticises . . .

And so on. And so on. Once *The Times*, the most respected of British newspapers, might have commented authoritatively on these excesses. But now it
was only *The Sun*'s success that enabled *Times* leader-writers to feed their
families. Anything in *The Times* about press standards simply sounded idiotic.

It was possible for MacKenzie to go too far. The interview with the Falklands widow, Mrs Marica McKay – who had refused to speak to *The Sun* –
was too blatant a fake to pass unnoticed. It touched on the very territory *The
Sun* had defined for itself: the heroism of the forces in the Falklands. Murdoch was said to be furious. There were waves. But in general the alliance
of Thatcher, Murdoch and MacKenzie was unshakeable. Smaller incidents
made only the tiniest ripples.

One early case was recorded by the writer and Labour MP Roy Hattersley.
It involved the actor Joss Ackland, whose son Paul had died suddenly in
confused circumstances. Ackland tried to head off the expected siege from
the popular press by giving interviews to *The Guardian* and *The Observer*,
hoping that the others would then lose interest. Ackland told the two papers
his son was not a drug addict. *The Sun* ran the interview under the headline

THE HELL OF HAVING A DRUG ADDICT SON

'The article in the *Sun*', wrote Hattersley, 'was a literal pastiche, the *Guardian*
and *Observer* interviews cut up into pieces and rearranged in a way that made
it look as if Mr Ackland had actually been interviewed by that paper . . . They
certainly never spoke to Joss Ackland. All they did was steal somebody else's
copy. The episode is made more poignant and more repulsive by the nature
of the story which they stole.'[30] Hattersley was about to become deputy leader
of the Labour Party; but in the 1980s that was not a position which offered
the opportunity to influence the direction of British society.

The early 1980s had much in common with the early 1930s: great opportunities for wealth creation mixed with high unemployment; and frenzied
competition among the newspapers themselves. But there was an added

element. It was no longer enough for the papers simply to beat each other. They had to offer a reason for people who would have seen news and images on their television screens the previous night to pay for a paper the following day, or risk the demise of the whole industry.

But British newspapers were dominated by one man. Rupert Murdoch owned the biggest-selling Sunday paper (plus the leading quality Sunday paper, the *Sunday Times*) as well as the biggest-selling daily paper. Even Northcliffe had never managed that. It was a position offering enormous power to influence the nature and quality of both journalism and society; yet these were not subjects that interested him. It is impossible to avoid the conclusion that at the heart of the Murdoch empire there was a vacuum, a moral void. Thus the newspapers developed an amorality of their own, inspired largely by MacKenzie.

The process of reporting changed as well as the newspapers themselves. Doorstepping was and is one of the most baffling of all British newspaper traditions. Photographers and reporters descend on the home of a person touched by scandal or tragedy – the two merge into one for these purposes – and wait, in the hope of a picture of one of the actors in the drama or, far less probably, a comment. It is a tiresome and, for the reporters, almost always a pointless chore, unless they are actually paying to buy the story. 'I've done hundreds of doorsteps,' said Jim Lewthwaite, twenty-two years on *The Sun*, 'and I doubt if half a dozen have given anyone a story.'

Until the 1970s all the reporters on the case would almost certainly know all the others, and they could do the job in shifts. Now, as the number of news media outlets increased, the doorstepping brigade would swell to vast numbers, and there would be desperate youngsters on the make who wouldn't dare leave and would keep knocking on the door, regardless of the sensitivities involved. And the *Sun* reporters would never be allowed to leave, until the story was so old that people could hardly remember who on earth they were doorstepping and why, or until the *Daily Mail*, most relentless of their opponents when it came to pursuing a quarry, also left – whichever came second. (Communication between office and doorstep is, however, easier now with mobile phones; and Norman Smart, an *Express* reporter of the 1930s, said it was infinitely worse before motor cars.)

The Royal Family were permanent candidates for this treatment. And when editors were summoned to Buckingham Palace to be asked to allow the pregnant Princess Diana a little peace, MacKenzie refused to attend and certainly never instructed his staff to allow her any peace. The Royals were permanent stars of the soap opera being played on the *Sun* pages. 'Mac-Kenzie, who had no strong feelings about them, treated them rather like partridges – dumb creatures to be kept in good health so that they could be shot down whenever he felt like it.'[31] The rest of the cast shifted fast according to MacKenzie's devastatingly accurate perceptions of public taste: Page Three girls Samantha Fox and Linda Lusardi; pop stars like Boy George and Wham!; the comedian and Lothario, Jim 'Nick-Nick' Davidson; sexy newsreader Selina Scott; Dempsey and Makepeace, TV 'tecs who were conducting a real-life romance. But what was real and what was fictional? It was becoming hard to tell.

In 1985 the BBC began a new TV soap opera, a Cockney version of *Coronation Street* called *EastEnders*. Its characters all looked and sounded like *Sun* readers and MacKenzie correctly divined that this was going to be big. The newspaper and the programme developed a symbiotic relationship. It began with a genuine and amazing story that the star of the show – Leslie Grantham, who played the pub landlord 'Dirty Den' – had been convicted of murdering a taxi driver years earlier. Dirty Den the actor merged into his character; reality and fantasy seemed to be mixed. It became hardest of all to tell how much of the coverage was being orchestrated by TV publicists, what was legitimate reporting, what was harassment and what was simply invention. And less and less did anyone seem to care.

XIII

The second half of the 1980s was a golden age of British journalism. This, like many introductory paragraphs written during that era, is the truth, if not the whole truth.

The newspaper proprietors had a couple of extraordinary bits of luck. The first was that the Reuters news agency, in which the Fleet Street papers were major shareholders, had slowly transformed itself from a rickety old firm that provided accurate and, best of all, cheap foreign news into a slick organization selling financial information systems. In 1973 it made £700,000 profit; in 1983 it made £55 million. Displaying unusual devotion to the common cause, the owners cashed in by floating the organization on the Stock Exchange. It was like discovering that the dusty old picture in the attic was a Caravaggio.

Their second bit of luck was that they had Murdoch to lead the way. The Reuters money was a drop in the bucket to Rupert Murdoch. He needed to maximize the revenue *The Sun* and the *News of the World* were capable of producing in order to finance his global ambitions. Finally, he managed it.

In January 1986 the print unions on Murdoch's London newspapers went on strike, as they had done so often over the previous seventeen years. They were protesting against the owner's plans to move publishing and production to a new plant at Wapping, two miles east of Fleet Street. This time, however, they did not succeed in wringing concessions from an exasperated management. This time, they walked straight into a lovingly constructed heffalump trap from which they never escaped. For *The Times* it was a reprise of the events of 1814.

The haphazard labour relations of Fleet Street had at last taken Murdoch past boiling point. By 1985 linotype operators on the *Daily Express* were reported to be earning £1,100 for a sixteen-hour week[32] – doing a job in a manner that dated back to Northcliffe's time, and which was now wholly unnecessary: it was far more efficient for the journalists to type their own copy directly into the computer system. This was only a slightly extreme case.

Through 1985 Murdoch's employees equipped the Wapping plant while pretending to be preparing for the launch of a phantom newspaper, the *London Post*. The unions refused to work at Wapping and performed the most carefully practised of all their ancient arts: they went on strike. They were deemed to have dismissed themselves, an idle threat that had been uttered many times before. But this time they stayed dismissed. *The Sun*, *The Times*, the *News of the World* and the *Sunday Times* continued from Wapping, without the unions, using the men, machinery and distribution system that had been secretly put in place. The stratagem was made possible primarily by the new computerized technology, which was in use in newspapers throughout even the Third World, though not in the primeval swamp of Fleet Street; by the Thatcher Government's new industrial relations law, which heavily constrained the unions' ability to counter-attack; and by Murdoch's possession of the resources, the will and the audacity to carry the plan through.

In the wake of the Murdoch coup the other national newspapers were able to persuade their print workers that the game was up, and used their Reuters windfall to pay redundancy money and invest in new equipment. The recession of the early 1980s turned into a boom leading to a surge in advertising. In 1986 two new daily newspapers began: *Today*, owned by Eddy Shah, and *The Independent*, started by three ex-*Telegraph* journalists. Other hacks found that the labour market had turned more sharply in their favour than at any time in memory, perhaps in history.

Sun journalists, with a handful of exceptions, had agreed to go to Wapping, after a speech by MacKenzie that encapsulated the whole history of newspaper production in a few Kelvinesque sentences: 'In a minute-by-minute industry, when they've got you by the balls, you've got to listen. Well, they haven't got us by the balls any more . . . The only people who matter any more are the journalists.' They were each promised a £2,000 bribe and free health care. None of them needed reminding that the one time print workers could be relied on not to go on strike was when the journalists were in dispute, as during the Falklands, when the printers had cheerfully crossed NUJ picket lines.

But while Wapping did indeed give journalists new freedom, it gave proprietors, and their manic editors, even more. Outside the razor wire, the print workers – or at any rate their left-wing supporters – were screaming abuse. Inside the hideous new building, the editor of *The Sun* was doing the same. In Bouverie Street, MacKenzie had been constrained by the layout of the building. Now all the editorial staff were on one floor, and he was able to patrol it constantly. One reporter compared him to Captain Peacock, the store floorwalker in *Are You Being Served?*

By shouting, intimidating, cajoling, MacKenzie was able more than ever before to construct the kind of paper he wanted. And on 13 March, six weeks after the move to Wapping, he came up with the headline that will stand alongside GOTCHA as the epitaph of the MacKenzie era:

FREDDIE STARR ATE
MY HAMSTER

Zany comic Freddie Starr put a live hamster in a sandwich and ATE it, model girl Lea La Salle claimed yesterday.
 . . . She said: 'I was sickened and horrified. He killed my pet.' . . .

'Anyone could have written that headline,' the former *Sun* editor Bernard Shrimsley said years later. 'Only Kelvin could have put it on the front page.' But only in MacKenzie's paper could such a story have crawled out from under its stone. The incident had happened three years earlier. It was apparently an exaggeration of a joke in which Starr had pretended to eat the hamster. And lurking close to the story was Starr's PR man, Max Clifford, who was to become the Lucifer of the booming netherworld where truth, half-truth, exaggeration and publicity met and mingled.

The constant stream of *EastEnders* stories continued throughout 1986 and into 1987, generally outshouting anything connected with the real world, but occasionally interacting with it.

SEARCH FOR REAL-LIFE DIRTY DENS

EASTENDERS KILLED OUR MARRIAGE

and

LOVE ROW ENDS WITH
THREE SUICIDES

Three young friends killed themselves
after a lovers' tiff – and a fourth was left
fighting for her life . . . Last night, one
mother blamed at least two of the deaths
on the TV soap opera *EastEnders*. The
hit BBC show featured an overdose
drama at the Queen Vic pub last month.

For the most part, stories about the Royal Family were allowed to continue
in the newspaper without necessarily having an *EastEnders* angle, but even
this was not assured. As a follow-up to the news of the engagement of Prince
Andrew and Sarah Ferguson, *The Sun* reported that Leslie Grantham – Dirty
Den – had sent a message congratulating them and added 'Thanks for keeping
me off the front page.' There was also a story that the actor who played Pete
Dean in the series was living with a woman who had been out with Prince
Charles. As the old song might have gone: 'I danced with a man who danced
with a girl who danced with an actor in *EastEnders*.'

Observing MacKenzie in these years was like watching a tightrope act.
From the day it started, Murdoch's *Sun* had the ability to play to male sexual
tastes without alienating women. Under MacKenzie it was able to hint at
racism –

FREEBIE TRIPS FOR BLACKS, BUT WHITE KIDS MUST PAY

– while still maintaining a substantial black readership. Overt racism was
reserved for the French and Germans, the Frogs and Krauts, who were not
in the paper's circulation area. There were racial undertones to the campaign
against the Loonies, the Labour left-wingers whose last operational base was
the increasingly powerless local councils. There was, for instance, this classic,
on 20 February 1987:

BAA-BAA BAN ON SAD
LITTLE DAN

Handicapped tot Daniel Griffin delighted his mum by reciting Baa Baa
Black Sheep but loony leftie teachers
banned it – for being racist! . . . They
put a note in the five-year-old's progress
book complaining: We do not encourage
the rhyme . . . It has been identified as
racially derogatory and is actively dis-
couraged by Islington Council.

In so far as one can ever uncover the provenance of such stories, it appears that no council ever did ban Baa Baa Black Sheep, but teachers believed they had done, having read it in the newspapers.

It was six years before MacKenzie even began to wobble on the tightrope. The first major problem came with a story about the pop star Elton John that appeared on 25 February 1987:

ELTON IN VICE BOYS SCANDAL

with a follow-up the next day

ELTON'S KINKY KICKS

which was billed as a SUN WORLD EXCLUSIVE. It had to be, because the whole thing was a fabrication. But before the full consequences of this could unfold, *The Sun*'s phenomenal success caused one of its rivals to press the panic button.

XIV

Not every proprietor was still standing when the time came to collect the post-Wapping prize money. In 1985 Lord Hartwell, chairman of the *Telegraph*, a-weary of the struggle, took fright at his paper's economic position and sold to a right-wing Canadian tycoon, Conrad Black. The *Mirror*'s owners had merged with a firm of paper manufacturers and emerged as Reed International, a conglomerate that grew increasingly bored with funding a newspaper whose anti-Tory editorial views were almost as incomprehensible as its labour practices. Reed decided to float the company on the Stock Exchange, promising not to allow control to pass to a single bidder, which was code for Robert Maxwell. However, Maxwell made an offer so far above Reed's expectations, £113 million, that business overwhelmed scruples. The chief executive, Clive Thornton, got the news when he found Maxwell sitting at his desk.

In his seven years in charge of the *Mirror*, Maxwell never threatened to increase its circulation back above that of *The Sun*.[33] Indeed, in the early months, when he insisted on filling it with pictures of himself, he showed some signs of wanting to reduce it to zero. In keeping with Fleet Street tradition, he was a megalomaniac. Unlike the others, he was a megalomaniac even before he owned newspapers. He was also a thief on a grand scale. He was not wholly unsuccessful: with his own brand of bluster and brinkmanship, he did a good deal to intimidate the unions and bring down the *Mirror*'s unnecessary labour costs even before Wapping. But his comic-book capriciousness enfeebled the *Mirror* editorially, and made life even easier for Murdoch.

The Express group had been sold again. Trafalgar House, who had bought the company from Sir Max Aitken, had floated the company on the Stock Exchange for 20p a share. Four years later, the share price inflated by the Reuters windfall, it was bought by United Newspapers, owners of *Punch* and a string of grey provincial papers, who after years of sleepy profitability were now anxious to take a slice of the go-getting eighties. The firm's chairman, David Stevens, a city financier with no journalistic background, ensured that the once-vibrant columns of the *Express* cheered slavishly whatever the leadership of the Conservative Party happened to be saying at any given moment. And as Mrs Thatcher won her third successive election in 1987, he collected his statutory peerage.

But there was another newcomer to this eccentric club. In 1986 David Sullivan, publisher of masturbatory magazines like *Parade* and *Readers' Wives*, joined in the boom by starting *Sunday Sport*, a publication that established a new market of its own: it was part-newspaper (it did publish football reports and the occasional paragraph of traditional news), part-pornography and part-send-up. It rocketed to a circulation above half a million by publishing pin-ups of women some of whose bosoms had swelled to twice the size of anything *The Sun* had ever printed and front-page splashes that were cheery pastiches of Kelvin MacKenzie's wilder excesses. One week a B-52 bomber was reported to have been found on the moon. Literalists asked for evidence, so the following week the paper announced, with an equal flourish, that it had disappeared. A London bus turned up mysteriously in the Antarctic. A husband stuffed his wife down the plughole. And a giant green sprout from Venus ate a man in Tamworth.

Unfortunately, Lord Stevens did not have much sense of humour. And he was particularly unamused by the performance of *The Star*. (For obscure reasons, it had temporarily dropped the *Daily*.) It had its successes in the way journalists judge such matters: in March 1987 it was reckoned to have come off better in a tug of love with *The Sun* for Blackie the Donkey, which was alleged to be on the brink of being ritually slaughtered as part of a local fiesta in a remote Spanish mountain village. At any rate, *The Star* got possession of the donkey.

Blackie was heir and successor to all the animals who have punctuated Fleet Street history from Jumbo the Elephant onwards: Goldie the Escaped Eagle in the 1960s; Victor the Giraffe, who collapsed in a Hampshire zoo and could not get up; and the Nottingham Lion, definitively sighted by about half the local population in the hot and deranged summer of 1976, which turned out on closer inspection to be a brown paper bag.

However, *The Star* gained little from its triumph except one donkey. Since *The Sun* had neutralized its initial bingo advantage *The Star* had lost a third of its circulation – above 1.6 million in late 1984 – in three years. It had also foolishly lifted a story from the *News of the World* about the politician, author and litigant Jeffrey Archer and a prostitute. After a trial better than any donkey-show, *The Star* had been obliged to pay a record £500,000 in libel damages and the editor, Lloyd Turner, had paid the supreme penalty.

Sunday Sport was printed on United Newspapers' regional presses and the firm's managers noted how its print-run was getting bigger and bigger. There were rumours that it might be turned into a daily paper. And then what?

Stevens might have closed *The Star* there and then. Instead, he talked to Sullivan. Express Newspapers took a £2 million stake in his company. In return, Sullivan would help revamp *The Star*, with Michael Gabbert, editor of *Sunday Sport*, moving over to become *The Star*'s editor, and Sullivan would get a ¹/₂p royalty on every extra copy sold, thus reviving, in a sense, the ancient Northcliffean ideal of the ha'penny press. There was nothing else about *The Star* that Northcliffe would recognize.

On 7 September 1987 *The Star* printed a front-page picture of a well-developed teenager who was starting to unzip an already skimpy costume:

SHE'S 15. SHE'S GOT A 40 INCH BUST. SHE'S GOING TOPLESS IN 34 DAYS. IF YOU WERE HER MUM WOULD <u>YOU</u> LET HER?

This was Natalie Banus. And there was more of her, if not yet her nipples, on the centre spread:

THE SEXIEST 15-YEAR-OLD IN BRITAIN

Natalie first noticed that she had something special at ELEVEN. Her boobs started sprouting . . . At 14, she applied to join the Italia Conti stage school in London. The boys went crazy! One gangly youngster was so amazed by her looks that she thought he was trying to rape her in the girls' locker room. 'He ripped off my tie . . . tore open my shirt and put his hands down my breasts. Then he kissed me, ramming his tongue down my throat. I quite enjoyed that, but I didn't like the way he was treating me' . . . But Natalie has no qualms about her first topless photo session, already booked for her 16th birthday on October 11. 'I can't wait,' she says. And her mum reckons: 'If you've got it, flaunt it.'

And that was merely the start. *The Sun* had already popularized the use of the word 'bonk', which had started as slang for sexual intercourse among upper-class youngsters. Sub-editors had latched on to it enthusiastically, since it was euphonious and the perfect length for a tabloid headline, without any of the taboos that surrounded the synonym 'fuck'. Twenty years earlier, the *Daily Mirror* had fatally failed to catch on to any of the changes in society symbolized by what became known as the Summer of Love. Now *The Star* created the Autumn of Bonk:

BED AND BONK

HEAP BIG BONKUM

TAUNTED BY A BONKING WIFE

A BONK IS THE BOTTOM LINE

The word dominated what passed for news stories as well: 'Swinging southerners are the biggest bonkers in Britain,' said a report on an alleged survey of sexual behaviour. 'Everybody's at it in EsSEX, they can't get enough in SusSEX – and MiddleSEX is the lust paradise . . .' This might have been an attempt to counteract *The Star*'s perceived northern bias. There was even the odd attempt to interest women readers.

MACHO OF THE DAY!

> Giant soccer star Jiri Rantanen is just
> too big for his – shorts. Leicester City's
> Finnish striker has outstanding talents,
> as lady fans have been quick to spot. But
> now his chairman has ordered a
> cover-up.

The Star began selling T-shirts with the slogan 'The Star: I Get It Every Day' for people who, one suspected, did not. The paper had always specialized in a rather more voluptuous sort of pin-up than *The Sun*. Now the women who sprawled over the pages grew to *Sunday Sport* proportions, and were rechristened STAR STUNNAS instead of STARBIRDS. Meanwhile, the staff dwindled as a succession of journalists resigned on principle. The features editor, Ian Mayhew – echoing the remarks of the founder, Victor Matthews, at the paper's birth – said: 'It's become a newspaper that I can't take home because I have two young children.' The chief leader-writer David Buchan was fired after calling *The Star* 'a soft-porn rag'. These departures may not have been too distressing to the management: the objective was to make the paper profitable, and bonk-journalism did not actually need a vast number of journalists.

But most telling was the departure of the women's editor, Alix Palmer, who ran a Proopsian agony column which she took very seriously. At his first editorial conference, she said, Gabbert had told her that he wanted her to use letters that were both shorter and raunchier, 'about how my husband is tearing my sister's knickers off, that sort of thing'. Palmer said she did not actually get many letters like that. Gabbert said that on *Sunday Sport* they had never been able to use any real letters, either because they were too boring or because they were too filthy even for *Sunday Sport*. He denied instructing Palmer to make things up. But within days he had announced that the column would be written by a feature writer called Moira Petty under the title NOTHING SHOCKS MOIRA! This was not exactly the case. Petty said Gabbert had told her the column should be 'a masturbatory device for readers, male or female'. She was horrified, never mind shocked, and resigned too.[34]

The column eventually appeared as NOTHING SHOCKS SHIRL!

> I've got to tell someone – but please be
> gentle with me.
> I'm 17 and I simply can't say 'No'.
> I'm a nymphomaniac. I know, be-
> cause I looked it up in my dad's dic-
> tionary.

It was never made clear who Shirl was, but one got the impression she was male, and a trusted associate of Gabbert.

Circulation did increase during the first few weeks of the *Daily Bonk*, but only – on the paper's own claims – by 3.5 per cent, a fraction of what had already been lost. And a good deal of these must have been curiosity-seekers. The most extraordinary feature of Gabbert's *Star* was that the anarchic, almost subversive, humour of *Sunday Sport* failed to translate into a daily paper. Even the slogan was absurd: It was billed as 'Britain's most with-it paper', though 'with-it' had been dated twenty years earlier. The prevailing tone, when not straightforwardly obscene, was defensive, bordering on the petulant, even spiteful:

Linda Lusardi was twice Starbird of the Year. The money *The Star* dished out helped pay for her house. We MADE her. So you'd think Linda would be the last person to slag off your favourite paper.

But that's what she did – both off-screen and on – when she went on TV-AM yesterday with Anne Diamond.

Oh, Linda, what a hypocrite! On the left is the sort of lovely picture of you *The Star* likes to delight readers with.

Below it is the sort of picture you posed for in *Penthouse* magazine – we've had to censor it, as you can see.

Within a month this had turned into a childlike delight that *The Star* had attracted enough attention to be the subject of the ITV documentary programme *This Week*:

WATCH US ON TELLY TONIGHT!

And the following day this was thought worthy of a leader:

> Who could have watched *This Week*'s
> fly-on-the-wall look at how *The Star* is
> produced and not ended up agreeing that
> above all else it's FUN.
> There we all were – warts and all –
> doing our best to make *The Star* Britain's
> most with-it paper.

To an objective observer, however, *The Star*'s warts were, with the obvious exception of the breasts, the programme's most prominent anatomical feature. Gabbert himself was not an attractive defender of the paper's qualities: 'I think in certain elements a pop paper ought to be a bit of a turn-on. Of course I'm not going to deny that.' If Beaverbrook had been a pedlar of dreams, Gabbert, someone remarked, was a pedlar of wet dreams. The cameras spent much of the time observing his enthusiasm for a story about a Birmingham pop group called Dream, comprising a male singer and two sisters, all of whom, according to the singer, Matt Nelmes, had sex with each other:

POP GROUP 3-IN-A-BED SHOCKER

Unfortunately, the girls' parents had been understandably upset by this revelation and when *This Week* interviewed Nelmes he was, very convincingly, denying the whole thing: 'We're just a band that's trying to make it, and a piece of publicity for us is a slice of the action.' Lord Stevens declined to appear. There was no sign, either, of the group's managing director Andrew Cameron who, when the original deal was done, had announced: 'I'm a businessman not a moralist. Porn is in the eye of the beholder.'[35] Even fifteen-year-old Natalie Banus let the side down. She denied ever saying that she had enjoyed any part of the sexual attack the paper had described.

It was the beginning of the end. There was time for Natalie to do what she had promised. *The Star* had published the answer to the original question – What Do You Think? – on 28 September, under the headline:

YES, MY DARLING
DAUGHTER
WOW! What a surprise the result was.
For 62 per cent of WOMEN readers said:
'Yes – pose away.' But 61 per cent of
MEN readers said: 'She's too young.'
So the GALS are more liberal-minded
than the GUYS!

There was no mention of the problem that, if, as was assumed, the readership of the new paper was overwhelmingly male, this meant a majority against.

On 15 October, the forty-inch breasts of Natalie Banus, aged sixteen years four days, were revealed to *Star* readers. They were indeed impressive. But after fifteen more days, an increasing number of 'amateur stunnas', topless pictures of readers rather than models, which was one way of filling the paper cheaply, and a few more headlines –

BONKING MP WIFE'S FURY

A BONK IN THE EYE

NO BONKING – IT'S A DRAG

– there was a discreet notice on page two:

> Express Newspapers, publishers of *The Star*, last night severed its links with the publishers of *Sunday Sport*.
> Editor Mr Mike Gabbert has now left the company.

It was 30 October. The whole business had lasted less than two months. The crucial vote had come from the advertisers, led by Tesco and Co-op: concerned tactically about the logic of aiming advertising at housewives in a paper aimed primarily at young men, concerned strategically about the effect on their reputation if they were seen keeping company with a paper whose idea of women's interest was a story about a footballer whose testicles were almost hanging out.

A leader in *The Guardian* the following day theorized that Gabbert had in fact been engaged in a subtle attempt to widen his readers' horizons.

He ran frequent stories about labour relations ('I whacked Scargill on his conk'), foreign affairs ('Evil Idi Amin was nowhere to be seen when his wife applied for a divorce') and higher education ('A professor's daughter came to our house one night and she was the worst of the lot').

Nor did he flinch from history ('Doctors have discovered why Napoleon had to tell Josephine "Not tonight" ... the diddy dictator had syphilis, cystitis, chronic piles, skin disease, stomach ache and acute depression') or even haute cuisine ('Curvy Carol Anne was a waitress in a cafe where customers voted her dish of the day').

Religion ('Our city of shame, by a bishop's wife'), medicine ('I'm no fondler, claims dentist') and even linguistics ('grumpy blonde Lynn Luxton was sacked after yelling "bollocks"') – none was considered too tough or intellectually demanding ... Mr Gabbert's dreams of a mammary-led British intellectual renaissance lie shattered in the gutter of destiny ... *The Star*, as he recreated it, has gone for ever. We shall not, with any luck, look on its like again.

Nor have we. This largely forgotten interlude is in fact crucial to British journalistic history. Everything that had happened since Day One of the Northcliffe Revolution years earlier, indeed since the abolition of stamp duty in 1855, pointed in one direction. Daily newspapers thrived by lowering their sights to encompass a greater proportion of the population and, in the process, lowering their standards. Now someone had been in danger of going broke by underestimating the intelligence of the British public.

Gabbert was to die, aged only 53, the following year. Sullivan did start a *Daily Sport*, as Stevens feared all along, and had a full seven-day operation by late 1991. But its circulation remained insignificant. An experienced old hand, Brian Hitchen, was sent to *The Star* to nurse it back to health, though its circulation grew ever more delicate and its spirit never really recovered. Certainly, no one ever took much notice of it again.

On the face of it, this was another triumph for *The Sun*. Its profits were rocketing: MacKenzie was still strutting round Wapping, apparently as unconquerable as his heroine Mrs Thatcher. 'By now,' wrote the paper's biographers, 'he had cranked the paper up into an outrage machine that was the journalistic equivalent of the Sex Pistols, metaphorically gobbing over anyone, or any institution, it chose.'[36] *The Sun* was the Government's Praetorian Guard, its KGB, its Stasi; fastidious people might regret its excesses but, if it was over-zealous, it was over-zealous in the regime's interests. It was a very satisfactory arrangement.

But it was still, just about, possible for a Murdoch paper to slip beneath permissible rock-bottom. By the mid-1980s the old rascal of British journalism, the *News of the World*, was once more gaining readers. The cross-promotion of bingo with *The Sun*, the advent of a colour magazine, plus the final, belated decision to go tabloid in 1984 helped arrest the fall of the 1970s and put an end to any idea that the British public had grown out of the paper. By 1985 circulation was back up from four million to five million, and the *Sunday Mirror* and the *Sunday People* – both under the leaden hand of Maxwell – were each two million behind.

The *News of the World* had lost much of its old identity, however. Much of the time, it now seemed like a slightly pallid weekend version of *The Sun*, using the same cast of stock characters, though sometimes in more compromising positions. In 1987 MacKenzie's old protégée, Wendy Henry, became the first woman to edit a national newspaper since the first few feminine weeks of Northcliffe's *Daily Mirror*. In the intervening eighty-three years it had generally been thought that ladies were too delicate for the rough trade of editing. This one may have over-compensated. Under Wendy Henry the *News of the World* gained a twist new even to a paper that one would have thought had seen everything. Stories had to be pushed to the outermost limits of truth. 'Has this one been Wendified yet?' became the office catchphrase – i.e. had she given the report her own particular imprimatur?

If MacKenzie's *Sun* was cheerfully irresponsible and Gabbert's *Star* pathetically sex-obsessed, Henry's *News of the World* was downright horrid:

NOW YOU'VE GOT AIDS SNEERED BOWIE

MY LOVE HAS GOT CANCER

BRIDE QUIZ MAN IS RAPIST

TV BEAUTY'S SECRET DRUG SHAME

This was just a sample from late 1987. (It is a curiosity of British tabloids that mention of drugs is nearly always followed by the word 'shame', an emotion rarely felt by those actually using them.) It was not that the individual stories were out of the run of anything the *News of the World* had been reporting; it was the unrelenting unpleasantness that was so striking. The week before Christmas in 1987 the splash story was

MY BLIND DATE WAS CHEATING RAT

followed the next week by:

EVIL MYRA'S CANCER OP

All very festive. In 1988 the *News of the World* was published on fifty-one Sundays (the fifty-second was Christmas Day). A quick count suggests that on twenty-five of these occasions the main story involved some kind of illicit heterosexual liaison and on eleven some form of sexual deviance, including the latest manifestation of the time-honoured sex-change standby,

HERO COP SAYS CALL ME CAROL

while ten involved the Royal Family. These categories were not mutually exclusive. There was, for instance,

LADY SARAH TWO-TIMES HER LOVER

FERGIE'S DAD IN VICE SHOCK

and

ROYAL COMIC IN RENT BOY SHAME

By December even Murdoch had had enough and asked Henry to calm the paper down. She refused, and resigned.[37]

XVI

In the general election of June 1987 *The Sun*'s heroine, Margaret Thatcher, retained power with an only slightly decreased majority. But both she and *The Sun* were forced to fight a little harder this time.

This campaign included a

SPECIAL NIGHTMARE ISSUE

three days before the vote, with a faked picture of the Labour leader Neil Kinnock waving outside Downing Street with the caption 'Wake up, folks, this is just a bad dream.' There was the odd smear story. And *The Sun* had asked 'medium and psychic investigator Nella Jones' to contact dead luminaries and ask them how they would vote. Stalin was for Labour; Churchill, Nelson and Boadicea ('When I hear the words of Kinnock and his treacherous ilk I feel ashamed for England . . .') were all for Maggie; Keir Hardie was voting SDP and Genghis Khan said he Didn't Know. It was a pity the medium did not try to re-establish contact with Northcliffe. He might have said something pertinent.

Nemesis is supposed to follow hubris as rapidly as the dust-cart lumbers on to the scene after the Lord Mayor's Show. In Kelvin MacKenzie's case it took its time. His Waterloo was a long way off, but various events in the late 1980s might collectively be described as his Austerlitz: from then on his path was not upwards.

The first and most symbolic setback came with the haunting pictures of a cross-Channel ferry on its side outside Zeebrugge harbour in March 1987; 193 people drowned, many of them *Sun* readers on a special £1 promotional deal. The ship was called the *Herald of Free Enterprise*.

In October that year the stock market slumped. This was followed in 1988 – bringing far more widespread grief to *Sun* readers – by the collapse of the property boom that the Government had so lovingly been fuelling. By then, Dirty Den had been displaced as *The Sun*'s most prominent stock character by 'Loadsamoney', created by the comedian Harry Enfield, an obviously *Sun*-reading Cockney yob who typified the get-rich-quick attitudes of the era. But Loadsamoney's world was falling apart. As Mrs Thatcher became increasingly unpopular, MacKenzie, in a brilliant tactical ploy, effectively separated her from the Government. The smug-looking Chancellor of the Exchequer, Nigel Lawson, was appointed villain. When he resigned in 1989 he was waved off by the *Sun* headline

GOODBYE AND GOOD RIDDANCE

Thus it was in *Animal Farm* after Napoleon had driven out Snowball.

Some situations were less easily dealt with. *The Sun* was obliged to pay £100,000 to charity for printing a stolen copy of the family picture used on the Queen's Christmas card. The Elton John case ended in a £1 million libel pay-out. The sums of money were trivial compared to *The Sun's* profits but, as Mrs Thatcher's power waned, the Murdoch press was no longer beyond political criticism.

On Saturday 16 April 1989, ninety-five Liverpool football supporters were crushed to death at the Hillsborough ground in Sheffield. On the Monday morning several papers printed pictures of the dying that were widely regarded as offensive. There was also intense debate about where the blame for the tragedy might lie. It was a complex problem, and *The Sun* had its own way of cutting through complexities. On the Tuesday, 19 April, the front page was dominated by this headline:

THE TRUTH
By Harry Arnold and John Askill

Drunken Liverpool fans viciously attacked rescue workers as they tried to revive victims of the Hillsborough soccer disaster, it was revealed last night.

Police officers, firemen and ambulance crew were punched, kicked and urinated upon by a hooligan element in the crowd.

Some thugs rifled the pockets of injured fans as they were stretched out unconscious on the pitch.

In one shameful episode, a gang of Liverpool fans noticed the blouse of a girl trampled to death in the crowd had risen above her breasts.

As a policeman struggled in vain to revive her, they jeered: 'Throw her up here and we will **** her.'

If this was the truth, it was nothing like the whole truth. These were allegations that were never substantiated. That had not stopped *The Sun* before. But this time it was not some hapless victim who was being alienated, it was an entire city. People on Merseyside began boycotting *The Sun*, and circulation fell significantly. The folks were now being offended, and that was unforgivable.

And so, simultaneously, were the politicians. By coincidence, a Labour MP's Private Member's Bill offering a statutory right of reply in newspapers was to be debated the following Friday. The Bill was doomed to fail: the Government opposed it. But such Bills might not be doomed for ever, if the press carried on this way. David Mellor, the junior minister at the Home Office, warned that the press were now drinking in the Last Chance Saloon. MacKenzie, in a rare interview, was forced to admit that he had made 'a rather serious error'.[38] Sorry, Elton. Sorry, Ma'am. Sorry, Liverpool. It was getting to be a habit.

XVII

At the beginning of the 1990s two books were published about the Murdoch empire. Both made a blatant error in the most conspicuous place imaginable.

Peter Chippindale and Chris Horrie wrote a very funny book which is accepted as being largely accurate. Unfortunately, they called it *Stick It Up Your Punter!: The Rise and Fall of The Sun*. A more serious volume on Rupert Murdoch's financial manoeuvrings, by R. Belfield, C. Hird and S. Kelly, was entitled *Murdoch: The Decline of an Empire*. But *The Sun* had not fallen, and Murdoch's empire was not in decline, as Belfield, Hird and Kelly were forced to admit when they retitled the paperback edition *Murdoch: The Great Escape*.

The proprietor was having a few difficulties. He was now embroiled in the most perilous of his global adventures, trying to add British and American television simultaneously to the range of his conquests. He was no longer just Lord Northcliffe; he was more like Alexander the Great. The continued success of *The Sun* was crucial to his objectives. But his conquests had been funded on the creative use of debt. The short-term debts were now mounting and his British satellite station, Sky TV, which started transmitting in 1988 to an audience of approximately zero, was losing £2 million a week as it battled against a rival consortium, BSB. The banks were starting to panic. However, those convinced that Murdoch was about to fall forgot the old truth that if you owe the bank a pound you have a problem, but if you owe the bank a billion pounds, the bank has a problem. And in the battle of the satellite TV stations, the opposition blinked first. The rivals merged under Murdoch's effective control, giving him a potentially infinite number of television channels. By November 1990 'he was virtually bankrupt – and would have been but for the Sky–BSB deal.'[39] But he escaped, to rebuild the edifice of his empire ever more toweringly. Another apparently invulnerable figure of the 1980s did not.

In November 1990 Margaret Thatcher was forced out by Conservative

MPs who now believed the evidence of the opinion polls more than they believed Kelvin MacKenzie:

WE STILL NEED MAGGIE THE LIONHEART

When she realized this was no longer the view of a significant majority of her MPs, she resigned, to be ranked by *The Sun* with Churchill, Montgomery, Nelson and Wellington. It even claimed she looked younger than when she had come to power eleven years earlier. 'What a gutless rabble,' sneered the paper's star writer Garry Bushell as he contemplated the Tory Party. 'What a bunch of spineless saps. Who wanted Maggie to be ditched? Not the voters.'

The magical symbiosis between the newspaper and the popular mood seemed to have snapped. In the summer, years of sniping at the England football manager Bobby Robson and his team had culminated in the 1990 World Cup in Italy:

PATHETIC! ARROGANT! SMUG!

WORLD CUP WALLIES

YOU'RE BONKERS BOBBY

WE'RE A CARBUNCLE ON THE FACE OF SOCCER

PATHETIC BORING RUBBISH

England reached the semi-finals of the World Cup before losing to Germany in a penalty shoot-out. *The Sun* had to reverse very abruptly and start referring to 'our soccer heroes'.

In the autumn MacKenzie began his campaign of vilification of the French in general and the president of the European Commission, Jacques Delors, in particular. On 1 November, under the headline,

UP YOURS DELORS

readers were instructed to go into a public place at noon the following day, face France and tell Delors where to stuff his plans for a single currency. Murdoch said later that it was 'good-natured fun'.[40] It was the culmination, perhaps, of a process begun with Northcliffe telling readers what bread to eat and what hat to wear. But it was hopelessly mistimed. If anyone obeyed, we have only *The Sun*'s very unconvincing word for it. Instead, on the appointed day, there was a genuine story: the Deputy Prime Minister, Sir Geoffrey Howe, resigned, setting in train the series of events that were to lead to Mrs Thatcher's downfall four weeks later.

Murdoch's financial troubles were impinging on Wapping. Money was tight, tighter than it had been since the first, mad weekend in Bouverie Street. Circulation was drifting down. Morale was slumping. At the 1992 election, for the first time in *The Sun*'s history, the paper was forced to support the party that looked like losing. MacKenzie took to going round the editorial floor at Wapping pulling an imaginary chain as its support of Mrs Thatcher's successor, John Major, and its attacks on the man who looked like replacing him, Neil Kinnock, grew ever more extreme. *The Sun* alleged that Labour would admit 'tens of thousands' of immigrants and make it impossible for homebuyers to get a mortgage: NIGHTMARE ON KINNOCK STREET – HE'LL HAVE A NEW HOME, YOU WON'T. But, amid the mendacity, MacKenzie's gallows humour within the office still got through to the paper. This was the election day front page:

> ### IF KINNOCK WINS TODAY WILL THE LAST PERSON TO LEAVE BRITAIN PLEASE TURN OUT THE LIGHTS
>
> You know our views on the subject but we don't want to influence you in your final judgment on who will be Prime Minister.
>
> But if it's a bald bloke with wispy red hair and two K's in his surname, we'll see you at the airport!
>
> Goodnight and thank you for everything.

XVIII

MacKenzie had not lost his touch. It was harder even than in 1945 to find people who could convincingly say they knew it all along. But the bald bloke did not become Prime Minister. John Major won a narrow but workable majority. The joint *imperium* of *The Sun* and the Conservative Party seemed set to roll on for ever. Two days after the election, the paper quoted the Tory victor of the swing seat of Basildon in Essex, David Amess, to the effect that *The Sun*'s front page had made the difference, under the headline

IT'S THE SUN WOT WON IT

The psephological validity of this may be debated indefinitely, though the most detailed study, by Martin Linton, suggested that *The Sun* may never have spoken a truer word: there was an 8 per cent swing to the Tories among *Sun* readers in the three months before the election; *Mirror* readers did not shift at all.[41] But the voters had to be ready to be convinced: they were doubtful that Kinnock was a suitable Prime Minister and *The Sun* played on those fears. Kinnock promptly resigned as Labour leader, to be followed by two more plausible figures: John Smith and, after his death, Tony Blair, neither of whom could be painted as irresponsible or nightmarish.

But a Labour Government, which might be far readier to curb the excesses of the press, was a problem now postponed into the indefinite future. The next twenty months were to produce the last, blazing hurrah of MacKenzie's editorship, the apotheosis of the process of popularization that Northcliffe had begun. Even in his final weeks of delirium, however, he could never have imagined the direction in which his revolution was to head.

On 19 June 1992 *The Sun* ran its most famous headline a third time:

GOTCHA

This time the victim was not 'Billy Liar' Tobin or even a thousand Argentine sailors but the daughter-in-law of the man who was once Rupert Murdoch's most potent rival, Robert Maxwell, the former owner of the *Daily Mirror*, who was now not merely dead but disgraced, leaving his sons to face charges of fraud and theft.

> The wife of Kevin Maxwell yelled at detectives swooping to arrest her husband: 'p*** off, we don't get up for an hour.'
>
> Pandora Maxwell, 32, leaned from her bedroom window to tell bemused fraud squad officers: 'I'm about to call the police.'
>
> A detective retorted: 'Madam, we are the police.'

It is hard to imagine that anyone outside the Maxwell family failed to find that funny. The word GOTCHA, so shocking ten years earlier, now seemed very humorous, a cultural reference-point.

Something else happened in 1992 that sealed *The Sun*'s place at the heart of British society. For the first time since *The Times* reviled George IV, the Royal Family ceased to be above criticism. It became public knowledge that the only fairy-tale aspect of the marriage of the Prince and Princess of Wales was the one the papers and the population had woven around it. In December the couple formally separated. Princess Anne was already divorced. And Prince Andrew's estranged wife, the Duchess of York, was pictured on the front page of *The Sun*, topless, by a pool in the South of France with a man who was not her husband.

As the Royal Family fell from grace, so also did the Government. The glow of its unexpected election victory lasted barely three months before David Mellor, would-be landlord of the Last Chance Saloon and newly appointed Secretary of State for the National Heritage, was forced to resign after an affair with an actress and allegations of taking free trips. When the Government was obliged to pull out of the European Exchange Rate Mechanism, MacKenzie was able to fill the front page with the line:

Now we've ALL been screwed by the Cabinet

A month later, after the President of the Board of Trade, Michael Heseltine, had announced plans to close most of Britain's coal mines, the front page consisted of white space surrounding a small box containing a picture of the minister and these words:

> This page is dedicated to Michael Hesel-
> tine. It represents all that he understands
> about the worries and fears of the ordi-
> nary working people in depression-hit
> Britain. Nothing. Absolutely nothing.

Over the next fifteen months the troubles of both the Government and the Royal Family deepened. A succession of ministers were obliged to resign for Melloresque misdemeanours. *The Sun*, turning away from its old partisan-ship, revelled in the chase. Bobby Robson's successor as England football manager, Graham Taylor, who failed even to get the team into the last twenty-four of the 1994 World Cup, posed a problem since all the standard epithets had been hurled at his predecessor. *The Sun* depicted him as a turnip. It was coarse and demented journalism. But it seemed like a coarse and demented country.

Murdoch's financial troubles were behind him, and the dishes to receive his television programmes sprouted on the south-facing walls of Britain, where once there might have been roses or wistarias. But the alliance between *The Sun* and the Conservative Party was no longer safe. In January 1993 MacKenzie was forced to appear before the National Heritage select commit-tee, which was considering the possibility of laws to protect the privacy of individuals. He seemed unconquerable. 'You guys', he said at one point, 'must be nuts.'

It had to end sometime. On 21 January 1994 Kelvin MacKenzie ceased to be editor of *The Sun*, to be replaced by his deputy Stuart Higgins; he was appointed managing director of Murdoch's Sky-TV. 'It was a huge challenge,' he said. Maybe it was a promotion, but he left the organization soon after-wards. Possibly Murdoch felt MacKenzie had become too entrenched, too visible, too dangerous; it had not been a good idea to tell the MPs they were nuts.

And *The Sun*'s attacks on the Government had become ever more strident in 1993; it now looked less like the Praetorian Guard and more like the mob at the gate. The Chancellor, Kenneth Clarke, had been contemplating VAT on newspapers in his November budget, which would have done severe damage to every newspaper; just before that budget Murdoch dined with the Prime Minister; the Chancellor did not put VAT on newspapers.

Was a deal done? 'You stop VAT – I'll get rid of Kelvin and calm *The Sun* down.' We shall probably never know. The truth about newspapers is usually murkier than the truth within them.

PART SEVEN

Nothing New Under The Sun

The Popular Press after 1996

On 27 May 1993 *The Sun* issued a Code of Practice to its journalists. Item no. 1 was headed ACCURACY: 'The first and foremost requirement of journalists in the 1990s', it said, 'is accuracy. So if you are not 100 per cent sure of your facts don't write the story.'

The telling part of that sentence is the reference to the 1990s. Delete it from the instruction and you have what an innocent might take to be an immutable journalistic law, one that might have been endorsed by Northcliffe or C. P. Scott or R. D. Blumenfeld. By adding the three little words 'in the 1990s', *The Sun* was issuing a fashion note. Accuracy was in fashion, like shorter skirts and baggy tops.

There was a good reason for this. In the strange atmosphere of the 1990s when even the monarchy, for the first time in more than 150 years, had ceased to command public adulation, all the institutions of the country were in just about as big a mess. The aristocracy and the clergy had been irrelevant for years. The House of Commons, by-passed by international business and the new power centre in Brussels, was going the same way. So, in a sense, the press, the unofficial Fourth Estate of the Realm, was better off than the other three.

Among voters and newspaper-buyers, contempt for the Government was close to universal, and even newspapers where the 'first and foremost requirement' had often been to show the Conservative Party in a favourable light found themselves obliged to amend their policy. The papers' attitude was both a cause and an effect of the prevailing mood. Possibly some people in public life were conducting their private lives in a boringly conventional fashion; most weeks, a newspaper – generally the *News of the World*, in keeping with its time-honoured role – managed to discover one who was not.

BISHOP OF DURHAM IN GAY SEX SCANDAL

TOP TORY 'ENJOYED' LESBIAN SEX SHOW

CHIEF OF DEFENCE IN SEX AND SECURITY SCANDAL

JUDGE'S DRUGS AND SEX ROMP WITH JAILBIRD HOOKERS

The fitness of the people running the country to do their jobs did seem to be compromised by their inability to find sexual gratification from people who could be trusted not to shop their lovers to the press for large sums of money. But the nature of stories like this is that they absolutely do have to be accurate. A wrong one, or an ill-advised one –

DI'S SISTER IN BOOZE AND BULIMIA CLINIC

– inevitably brought forth demands for new laws to curb the press. These were held at bay, partly because the papers generally stuck to *The Sun's* watchword for the 1990s, and partly because the Government, whose ministers and backbench supporters were the people whose sexual habits were most often being exposed, lacked the authority to take action.

The stories came and went. By the time the last reporter had left the doorstep, and the person exposed began to piece together his or her shattered life, the average reader had almost certainly forgotten who they were and what on earth they had done. With a notable exception. The most enduring stories of the mid-1990s related to a family which, ten – even five – years earlier, had been beyond criticism even from the *News of the World*. What was unthinkable in the 1980s was now a Sunday morning routine:

DI FOUND KNICKERS IN CHARLES' POCKET
CHARLES BEDDED CAMILLA AS DIANA SLEPT UPSTAIRS
I SPIED ON DI AND HEWITT MAKING LOVE IN GARDEN

and even, on Christmas Eve 1995,

ROYAL SEX ORGY SHAME

Not much earlier, most people who consider themselves thoughtful would have agreed with the Buckingham Palace press officer who said there were only two types of stories about the Royal Family: the sentimentally inaccurate and the maliciously inaccurate. But the tabloids had been trying to say for years that all was not well in the marriage of the Prince and Princess of Wales. And eventually publications like *The Spectator* and *The Guardian*, which used to cover royal stories only to mock the popular press's coverage of them, had to give credit where it was due: 'Today, with scores of other journalists, I feel deeply humble. It was all true . . . gutter press they may be – but they were right, absolutely right.'[1] 'For once, yellow journalism is exculpated. Next time anyone asks "what use are the tabloids?" point to the gradual peeling away of the Great Royal Lie.'[2]

But if 1995 was a time of vindication for the popular press, it was an uneasy triumph. The fat years ushered in by Rupert Murdoch's coup at Wapping gave way to thinner years, characterized by a long recession and then a sudden rise in paper costs. Even Murdoch suffered, or a line on his balance sheet did. *Today*, which closed in November 1995, was the first well-established paper to disappear since the *Daily Sketch* in 1971. It was not impossible that the *Daily Star* and *The Independent* would follow suit, leaving only the six daily papers which at some time or other have been the top-sellers, as chronicled in this book, plus *The Guardian*.

Employment prospects for journalists were thus gloomier than at any time in two decades. And the same went for their editors, who began to come and go as rapidly and confusingly as the football managers whose exits and entrances were the staple fare of their sports pages. And for the same reason: failure cost money. At the start of 1996, no editor, daily or Sunday, had been in place longer than three and a half years; most had been appointed in the previous twelve months.

Fleet Street existed as a generic title for national papers, and as a geographical entity, but the two no longer had much to do with each other. The Press Association, the national news agency, moved its journalists to Vauxhall Bridge Road in August 1995, leaving only a couple of dozen journalists working for the eccentric Scottish firm, D. C. Thomson, at no. 185, supposedly the site of Sweeney Todd's barber shop. Sometimes the more sentimental old hacks might return for a drink or a memorial service at St Bride's. But the pubs – the Bell, the Punch, the Harrow, the Albion – once as famous in the business as the papers themselves, were full of bankers. And the City Golf Club, where there was no golf but a formidable amount of drinking, was now the Wynkyn de Worde wine bar, serving Wynkyn's Fayre and Compositor's Salads, heaven help us all.

Even the journalists, in their new surroundings, behaved a little less like journalists. The teetotal regime imposed by the Diet Coke drinker Kelvin MacKenzie at *The Sun* had once seemed unimaginable anywhere else. Now, as journalists walked round the ground floor of Canary Wharf, home of the *Telegraph*, *Mirror* and *Independent*, with a polystyrene cup in one hand and a mobile phone in the other, there was a different mood. At Wapping, where *The Sun* and *The Times* were bedded down in a conjunction that would once have been as improbable in public as the Prince of Wales and his mistress's knickers, the razor wire remained in place, long after the protesters who made it necessary had vanished. There were a few picnic tables on the lawn behind the security guards at the main entrance now. But it remained a weird and dispiriting place: inside, more like Ford's Dagenham plant than the traditional happy chaos of a newspaper office; outside, like Checkpoint Charlie, or, at the very least, Butlin's Skegness.

Of the papers that once outsold all the others, *The Times*, at the beginning of 1996, was selling more than at any time in its history: over 600,000 per day. This was the direct result of a promotional stunt whereby the paper that a hundred years ago cost three or six times as much as its rivals (threepence against a penny or a ha'penny) became, for much of 1995, the cheapest paper in the kingdom, at 20p. Railway trains coming into the London termini in the morning rush hour would be littered with leftover copies, bought cheaply, glimpsed quickly, then chucked away like a free sheet. Or you could obtain a free copy in exchange for four special promotional wrappers from King Size Mars Bars. All this was made possible by subsidy from other parts of the Murdoch empire. *The Times*'s editorial opinions were taken seriously by a few old people and foreigners.

The *Daily Telegraph*, forced against its proprietor's wishes to cut its own price to compete with *The Times*, continued to sell more than a million a day, but only just, helped by its own giveaway promotions. It had modernized itself stealthily, and rather cleverly. It continued to print details of the murkier sort of court cases, and displayed them rather more beguilingly. A hasty newspaper reader waking after a forty-year sleep might assume that all the broadsheet papers of 1996 were the lineal descendants of the *Express* or *Mail*, rather than anything to do with their old selves.

Northcliffe would still recognize the spirit, if not the look, of the *Daily Mail*: successful, professional, respected, competitive, forceful, well-written and, *in extremis*, particularly during elections, thoroughly mendacious. His great-nephew, the third Lord Rothermere, invested money in journalism, found good staff and paid them well, just as Northcliffe did. The *Mail* now had the two most original popular-paper columnists in the business, having signed Keith Waterhouse from the *Mirror* and Richard Littlejohn from *The Sun*. Its circulation had been essentially static for years. But it felt like a success.

In contrast, the *Express* and *Mirror* languished under managements that were more interested in rapid profits than in long-term investment. Both, at the start of 1996, were showing vague, but very belated, signs of stirring under new, young editors: Richard Addis and Piers Morgan. Lord Cudlipp was still prone to say, if asked whether he had ever had anything to do with the *Daily Mirror*, that he was, in fact, a retired deckchair attendant from Bognor. The left-wing opinions the *Mirror* felt obliged to maintain were entirely at odds with the businesslike views and methods of the management. To cover its insincerity, the paper tended to shout. Uncertain whether it was still the old, caring *Mirror* or just another brawling tabloid, it sometimes stooped to journalistic tricks – buying snatched photos of Princess Di at her gym, for instance – which had the potential to backfire, and which the more practised Murdoch press knew to avoid. Worst of all, the *Mirror* had become a humourless paper. Morgan said he wanted to change that, but admitted frankly that his job was to compete with *The Sun*.[3]

Neither Lord Beaverbrook nor Arthur Christiansen has been available, these past thirty years and more, to rasp down the telephone or post a bulletin on the current state of the *Daily Express*. But if there is an afterlife, someone is going to cop it. When *Today* closed, its editor Richard Stott was linked with the vacant *Express* editorship. He rejected the idea, saying: 'I want to stay in journalism.' After years of under-investment, lack of imagination and political opinions that unwaveringly reflected the Tory Party line, whatever that happened to be, it was generally held, whenever journalists met over a foaming polystyrene cup or two, that only a genius could revive it. Addis's initial attempts at least showed a respect for the paper's traditions: he revived Beachcomber and the Hickey column.

The *Express* also maintained more substantial Fleet Street traditions. When the offices were moved from the sausage shop, they went only to the other side of Blackfriars Bridge, to a building that looked like a newspaper office. It even had an in-house pub. There the *Daily Star* continued too. Its original purpose, as a make-work scheme for unsackable labour, was irrelevant following the crushing of the print unions. And, after the Daily Bonk disaster, its journalistic *joie de vivre* ebbed away as well. Sometimes it would outshine all the papers. When the rogue banker Nick Leeson was arrested in March 1995 it showed him under guard with the headline:

CAN WE HAVE A WORD ABOUT YOUR OVERDRAFT, SIR . . .

but hardly anyone noticed, because hardly anyone read it.

No paper, since *The Times* came to the fore in the early nineteenth century, has been the no. 1 daily seller for more than about forty years. *The Sun*, in 1996, was coming up to half that span. There was no obvious threat. Kelvin MacKenzie had been gone as editor for almost two years and was now on the twenty-first floor of Canary Wharf, where he presided over the *Daily Mirror*'s cable TV operation, almost wholly unwatched, though rumour said it showed topless darts. Back at *The Sun*, there was not much evidence that he had gone. The paper continued to set the agenda for the news media more often than any of its rivals. Indeed, sometimes it seemed to be setting the agenda for the entire country:

QUEEN ORDERS DIVORCE

it said, exclusively, in its issue of 21 December 1995. And before the 21st had dawned, there was confirmation from the Palace. This was not just a piece of news-gathering; someone high up wanted *The Sun* to have the story. Nor was it untypical. The police-killer Harry Roberts had wearily told the *Evening Standard* the previous May that his chances of release depended on

The Sun, which dictated prisons policy to the Government. And Roberts was already locked up when Rupert Murdoch bought the paper.

The Sun's editor, Stuart Higgins (once christened by MacKenzie 'Higgy the Human Sponge'), was sometimes seen as John Major to MacKenzie's Thatcher: less tyrannical, and also less effective. *The Sun* read like MacKenzie's *Sun* while he was on holiday. The formula was the same, without the extra hint of danger. Higgins would not contemplate (as MacKenzie did) running a competition for the tomboyish athlete Fatima Whitbread's razors, or offering a lucky *Sun* reader a free trip to Japan to dance on Emperor Hirohito's grave. *The Sun* got the stories, still, but the stories were more conventional now, and mostly, in 1995 and early 1996, about the National Lottery. Its day-to-day politics were more plain right-wing than populist. The paper of 22 September 1995 displayed thirty-four nipples (though only thirty-three were female; one belonged to the boxer Naseem Hamed), exactly twice the number that induced David Buchan to call the *Daily Star* pornographic and get fired in 1987. *The Sun*'s obsession with breasts ('assets') was increasingly modified by a new penis-fixation, usually referred to by the nonce euphemism 'manhood'.

The *News of the World*, meanwhile, seemed to be blossoming. In 1995 it acquired its thirteenth editor in Murdoch's twenty-six-year proprietorship: Phil Hall. But under no. 12, Piers Morgan, it had won several major journalistic prizes, including a special award for Scoops of the Year from the TV programme *What The Papers Say*. The chairman of the Press Complaints Commission, Lord Wakeham, was thus obliged to be seen applauding the *News of the World*. In their citation, the judges approvingly parroted Morgan's remark that he had moved the paper towards the middle market. They did not explain, if a paper with front-page splashes like

MARGARET'S BUTLER BEDS PERVERT AT PALACE

SETH'S 6-YEAR AFFAIR WITH A GENDER BENDER

and

MAJOR'S BOY <u>DID</u> GET A LEG OVER!

was in the middle market, where on earth the bottom might lie.

The *News of the World*'s proprietor continued to defy encapsulation or easy categorization. By 1996 his domain had grown to astonishing proportions: 132 newspapers, magazines, TV stations (terrestrial, satellite and cable), movie studios, home videos and publishers – including 'the dominant publisher of religious books', Zondervan. The magazine *Business Week* summed it up in the headline

MAN BUYS WORLD

– and the Zondervan subsidiary suggests he may also have his eye on the next one.

All this power makes the great media tycoons of the past seem insular, even provincial. But it has been possible only because he has offered himself in many different guises, shmoozing simultaneously with the Gingrich Republicans in Washington and the Communist dictators in China. In India he could be a puritan, musing that Page Three was something that might soon disappear, and that it had been nothing to do with him, anyway: 'The editor did it while I was away.'[4] His papers have been just as adaptable. In 1996 *The Sun* was dickering with backing Labour, the likely winners of the next election. Even in 1992 the Scottish edition had backed the Scottish National Party –

THE SUN SPEAKS ITS MIND – RISE NOW AND BE A NATION AGAIN

– while the English editions were acting as Tory shock troops. This sort of discrepancy used to be confined to differing interpretations of football matches for different regions. Rupert Murdoch's power is thus at once infinitely greater, and yet curiously smaller, than that of Northcliffe or Beaverbrook, who used their newspapers to proclaim messages. At the heart of Rupert Murdoch's vast empire is nothing, because he believes in nothing. In that sense, he truly might be the Wizard of Oz. And though he has trampled the globe, his footprints may fade far faster than those of many less overtly successful men. As one TV executive put it: 'I believe that we're talking about Genghis Khan, not the Roman Empire.'[5]

But the first century of popular newspapers has ended amid the nihilism which Murdoch created, and it will take a long time to recover. As we have seen, there is nothing new under *The Sun*. Intrusive journalism is not new; distortions are not new; political twisting is not new; mendacity is not new; even public warfare between the heir to the throne and his wife is not new. (Praise for the gutter press in *The Guardian* and *The Spectator* may well be new, but it is probably fleeting.) In America at the turn of the century, 'personal privacy was no more sacred to the newspaper of that day than the Golden Rule to the Hottentot'.[6] As we have seen, the same phenomenon has come in waves, which in the 1930s and the 1980s almost burst the sea wall. In all likelihood, there will be another tidal surge before long. But this writer is not going to fall into the R. D. Blumenfeld trap and predict what the paper of the future is going to be like so that some clever dick can discover this book in a dusty corner fifty years hence and make mock.

By that time, it is of course possible that newspapers will have ceased to exist completely. It is certainly possible that the centrally printed newspaper of today will have disappeared, to be replaced by something clicking and whirring out of a home computer. I have a personal fantasy about a completely customized paper, adjusting the balance of the day's news to the reader's own tastes, weighing the importance of Auntie Doris's varicose veins and your near-miss in the Lottery against royal sexual frolics and the situation in Rwanda. That seems far more likely than Blumenfeld's dream of a truly responsible press, unless the human race changes. (And what would a nation entirely composed of *Guardian* readers actually make? Documentaries about each other?) But for as long as literacy survives, people will still need to read something. 'I am absolutely optimistic about the future of the tabloid business,' said Kelvin MacKenzie. 'A hundred years from today, some mad man or mad woman will be running round shouting out "Up yours, Delors", or the equivalent of its time.'[7]

Yes, I am afraid of that. But people are always going to want to be tickled. Somehow or other. And it is remotely possible, through the tangled and often barbed wires of the journalistic process, that now and again we might even learn something.

Notes

Part One

1 Kennedy Jones, *Fleet Street and Downing Street* (1920), pp. 30–1.
2 F. S. Siebert, *Freedom of the Press in England* (1952), p. 30.
3 Wickham Steed, *The Press* (1938), p. 108.
4 In 1797 it shot up from 2d to 3½d, and then in 1815 went up to 4d, where it stayed until 1836, when it was reduced to a penny again before finally being abolished in 1855.
5 George Crabbe, 'The Newspaper' (1785).
6 Alexander Andrews, *The History of British Journalism* (1859), vol. 2, p. 16.
7 Ibid., vol. 2, p. 32.
8 *The History of the Times*, vol. 1 (1935), p. 3.
9 Quoted in *World's Press News*, 3 August 1933.
10 The hangman.
11 *Cambridge Social History of Britain*, vol. 3 (1990), pp. 122–5.
12 E. P. Thompson, *The Making of the English Working Class* (1963), p. 787.
13 James Curran and Jean Seaton, *Power Without Responsibility: The Press and Broadcasting in Britain*, 4th edn (1991), p. 14.
14 Thompson, *Working Class*, p. 789.
15 Originally the *British Gazette and Sunday Monitor*.
16 Stanley Morison, *The English Newspaper* (1932), p. 249.
17 Andrews, *History of British Journalism*, vol. 2, p. 341.
18 R. Power Berrey, *The Romance of a Great Newspaper* (1933), p. 40.
19 Curran and Seaton, *Power Without Responsibility*, p. 29.
20 Both the *Chronicle* and the *Herald* were to expire in the 1860s, presumably because of the *Telegraph*'s success. The *Chronicle* was then being run by a Mr Stiff.
21 Lord Burnham, *Peterborough Court: The Story of the Daily Telegraph* (1955), p. 13.
22 Ralph Straus, *Sala* (1942), p. 30.
23 Duff Hart-Davis, *The House the Berrys Built: Inside the Daily Telegraph* (1990), p. 41.

24 John M. Robson, 'Marriage or Celibacy? A Victorian Dilemma', in Joel H. Wiener, ed., *Papers for the Millions* (1988), p. 190.
25 It was not only Jumbo who liked beer and whisky. It was rumoured that on this occasion both keeper and elephant were drunk.
26 Jumbo's hide was preserved in Tufts College, Massachusetts. His successor, Jingo, never attained the same popularity: he was sold to America at a similar age for just £200 in 1903, and no one noticed. He died at sea and was thrown into the Atlantic. For more on the Jumbo story see Eric Mathieson, *The True Story of Jumbo the Elephant* (1963) and Wilfrid Blunt, *The Ark in the Park* (1976).
27 J. Hall Richardson, *From the City to Fleet Street* (1927).
28 A student of phrenology explained that, merely by studying the person's head, the true character of an intended spouse could be discerned in five minutes. He insisted: 'This science will in future prevent many long and useless engagements and unhappy marriages.'
29 Miss Mary Anderson, the actress.

Part Two

1 Brian Masters, *Now Barabbas was a Rotter* (1978), p. 3.
2 Reginald Pound and Geoffrey Harmsworth, *Northcliffe* (1959), pp. 36–8.
3 Paul Ferris, *The House of Northcliffe* (1971), p. 32.
4 The *Daily Mail* has now, pleasingly, revived the name and the idea of 'Answers to Correspondents' as a regular feature.
5 A third of these snippet-magazines, *Pearson's Weekly*, was founded in 1890 by C. Arthur Pearson, who ten years later started the *Daily Express*. That, like *Answers*, closed long ago. Something called *Tit-Bits* survives, but it is now sold on the top shelves of newsagents, the tits and the bits being totally different from those Newnes published.
6 W. MacQueen-Pope, *Twenty Shillings in the Pound* (1948), pp. 246–7.
7 Quoted in *The Guardian*, 28 December 1994.
8 Lucy M. Brown, *Victorian News and Newspapers* (1985), p. 254.
9 Arnot Reid, 'The English and the American Press', in *The Nineteenth Century*, August 1887, p. 231.
10 The *Post* merged with the *Telegraph* in 1937. It depended on Situations Vacant and Wanted adverts for domestic servants. According to Lord Deedes, probably the *Post's* last surviving journalist, it was the decline of this market after the First World War that put the *Post* out of business.
11 It survived in that guise until 1994.
12 Jones, *Fleet Street and Downing Street*, p. 124.

13 Hamilton Fyfe, *Sixty Years of Fleet Street* (1949), p. 80. Local newspapers in the 1970s, I recall, would work on a similar principle, with equally tedious results.

14 Meaning that it sold most in London itself. The *Chronicle* had grown out of the *Clerkenwell News* in 1870.

15 The *Mail* did not go tabloid until 1971.

16 Max Pemberton, *Lord Northcliffe: A Memoir* (1922), p. 60.

17 *Sell's Dictionary of the World Press* (1896), p. 63.

18 It closed in 1916.

19 Paul Rubens, 'When I Leave Town', from *Florodora, a Musical Comedy*, produced at the Lyric Theatre in 1899.

20 Chamberlain.

21 Written by Ernest Shand.

22 Hart-Davis, *The House the Berrys Built*, p. 32.

23 The word 'thrill' had slightly different connotations then; 'shudder' would now come closer to the meaning.

24 No such claims are made for the multiple murders by Dennis Nilsen in Muswell Hill in the 1980s.

25 R. A. Scott-James, *The Influence of the Daily Press* (1913), pp. 259–60.

26 F. W. Memory, *Memory's* (1932), p. 298.

27 William Colley, *News Hunter* (1936), p. 74.

28 R. Macnair Wilson, *Lord Northcliffe: A Study* (1927), pp. 9–10.

29 James Dunn, *Paperchase: Adventures In and Out of Fleet Street* (1938), p. 15.

30 Alex M. Thompson, *Here I Lie: The Memorial of an Old Journalist* (1937), p. 230.

31 F. W. Wile, *News is Where You Find It* (1939), p. 148.

32 Margaret Lane, *Edgar Wallace: A Biography* (1938), pp. 201ff. Shortly afterwards, Wallace got the paper into another libel action, involving a court martial in Portsmouth, and was sacked. The writer responsible for most of the soap stories, a man called Bolton, simply disappeared; he was rumoured to have emigrated to Canada.

33 For countless examples see Piers Brendon, *The Life and Death of the Press Barons* (1982).

34 The *Mirror* temporarily overtook the *Mail*; see Part Four.

35 See Part Three.

36 Hamilton Fyfe, *Press Parade* (1936), p. 84

37 *World's Press News*, 7 May 1936.

38 The *Mail* revived the competition in 1995.

39 This is believed to be neither fact nor a newspaper invention, but a later piece of imagination, probably from Neville Cardus.

40 For more on this see I. F. Clarke, *Voices Prophesying War* (1966).

Part Three

1 These selective extracts are not entirely fair to Ralph Blumenfeld. He was taking tea with H. G. Wells on 28 June 1914 when he heard that Franz Ferdinand had been assassinated at Sarajevo and remarked 'That will mean war.' But they do give a reasonable flavour. And this is a book about journalism, and cannot be entirely free from the vices of the profession.

2 E. T. Raymond, *Portraits of the New Century* (1928), pp. 120–1.

3 Sidney Dark, *Not Such a Bad Life* (1941), p. 59.

4 Anne Chisholm and Michael Davie, *Beaverbrook: A Life* (1992), p. 71.

5 Ibid., p. 99.

6 The *Globe, Pall Mall Gazette, Westminster Gazette, Star, Evening News* and *Evening Standard*. The first three closed in the 1920s, the *Star* in 1960 and the *Evening News* (save for a brief revival) in 1980. There had been nine before 1905 when *The Echo* and *St James's Gazette* both folded, followed in 1906 by *The Sun*. Since the closure of the *Evening Press*, Dublin, in 1995, nowhere in the English-speaking world has competing evening newspapers.

7 Wareham Smith, *Spilt Ink* (1932), p. 13. Glover cannot have been that ordinary. He spoke four languages and doubled up as the office interpreter. He did not actually take charge of the department, but he provided Northcliffe with regular reports.

8 Ferris, *The House of Northcliffe* (1971), p. 273.

9 Tom Clarke, *My Northcliffe Diary* (1931), pp. 173–4.

10 Robert Graves and Alan Hodge, *The Long Week-end* (1940), p. 15. This is a marvellous evocation of Britain in the inter-war years.

11 *Daily Mail*, 25 October 1924. For the accepted view see Lewis Chester, Stephen Fay and Hugo Young, *The Zinoviev Letter* (1967). The old romantic right-wing view that the letter was genuine was raised again by Frank Johnson in the *Daily Telegraph*, 23 February 1995.

12 Chisholm and Davie, *Beaverbrook*, p. 212.

13 William Barkley, *Reporter's Notebook* (1959), p. 18.

14 *Newspaper World*, 20 May 1922.

15 *World's Press News*, 16 May 1935.

16 Louise Owen, *The Real Lord Northcliffe* (1922), p. 51.

17 Tom Driberg, *Swaff: The Life and Times of Hannen Swaffer* (1974), pp. 123–4.

18 Chisholm and Davie, *Beaverbrook*, p. 215.

19 Interview, 13 June 1995.

20 Dunn, *Paperchase*, p. 99.

21 Sir Percival Phillips, *The Red Dragon and the Black Shirts* (1922), pp. 8–14.

22 Collin Brooks, *Devil's Decade: Portraits of the 1930s* (1948), p. 144.

23 Ferris, *The House of Northcliffe*, p. 291.

24 It is a curiosity that British press lords of this era invariably took titles that had nothing to do with their surnames and made them sound rather like seaside bungalows.

25 All this and much more is in Logan Gourlay, ed., *The Beaverbrook I Knew* (1984).

26 *Political Quarterly*, 1930, p. 164.

27 Hugh Cudlipp, *At Your Peril* (1962), p. 260.

28 Malcolm Muggeridge, *The Thirties* (1940), p. 86. This process could be helped in other ways. Anyone who smoked Black Cat cigarettes in the early 1930s could get enough coupons for a sports jacket from 120 packets of 20, while by my calculations anyone who smoked 80 Private Seal a day would get a new pair of silk stockings every week.

29 From a letter to the *Glasgow Evening Times*, quoted in *World's Press News*, 2 February 1933.

30 Fyfe, *Press Parade*, p. 40.

31 Ibid., pp. 112–13.

32 Graves and Hodge, *The Long Week-end*, p. 286.

33 Interview with Reg Foster, 13 June 1995.

34 *World's Press News*, 26 May 1932.

35 Ibid., 30 June 1932.

36 The *New York World* Telegram, quoted in *World's Press News*, 30 April 1936.

37 J. B. Priestley, *An English Journey* (1934), p. 401.

38 Hugh Cudlipp, *Publish and Be Damned!* (1953), pp. 255–6.

39 Cecil King, *The Future of the Press* (1967), p. 57.

40 Shading Geoffrey Dawson of *The Times*, Harold Evans of *The Sunday Times*, J. L. Garvin of *The Observer*, C. P. Scott of the *Manchester Guardian* and Kelvin MacKenzie of *The Sun* (of him, much more later). Hugh Cudlipp is primarily known for his work on the *Daily Mirror* which, in theory, he never edited, rather than his three stints as editor of the *Sunday Pictorial*. Michael Foot, later leader of the Labour Party, is rather more famous for that than for his brief wartime editorship of the *Evening Standard*. Derek Jameson, who edited the *Daily Express* and the *News of the World*, subsequently acquired a public following among people who do not habitually know the names of newspaper editors by becoming a disc jockey on BBC Radio 2.

41 Arthur Christiansen, *Headlines All My Life* (1961), p. 152.

42 Allen Hutt, *The Changing Newspaper* (1973), pp. 117–18.

43 Cudlipp, *Publish and Be Damned!*, p. 255.
44 Tom Baistow, *Fourth-rate Estate* (1985), p. 43.
45 Christiansen, *Headlines All My Life*, p. 144.
46 In a letter to Kingsley Martin, 1965, quoted in Adam Sisman, *A. J. P. Taylor* (1994), p. 114.
47 Christiansen, *Headlines All My Life*, p. 104.
48 Ibid., p. 142.
49 Ibid., p. 122.
50 Ibid., p. 148.
51 Richard Bourne, *Lords of Fleet Street: The Harmsworth Dynasty* (1990), p. 147.
52 Letter to Frank Gannett, quoted in Chisholm and Davie, *Beaverbrook*, p. 347.

Part Four

1 Fyfe, *Sixty Years of Fleet Street*, p. 115.
2 Maurice Edelman, *The Mirror: A Political History* (1966), p. 3.
3 In 1988, Eddy Shah, the founder of *Today*, began something called *The Post*, with similar intentions. It did better than the *Daily Paper*; it lasted thirty-three issues.
4 Pound and Harmsworth, *Northcliffe*, p. 278.
5 Ibid., p. 391.
6 Cudlipp, *Publish and Be Damned!*, p. 34.
7 Sisman, *A. J. P. Taylor*, p. 94.
8 Interview with Lord Cudlipp, 1 August 1995.
9 Interview, 21 September 1995.
10 Dorothy Dix's name and column lasted longer in other countries. I have heard New Zealand cricket-lovers of a certain age refer to a six-hit as a 'Dorothy', a piece of rhyming slang long gone from Britain, if it ever existed.
11 Muggeridge, *The Thirties*, p. 39.
12 Cudlipp, however, insists that Winn was a very assiduous reporter.
13 Hugh Cudlipp, *Walking on the Water* (1976), p. 60.
14 Ibid., p. 59.
15 Interview, 14 June 1995.
16 Harry Procter, *The Street of Disillusion* (1958), pp. 59–60. *Mirror* news editors remained famously fierce, and Audrey Whiting, who later became the *Mirror*'s royal reporter, told me that after the war any error could be a sacking offence. It certainly became a more indulgent paper later.
17 The row also does no justice to Zec's contribution to national morale.

He drew marvellous cartoons, full of light and shade, that summed up complex situations in an instant.

18 Jane appeared in the *Daily Mirror* from 1932 to 1959, when she was married off rather than killed off. She returned for a short time during Robert Maxwell's proprietorship.

19 Allighan's later career was less glorious. Elected for Gravesend in the 1945 landslide he helped to foment, he was expelled from the Commons in 1947 for 'offences against parliamentary privilege and decorum'.

20 Harold Nicolson, *Diaries and Letters 1939–45* (1967), p. 473.

21 Interview with Lord Cudlipp, 1 August 1995.

22. Speech by Beaverbrook in New York, 23 April 1942, quoted in Chisholm and Davie, *Beaverbrook*, pp. 434–5.

23 Quoted by Anthony Howard in Michael Sissons and Philip French (eds), *Age of Austerity* (1963), p. 16.

24 Christiansen, *Headlines All My Life*, pp. 240–1.

25 Peter Hennessy, *Never Again* (1992), pp. 326–7.

26 Similar surveys have come up with equally startling findings on this subject over the years. The 1949 figures show half the readers of the *Express* as Conservative, and a quarter Labour (Mass-Observation, *The Press and its Readers*, 1949, pp. 110–11).

27 *Encounter*, July 1957, pp. 8–14.

28 Quoted in Michael Leapman, *Treacherous Estate* (1992), p. 225. Actually, the *Mirror* had its own reasons for being impatient. At the Coronation in 1953 the *Mirror* reporter Audrey Whiting had seen Margaret go up to Townsend, then an equerry, and lift a piece of loose thread off his jacket. Whiting, with a woman's certainty, informed the news desk that they were in love. The *Mirror* did not dare run the story.

29 Interview, 13 June 1995.

30 Mike Randall, *The Funny Side of the Street* (1988), p. 43.

31 Ferris, *The House of Northcliffe*, p. 306.

32 Christiansen was ill and Sir Edward Pickering, his deputy, takes the credit.

33 Despite this, the absurd 'A' classification persisted until well into the 1960s.

34 Lord Moran, *Winston Churchill: The Struggle for Survival* (1966), p. 500.

35 She had been made a judge.

36 Cecil King, *The Future of the Press* (1967), p. 111.

Part Five

1 Cyril Bainbridge and Roy Stockdill, *The News of the World Story* (1993), p. 245; interview with Bernard Shrimsley, 12 September 1995.
2 John Wigley, *The Rise and Fall of the Victorian Sunday* (1980), p. 185.
3 The *Sunday Telegraph* did not poke its head above the parapet until 1961 or the *Mail on Sunday* until 1982.
4 Wigley, *Victorian Sunday*, p. 28.
5 E. T. Raymond, *Portrait of the Nineties* (1921), p. 291.
6 *Newspaper World*, 14 March 1931.
7 G. Binney Dibblee, *The Newspaper* (1939), p. 199.
8 Lord Riddell, *More Pages from My Diary* (1934).
9 Berrey, *The Romance of a Great Newspaper*, p. 50.
10 Bainbridge and Stockdill, *The News of the World Story*, p. 81.
11 Hamilton Fyfe, *Northcliffe: An Intimate Biography* (1930), p. 114.
12 *The Times*, 17 April 1926.
13 *Newspaper World*, 25 December 1926.
14 George Orwell, 'Decline of the English Murder', first published in *Tribune*, 1946.
15 This was a huge sum then; but £1,600 was earmarked to pay off debts by his wayward son Randolph. See Martin Gilbert, *Winston S. Churchill*, vol. 5 (1976), pp. 438–9.
16 A paper called the *Sunday News* opened, offering a new insurance deal and using the slogan 'You get ill – we pay the bill'. Surprisingly, it closed rapidly.
17 Bainbridge and Stockdill, *The News of the World Story*, p. 102.
18 Stafford Somerfield, *Banner Headlines* (1979), p. 44.
19 Ibid., p. 106.
20 See also Part Four above.
21 Somerfield, *Banner Headlines*, p. 111.
22 Ibid., p. 112.
23 Ibid., p. 157.
24 Ibid., p. 188.

Part Six

1 R. D. Blumenfeld, *The Press in My Time* (1933), pp. 234–48.
2 Leslie Sellers, *Doing it in Style* (1968), p. 137.
3 See e.g. Michael Leapman, *Barefaced Cheek* (1983), p. 19.
4 William Shawcross, *Murdoch* (1992), p. 57.
5 Ibid., p. 110. The Sydney *Sun* was finally seen off: it closed in 1988,

giving Murdoch a monopoly of the city's afternoon sales. He then merged the *Mirror* with his morning tabloid, the *Telegraph*.

6 This figure excludes the communist *Morning Star*, the capitalist *Financial Times*, the *Morning Advertiser*, by now solely for publicans, the shipping paper *Lloyd's List* and the racing papers, none of which was truly general.

7 Hart-Davis, *The House the Berrys Built*, p. 11.

8 Interview with Sir Edward Pickering.

9 James Cameron, *Point of Departure* (1967), p. 281.

10 Interview, 1 August 1995.

11 *Private Eye*, 26 September 1969.

12 For more details see Larry Lamb, *Sunrise* (1989), pp. 1–24, and Peter Chippindale and Chris Horrie, *Stick It Up Your Punter! The Rise and Fall of the Sun* (1900), pp. 14–21.

13 *The Independent*, 7 November 1989.

14 Interview, 12 September 1995.

15 Derek Jameson, *Touched by Angels* (1988), p. 262.

16 *New York Times*, 18 April 1976.

17 Chippindale and Horrie, *Stick It Up Your Punter!*, p. 31.

18 Lamb, *Sunrise*, p. 160.

19 Chippindale and Horrie, *Stick It Up Your Punter!*, p. 56.

20 Lamb, *Sunrise*, p. 158.

21 *Punch*, 4 November 1981.

22 Quoted in Dennis Griffiths, ed., *The Encyclopedia of the British Press* (1992), pp. 187, 407. Matthews died in 1995.

23 Jameson, *Touched by Angels*, p. 11.

24 In Northcliffe's day, they tended to live in Brixton because it had the best late-night transport from Fleet Street. Later Orpington was favoured for the same reason. The geography is more confused now that newspapers are a diaspora.

25 Before MacKenzie came to power, Nicklin reputedly closed an argument by telling him it was a question of mind over matter: 'I don't mind and you don't matter.'

26 Chippindale and Horrie, *Stick It Up Your Punter!*, p. 119.

27 Robert Harris, *Gotcha! The Media, the Government and the Falklands Crisis* (1983), p. 48.

28 Chippindale and Horrie, *Stick It Up Your Punter!*, p. 100.

29 Harris, *Gotcha!*, p. 48.

30 *Punch*, 24 November 1982, reprinted in Roy Hattersley, *Press Gang* (1983).

31 Chippindale and Horrie, *Stick It Up Your Punter!*, p. 103.

32 Quoted in Linda Melvern, *The End of the Street* (1986), p. 34.

33 Except by massaging the figure and including the sale of the *Mirror's* sister paper, the *Daily Record*, overwhelmingly the biggest seller in Scotland. This was not wholly unfair, because the *Mirror*, alone of the Fleet Street papers, has never been distributed north of the border. However, the papers are clearly separate; even the cartoon strips are different.
34 Alix Palmer and Moira Petty, interviewed by *This Week*, Thames TV, 1 October 1987.
35 *The Guardian*, 4 September 1987.
36 Chippindale and Horrie, *Stick It Up Your Punter!*, p. 228.
37 Ibid., pp. 332–3.
38 *The World This Weekend*, BBC Radio Four, 31 July 1989.
39 Shawcross, *Murdoch*, p. 513.
40 Raymond Snoddy, *The Good, the Bad and the Unacceptable* (1992), p. 126.
41 *The Guardian*, 30 October 1995.

Part Seven

1 *The Spectator*, 25 November 1995.
2 *The Guardian*, 22 December 1995.
3 *The Guardian*, 29 January 1996.
4 Interview with *India Today*, quoted in *The Guardian*, 25 February 1994.
5 Roger Laughton, quoted in the *New Yorker*, 13 November 1995.
6 Silas Bent, 'Journalism and Morality', *Atlantic Monthly*, 1926, p. 761.
7 Interview, 26 July 1995.

Bibliography

Some volumes have been used in more than one Part; in these cases either the first or the main use is cited. Works listed are published in the UK unless otherwise stated.

General

Audit Bureau of Circulations, *National Newspaper Circulation Figures, 1931–1994*, 1994

Baistow, Tom, *Fourth-Rate Estate*, 1985

Butler, David, and Sloman, Anne, *British Political Facts 1900–1979*, 1980

Cambridge Social History of Britain 1750–1950, volume 2, 1990

Cook, Chris, and Keith, Brendan, *British Historical Facts, 1830–1900*, 1975

Cudlipp, Hugh, *Publish and be Damned!*, 1953

Griffiths, Dennis, *The Encyclopaedia of the British Press 1422–1992*, 1992

Hutt, Allen, *The Changing Newspaper*, 1973

Koss, Stephen, *The Rise and Fall of the Political Press in Britain* (2 vols), 1981/1984

Linton, David, *The Twentieth-Century Newspaper Press in Britain: An Annotated Bibliography*, 1992

Royal Commissions on the Press, Reports, 1949, 1962, 1976

Various authors, *The British General Election of 1945* (and following election years)

Wadsworth, A. P., *Newspaper Circulations, 1800–1954 (Transactions of the Manchester Statistical Society)*, 1955

Williams, Francis, *Dangerous Estate*, 1957

Williams, Raymond, *The Long Revolution*, 1961

Wintour, Charles, *The Rise and Fall of Fleet Street*, 1989

Part One

Ackroyd, Peter, *Dickens*, 1990

Andrews, Alexander, *The History of British Journalism* (2 vols), 1859

Blumenfeld, R. D., *The Press In My Time*, 1933

Blumenfeld, R. D., *RDB's Diary 1887–1914*, 1933

Blumenfeld, R. D., *What Is A Journalist?*, 1930

Blunt, Wilfrid, *The Ark in the Park: The Zoo in the Nineteenth Century*, 1976

Boston, Richard, ed., *The Press We Deserve*, 1970

Boyce, G., Curran, J. and Wingate, P., *Newspaper History from the Seventeenth Century to the Present Day*, 1978

Brown, Lucy, *Victorian News and Newspapers*, 1985

Burnham, Lord, *Peterborough Court: The Story of the Daily Telegraph*, 1955

Cranfield, G. A., *The Press and Society: From Caxton to Northcliffe*, 1978

Curran, James, and Seaton, Jean, *Power Without Responsibility*, 1991

Dibblee, G. Binney, *The Newspaper*, 1913

Ensor, R. C. K., *England 1870–1914*, 1936

Falk, Bernard, *Bouquets for Fleet Street*, 1951

Fleming, G. H., *Victorian Sex Goddess: Lady Colin Campbell*, 1989

Fyfe, Hamilton, *Press Parade*, 1936

Fyfe, Hamilton, *Sixty Years of Fleet Street*, 1949

Fox Bourne, H. R., *Chapters in the History of Journalism* (2 vols), 1887

Heppenstall, Rayner, *Reflections on the Newgate Calendar*, 1975

Howard, Philip, *We Thundered Out: 200 Years of The Times 1785–1985*, 1985

James, Louis, *Print and the People*, 1976

Jones, Kennedy, *Fleet Street to Downing Street*, 1920

'A Journalist', *Bohemian Days in Fleet Street*, 1913

Kieve, Jeffrey, *The Electric Telegraph: A Social and Economic History*, 1973

King, Cecil, *Without Fear or Favour*, 1972

Knightley, Phillip, *The First Casualty*, 1975

Mathieson, Eric, *The True Story of Jumbo the Elephant*, 1963

Morison, Stanley, *The English Newspaper 1622–1932*, 1932

Mott, F. L., *American Journalism*, 1941 (New York)

Pearson, Geoffrey, *Hooligan: A History of Respectable Fears*, 1983

Raymond, E. T., *Portraits of the Nineties*, 1921

Richardson, J. Hall, *From The City to Fleet Street*, 1927

Siebert, F. S., *Freedom of the Press in England 1476–1776*, 1952 (Urbana, Illinois)

Simonis, H., *The Street of Ink*, 1917

Spater, George, *William Cobbett*, 1982

Stead, W. T., *A Journalist on Journalism*, 1892

Steed, Wickham, *The Press*, 1938

Stephens, Mitchell, *A History of News*, 1988 (New York)

Straus, Ralph, *Sala*, 1942
Symon, J. D., *The Press and its Story*, 1914
Thompson, E. P., *The Making of the English Working Class*, 1963
The Times, *The History of the Times: The Thunderer in the Making, 1785–1841*, 1935
The Times, *The History of the Times: The Tradition Established, 1841–1884*, 1939
The Times, *The Times: Past, Present, Future*, 1985
Wickwar, W. H., *The Struggle for the Freedom of the Press*, 1928
Wiener, Joel H., ed., *Papers for the Millions*, 1988

Files of: *Daily Telegraph, The Echo, Nineteenth Century, The Star, The Times, The Newspaper Owner, World's Press News*

Part Two

Angell, Norman, *The Press and the Organisation of Society*, 1922
Bourne, Richard, *Lords of Fleet Street: The Harmsworth Dynasty*, 1990
Brendon, Piers, *Life and Death of the Press Barons*, 1982
Brex, Twells, comp., *Scaremongerings from the Daily Mail, 1896–1914*, 1914
Carson, William E., *Northcliffe: Britain's Man of Power*, 1918 (New York)
Clarke, I. F., *Voices Prophesying War, 1763–1984*, 1966
Clarke, Tom, *My Northcliffe Diary*, 1931
Clarke, Tom, *Northcliffe in History: An Intimate Study of Press Power*, 1955
Coleridge, Nicholas, *Paper Tigers*, 1993
Colley, William, *News Hunter*, 1936
Coster, Ian, *Friends in Aspic*, 1939
Crosland, T. W. H., *The Suburbans*, 1905
Dark, Sidney, *Not Such a Bad Life*, 1941
Dunn, James, *Paperchase: Adventures In and Out of Fleet Street*, 1938
Falk, Bernard, *Bouquets for Fleet Street*, 1951
Ferris, Paul, *The House of Northcliffe: The Harmsworths of Fleet Street*, 1971
Furneaux, Rupert, *News of War*, 1964
Fyfe, Hamilton, *Northcliffe: An Intimate Biography*, 1930
Gardner, A. G., *The Daily Mail and the Liberal Press: A Reply to 'Scaremongerings'*, 1914
Gibbs, Philip, *The Pageant of The Years*, 1946
Gibbs, Philip, *Street of Adventure*, 1909
Greenwall, Harry J., *Northcliffe*, 1957

Hammerton, J. A., *With Northcliffe in Fleet Street*, 1932

Harris, José, *Private Lives, Public Spirit: Britain 1870–1914*, 1993

Harris, M., and Lee, A. J., eds, *The Press in English Society from the 17th to the 19th Century*, 1986

Herd, Harold, *The Newspaper of Tomorrow*, 1930

Jenkins, Roy, *Asquith*, 1965

Jenkins, Simon, *The Market for Glory: Fleet Street Ownership in the 20th Century*, 1986

Juergens, George, *Joseph Pulitzer and the New York World*, 1966 (Princeton, NJ)

Lane, Margaret, *Edgar Wallace: A Biography*, 1938

Lee, Alan J., *The Origins of the Popular Press, 1855–1914*, 1976

McGee, Harold, *On Food and Cooking: The Science and Lore of the Kitchen*, 1986

Marwick, Arthur, *Britain in the Century of Total War*, 1968

Marwick, Arthur, *The Deluge*, 1965

Masters, Brian, *Now Barabbas Was a Rotter*, 1978

Memory, F. W., *Memory's*, 1932

Morris, A. J. A., *The Scaremongers: The Advocacy of War and Rearmament*, 1984

Morris, Jan, *Pax Britannica*, 1968

The Mystery of the Daily Mail, 1896–1921, 1921

News in our Time 1896–1946: Golden Jubilee Book of the Daily Mail, 1946

Northcliffe, Lord, *Newspapers and their Millionaires*, 1922

Owen, Louise, *Northcliffe: The Facts*, 1931

Owen, Louise, *Northcliffe's Views Upon the Christ*, 1925

Owen, Louise, *The Real Lord Northcliffe: Some Personal Recollections of a Private Secretary, 1902–1922*, 1922

Pemberton, Max, *Lord Northcliffe: A Memoir*, 1922

Perkin, Harold, *The Structured Crowd*, 1981

Phillips, Sir Percival, *The 'Red' Dragon and the Black Shirts: How Italy Found its Soul*, 1922

Ponsonby, Arthur, *Falsehood In War-time*, 1928

Pope, W. J. M., *Twenty Shillings in the Pound*, 1948

Pound, Reginald, and Harmsworth, Geoffrey, *Northcliffe*, 1959

Pyke, Magnus, *Food and Society*, 1968

Raymond, E. T., *Portraits of the New Century*, 1928

Royle, Trevor, *The Kitchener Enigma*, 1985

Ryan, A. P., *Lord Northcliffe*, 1953

Scott-James, R. A., *The Influence of the Daily Press*, 1913

Smith, Wareham, *Spilt Ink*, 1932

Springfield, Lincoln, *Some Piquant People*, 1924

A Study in Malevolence: An Open Letter to Lord Northcliffe from an MP, 1920

Swaffer, Hannen, *Northcliffe's Return,* 1925

Taylor, A. J. P., *Essays in English History,* 1976

Taylor, A. J. P., *The Struggle for Mastery in Europe,* 1954

Thompson, Alex M., *Here I Lie: The Memorial of an old Journalist,* 1937

Thompson, Paul, *The Edwardians: The Remaking of British Society,* 1976

Trevelyan, G. M., *British History in the Nineteenth Century and After,* 1937

Tuchman, Barbara, *The Proud Tower,* 1967

Wile, F. W., *News Is Where You Find It,* 1939 (Indianapolis)

Wilson, R. Macnair, *Lord Northcliffe: A Study,* 1927

Files of: *Daily Chronicle, Daily Courier, Daily Mail, Daily News, Daily Sketch, Daily Telegraph, Morning Post, New Statesman, The Newspaper Owner and Modern Printer, The Standard, The Times*

Various volumes of: *Dictionary of National Biography, Sell's Dictionary of the World Press*

Part Three

Allen, Robert, *Voice of Britain,* 1983

Barkley, William, *Reporter's Notebook,* 1959

Baxter, Beverley, *Strange Street,* 1931

Beaverbrook, Lord, *Politicians and the Press,* 1924

Beaverbrook, Lord, *Success,* 1921

Blake, Robert, *The Decline in Power, 1915–1964,* 1985

Blumenfeld, R. D., *All in a Lifetime,* 1931

Blumenfeld, R. D., *Do's and Don't's for Reporters and Sub-editors,* 1930

Brooks, Collin, *Devil's Decade: Portraits of the 1930s,* 1948

Carter, Frederick W., *Secrets of Your Daily Paper,* 1929

Chester, L., Fay, S., and Young, H., *The Zinoviev Letter,* 1967

Chisholm, Anne, and Davie, Michael, *Beaverbrook: A Life,* 1992

Christiansen, Arthur, *Headlines All My Life,* 1961

Cockburn, Claud, *The Devil's Decade,* 1973

Cudlipp, Hugh, *At Your Peril,* 1962

Daily Express, These Tremendous Years, 1938

Driberg, Tom, *Beaverbrook: A Study in Power and Frustration,* 1956

Driberg, Tom, *Ruling Passions,* 1977

Driberg, Tom, *Swaff,* 1974

Gannon, Franklin R., *The British Press and Germany, 1936–39,* 1971

Goodman, Arnold, *Tell Them I'm On My Way*, 1993

Gourlay, Logan, ed., *The Beaverbrook I Knew*, 1984

Graves, Robert, and Hodge, Alan, *The Long Weekend*, 1940

Herd, Harold, *The Making of Modern Journalism*, 1927

Hindle, Wilfred, *The Morning Post 1772–1837: Portrait of a Newspaper*, 1937

Jameson, Derek, *Touched by Angels*, 1988

London Press Club, *Fleet Street: The Inside Story of Journalism*, 1966

Mackenzie, F. A., *Beaverbrook*, 1931

Middleton, Edgar, *Beaverbrook: The Statesman and the Man, c.1931*

Minney, R. J., *Viscount Southwood*, 1954

Muggeridge, Malcolm, *The Thirties*, 1940

Political and Economic Planning, *Report on the British Press*, 1938

Priestley, J. B., *English Journey*, 1934

Rothermere, Lord, *Warnings and Predictions*, 1939

Sharf, Andrew, *The British Press and Jews under Nazi Rule*, 1964

Shepherd, C. W., *Let's Walk Down Fleet Street*, 1947

Sisman, Adam, *A. J. P. Taylor*, 1994

Smith, A. C. H., *Paper Voices: The Popular Press and Social Change, 1935–1965*, 1975

Taylor, A. J. P., *Beaverbrook*, 1972

Taylor, A. J. P., *English History 1914–1945*, 1965

Turner, William R., *Eyes of the Press*, 1935

Wheen, Francis, *Tom Driberg: His Life and Indiscretions*, 1990

Ziegler, Philip, *Diana Cooper*, 1981

Files of: *Daily Express, Daily Mail, The Economist, The Newspaper Owner and Modern Printer, The Newspaper World, New Statesman, New York Times, Political Quarterly, The Times, World's Press News*

Part Four

Abrams, Mark, *Education, Social Class and Newspaper Reading*, 1931

Abrams, Mark, and Rose, Richard, *Must Labour Lose?*, 1960

Allen, Robert, *Daily Mirror*, 1981

Allsop, Kenneth, *The Angry Decade*, 1958

Barker, Ernest, ed., *The Character of England*, 1947

Booker, Christopher, *The Neophiliacs*, 1969

Boston, Richard, ed., *The Press We Deserve*, 1966

Campbell, Doon, ed., *The British Press: A Look Ahead*, 1978

Cameron, James, *Point of Departure*, 1967

Camrose, Viscount, *British Newspapers and their Controllers*, 1947
Cassandra at his Finest and Funniest, 1967
Cleverley, Graham, *The Fleet Street Disaster*, 1976
Connor, Robert, *Cassandra: Reflections in a Mirror*, 1969
Cudlipp, Hugh, *The Prerogative of the Harlot*, 1980
Cudlipp, Hugh, *Walking on the Water*, 1976
Edelman, Maurice, *The Mirror: A Political History*, 1966
Edwards, Robert, *Goodbye Fleet Street*, 1988
Hart-Davis, Duff, *The House the Berrys Built: Inside the Telegraph, 1928–1986*, 1990
Hennessy, Peter, *Never Again: Britain 1945–1951*, 1993
Hopkins, Harry, *The New Look*, 1964
Jameson, Derek, *Touched by Angels*, 1988
Jenkins, Simon, *Newspapers: The Power and the Money*, 1978
King, Cecil, *The Cecil King Diaries 1965–1970*, 1972
King, Cecil, *The Future of the Press*, 1967
King, Cecil, *Strictly Personal*, 1969
King, Cecil, *With Malice Toward None: A War Diary*, 1970
King, Cecil, *With Fear or Favour*, 1971
Levin, Bernard, *The Pendulum Years*, 1970
Levy, Philip, *The Press Council: History, Procedures and Cases*, 1967
Mass-Observation, *The Press and its Readers*, 1949
Matthews, T. S., *The Sugar Pill*, 1957
Moran, Lord, *Winston Churchill: The Struggle for Survival*, 1966
Nicolson, Harold, *Diaries and Letters 1939–45*, 1967
Patmore, Angela, *Marje*, 1993
Procter, Harry, *The Street of Disillusion*, 1958
Randall, Mike, *The Funny Side of the Street*, 1988
The Romance of the Daily Mirror 1903–1924, 1924
Sampson, Anthony, *Anatomy of Britain Today*, 1965
Sissons, Michael, and French, Philip, *Age of Austerity 1945–1951*, 1963
Waterhouse, Keith, *Daily Mirror Style*, 1981
Winn, Godfrey, *The Infirm Glory*, 1967
Winn, Godfrey, *Personality Parade*, 1937
Wintour, Charles, *Pressures on the Press*, 1972
Zec, Donald, *Some Enchanted Egos*, 1972

Files of: *British Journalism Review, Daily Express, Daily Mirror, Encounter, Master Printer and Newspaper Owner, New York Times, Newspaper World, The Observer, The Spectator, World's Press News*

Part Five

Bainbridge, Cyril, and Stockdill, Roy, *The News of the World Story*, 1993
Berrey, R. Power, *The Romance of a Great Newspaper*, 1922
Catling, Thomas, *My Life's Pilgrimage*, 1911
Good Stories from the News of the World, 1931
Henry, Harry, ed., *Behind the Headlines: The Business of the British Press*, 1978
Hoggart, Richard, ed., *Your Sunday Newspaper*, 1967
Kersh, Cyril, *A Few Gross Words*, 1990
Reid, J. C., *Bucks and Bruisers: Pierce Egan and Regency England*, 1971
Riddell, Lord, *More Pages from My Diary, 1908–1914*, 1934
Smith, Anthony, *The Newspaper: An International History*, 1979
Somerfield, Stafford, *Banner Headlines*, 1979
Thompson, F. M. L., *The Rise of Respectable Society*, 1988
Wilson, Charles, *First with the News: The History of W. H. Smith, 1792–1972*, 1985
World's Press News Inky Way Annual, Book Two, 1948

Files of: *British Journalism Review, Daily Telegraph, Lloyd's Weekly Newspaper, News of the World, Newspaper Owner and Modern Printer, Newspaper World, Reynolds's Newspaper, UK Press Gazette, World's Press News*

Part Six

Belfield, R., Hird, C., and Kelly, S., *Murdoch: The Decline of an Empire*, 1991
Belfield, R., Hird, C., and Kelly, S., *Murdoch: The Great Escape*, 1994
Burn, Gordon, *Fullalove*, 1995
Chester, L., and Fenby, J., *The Fall of the House of Beaverbrook*, 1979
Chippindale, Peter, and Horrie, Chris, *Stick it Up Your Punter!*, 1990
Clarkson, Wensley, *Dog Eat Dog*, 1990
Essery, John, ed., *Gotcha: Classic Headlines from The Sun*, 1993
Evans, Harold, *Good Times, Bad Times*, 1983
Goodhart, David, and Wintour, Patrick, *Eddie Shah and the Newspaper Revolution*, 1986
Greenslade, Roy, *Maxwell's Fall*, 1992
Grose, Roslyn, *The Sun-Sation*, 1989
Harris, Robert, *Gotcha! The Media, The Government and the Falklands Crisis*, 1983

Hattersley, Roy, *Press Gang*, 1983
Lamb, Larry, *Sunrise*, 1988
Leapman, Michael, *Barefaced Cheek: The Apotheosis of Rupert Murdoch*, 1983
Leapman, Michael, *Treacherous Estate*, 1992
Melvern, Linda, *The End of the Street*, 1986
Munster, George, *Rupert Murdoch: A Paper Prince*, 1984
Porter, Henry, *Lies, Damned Lies and Some Exclusives*, 1984
Regan, Simon, *Rupert Murdoch*, 1976
Robertson, Geoffrey, *People against the Press: An Enquiry into the Press Council*, 1983
Searle, Chris, *Racism and the Press in Thatcher's Britain*, 1989
Sellers, Leslie, *Doing it in Style*, 1968
Shawcross, William, *Murdoch*, 1993
Snoddy, Raymond, *The Good, the Bad and the Unacceptable*, 1992
Taylor, S. J., *Shock! Horror! The Tabloids in Action*, 1991

Files of: *British Journalism Review, Journalism Studies Review, Daily Mirror, Daily Star, The Guardian, New York Times, The Sun, The Times, UK Press Gazette*

Daily Newspapers, 1896–1996

Papers still in existence at January 1996 are shown in bold italics, defunct papers in italics. All circulation figures are six-monthly statistics issued by the Audit Bureau of Circulations (ABC). Figures for 1995 are July to December.

Fringe, specialist and overtly pornographic publications have been excluded from this list, as have those not circulating in London.

Daily Citizen Official Labour paper. Founded 1912. Closed 1915.

Daily Chronicle Liberal paper with strong circulation within London. Developed from local titles after 1869. Owned by Lloyd George and associates 1918–26. Merged with *Daily News* 1930.

Daily Courier Sir George Newnes's ha'penny rival to *Daily Mail*. Beat *Mail* by launching 11 days earlier, in April 1896. Closed in August, after 98 issues.

Daily Express Founded 1900 by C. Arthur Pearson. Acquired gradually by Lord Beaverbrook during First World War. Top-selling daily c.1937–49. Bought by Trafalgar House 1977, by United Newspapers 1985. Peak circulation: 4,220,952 (first half 1950). 1995 circulation: 1,261,977.

Daily Graphic First morning picture paper. Merged with *Daily Sketch* 1926, but temporarily changed name back to *Daily Graphic* 1946–52.

Daily Herald Labour Party daily paper from 1912 (though published weekly during First World War). After 1929, 51 per cent of shares held by Odhams Press, 49 per cent by TUC. Odhams taken over by *Daily Mirror* 1961. Name changed to *The Sun* 1964. In 1930s became first paper to claim two million sale. Circulation before name-change: 1,265,020.

Daily Mail Founded by Alfred Harmsworth (later Lord Northcliffe) May 1896. Top-selling daily 1896–c.1930 (overtaken by *Daily Mirror* before and during First World War). Became tabloid 1971. Ownership essentially the same for 100 years; now controlled by 3rd Lord Rothermere,

	Northcliffe's great-nephew. Peak circulation: 2,293,565 (second half 1950). 1995 circulation: 1,876,991.
Daily Mirror	Founded by Alfred Harmsworth as women's paper 1903. Became pictorial paper 1904. Sold to Harmsworth's brother, Lord Rothermere, 1914. Rothermere sold shares in the 1930s, after which paper had no overall control. Bought by Reed International (1970), then Robert Maxwell (1984). Floated as public company after his death and revelations of his fraud. Top-selling daily 1949–78. Peak circulation: 5,282,137 (second half 1967). 1995 circulation: 2,533,150.
Daily News	Liberal paper founded 1846. Charles Dickens editor for first 17 issues. Merged with *Daily Chronicle* 1930.
Daily Paper	'A paper for the abnormally scrupulous' edited by W. T. Stead. Founded 1904. Closed after 32 issues.
Daily Sketch	Conservative tabloid picture paper. Founded 1908 by Sir Edward Hulton. Originally Manchester-based. Sold to Lord Kemsley 1928 (renamed *Daily Graphic* 1946–52) and Lord Rothermere 1953. Merged with *Daily Mail* 1971. Peak circulation: 1,304,892 (first half 1947). Circulation before closure: 764,187.
Daily Star	Founded 1978 as down-market tabloid sister of *Daily Express*. Originally Manchester-based. Peak circulation: 1,633,263 (second half 1984). 1995 circulation: 749,650.
Daily Telegraph	Started as Liberal paper 1855 by Col. Arthur Burroughes Sleigh. Sold to Moses Levy (within weeks), Berry family (1928) and Conrad Black (1985). Top-selling daily from just after its launch to 1896. Peak circulation: 1,510,766 (second half 1979, when *Times* mostly not published – otherwise 1,454,581, first half 1971). 1995 circulation: 1,052,928.
The Guardian	Founded as *Manchester Guardian* 1821. Became daily 1855. Paper renamed *The Guardian* 1959 and published in London from 1961. Peak circulation; 524,264 (first half 1986). 1995 circulation: 395,130.
The Independent	Founded 1986 by three former *Telegraph* journalists. Acquired 1994 by consortium headed by *Daily Mirror* and Irish businessman Tony O'Reilly. Peak circulation: 414,357 (first half 1990). 1995 circulation: 292,827.
Morning Herald	Founded 1892. Merged with *Daily Express* 1900.

Morning Leader   Liberal paper owned by Colman's, the mustard family. Founded 1892. Merged with *Daily News* 1912.

Morning Post   Conservative paper. Founded 1772. Absorbed by *Daily Telegraph* 1937. Circulation before closure: 116,681.

News Chronicle   Liberal paper born when *Daily News* and *Daily Chronicle* merged 1930. Absorbed by *Daily Mail* 1960. Peak circulation: 1,633,207 (second half 1946). Circulation before closure: 1,162,194.

The Post   Tabloid launched by Eddy Shah November 1988. Closed after 33 issues.

The Standard   Businessmen's paper. Founded 1857. Closed 1917; sister paper, *Evening Standard*, survives.

The Sun   New name of *Daily Herald* from 1964. Bought by Rupert Murdoch and relaunched as a tabloid 1969. Top-selling daily 1978 to date. Circulation before Murdoch: 1,009,182. Peak circulation: 4,219,052 (second half 1988). 1995 circulation: 4,027,850.

The Times   Founded as *Daily Universal Register* 1785. Changed name 1788. Owned by the Walter family until 1908. Bought by Lord Northcliffe (1908), Lord Astor (1922), Lord Thomson (1966), Rupert Murdoch (1981). Top-selling paper early nineteenth century to *c.*1855. Peak circulation: 682,419 (first half 1995). Circulation second half 1995: 668,756.

Today   Founded by Eddy Shah 1986 as Britain's first full-colour, post-print-union paper. Rapidly sold to Lonrho and then Rupert Murdoch, who closed it in November 1995. Peak circulation: 589,235 (second half 1989). Circulation before closure: 566,302.

Tribune   Liberal daily, founded 1906, closed 1908.

Index